AF760896

CLINICIAN'S GUIDE TO VALIDITY ASSESSMENT AND MANAGEMENT IN NEUROPSYCHOLOGY

Evidence-Based Practice in Neuropsychology

Kyle Brauer Boone, Series Editor

Clinical Practice of Forensic Neuropsychology:
An Evidence-Based Approach
Kyle Brauer Boone

Psychological Assessment:
A Problem-Solving Approach
Julie A. Suhr

Validity Testing in Child and Adolescent Assessment:
Evaluating Exaggeration, Feigning, and Noncredible Effort
Michael W. Kirkwood, Editor

Neuropsychological Report Writing
Jacobus Donders, Editor

Assessment of Feigned Cognitive Impairment:
A Neuropsychological Perspective, Second Edition
Kyle Brauer Boone, Editor

Validity Assessment in Clinical Neuropsychological Practice:
Evaluating and Managing Noncredible Performance
Ryan W. Schroeder and Phillip K. Martin, Editors

Clinician's Guide to Validity Assessment and Management
in Neuropsychology
Ryan W. Schroeder and Phillip K. Martin

Clinician's Guide to Validity Assessment and Management in Neuropsychology

Ryan W. Schroeder
Phillip K. Martin

Series Editor's Note by Kyle Brauer Boone

THE GUILFORD PRESS
New York London

Printed in the United States of America

This book is printed on acid-free paper.

For product and safety concerns within the EU, please contact *GPSR@taylorandfrancis.com*, Taylor & Francis Verlag GmbH, Kaufingerstraße 24, 80331 München, Germany.

Last digit is print number: 9 8 7 6 5 4 3 2 1

Library of Congress Cataloging-in-Publication Data is available from the publisher.

ISBN 978-1-4625-5785-1 (paperback)
ISBN 978-1-4625-5786-8 (cloth)

Disclosure of Interest: The authors' work on this project was not associated with or supported by their employment at any institution. The views and content within this book are those of the authors, and they should not be seen as representing the views of the U.S. Department of Veterans Affairs, the U.S. Government, or any university or institutional body.

About the Authors

Ryan W. Schroeder, PsyD, ABPP-CN, is a board-certified neuropsychologist practicing both clinical and forensic neuropsychology. He engages in clinical work at the Robert J. Dole VA Medical Center in Wichita, Kansas, and he engages in forensic work through his private practice. Additionally, he is a volunteer Associate Professor in the Department of Psychiatry and Behavioral Sciences at the University of Kansas School of Medicine–Wichita and Adjunct Faculty in the Clinical Psychology Program at Wichita State University. Dr. Schroeder has published and presented widely on neuropsychological validity assessment and has served on expert committees related to validity assessment and test security. He is a recipient of early career awards from the National Academy of Neuropsychology (NAN) and the American Psychological Association (APA), and is a Fellow of NAN and APA.

Phillip K. Martin, PhD, ABPP-CN, is a board-certified clinical neuropsychologist and Associate Professor in the Department of Psychiatry and Behavioral Sciences at the University of Kansas School of Medicine–Wichita. He is an active clinician, supervisor of neuropsychology trainees, teacher, and researcher. Dr. Martin has published on multiple topics, including but not limited to neuropsychological validity assessment. He has made unique contributions to the validity assessment literature with his scholarly articles pertaining to professional beliefs and practices, the management of clinical patients who produce invalid test performance, and meta-analysis of specific validity measures. In addition to his published research, Dr. Martin's participation in the evolving discussion of neuropsychological validity assessment practice has included serving as an expert committee member and a recurrent national conference speaker.

Series Editor's Note

In this guide for how to expertly handle validity issues in a clinical neuropsychology exam, Drs. Schroeder and Martin walk the reader through each step in the process. While there are publications in the field that provide consensus recommendations as to how to address validity issues in neuropsychological exams (e.g., Sweet et al., 2021) and summaries of the voluminous literature on cutoffs and classification statistics for various performance validity tests (PVTs) and validity indexes (e.g., Boone et al., 2021), there has not been a hands-on guide that covers each step of the clinical evaluation process, from clarifying referral questions and goals of the exam through a completed report and feedback to patients. Without a step-by-step guide, clinicians can often feel unsure as to how to seamlessly integrate PVT practice recommendations and evidence-based research into their neuropsychological evaluations.

When approaching validity issues in neuropsychological exams, early career neuropsychologists often experience some trepidation because the mishandling of validity concerns ostensibly could lead to patient harm, rupture of the patient–clinician relationship, and risk for the practitioner. Hence, there is often an impulse to "ignore" validity issues, as reflected in comments heard by practitioners in other disciplines who say that their default setting is "to assume what the patient is saying as true." In Chapter 1, Schroeder and Martin lay to rest eight "myths" that often lead clinicians to avoid addressing validity concerns in their exams, and show that avoidance of validity assessment can actually lead to harm to both patients and the larger society.

In Chapter 2, Schroeder and Martin carefully walk the reader through situations in which secondary gain issues are—or may be—present in referrals for clinical exams, and they discuss the pros and cons of accepting such referrals. The clinician needs to be able to navigate these situations because they are far from atypical; for example, patients with disabling conditions who would benefit from clinical exams to guide their care also constitute the pool of patients applying for disability (secondary gain). The chapter provides sample conversations to have with patients that illustrate how to educate them, prior to their giving consent to proceed with an exam, regarding potential negative repercussions from clinical exams affected by forensic considerations.

Chapter 3 offers a master class on how to conduct an interview, from clinician behavior (the importance of conveying interest and respect to the patient) to the advantages of an "open-ended" and conversational approach regarding eliciting symptoms and history. The clinician is counseled to be attentive to how the patient reports symptoms (e.g., whether hyperbole is present), whether reported symptoms are plausible for the claimed condition, whether cognitive symptoms are in fact observed in spontaneous interview interactions, and potential factors that could serve to foster or encourage invalidity. The clinician is recommended to gather information on how the patient spends a "typical day," as a means of gaining insight to functionality in daily life activities. The clinician ends the interview by summarizing key data provided by the patient (nature and perceived cause of symptoms, co-occurring issues, etc.), and obtaining agreement with the patient as to the goals of the exam. The authors discuss how to introduce the subsequent testing, including the importance of performing to true ability, and they also describe how information gleaned during the interview is then used in the selection of specific validity tests to be subsequently administered in the exam.

Chapter 4 introduces commonly used stand-alone PVTs (validity measures used to verify that test takers have performed to their actual ability on cognitive testing), and Chapter 5 reviews frequently employed "embedded" PVTs (i.e., validity measures contained within standard neurocognitive tests). Discussion of validity score classification terms (sensitivity, specificity, positive and negative predictive power, false-positive errors) is succinct and easy to digest. The chapters cover the strengths and weaknesses of each PVT and common cutoffs and associated classification rates, as well as the critical importance of using multiple PVTs within a test battery.

Chapter 6 is devoted to the process of interpreting symptom validity tests (SVTs), which are validity measures that assess for the veracity of symptom report. The authors provide the pivotal rationale for use of SVTs, namely, that without the use of SVTs, the veracity of self-reported symptoms—psychological, physical, and cognitive—is unknown. The chapter summarizes relevant research on various SVTs "embedded" within standard psychological symptom inventories, as well as stand-alone SVTs. The authors provide summaries of the validation research for each SVT, from which they generate cutoff recommendations. Importantly, the authors also discuss how to interpret PVT and SVT data in combination; they point out that when a patient fails PVTs, as well as SVTs involving a cognitive symptom report, the clinician can be highly confident that the PVT failures are not false-positive findings since the patient has also engaged in nonplausible overstatement of cognitive symptoms.

Chapter 7 returns to interpreting PVT data, and then how to weave together PVT, SVT, and clinical observations for a determination of validity/invalidity. The authors describe the selection process for embedded and stand-alone PVTs for specific types of patients, including where to place the measures within a battery, and they provide sample "PVT batteries" for differing types of patients. While two or more PVT failures is considered robust evidence for invalidity in patients without a major neurocognitive disorder, the authors discuss situations in which it is appropriate to use a single PVT failure as evidence of invalidity (i.e., when the score is associated with 100% specificity), or to even conclude invalidity when all PVTs are passed. Importantly, the authors clarify what is meant by significantly below chance performance on a forced choice PVT.

Chapter 8 provides important guidance as to what can and cannot be viewed as causes for PVT failures, concluding that there is no empirical evidence that depression and anxiety, "cry for help," or physical factors (pain, fatigue, medications, apathy) account for PVT failures. The authors also cover the pros and cons of using the term "malingering," as well as the differential diagnosis of malingering versus factitious disorder and somatic symptom disorder. The chapter concludes with a discussion of specific populations at increased risk for elevated rates of invalidity, including mild traumatic brain injury, adult ADHD, work issues (e.g., disability claimants, Workers' Compensation), veterans, patients injured in accidents, criminal defendants, and younger adults with no medical conditions to account for significant cognitive decline.

Chapter 9 addresses the anxiety-producing situation of providing feedback regarding invalid test findings to patients. The authors outline an approach that is objective and does not "skirt the issue," while still conveying compassion and validation to the patient and an offer to further collaborate with the clinician on treatable issues. Specific examples of sample conversations to have with the patient when conveying findings of invalidity are provided.

Chapter 10 covers report writing in cases of invalidity, including sample language for discussing PVT results, and how, despite invalid test findings, the clinician can still provide useful recommendations (i.e., what conditions the person has that could be treated and be of help to the patient). The chapter concludes with a redacted sample report that illustrates how to formulate accurate, thorough, and compelling reports. Chapter 11 provides a useful summary of the entire exam process, by having the reader follow a redacted case example from receipt of the referral to completion of the report, which is included at the end of the chapter.

This book, with its common sense, easily digestible, and thorough guidance, will provide important reassurance and confidence as the clinician tackles the critical task of assessing for validity in clinical neuropsychological exams.

Kyle Brauer Boone, PhD
Private Practice
Torrance, California

REFERENCES

Boone, K. B. (Ed.). (2021). *Assessment of feigned cognitive impairment* (2nd ed.). Guilford Press.

Sweet, J. J., Heilbronner, R. L., Morgan, J. E., Larrabee, G. J., Rohling, M. L., Boone, K. B., . . . Conference Participants. (2021). American Academy of Clinical Neuropsychology (AACN) 2021 consensus statement on validity assessment: Update of the 2009 AACN consensus conference statement on neuropsychological assessment of effort, response bias, and malingering. *The Clinical Neuropsychologist*, *35*(6), 1053–1106.

Preface

In an upcoming book chapter currently titled "Deception, Response Bias, Malingering, Effort, and Invalidity: The Conceptual Evolution of Neuropsychological Validity Testing" we detail the history of performance validity assessment. In brief, psychologists began developing performance validity assessment methods for forensic use in the early 1900s. In the 1940s, Dr. André Rey began developing more modern performance validity tests, motivated by concerns that claimants were feigning cognitive impairment. The next major advancement came in the 1970s–1980s when Dr. Loren Pankratz and colleagues began publishing on a forced choice method to detect invalid presentations and malingering. Dr. Pankratz's work led to the development of multiple performance validity tests, which started being published in the late 1980s and early 1990s. Early research on these performance validity tests was nearly exclusively forensic in nature, typically investigating how well the tests could detect malingering or simulated malingering. Through the 1990s, forensic research continued to dominate the performance validity assessment literature base, but a growing number of articles began to evaluate performance validity assessment within clinical settings. The findings from this emerging arm of research were compelling enough to lead the National Academy of Neuropsychology Policy and Planning Committee to state that "assessment of response validity, as a component of a medically necessary evaluation, is medically necessary" (Bush et al., 2005, p. 419). Likewise, just two years later, the American Academy of Clinical Neuropsychology Board of Directors published practice guidelines indicating "the assessment of effort and motivation is important in any clinical setting, as a patient's effort may be compromised even in the absence of any potential or active litigation, compensation, or financial incentives" (Board of Directors, 2007, p. 221).

While professional organizations started to promote the necessity of evaluating for performance and symptom validity in clinical settings, minimal literature was published on how to apply validity assessment research to clinical settings, how to conceptualize validity test failure in clinical settings, and how to manage noncredible performances in clinical settings. Because of this gap in the literature, we conducted multiple research projects, which have been published in various journals. We desired, however, to create a single resource for clinicians, which would be authored by multiple experts in all areas of validity assessment. Hence, the idea for our first book, *Validity Assessment in Clinical Neuropsychological Practice: Evaluating and Managing Noncredible Performance*, was born (Schroeder & Martin, 2022e). Dr. Kyle Brauer Boone was instrumental in helping to get this project off the ground. She faithfully encouraged us to proceed with the book, and she recommended us to Ms. Rochelle Serwator, Senior Editor at The Guilford Press. Ms. Serwator was very professional and generous in helping us to efficiently navigate our new endeavor. After completing the book, she recommended that we consider authoring a follow-up book, which is this one.

The current book differs from *Validity Assessment in Clinical Neuropsychological Practice: Evaluating and Managing Noncredible Performance* in that it is intended to be a hands-on book that walks through each step of the evaluation process focusing on validity assessment issues, and it is a book that provides examples of how we, ourselves, evaluate for and manage noncredible presentations in clinical practice. After discussing validity assessment as a medically necessary standard in clinical settings (Chapter 1), we walk through the evaluation process. This starts with discussions of managing potentially complicated referrals (Chapter 2) and it ends with discussions of providing feedback (Chapter 9) and report writing (Chapter 10) when invalid testing is obtained. We then conclude the book by "putting it all together" in a case demonstration (Chapter 11). By writing this book, we hope that it will help readers effectively navigate clinical evaluations in which noncredible performances are obtained. We echo Dr. Pankratz's previous statement that the purpose of evaluating for valid reporting of symptoms and test-taking behavior in clinical practice is not necessarily to catch lies but to identify and treat proper problems (Pankratz, 2003).

In closing, we would like to acknowledge individuals for whom we are extremely grateful to have in our professional lives. Ryan would like to thank everyone who has contributed to his professional training as a psychologist and neuropsychologist. He would also like to specifically thank Drs. Paul Marshall, Lyle Baade, Kyle Brauer Boone, and Glenn Larrabee, who heavily shaped his conceptualization of and provided mentorship in validity assessment. He would also like to thank Drs. Jerry Sweet, Joel Morgan, and Robert Heilbronner for providing additional opportunities to contribute to significant validity assessment projects. Furthermore, he would like to thank Dr. Phillip Martin for all of the discussions and collaborative work that have occurred over the years and led to the publication of our articles and books. Phillip would like to thank Drs. Laurence Levine and Ryan Schroeder for helping to foster both his interest in and conceptualization of validity assessment issues in clinical practice, as well as Drs. Don Morgan, Charles Golden, and Lyle Baade for their training, mentorship, and professional guidance. Finally, both Ryan and Phillip would like to thank Dr. Kyle Brauer Boone for her great generosity in all that she has done for us. We would also like to thank Ms. Rochelle Serwator for her guidance and support throughout both of our book projects. Lastly, we would like to thank all of our colleagues, who are too many to specifically name, who contributed to validity assessment writings in our first book and who continue to contribute to validity assessment writings outside of that book.

Contents

Purchasers of this book can download and print copies of Appendices 3.1 and 3.2 at *www.guilford.com/schroeder3-forms* for personal use or use with clients (see copyright page for details).

CHAPTER 1

Understanding Validity Assessment as a Medically Necessary Standard of Practice

The tests that neuropsychologists utilize to assess cognitive and emotional functioning differ from other common diagnostic tests, such as laboratory blood tests and neuroimaging, in that they are interactive tests that rely heavily on patient motivation, engagement, and cooperation (Bianchini, Mathias, & Greve, 2001; Schroeder & Martin, 2022a). If a patient provides less than optimal motivation or engagement, lacks cooperation, or even produces inaccurate data with the intention of deceiving the clinician, his or her functioning will not be accurately captured, which can result in inaccurate clinical formulations, diagnoses, and treatment recommendations. Given this, the field of neuropsychology has come to embrace the fact that the accuracy of neuropsychological test data must be verified in an objective and evidence-based manner through the application of empirically vetted performance and symptom validity tests.

The need to assess performance and symptom validity was recognized as early as the 1940s when the seminal Swiss neuropsychologist, Andre Rey, began creating performance validity tests, and the publication of the Minnesota Multiphasic Personality Inventory (MMPI) underscored the need to routinely utilize symptom validity scales. While recognized at that time, no formal position statements on the topic of validity assessment were published until 2005. The first major position statement, released by the National Academy of Neuropsychology (NAN; Bush et al., 2005), emphasized the importance of validity assessment stating that "adequate assessment of response validity is essential in order to maximize confidence in the results of neurocognitive and personality measures and in the diagnoses and recommendations that are based on the results" (p. 419). The NAN position paper further declared that "assessment of response validity, as a component of a medically necessary evaluation, is medically necessary" (p. 419), indicating that validity assessment should be considered essential, not only in forensic evaluations, but also in clinical evaluations. Shortly after this position statement was released, the American Academy of Clinical Neuropsychology (AACN) published practice guidelines for neuropsychological assessment and consultation (Board of Directors, 2007). These guidelines expanded upon the previous validity assessment guidance, stating that "the assessment of effort and motivation is important in any clinical setting, as a patient's effort may be compromised even in the absence of any potential or active litigation, compensation, or financial incentives" (p. 221). These papers not only cemented the importance of validity assessment in forensic evaluations, but they also highlighted that invalid symptom report and test performance can occur in clinical evaluations.

Coinciding with the professional organization guidance related to evaluating validity status, a burgeoning in empirical research on the topic of validity assessment started occurring. As illustrated in Figure 1.1, articles pertaining to validity assessment comprised just over 5% of articles published in *The Clinical Neuropsychologist* and *Archives of Clinical Neuropsychology* in the mid- to late 1990s but expanded to around 25% of articles published in these two journals by the mid-2010s. This empirical research resulted in a robust scientific foundation for the assessment of validity status in neuropsychology, and it provided clinicians with empirically based

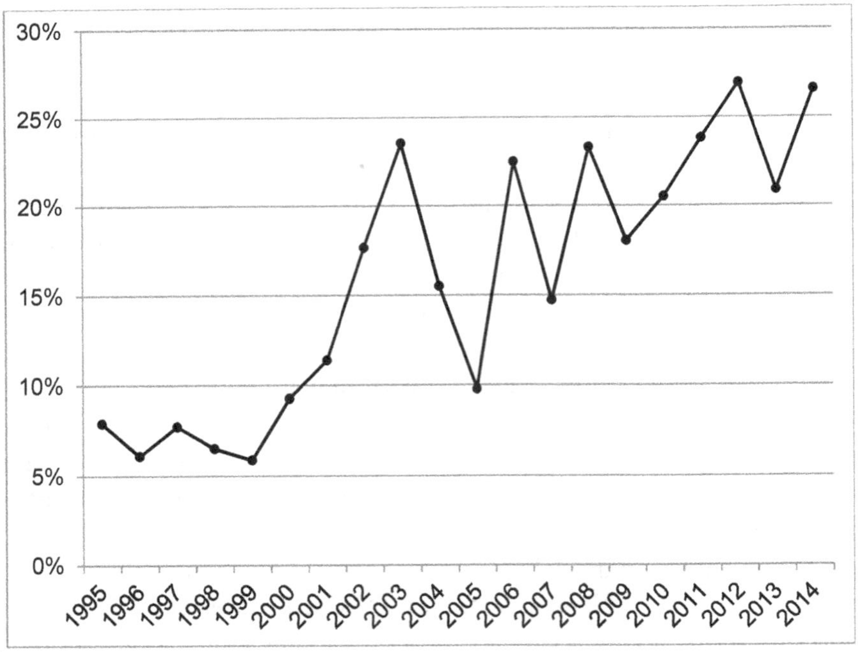

FIGURE 1.1. Average proportion of articles published on neuropsychological validity assessment by year in *The Clinical Neuropsychologist* and *Archives of Clinical Neuropsychology*. Data compiled by Martin, Schroeder, and Odland (2015). From Schroeder and Martin (2022a). Reprinted with permission from The Guilford Press.

methods for meeting the needs articulated by the early NAN and AACN position papers.

In addition to increasing the volume of literature, validity assessment research has shifted and expanded in focus (Suchy, 2019). Whereas early validity assessment research focused primarily on the detection of *malingering* in forensic examinees, research over the last two decades has pivoted to identifying *invalidity*, regardless of cause in clinical, forensic, and mixed clinical/forensic samples. This research has not only demonstrated that validity tests can be accurately used in clinical settings, but it has also highlighted that invalid test performance occurs in clinical examinees, sometimes for reasons other than malingering. Likely as a result of both this research and guidance by professional organizations, conceptualizations of validity assessment have expanded over time. In fact, the term "validity assessment," which is the term used throughout this book, is a relatively newer term, replacing more specific terms like "malingering" and "effort" assessment that do not accurately generalize to all instances of invalidity. Figure 1.2 demonstrates how this trend is reflected in published neuropsychological literature across time. A PsycInfo search, conducted on December 9, 2020, showed that the number of publications including the terms "malingering" and "neuropsychological" began declining in 2013, while the terms "performance validity" and "neuropsychological" began steadily increasing. By 2019, the number of neuropsychological articles utilizing the term performance validity outnumbered those utilizing the term malingering.

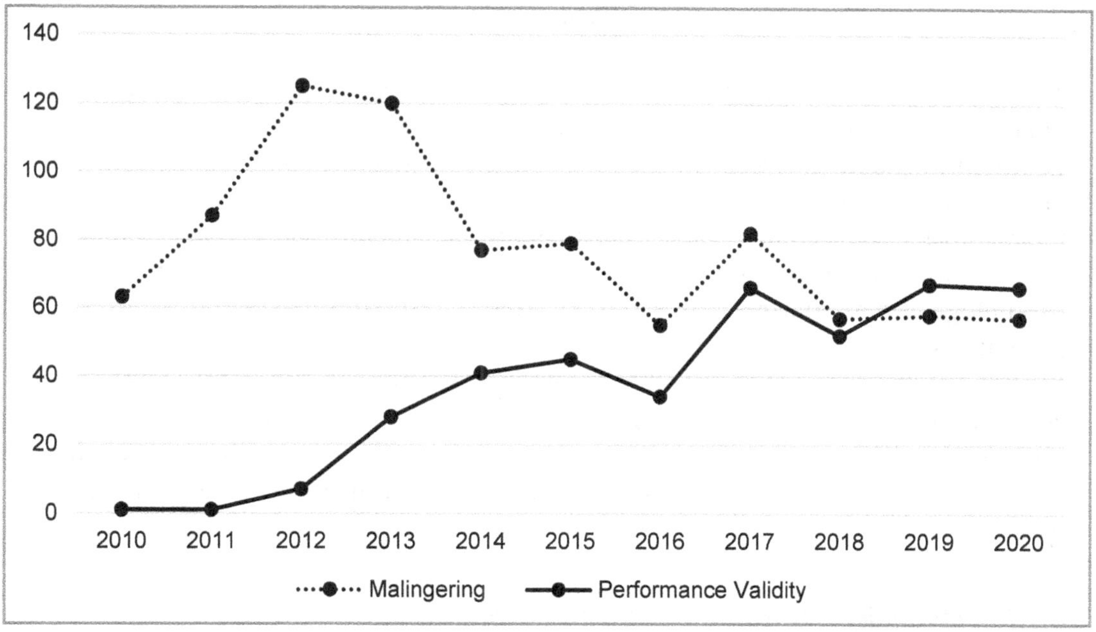

FIGURE 1.2. The number of publications utilizing the terms "malingering" and "neuropsychological" versus "performance validity" and "neuropsychological" per a PsycInfo search.

Likely as a result of this growing literature base, use of validity testing has evolved from being a practice espoused by only some clinicians in some circumstances to a practice viewed by the vast majority of neuropsychologists as being important across evaluation contexts (Martin, Schroeder, & Odland, 2024). To this point, a survey by Sharland and Gfeller in 2007 revealed that only 56% of neuropsychologists regularly used validity tests in their evaluations, and it was common for neuropsychologists to rely more heavily on clinical judgment-based methods than objective validity tests to assess validity. In contrast, by 2015, greater than 90% of surveyed North American neuropsychologists indicated that they often or always used stand-alone and embedded validity tests in their evaluations, similar to the rates that subjective approaches were utilized (Martin, Schroeder, & Odland, 2015). In an even more recent survey (Martin et al., 2024), it was found that greater than 98% of neuropsychologists believe validity testing to be mandatory or desirable when evaluating adults and older adults in forensic settings, more than 96% of clinicians believe validity testing to be mandatory or desirable when evaluating adults in clinical settings, and nearly 89% believe validity testing to be mandatory or desirable when evaluating older adults in clinical settings. Additionally, the vast majority of surveyed neuropsychologists indicated that a neuropsychological evaluation with few to no validity tests interspersed throughout the test battery is of lesser quality than one with multiple validity tests incorporated.

IMPORTANCE OF VALIDITY TESTING IN CLINICAL EVALUATIONS: ADDRESSING MYTHS

Taken together, the neuropsychological literature base, comprised of professional organization position papers, empirical research, and surveys of neuropsychologists' beliefs and practices, allows for several important conclusions. First, professional organizations in neuropsychology direct neuropsychologists to evaluate validity in their assessments. Second, there is robust research supporting the accuracy of validity assessment methods as applied to both forensic and clinical settings. Third, neuropsychologists view routine employment of validity testing as a standard of practice, a point also emphasized by professional organizations (Sweet et al., 2021). Yet, a skeptical perspective might, nonetheless, question whether validity assessment is necessary, accurate, and/or beneficial, particularly in clinical settings, where validity has historically been less of a focus. This section addresses potential myths, which, while superficially reasonable, are not borne out by the extant neuropsychology literature base.

Myth 1: Invalidity Is Uncommon in Clinical Settings

In general, invalid test performance is known to occur at greater base rates in forensic settings than clinical settings (Mittenberg, Patton, Canyock, & Condit, 2002;

Martin & Schroeder, 2020; Sweet et al., 2021). Because of this, it might be argued that validity assessment is less necessary in clinical than forensic settings. However, research indicates that rates of invalidity in clinical settings are not insignificant. For example, empirical research has demonstrated that 45% of clinical patients considering disability, 33% of patients involved with Workers' Compensation, 32% of clinically evaluated VA patients, and 20–25% of individuals evaluated for adult ADHD fail validity testing (Bianchini, Curtis, & Greve, 2006; Schroeder, Clark, & Martin, 2022; Shura, Denning, Armistead-Jehle, & Axelrod, 2022a; Suhr, Lee, & Angers, 2022). Surveyed neuropsychologists (Martin & Schroeder, 2020) estimate that 15% of patients across all nonforensic neuropsychological evaluations invalidate testing, with base rates ranging from 5 to 50% depending on the context and setting of the nonforensic evaluation (see Table 1.1). Perhaps unsurprisingly, neuropsychologists perceived clinical contexts associated with the potential for external incentive goals (e.g., patients who are clinical referred for a workup but are also thinking about litigation or are pursuing disability benefits) to have base rates of invalidity approximating those seen in forensic settings.

One might assume that validity assessment is only of particular relevance when clinical patients are identified as having an external incentive; however, surveyed neuropsychologists also note high rates of validity test failure in individuals with somatic symptom disorder or medically unexplained symptoms (50%), patients who

TABLE 1.1. Survey Findings of Estimated Base Rates of Invalidity within Clinical Contexts

Clinical context or setting	Median base rate
Patients involved in an accident who might be thinking about civil litigation	40.0%
Patients who might stand to obtain Veterans' benefits	40.0%
Patients who have Workers' Compensation involved	33.5%
Patients considering disability	25.0%
Patients undergoing adult ADHD evaluations	20.0%
Patients with somatoform disorders or medically unexplained symptoms	50.0%
Patients with oppositional attitudes toward testing	37.5%
Patients with psychiatric or mental health issues	22.0%
Patients with mild TBI who do not report having an external incentive	21.0%
Patients undergoing dementia evaluations	5.0%
Patients with none of the above histories and for whom validity failure is unexpected	5.0%
All clinical patients across all clinical contexts	15.0%

Note. Data from Martin and Schroeder (2020).

demonstrate oppositional attitudes toward testing (40%), and patients with psychiatric/mental health issues (22%), regardless of whether external incentives are present (Martin & Schroeder, 2020). Additionally, research shows that a sizable number of clinical patients with external incentives do not discuss their external incentive goals with their clinician. For example, in anonymous surveys of outpatients seeking psychological treatment, Van Egmond and Kummeling (2002) and Van Egmond, Kummeling, and Balcom (2005) found that just over 40% of patients had expectations of external gains (e.g., Social Security, work, legal issues), yet only 6.0 to 9.5% of patients told their clinicians about these expectations. Of note, those patients with expectations of secondary gain had significantly poorer treatment outcomes than those patients without expectations of secondary gain.

Research also demonstrates that patients who present with just the *possibility* of an external incentive fail validity testing at relatively high rates, even when they deny having explicit external incentive goals during the evaluation. For example, Schroeder et al. (2022) found that nearly 40% of clinical patients who reported that they had thought about but were not actively pursuing Social Security Disability Insurance (SSDI) payments produced invalid cognitive test data. The results suggest that some clinical patients are committed to pursuing disability even when they tell the neuropsychologist otherwise and that such patients fail validity testing at high rates. Likewise, Chafetz, Prentkowski, and Rao (2011) found that almost 7% of individuals who were in a vocational rehabilitation program aimed at returning them to work failed validity testing. When Chafetz and colleagues analyzed the records of those individuals who failed validity testing, they found that all of them were either seeking or had obtained SSDI payments, suggesting to the authors that these individuals were invalidly performing to covertly obtain or retain disability benefits. These research findings, taken as a whole, inform us that even when no external incentives are known to the clinician, it is possible (and sometimes even probable) that external incentives could still be present and negatively contributing to evaluation and treatment outcomes.

Even when external incentives are not hidden, clinicians might overlook the fact that external incentives exist. For example, Schroeder et al. (2022) found that just under 60% of clinical patients who were already on SSDI failed validity testing, which was higher than the percentage of patients who were actively seeking SSDI benefits (i.e., approximately 45%). One might question why validity test failure rates were higher in the group of patients who were already receiving an external incentive (i.e., SSDI benefits). This was likely because Disability Determination Services reviews medical status periodically to ensure that patients still have a disability. This is generally communicated to patients, and patients are often aware that they may be asked for updated medical records from their health care providers to ensure that conditions meeting standards for disability remain present. Indeed, the current authors have periodically been told by patients that they requested that their primary care physicians refer them for an evaluation because they needed updated paperwork to maintain their disability status. Thus, patients who are already receiving financial benefits may have an external incentive to exaggerate symptoms in an attempt to ensure that they do not lose the financial benefits that they are already receiving and have become dependent upon.

In summary, it is clear that invalidity occurs in clinical settings, and, in certain contexts, it can even occur at rates similar to those seen in forensic settings. Clinical patients who attend the evaluation with external incentive goals are certainly at increased risk for invalidity, and it is important to realize that not all of these patients will share their goals with their clinicians. Additionally, clinical patients who have somatoform presentations or medically unexplained symptoms, and clinical patients who have oppositional attitudes toward testing, are believed to be at relatively high risk of invalidating testing in clinical settings.

Myth 2: My Patients Are Different

In the past, invalid test performance and noncredible presentations were often associated with malingering, which, as a term, has carried negative connotations often reserved for a select group of patients thought to be so deplorable that they would deceive their clinician for selfish purposes. The *Diagnostic and Statistical Manual of Mental Disorders* (5th ed., text rev; DSM-5-TR; American Psychiatric Association, 2022) seems to reinforce the belief that malingering is an act of bad people engaged in an act of nefarious behavior, as it indicates that malingering should be suspected when there is a medicolegal context, marked discrepancies, lack of cooperation, and antisocial behavior. If adopting such a conceptualization, it can be difficult to reconcile that a patient who is polite and seemingly cooperative might also be malingering. However, in reality, many individuals who malinger do not have antisocial personalities or approach the evaluation in an overtly uncooperative manner (Martin & Schroeder, 2022b). Conversely, in our experience, clinical patients who fail validity testing in the presence of external incentives are often likeable individuals who present with sympathetic circumstances, appear distressed by their symptoms, and even appear earnest in their appeal for clinical assistance. Likely for this reason, criteria for determinations of malingering in neuropsychology (i.e., Slick, Sherman, & Iverson, 1999; Sherman, Slick, & Iverson, 2020) make no mention of examinee characterological traits and are, instead, based on (1) indicators of noncredibility determined by test performance, discrepancies, and inconsistencies, and (2) the suspicion that an external incentive has resulted in an act of deception. In addition to noting that many patients who malinger might come across as likeable and invested in the evaluation, it is, again, important to be aware that patients can invalidate testing for reasons other than malingering and that external incentives aren't always known in clinical evaluations.

Even after recognizing that not all individuals who malinger are characterologically bad people and that issues outside of malingering can cause invalidity, it can still be easy to underestimate or even deny the possibility of invalidity in our clinical patients. As health care professionals, we recognize that the vast majority of our patients are suffering and that our patients are often seeking help to minimize that suffering. Because of this view and because we are often wanting to see the best in our patients, it is understandable to view our patients as inherently good people who want help, report their symptoms accurately to receive accurate help, and do not underperform on testing. It can, therefore, be tempting to believe that the base rates listed in Table 1.1 might not apply on the individual patient level. The temptation might even arise to only use validity tests in cases that are highly atypical and/or suspicious for invalidity. A consequence of such an approach could be the formation of an inaccurate estimate of base rates of and schemas for invalidity in one's own clinical sample. For example, consider a clinician who does not routinely administer validity testing and then views cognitive test data obtained in cases where validity tests are not administered as accurate because the cognitive profiles *appear* realistic (despite the fact that research indicates that clinicians are not consistently accurate in identifying invalidity based on cognitive profile analyses). The clinician's belief that their patients are accurate in reporting symptoms and producing cognitive test data would then be reinforced. The clinician might then reason that validity testing is unnecessary for their particular practice or with certain groups of patients, creating a feedback loop involving circular reasoning and confirmation bias (i.e., interpreting information in a way that confirms one's previous hypotheses; Tversky & Kahneman, 1974).

Finally, outside of the factors described above, health care professionals might believe that their patients will not invalidate testing if positive and strong rapport is developed during the clinical evaluation. While this rapport might potentially serve as a mechanism to keep some patients positively engaged with the evaluation, having a positive and strong rapport is unlikely to stop all patients from invalidating testing if the patient believes that performing poorly on testing will allow him or her to gain a highly desirable incentive. As Suhr (2015) points out, invalid test results can serve as a form of communication and, in some cases of malingering, the communication that is being provided through invalid testing might be that the person believes that he or she is in need of an external incentive (e.g., disability payments) to survive. Arguably, then, by having a positive and strong rapport with the patient, the patient is no less likely to invalidate testing, as they may feel that the clinician with whom they have positive rapport may help them achieve their goals, which might include obtaining "help" in the form of assisting with getting an external incentive that is perceived and communicated as needed.

Myth 3: I Can Tell When Patients Are Not Being Forthright

It also might be tempting to believe that one can tell when a patient is not being forthright solely by identifying atypical symptoms and unusual behaviors and/or by examining obtained neuropsychological test scores for atypical patterns of cognitive dysfunction. However, such a stance is not empirically supported. In early studies on this topic, Heaton, Smith, Lehman, and Vogt (1978) and Faust, Hart, Guilmette, and

Arkes (1988) found that neuropsychologists provided with test data (minus validity test data) could not accurately differentiate cognitive profiles of patients with brain injuries from cognitive profiles of individuals simulating brain injuries. Additionally, it was found that the accuracy of validity determinations was no better for those clinicians with more years of clinical experience or those who expressed having greater confidence in their determinations. In a more recent study on the topic, Dandachi-FitzGerald, Merckelbach, and Ponds (2017) found that neuropsychologists were unreliable in making predictions of validity test performance in their own "real world" patients. After reviewing medical records and conducting clinical interviews, clinicians predicted how patients would perform on validity testing. These clinical impressions of validity status were incongruent with actual validity test performance in approximately 25% of cases, with the majority of errors (but not all of the errors) occurring when neuropsychologists thought that invalidity would be present. Thus, research to date indicates that clinicians are unable to reliably identify if patients are being forthright when clinical judgment alone is used for the determination.

Myth 4: Validity Tests Are Frequently Inaccurate

While determinations of validity that are based solely on clinical judgment are not empirically supported, research demonstrates that accurate determinations of invalidity can be made with appropriate utilization of empirically validated validity tests (e.g., Larrabee, 2014; Victor, Boone, Serpa, Buehler, & Ziegler, 2009). The superiority of validity testing to clinical judgment is now recognized by most neuropsychologists as is demonstrated by survey findings that show that the vast majority of neuropsychologists report that they will change their clinical impressions of a patient's credibility when validity test results are discrepant from their initial clinical impressions (Martin et al., 2024).

To understand why validity tests are accurate, it is helpful to first understand the process by which validity tests are developed and researched. The basic tenant of validity test development is that validity tests should be able to identify invalid test taking and, simultaneously, be largely unaffected by genuine cognitive dysfunction (Schroeder & Martin, 2022b). A validity test's ability to accurately identify invalid test takers is captured by its sensitivity rate, which, in a general sense, refers to the proportion of individuals with a condition who are classified as positives by a diagnostic test. A validity test's ability to accurately identify those who are providing valid test performance is captured by its specificity rate, which, in a general sense, refers to the proportion of individuals without a condition who are classified as negatives by a diagnostic test. As is the case with all diagnostic testing, a trade-off exists between a validity test's sensitivity and specificity. That is, sensitivity can be improved by using less conservative methods or cutoffs but this results in a sacrifice of specificity. Likewise, specificity can be improved by using more stringent methods or cutoffs but this results in a sacrifice of sensitivity. Because misclassifying a patient as invalidly performing when they are providing valid data could result in undue harm to the patient, methods and cutoff values for validity tests generally optimize specificity at the loss of sensitivity, with cutoffs typically set at levels demonstrating 90% or greater specificity. Therefore, individual validity tests inherently contain a low false-positive risk. Additionally, empirical research indicates that utilizing multiple validity tests can help to increase sensitivity while still maintaining specificity around 90%. For example, Victor et al. (2009) found that sensitivity was 84% and specificity was 94% when four validity tests were administered and failure of two or more validity tests was the criterion for identifying invalidity. Similarly, Larrabee (2014) found that sensitivity was 98% and specificity was 89% when seven validity tests were administered and failure of two or more validity tests was the criterion for identifying invalidity.

While empirical research indicates that false-positive rates of validity test failure are typically not high, there are a few conditions that can potentially cause elevated false-positive rates on some validity tests (e.g., Drane et al., 2016; Martin, Schroeder, & Olsen, 2022a; Meyers & Volbrecht, 2003; Smith, Peterssen, Iynik, Malc, & Tangalos, 2014). These conditions are outlined in Table 1.2; in general, they include conditions marked by cognitive impairment significant enough to interfere with independent completion of instrumental activities of daily living (e.g., cognitive impairment within the context of dementia, intellectual disability, or clearly impactful large strokes) or conditions that cause transient but significant altered mental status (e.g., epileptic seizures occurring in close proximity of testing). Even for individuals with these conditions, validity testing is still recommended; however, different validity tests and/or different validity test cutoffs are often required (further details are described in Chapters 4 and 5 in this book). In cases of lesser cognitive dysfunction, though, conventional validity tests at standard cutoffs can typically be utilized without concern for increased risk of false-positive errors.

In summary, validity tests are developed to minimize false-positive errors and, beyond this, there are multiple ways clinicians can further reduce the likelihood of making a false-positive determination of invalidity. These are discussed throughout the book but, in brief, include (1) knowing base rates of invalidity in clinical settings so that one understands the likelihood of invalid performance when certain conditions

TABLE 1.2. Conditions That Could Potentially Cause False-Positive Findings on Some Validity Tests

- Dementia-level cognitive impairment sufficient to cause impaired activities of daily living
- Intellectual disability
- Frequent epileptic seizures with seizure activity occurring in close proximity of testing
- Large and clearly identifiable cerebrovascular accidents

are met, (2) choosing validity tests that are appropriate for the patient's suspected degree of cognitive impairment, (3) aggregating multiple validity tests to ensure that classification accuracy rates are optimal, (4) recognizing degree-of-validity test failure which can allow for more confident determinations of invalidity, and (5) being aware of conditions that might increase the risk of false-positive findings.

Myth 5: Using Validity Tests Takes Too Much Time

Within health care settings, clinicians are often confronted by the need to limit the length of the exam due to (1) restrictions in how much time will be reimbursed by health insurance, (2) patient tolerability of the exam, and/or (3) institutional demands to see a greater volume of patients. As a result, clinicians are tasked with accurately collecting data in the most time efficient manner possible. Unfortunately, as more tests are added to a test battery, more time, which may not be reimbursable, is typically needed.

Given that testing time is an important practical consideration in clinical settings, it is pertinent to note that validity test batteries can be constructed in such a manner that minimal time is added to the test battery. As discussed in Chapters 4 and 5, clinicians now have access to many well-validated embedded validity tests that do not take any additional time to administer, brief stand-alone validity tests that take no more than about 5 minutes to administer (e.g., Dot Counting Test [DCT] and Rey 15-Item Test with recognition), and well-validated shortened/abbreviated forms of frequently utilized stand-alone validity tests (e.g., Test of Memory Malingering [TOMM] Trial 1). Thus, a clinician can still employ a validity test battery that spans multiple cognitive domains (e.g., attention/working memory, mental processing speed, verbal memory, visual memory) without adding more than roughly 10 minutes of time to the length of testing.

Myth 6: There Is Greater Harm in Assessing Invalidity Than Not

It is understandable to be concerned about the possibility of making a false-positive determination of invalidity, as it can be harmful to suggest that a patient is providing inadequate testtaking effort or not being forthright when such is not the case. At the same time, it is also important to consider the harm to patients, the field of neuropsychology, and society when invalidity occurs but is not identified.

Not identifying invalidity can cause iatrogenesis to patients. Patients invalidating testing due to factors outside of malingering, and even patients invalidating testing due to malingering, might hold inaccurate beliefs regarding symptom severity, attribution of their symptoms to certain injuries or illnesses (e.g., mild traumatic brain injury [mTBI]), or the impact of symptoms on aspects of daily functioning (e.g., ability to work). By failing to identify invalid test data in such patients and accepting the data as reflecting deficits that are not actually present, clinicians can reinforce unwarranted beliefs of illness, disability, and dysfunction. In many of these cases, unnecessary recommendations for treatment, testing, and referral to additional specialists can occur. In addition to such recommendations leading to unwarranted costs, they can divert treatment attention from conditions in need of care. Additionally, unwarranted diagnostic testing and specialist referral can ferment patients' disillusionment with the health care system when it results in even more encounters with clinicians perceived as skeptical and unsympathetic to medically unexplained symptoms.

Consider an example of a patient who sustained a concussion and has co-occurring major depression. The patient may be experiencing amotivation, attention issues, pessimism, and a loss of hope, which reinforces his belief that his brain injury caused these issues, that his problems are permanent, and that he is disabled and unable to meaningfully engage in daily tasks including working. He undergoes a neuropsychological evaluation and invalidates testing to help ensure that the neuropsychologist provides documentation to get him SSDI payments, which he feels that he needs. If the invalidity is not identified, and he obtains disability based on an invalid assessment, he may subsequently become more isolated from others due to not working, experience less fulfillment in his life, obtain less financial support as compared to when working, and experience worsened depression and lowered quality of life as a result. If, however, invalidity is identified, psychoeducation is provided on recovery after concussion, and adequate treatment of the major depression (which was the actual cause of the patient's symptoms) is carried out, the patient's depression, his view of himself and his capabilities, and his quality of life might improve.

In addition to potentially causing harm to patients, not identifying invalidity can potentially harm the profession in that perceptions regarding the quality of our work lessen. If testing (along with diagnoses and clinical recommendations) is reported as being valid despite it being invalid, it might conflict with conceptualizations held by other related health care professionals such as neurologists and psychiatrists. If this happens with enough frequency, those related professionals may form a negative view of the field of neuropsychology, perceiving findings to be inaccurate and believing neuropsychologists to be inept. This can result in those professionals not referring patients for evaluations when evaluations could be helpful for their patients.

Finally, not identifying invalidity can also negatively impact society. For example, Chafetz (2011) indicated that an estimated payout of approximately $180 billion occurs for feigned disability across all SSDI program categories, with $20 billion being spent on malingered mental disorders (Chafetz & Underhill, 2013). Similarly, malingered brain injury claims within the Veterans Benefits Administration were estimated to be $136 million to $235 million in 2015 (Denning & Shura, 2019). In addition to these cost estimates, it should be considered that there is a loss of tax revenue for the common good, individuals who are working often have to pay increased costs for policies, and individuals who truly need financial assistance might be denied or postponed assistance due to programs having finite resources that are publicly available.

Myth 7: It's Better to Not Know

Arguably, some of the previous myths might be self-justified if a clinician does not want to address a potential underlying issue: he or she would rather be unaware of the test invalidity if it occurs. The old saying that "ignorance is bliss" might ring true. It can be difficult to determine how to move forward with an evaluation when data are known to be inaccurate, which can admittedly complicate diagnostic and treatment planning decisions. Most clinicians strive to be helpful to their patients and it is easy to feel uncomfortable when thinking about possibly confronting those for whom they are entrusted to provide care. There can be anxiety regarding how patients (and maybe even referring providers) might react to being told data are invalid, and there might even be fear that patients will respond negatively in the form of formal complaints. Furthermore, it can be difficult to know how to proceed in a clinically helpful way when testing is invalid, and it can sometimes feel unfulfilling when we are not able to speak to some aspects of the exam because data are invalid. The first step in addressing this issue, if present, is recognizing that these feelings are *normal*. The next step in addressing the issue is learning how to manage invalid presentations, doing so in an accurate and meaningful manner. In this book, we aim to discuss literature and provide our own recommendations to help clinicians navigate this potentially anxiety provoking but necessary endeavor.

CLOSING REMARKS

In conclusion, professional organization practice papers published over the past 15+ years (e.g., Bush et al., 2005; Board of Directors, 2007; Heilbronner et al., 2009; Sweet et al., 2021) indicate that validity assessment is essential and medically necessary in all settings, including nonforensic clinical settings. There has also been a shift in thinking on the topic of validity assessment: validity testing, especially within clinical settings, should not be utilized solely for the purpose of trying to determine if malingering might be present, but validity testing should be utilized to help determine if obtained test data are accurate. It is necessary to know when test results are not accurate to avoid potential harm to the patient, society, and field of neuropsychology. Equally important, if validity testing suggests that neuropsychological test results are accurate, clinicians can have increased confidence in the results of cognitive and psychological testing, which require patient motivation, engagement, and cooperation. Correspondingly, by having increased confidence that cognitive and psychological test results are valid, clinicians can also have increased confidence in their conclusions, diagnoses, and treatment recommendations, which will be more likely to help patients, referral sources, and the broader society. Table 1.3 summarizes these and other important considerations and shifts in thinking regarding validity assessment in clinical settings.

TABLE 1.3. Important Considerations and Shifts in Thinking Regarding Validity Assessment in Clinical Settings

1. To assess cognitive and emotional statuses, clinicians must utilize interactive neuropsychological tests that rely heavily on patient motivation, engagement, and cooperation.
2. In clinical settings, especially, there are a variety of factors that could potentially contribute to low motivation, engagement, and cooperation, resulting in inaccurate/invalid neuropsychological test findings.
3. Utilizing validity tests is the most accurate way to determine whether neuropsychological testing is valid. Clinicians should not rely on clinical judgment, qualitative data analyses, and/or patient characteristics or interactions as sole ways to determine if testing is valid.
4. It is possible to utilize validity tests without significantly adding to the length of the test battery, and one does not need to be an expert in validity assessment to accurately utilize validity tests.
5. Validity testing should *not* be thought of as a "malingering detection" tool. Validity testing *should* be thought of as a tool that allows the clinician to have increased confidence that neuropsychological test results are accurate.
6. When invalid testing is identified, the clinician should *not* jump to the conclusion that malingering is present; instead, the clinician *should* conclude that neuropsychological testing is not an accurate portrayal of the patient's cognitive and/or emotional status.
7. When invalid testing is identified, the clinician should be cautious in assigning diagnoses and making conclusive prognoses, as these conclusions could be inaccurate and could harm the patient, the profession, and/or society.
8. Help can still be provided to the patient when testing is invalid. There are discussions of conceptualizing patients when invalid testing is present, models for providing feedback when testing is invalid, and there are resources for report writing when testing is invalid.
9. Due to the importance of obtaining accurate neuropsychological test data, multiple professional organizations have concluded that validity tests are essential and medically necessary in all evaluations, even clinical nonforensic evaluations.

CHAPTER 2

Reviewing Referrals

Managing Clinical Consults That Contain Forensic Elements

For most clinicians, clinical work begins before the initial face-to-face encounter with a patient. Typically, the first step is reviewing insurance information, referral letters, and/or medical notes to ensure that referrals are appropriate for evaluation by the clinician. For example, the clinician might consider the patient's age, reason or condition leading to referral, primary language, and potential for a dual relationship (e.g., if the clinician knows the patient personally).

In addition to screening for issues such as those discussed above, clinicians should also consider whether referrals are appropriate for clinical evaluations. If billing the patient's health insurance, this means that the clinician must determine whether the evaluation is medically necessary, as evaluations that are not considered medically necessary (i.e., they are not expected to affect medical/health care management of the patient) are typically not reimbursed by health insurance (Schroeder, Martin, & Walling, 2019a). Even if an evaluation is to be paid in cash, it is necessary to consider whether a clinical evaluation, which entails the development of a doctor–patient relationship, or a forensic evaluation, in which no doctor–patient relationship is established (Binder, 2019), is most appropriate. Within the context of validity assessment, two of the more common types of referrals requiring careful consideration are clinical referrals to document neuropsychological dysfunction to aide in seeking disability benefits and clinical referrals of individuals involved with or considering litigation. From our perspective, there are instances where such referrals are appropriate to accept clinically but also instances where such referrals should be declined. In the following sections, we discuss factors to consider when screening such cases, and we also provide guidance for communicating the advantages and disadvantages of proceeding with a clinical versus forensic evaluation when discussing the case with referral sources and potential patients.

CASES WITH DISABILITY INVOLVED OR POTENTIALLY INVOLVED

When patients are clinically referred for an evaluation, but disability pursuit is also present, the clinician will need to determine whether a clinical or nonclinical evaluation would be most appropriate. For many clinicians, deciding how to move forward will likely vary on a case-by-case basis. We discuss three types of cases where the presenting issues are all related to disability pursuit but other background factors are different. We then discuss how each case might be handled within a clinical setting.

Cases Where Disability Is the Sole Referral Question

When patients are referred to document cognitive and/or psychological functioning for the *sole purpose* of assisting in an application for SSDI benefits, it would likely be inappropriate to accept the patient for a clinical evaluation and bill that patient's health insurance. This is because accepting the case as a clinical one would establish a doctor–patient relationship when there is no intent of truly having such a relationship. Additionally, health insurance might not reimburse for the evaluation because determining disability is not a medically necessary question. In cases where it is clear that the only referral question is regarding assistance for SSDI, potential patients might instead be directed to contact a Disability Determination Services (DDS) case worker. The potential patient can then obtain a referral for a psychological consultative examination if deemed necessary by DDS. A psychological consultative examination is a fairly condensed and structured evaluation done by a psychologist who is credentialled with and paid by DDS for the evaluation (Schroeder & Chafetz, 2022). Within these evaluations, the examinee is not paying any money for the evaluation (DDS is paying the agreed-upon contracted cost) and the examinee's health insurance is not billed. The individual, however, is unlikely to get a thorough neuropsychological evaluation, and he or she is unlikely to obtain feedback from the clinician on the results.

As an alternative to directing the potential patient to DDS, the clinician could accept the individual for a quasi-forensic evaluation and require that the evaluation be self-pay instead of billed through health insurance. While this would be appropriate (and in some instances, maybe preferable for the examinee as it would likely be a more thorough evaluation with feedback on the results), it would obviously cost the individual money whereas obtaining an evaluation through a DDS contracted psychological consultant would not cost him or her money. For this reason, it would be ethically appropriate to discuss potentially obtaining a DDS referred evaluation prior to agreeing to see the potential patient for a self-pay evaluation. A discussion on this topic with the potential patient could be structured in a manner similar to following:

"Dr. Smith referred you for a neuropsychological evaluation, indicating that the evaluation is for assessment of your cognitive functioning to potentially aide in obtaining SSDI benefits. While I would be happy to conduct the evaluation, I do need to provide you with some information on this topic that might alter whether you want to move forward with the evaluation. Since the evaluation is not for health care purposes, but for potential disability attainment, it is not what health insurance companies consider medically necessary. Consequently, health insurance companies generally refuse to pay for these evaluations. To move forward, there are a couple of options that I would suggest. If you would like, I could perform this evaluation for you but without billing insurance, meaning that there would be an out-of-pocket expense for you. I would estimate that your expense for the evaluation would be around $1,000 (or whatever the estimated expense would be), but my billing specialist could provide you with a more precise estimate. Another option would be to contact an SSDI case manager to ask if they could refer you to one of their contracted psychologists to get an exam. If they believe it would be necessary to help determine whether you have a disability, they would refer you for an evaluation, and they would likely pay all of the associated costs. The evaluation would probably be less comprehensive, solely conducted to help determine whether you meet their standards for disability, and you probably won't directly get feedback on the results, but it would help to achieve the goal of obtaining documentation for disability pursuit."

Cases Where Disability Is Present and Medical Necessity Might Be Present

Unlike when it is clear that the evaluation is solely for disability-related purposes, there are times when a referring provider documents the presence of symptoms, presumably in need of diagnosis and treatment planning, but then only states in the referral note something along the lines of "Patient would like to pursue disability and we discussed referral for formal neuropsychometric evaluation." In some of these cases, the medical necessity for a neuropsychological evaluation could perhaps be inferred; however, there is also the possibility that the patient's health insurance will reject reimbursement given that disability is the stated reason for referral. In cases of poor or unclear documentation on the part of the referring provider, one might consider contacting the referring provider to (1) ensure that a medically necessary question exists and (2) document the medically necessary question in the referral information to reduce the likelihood of insurance rejection. If medical necessity is established via this contact, it could be appropriate to move forward with a clinical evaluation. In such cases, it would still be important to discuss with the potential patient the possible advantages and limitations of continuing with a clinical evaluation (potentially using one of the scripts in this chapter) since the individual appears primarily interested in assistance with their disability application.

Cases Where Disability and Medical Necessity Are Both Clearly Present

Finally, outside of those types of cases previously discussed, we have seen a number of referrals that are made where disability pursuit is present (or likely present) but there are also clear clinical questions that would impact medical management. In this instance, there would likely be medical necessity, and health insurance could reasonably be billed. Consider, for example, the following case which was an actual referral that one of the authors received. The referral was from a local neurologist; the patient was a 61-year-old female who was reporting depressive symptoms, cognitive decline, difficulties with completing instrumental activities of daily living, and problems with completing activities at work. The referral note from the neurologist read "Please evaluate to help plan treatment. Differential diagnosis is pseudodementia due to depression versus emerging dementia. Patient is also pursuing disability and would like documentation for this." In this case, it is clear that the referral is for two purposes: differential diagnosis which would impact medical management (which makes the referral medically necessary) and documentation for disability pursuit (which is not a medically necessary reason for an evaluation).

In a case such as that which was just described, we tend to discuss the dual referral question with the patient either before the appointment is scheduled or at the very beginning of the clinical interview. A statement similar to the following might be provided:

> "Dr. Doe referred you for an evaluation of your cognitive functioning. He stated that the evaluation would help to direct your medical care, and he also noted that you would like documentation for pursuing disability. Health insurance policies typically indicate that they will only cover costs associated with evaluations that will directly impact your health care treatment. For that reason, the evaluation that I would provide to you would be geared toward achieving that objective—providing you with a diagnosis and treatment recommendations. It would not specifically be conducted to provide documentation for SSDI, as health insurance companies do not consider that need to be medically necessary, and they would not cover the cost of this. At the same time, many patients send their medical notes to Disability Determination Services for review, which Disability Determination Services often considers sufficient for documentation. Now, I cannot guarantee the outcome of the evaluation, I cannot guarantee that the results will be viewed favorably or will get you disability benefits, and I must emphasize that Disability Determination Services makes that ultimate determination of whether you get disability benefits, not me. But, if you would like to move forward, I would be happy to conduct the clinical evaluation and, after we discuss the findings, you can decide if you want to send the findings to Disability Determination Services in addition to your referring provider. Would you like to move forward with the clinical evaluation?"

In our experience, nearly all patients agree to the clinical evaluation, and we proceed to conduct the evaluation as a clinical one, billing health insurance.

Conclusions

Like us, most neuropsychologists appear not to view the presence of disability questions as exclusionary in the context of clinical evaluations so long as there are also clinically appropriate questions regarding diagnosis or treatment planning. In a recent survey (data previously unpublished but collected as part of the survey described in Martin & Schroeder, 2020) we asked neuropsychologists the question: "A patient is clinically referred to determine degree of cognitive impairment and need for intervention. At the outset of the neuropsychological evaluation, the patient states that he hopes the evaluation will contribute to his treatment planning, but his primary goal is to use the clinical report in support of applying for disability. How likely are you to accept this patient as a clinical patient?" The most frequent response (i.e., the mode response), which was endorsed by approximately 30% of neuropsychologists, was that the patient would be accepted as a clinical patient 100% of the time. Additionally, the median response from all surveyed neuropsychologists was that the case would be seen as a clinical case 80% of the time. These data suggest that, even in cases where the patient's primary reason for the evaluation is to support a disability application, so long as there are medically necessary questions that can be answered, most neuropsychologists will proceed with the clinical evaluation in most cases.

CASES WITH LITIGATION INVOLVED OR POTENTIALLY INVOLVED

When individuals are clinically referred for an evaluation, yet are simultaneously involved in or considering litigation, the neuropsychologist must determine whether a clinical or forensic evaluation would be most appropriate. Even when such cases are appropriate to be seen clinically, they can present with a set of unique challenges that clinicians must consider. For one, when lawsuits occur, data and opinions from clinical evaluations can lose confidentiality and become part of a public record (Schroeder & Martin, 2022b). Furthermore, lawsuits are adversarial in nature, which means that the patient's neuropsychological report is likely to be scrutinized by attorneys and retained experts from both sides. Given this, as well as the increased likelihood for noncredible symptom report in the context of possible or active litigation, such cases often encourage a more thorough investigation of other sources and materials to corroborate the individual's reported history and symptoms. In some cases, this can include reviewing an increased quantity of medical records and/or reviewing records that one might not generally review within the context of standard clinical practice (e.g., accident reports that are not readily available in the medical record or scholastic records). Moreover, the clinician might consider utilizing more thorough and/or time-consuming testing when there is knowledge that the patient might look to introduce the exam findings into his or her lawsuit. While clinicians can (and should) bill for all of the time that is required to conduct accurate and skillful evaluations, time limit caps are sometimes provided by health care insurance (e.g., not allowing payment for more than 8 hours of the clinician's time). In these cases, health insurance might not pay for all of the activities and, even if a clinician were to do these activities for reduced fees or free, these activities might sometimes be so time consuming that doing them could cause clinicians to have less time to see other clinical patients who need care.

Given the considerations noted above, clinicians will need to determine their own willingness to engage in a mixed clinical/forensic case. In addition to this, though, other factors should also be considered. In discussing this topic further, we present three types of mixed clinical/forensic referrals that we believe are likely the most common scenarios seen within clinical neuropsychology.

Cases Where Future Legal Issues Could Be Pending in the Background

Sometimes clinical referrals of patients are made without any mention of future litigation. Consider, for example, the following case. A 63-year-old male was referred by his primary care physician after suffering a stroke following an orthopedic surgery. The referral note from the primary care physician read "Evaluate and treat. Patient had stroke and would like to get a cognitive baseline to help direct speech therapy." Upon meeting with the patient for the clinical interview, the patient described that he was considering suing the physician who performed the surgery. He stated that he was considering litigation because he had a known history of stroke, yet his surgeon did not discuss the possibility that another stroke could occur as a result of his elective surgery. The patient stated that, if he had known that another stroke was possible, he would not have undergone the surgery. In this case, the referral was for treatment planning purposes (which makes the referral medically necessary) but there was also a clear possibility of litigation, which could have resulted in the neuropsychological report being submitted as legal evidence if litigation were to be pursued.

In cases such as the one just described, where a patient is clinically referred for an evaluation to address a clinically relevant question, it is our perspective that such patients should not be denied care just because there is a stated potential for future litigation. During the clinical interview, however, we discuss with the patient that the evaluation is being completed for health care purposes and not for the purpose of pursuing litigation because doing the evaluation for litigation purposes and billing health care would not be permissible and could even potentially be considered health care fraud. We also note that, if the patient were to pursue litigation and request the neuropsychologist's work be involved, patient–doctor confidentiality would no longer apply, and information obtained from the evaluation could become part of a public record. It is our experience that patients generally agree to pursue this type of evaluation as a clinical one, and follow-up litigation does not always occur. Our specific discussion is often along the lines of the following:

"Before moving forward with the evaluation, I want to make sure that we are on the same page regarding a couple of issues that you brought up. First, if this evaluation is to be billed to health insurance, which I believe was our original plan, it has to be completed for a medical reason, not a litigation-related reason, as litigation-related matters are typically not considered medically necessary reasons for health insurance to pay for evaluations. If you decide to move forward with a lawsuit and you want to use findings from our clinical evaluation after the fact, you would be able to do so, but this evaluation would, again, be done to address your health care needs, not to address litigation-related matters if we bill health insurance. Would you be in agreement with that or would you prefer to obtain an evaluation to better address litigation-related matters? (Pause here to obtain the patient's response.) Next, I need to inform you that if you were to pursue litigation and request information from this appointment be used in litigation, all of the information obtained during the evaluation could lose patient–doctor confidentiality and become part of a public record related to your lawsuit. Do you understand that, and do you still want to continue with this evaluation as is?"

Cases Where Legal Issues Are Co-Occurring

Sometimes clinical referrals are made with an indication that the evaluation request is clinical in nature but there is co-occurring litigation. Consider the following referral: A neurologist referred a 42-year-old male who was involved in a motor vehicle accident 5 months earlier. Available medical records suggested that the patient sustained a mild traumatic brain injury. The patient complained to the neurologist of headaches, periodic dizziness, cognitive dysfunction, and mood lability. The referral note from the neurologist read "Patient hit head in MVA. Evaluate to determine if cognitive symptoms are due to brain injury and/or depression. Lawsuit is pending." In this case, it is clear that the referral is for differential diagnosis which would impact medical management, but there are also clear signs of active litigation related to the injury in question. In this type of case, we tend to have discussions with patients (ideally before seeing the patient for a clinical interview) to ensure that a clinical evaluation is warranted and wanted by the patient and to also ensure that patients understand the limitations of using a clinical evaluation in litigation. This discussion may be similar to the following:

"Dr. Smith referred you for an evaluation of your cognitive functioning. She stated that the evaluation would help to direct your medical care, and she also noted that you are pursuing litigation. Health insurance policies, however, typically indicate that they will only cover costs associated with evaluations that will directly impact your health care treatment. We cannot conduct an evaluation solely for litigation-related reasons and then bill your health insurance for it because that could be considered health care fraud. Additionally, there are other differences between a health care-related evaluation and a litigation-related evaluation that I want you to be aware of.

"If we were to move forward with a health care-related evaluation, the goal of the evaluation would be focused on achieving a diagnosis and health care-related treatment recommendations, not necessarily on determining whether your accident was the cause of any of your symptoms and whether any ongoing care needs are directly related to issues stemming from the accident. Therefore, the evaluation report will likely be insufficient in addressing questions of causation, so it may not be of great help in your lawsuit. Further, there is always the possibility that findings from the evaluation do not support claims made in the lawsuit. If that were to be the case, the evaluation could still be discoverable by either attorney, and it could be introduced into court. Finally, if we were to move forward with an evaluation and you later request the results be included in your lawsuit, all of the information obtained during the evaluation could lose patient–doctor confidentiality and become part of a public record related to your lawsuit.

"For all of these reasons, if your goal is to use this evaluation in litigation, I would suggest that you first talk to your lawyer. He or she might then contact us or another neuropsychologist to schedule a forensic evaluation. The goals of a forensic evaluation would be somewhat different as the focus would be on not only identifying the nature and severity of your symptoms but also determining their relation to your injury. In a forensic evaluation there would be a focus on documenting diagnoses, determining how those diagnoses relate to your accident, documenting functional issues that might result from those diagnoses, and making recommendations for treatment and other care or needs related to litigation. If pursuing this route, the neuropsychologist involved in the case would likely need to review additional records, which your attorney would help to obtain. Additionally, with this type of evaluation, you and your attorney decide what happens with the report—for example, if you want to use it in the lawsuit or if you want to keep it private. This litigation-related evaluation would likely be more helpful for your lawsuit, but the cost would not be covered by health insurance; it would need to be paid out of pocket, and it can be quite expensive."

After having this discussion with the patient, it is recommended that the clinician ask the patient which type of evaluation they believe would be most fitting (clinical or forensic). It is then recommended that they speak with their attorney to get the attorney's input as well.

After having the discussion outlined above, both the patient and the clinician need to decide which evaluation to pursue, with the ultimate decision of whether to accept the case as a clinical evaluation being determined by the clinician. We tend to accept the patient as a clinical patient if that is the patient's preference *and* if there appears to be a genuine need and desire for clinical care. Conversely, if (1) the patient and his or her attorney desire a forensic evaluation *or* (2) it is stated that they still want a clinical evaluation but there does not appear to be a genuine need or desire for clinical care, we will decline the clinical evaluation but offer a forensic evaluation or a referral for a forensic evaluation. If the patient and/or his or her attorney wants the clinical evaluation but we feel a clinical evaluation is inappropriate, we state that, while we understand they are asking for a clinical evaluation, we don't feel a clinical evaluation is suitable for the purpose, we are concerned about the possibility of committing health care fraud, and, consequently, we are going to have to decline the referral.

Cases Where Legal Issues Are Clearly the Impetus for the Evaluation

Sometimes clinical referrals are made when the evaluation is clearly intended to be forensic in nature. Consider the following referral: A primary care physician referred a 34-year-old female who was involved in a motor vehicle accident and diagnosed with a concussion. The referral note from the primary care physician read "Patient is involved in a lawsuit and is requesting a referral for neuropsychological testing." Within the medical records from the physician, there was no documentation of concerns about cognitive or psychological functioning. The clinician called the referring physician and asked about the medical necessity of the case. The physician indicated that he was referring the patient because the patient requested the referral (not seeming to realize that the lack of medical necessity would result in a likely rejection of health insurance coverage), and the physician did not think that the results would likely change his treatment plan. Consequently, our office contacted the referred patient and discussed that there was no medical necessity for completing the evaluation; thus, billing health insurance could not be ethically or legally done. The patient indicated that she asked her primary care physician for the referral at the request of her attorney, and she didn't realize it would be inappropriate to bill health insurance. She was directed to talk to her attorney about undergoing a forensic neuropsychological evaluation, which she stated that she would do.

In the previous case, it seems likely that the referring physician simply did not realize that the referral was not an appropriate clinical referral. Conversely, it seems possible that the patient's attorney, who directed the patient to ask for the referral, might have been intentionally trying to deceive the health care providers with the referral. When there is intention to deceive others with the purpose of the referral, we refer to these deceptive referrals as stealth referrals. Specifically, we define a *stealth referral* as the following: a stealth referral for a forensic evaluation is a referral that is *intentionally* deceptive in the sense that the referral was initiated with the goal of obtaining data for forensic purposes, but that goal is hidden under the guise of a clinical referral. The purpose of a stealth referral for a forensic evaluation is typically to have the evaluation billed to a party (e.g., health insurance) that is not involved in the forensic proceeding in an attempt to save money within the forensic proceeding.

As an example of a stealth referral, consider the following referral that one of us has received: An attorney contacted the clinician and indicated that the attorney's client was in a lawsuit related to a brain injury. The attorney indicated that his client is struggling with apathy, and it was not clear if the apathy was due to the brain injury or depression. The attorney indicated that the client is a very nice gentleman and throughout his work with the attorney, the attorney has become more and more concerned about his well-being. The attorney adamantly stated that he did not want a forensic evaluation of the client; instead, he was looking for a doctor to determine whether the client is experiencing increasing depression so that the client can receive help if that is the issue. While the attorney indicated (when asked) that he does not yet have an expert neuropsychologist retained, he "reassure(d)" the clinician that the clinical evaluation would not be used as part of the legal case.

While it is possible that the attorney was being genuine in his request for a clinical evaluation, this was very possibly an attempt at a stealth forensic evaluation. In this case, the clinician communicated to the attorney that it seemed quite possible that the report could be used in a legal manner and discussed the limitations of the evaluation and resultant report if they were to be relied on as evidence in the case. The clinician then described the advantages of obtaining a forensic evaluation, which could still include recommendations for treatment of depression, if present. The attorney stated that he would discuss this with his client and then follow up; no follow up ever occurred.

While the two cases just described are different, they share an important commonality: the intended goal of the evaluation was seemingly forensic. In these situations, we tend not to accept the referrals as clinical referrals. Surveyed neuropsychologists also indicate that they tend to decline referrals for clinical patients who plan to *primarily* utilize the evaluation for forensic purposes. Specifically, neuropsychologists were asked: "A patient is clinically referred to determine degree of cognitive impairment and need for intervention. At the outset of the neuropsychological evaluation, the patient states that he hopes the evaluation will contribute to his treatment planning, but his primary goal is to use the clinical report in support of pursuing personal injury litigation. How likely are you to accept this patient as a clinical patient?" The most frequent response (i.e., the mode), which was endorsed by approximately 25% of neuropsychologists, was that the patient would be accepted as a clinical patient 0% of the time. The median response from all surveyed neuropsychologists was that the case would be seen as a clinical case 25% of the time (data previously unpublished but collected as part of the survey described in Martin & Schroeder, 2020).

Conclusions

In conclusion, it is our perspective that, in most instances, it is not appropriate to conduct a clinical evaluation when patients pursue the evaluation for the *primary purpose* of supporting a lawsuit. In such cases, education can be provided about why referrals are not accepted as clinical referrals, and recommendations for appropriate forensic referrals can be made. However, in cases where appropriate clinical questions co-exist, a clinical evaluation might still be appropriate at the discretion of the neuropsychologist so long as there is a mutual understanding between the patient and clinician that (1) the goal of the evaluation will be to address a medically necessary question (e.g., treatment planning), and (2) topics pertinent to the lawsuit will likely not be adequately addressed by a clinical evaluation.

FACTORS ASSOCIATED WITH INCREASED POTENTIAL FOR NONCREDIBLE SYMPTOMATOLOGY

In addition to ensuring that referred cases are appropriate for clinical evaluations, it is recommended that clinicians be aware of factors that are associated with an increased potential for noncredible symptomatology when reviewing referral records. Factors that suggest the potential for noncredible symptomatology are listed in Table 2.1. Identifying that such factors are present can help to ensure that appropriate questions are asked during the clinical interview, including those questions that might "pull out" clearer indications of pursuits of external incentives.

In many cases, the factors listed in Table 2.1 are associated with an increased likelihood of noncredibility because they either represent or suggest the possibility of external incentives (e.g., Ardolf, Denney, & Houston, 2007; Bianchini et al., 2006; Marshall et al., 2010; Shura et al., 2022; Suhr et al., 2022). For example, indications of problems at work could suggest that the examinee might be considering leaving the workforce, which could mean they might be seeking documentation to support

TABLE 2.1. Factors That Could Suggest an Increased Risk of Noncredible Symptomatology

- Indications of problems at work
- Disability might be or is being pursued
- Workers' Compensation is involved
- Veteran status, particularly when a diagnosis could be linked to military service
- A note of an accident occurring in the medical record
- Litigation might be or is being pursued
- Patient has legal or criminal issues pending
- Indications of problems at school
- Somatoform presentations are suspected or known
- Mild traumatic brain injury with persistent cognitive complaints
- Adult attention-deficit/hyperactivity disorder is a diagnostic consideration
- There are prominent psychiatric or mental health issues potentially contributing
- Severe cognitive complaints without medical conditions expected to cause dysfunction
- Other health care providers use terms presented in Table 2.2.

TABLE 2.2. Terms That Physicians Sometimes Use to Signal Possible Poor Effort, Feigning, or Nonorganic/Somatoform Presentations

Term	Possible suggestion
Nonorganic or nonphysiological	Terms suggestive of non-neurological etiologies, possible somatoform issues or feigning
Functional disorder	A non-neurologic disorder, likely somatoform in etiology
Psychogenic symptoms	Symptoms that are likely somatoform in nature
Supratentorial issues	Symptoms are likely psychological in nature, possibly somatoform related
Collapsing weakness/give-away weakness	A finding suggestive of poor effort, feigning, or weakness related to nonorganic issues
Improvement with distraction	A sign that suggests somatoform issues or feigning
Hoover's sign	A sign suggestive of a somatoform presentation
Waddell signs	Signs suggestive of possible somatoform issues or feigning

a disability application. Other examples listed in Table 2.1 pertain to medical issues where persisting cognitive dysfunction is not anticipated (e.g., mTBI), which could suggest that the patient's report is influenced by an undisclosed external incentive or possible somatization. It is important to keep in mind that the presence of such factors is neither necessary nor sufficient to determine noncredibility; however, identifying such issues prior to evaluating the patient is helpful when planning the clinical interview, as will be discussed in Chapter 3.

Finally, referring providers will sometimes alert the neuropsychologist to the possibility of noncredible or invalid presentations. Davis (2022) provides an excellent discussion of terms that physicians and other health care providers sometimes use to signal the possibility that a patient might be providing poor effort, feigning, or have psychological or somatoform features contributing to their neurological complaints. We summarize these terms in Table 2.2 and refer the reader to Davis's work if additional detail is desired. If a clinician were to identify one or more of these terms in referral notes, it would likely be wise to consider this information when approaching the clinical interview.

CLOSING REMARKS

As discussed throughout the chapter, it is important to screen referrals and ensure that they are appropriate for clinical evaluations. If billing health insurance, it is essential that there is documentation indicating that the evaluation is medically necessary. Even if the evaluation is to be paid in cash, though, it is important to consider whether a clinical evaluation will be appropriate given the evaluation context and needs. When disability or litigation pursuit are noted in the consult or become evident after meeting with the patient, a clinician can still potentially perform a clinical evaluation, but the clinician will need to consider the appropriateness of and their comfort with moving forward in this manner. When such cases are accepted as clinical evaluations, the clinician should consider the increased risk for noncredible symptomatology given the presence of an external incentive, and the clinician should be aware that the evaluation results might be introduced into administrative or legal cases at a later date. Considering all of these factors and having clear discussions with the patient (and potentially other pertinent parties such as the patient's attorney), should increase the likelihood that the evaluation will be carried out in an ethical, legally appropriate, and clinically helpful manner.

CHAPTER 3

The Clinical Interview as a Foundational Step

Considerations, Lines of Inquiry, and Methods

IMPORTANCE OF THE CLINICAL INTERVIEW

For many reasons, the clinical interview is recognized as an essential component of most neuropsychological evaluations (Board of Directors, 2007). The clinical interview typically serves as the first interaction between the patient and clinician, and, therefore, sets the stage for the entire evaluation. It is during the interview that the clinician and patient form a clinical relationship and establish rapport. Additionally, it is during the clinical interview where the clinician can obtain information that helps to fill in gaps that remain after reviewing the medical record. Furthermore, because the neuropsychologist conducting a clinical evaluation must make formulations regarding, not only diagnosis, but also treatment planning, information collected during the interview is often pivotal in determining what recommendations are provided and how they are discussed during the feedback session.

In addition to establishing rapport and obtaining pertinent background information, the clinical interview is integral to validity assessment. Whereas most neuropsychologists view passing or failing of objective validity tests and indices as the most influential factor in determining validity status (Martin et al., 2024), validity test utilization and interpretation does not occur in a vacuum. In cases of potential noncredibility, neuropsychologists rely on the clinical interview to investigate for possible discrepancies and inconsistencies suggestive of symptom distortion, collect important observational data, develop hypotheses regarding potential causes of invalidity, and inform decisions about the test battery. The remainder of this chapter will discuss general considerations and specific elements of the clinical interview in the context of validity assessment and management.

GENERAL CONSIDERATIONS OF THE CLINICAL INTERVIEW

For most clinicians, key topics covered by the clinical interview include the reason for the referral and informed consent, an account of the presenting problem, the patient's daily functioning, medical and psychiatric history (including family history), educational and work history, social and cultural functioning, and goals for the evaluation. While the clinical interview should typically start by discussing the reason for referral and informed consent and it should typically end with concluding statements that pave the way for testing and feedback, we recommend that the clinician obtain the rest of the information in whatever manner flows most naturally when talking with the patient. This should be done via engaging in a smooth back-and-forth conversational style discussion where the clinician will appropriately guide the clinical interview along, but the patient is allowed some leeway to shift and expand upon topics as well. This is in contrast to a more structured interview style where a clinician might utilize a fixed and highly directed organizational scheme, which encourages the direct answering of questions rather than an opportunity for open dialogue. We view the conversational style interview as being quite important in clinical practice because it often helps to build rapport, illicit rich information on topics that might otherwise go unaddressed, and better allow the clinician to follow the patient's thought processes and attributions.

In addition to engaging in a conversational style clinical interview, reflective listening and genuine empathy should be provided as appropriate. Doing this will likely help to further build rapport with the patient. Additionally, by adopting an empathic perspective, the clinician is more likely to intuit how the patient might be affected by various circumstances, which can then generate hypotheses to be tested with follow-up questions. This approach can be especially important when evaluating patients with medically unexplained symptoms and/or external or internal incentives as such patients (1) may very well be experiencing some form of dysfunction and (2) are at risk for misattributing their dysfunction to inaccurate sources. By "stepping into the shoes" of such patients, the clinician is more likely to pick up on subtle hints about other (e.g., psychological, psychosocial, personality) factors that might provide alternative (and often more plausible) explanations for the dysfunction that is being reported. Thus, empathy, as a clinical tool, can be like an attractive pair of looking glasses that also work really well. That is, empathy, like fashionable looking glasses, will likely engender a positive response from others (i.e., your patients) while also helping you to see things that you might have otherwise missed.

As an example of the above, consider a patient who reports that they are confident that they can no longer work because of cognitive symptoms for which there does not appear to be a clear basis. If the clinician is perceived as aloof and/or skeptical, the patient is more likely to focus their efforts on convincing the clinician of the severity and impact of their cognitive symptoms. While this can be helpful for documenting extreme or unrealistic symptoms or functioning, it often does little to elicit additional information that might provide context to the situation. What if, instead, the clinician takes an empathic perspective, appreciating that, for whatever the reason, the patient finds work to be unfulfilling, undesirable, and/or unmanageable? In this instance, the clinician is more likely to be invested in learning about all of the potential factors contributing to their patient's complaints. Perhaps, this perspective then provides the opportunity for a conversation about a scrutinizing boss, conflicts with coworkers, difficult changes in job roles or demands, financial struggles, strain from marital or family relationships, untreated symptoms of depression and anxiety, etc. The point we are making is that, in our experience, conversations regarding underlying factors that are driving behaviors (including driving feigning behaviors) are most likely to occur when patients feel listened to and cared for, which, in turn, is more likely to be the case when patients are being asked insightful and relevant questions as a consequence of the clinician's genuine interest and empathy. As discussed later in the chapter, gaining awareness of such factors during the clinical interview is particularly important in guiding feedback and treatment recommendations when patients invalidate testing.

SPECIFIC ELEMENTS OF THE CLINICAL INTERVIEW

Keeping in mind that there should not be a single, fixed organization or flow to the clinical interview, we will discuss each element of the clinical interview individually (along with our patient check-in process), highlighting topics that pertain to validity assessment in clinical settings.

Check-In Process

In our clinical practices, we typically ask that the patient bring a collateral informant with them for the clinical interview (and feedback session if desired). Upon arrival at our clinic, patients are asked to sign documents that include an informed consent for the evaluation and releases of information. Patients are also asked to bring a completed history questionnaire (see Appendix 3.1 at the end of this chapter) which was mailed out prior to the evaluation. We find that history questionnaires such as ours can nicely complement the clinical interview. The questionnaires allow for the collection of a broad array of symptoms and aspects of background history that might not be in the medical records, which can help the clinician undertake the clinical interview in a more targeted and efficient manner. They can also be a way to inquire about potentially sensitive topics (e.g., childhood abuse) without diving too far into those topics. Questionnaires can also identify patients who endorse having a significant number of various physical health complaints without having to address every somatic complaint during the clinical interview. In some cases, the way a patient fills out the form can sometimes provide helpful qualitative data as well (e.g., frequent spelling mistakes, strong focus on specific types of symptoms, filling in the margins and the back side of the pages elaboratively describing a multitude of symptoms).

Such information can potentially aid in generating hypotheses to be considered during the clinical interview regarding the patient's perspective and relationship with their symptoms, level of insight, abnormal personality characteristics, and the possible presence of minimization or magnification of symptoms. The questionnaire can also ask whether the patient is involved with or considering litigation or if they have been awarded or are considering applying for disability, information which is important to be aware of before the interview begins. Finally, by having patients complete questionnaires before the clinical interview, they are more likely to anticipate the types of questions that could be asked during the clinical interview, allowing for a smoother discussion of topics.

Some clinicians also have patients sign a form indicating that the evaluation is for clinical reasons as opposed to forensic reasons (for an example, see Appendix 3.2 at the end of this chapter). One argument for utilizing this type of form is that it could potentially help to protect the clinician from a fraud complaint and/or investigation brought up by the patient's insurance carrier if the insurance carrier were to argue that the evaluation is truly for forensic reasons and, thus, does not constitute medical necessity. A second argument that is sometimes provided is that, if a patient were to pursue litigation and want to use the neuropsychological report as evidence in a lawsuit, the form might provide some type of protection or justification for the fact that a full forensic evaluation was not carried out. While we do not necessarily think negatively of this type of form, which is why we are providing an example form for those who might wish to use it, we and a variety of other clinicians do not use similar forms in our clinical practices. This is because we ensure that there is medical necessity in all evaluations accepted as clinical evaluations even if there are co-occurring legal issues or disability pursuit. Additionally, while we acknowledge that, in a clinical setting, we might not have as many records to review or as much time for testing as would be the case in a forensic evaluation, we attend to validity issues, and we do not make conclusions that are not justified by the available data. Finally, we also recognize that we do not have control over whether patients choose to use their health care records (including neuropsychological reports) in a lawsuit, and we don't have the right to try to prevent them from doing so if they so choose. Relatedly, having possession of a signed form stating that the evaluation is for clinical reasons as opposed to forensic reasons will not legally prevent the neuropsychologist from having to release the report and/or test data if the patient were to pursue litigation. Likewise, it does not preclude the scheduling of depositions or court appearances. Thus, in our opinion, it is not necessary to use this type of form in clinical practice.

Reason for Referral and Informed Consent

After reviewing the history questionnaire (which the receptionist hands to us while patients complete the rest of the paperwork), we meet the patient and his or her collateral informant in the waiting room and bring them back to our offices, making natural, unforced small talk along the way. Although such a practice might not be universal across settings, we find that patients generally view such efforts positively. We have had patients remark that it is unusual, yet appreciated, to be greeted in the waiting room by their clinician, instead of by a nurse, assistant, or trainee. Such a practice can communicate that the clinician is taking extra effort, and, when coupled with a warm and inviting approach, can be an easy initial step toward facilitating rapport. Such gestures can be especially helpful with individuals who have come to view the health care system as cold and unfriendly or health care providers as unhelpful, uncaring, and/or skeptical (perspectives sometimes held by those with medically unexplained symptoms and/or those potentially at risk for malingering).

Once in our offices, we typically start the clinical interview by making a statement along the lines of "Dr. Smith referred you here to meet with me, and she sent some records, which I've reviewed. I always like to start, though, by asking what your understanding is of this appointment." Starting the interview in this manner serves several purposes. The first purpose is to ensure that the patient is sufficiently aware of the reason for the evaluation in order to provide informed consent. Some patients respond that they do not know why they are at the appointment; they were just told to come by their referring provider, a family member, or a letter received in the mail from the office. When this occurs, the collateral informant often jumps in and provides a reason for the evaluation, but, if the collateral informant does not do so, the clinician can provide the stated reason for the referral and ensure that the evaluation is something that the patient wants to pursue. Other patients provide a statement that closely matches the statement in the referral note. In this case, the clinician can indicate that the patient's stated reason is the same reason that was provided in the referral letter. Other patients might provide a reason for the evaluation that is completely different from the reason provided in the referral note (in our experience, though, this is uncommon) or provide a reason that is stated in the referral note but also add another reason. For example, the patient might state that the reason for the referral is "To look into my memory problems" (which might be the stated referral reason) "and to see if I need disability" (which might not be a stated reason for the referral). In this latter instance, we provide clarifying information on the role of the evaluation and obtain informed consent to move forward with the evaluation in an ethical and appropriate manner, as described in Chapter 2.

In addition to obtaining informed consent, opening the clinical interview with the aforementioned question communicates thoroughness. When inquiring about the patient's understanding of the reason for the evaluation, it is important to ask in a manner that also communicates that you understand why they were referred. Otherwise, the patient might suspect that the referring provider did not adequately communicate with you, the neuropsychologist, or that you have not taken the time to review their records or prepare for the evaluation. Thus, by noting that we have already reviewed the patient's records and referral notes, it is clear that we are asking about the patient's understanding of the reason for the referral, not because we don't know why they were referred, but because we are interested in and care about their perspective, which can be helpful in building rapport. Starting the interview in an open and nonleading manner also creates the opportunity for the clinician to learn (1) if the patient has insight into the reason for the referral, (2) about the patient's attitude toward the evaluation, (3) what symptoms the patient is most concerned about communicating to the clinician, (4) what factors might influence the patient's accuracy in discussing their symptoms and functioning, and (5) if there are signs of obvious cognitive, speech, psychiatric, or personality dysfunction.

As an example, imagine a patient who responds to the question with the following:

> "I literally can't remember anything anymore. I've forgotten my entire childhood, and sometimes I forget that I'm married even though I've been married for 17 years. Last week, I was looking at photographs of me with my daughter on her first day of school, and I couldn't even remember the picture being taken. My mother passed away 10 years ago on my birthday, and sometimes I forget that she is dead. I drive a vehicle at work and will arrive somewhere and not remember anything about the drive. It's gotten to the point where driving for work has become a safety issue. So, I don't think I can work anymore. My husband tries to be understanding, but I feel really guilty because I can't help out the way I used to because I can't remember, and I'm always tired and in pain."

The patient's response, elicited at the very outset of the clinical interview, illuminates several pieces of key information. First, she provides a symptom report incompatible with plausible presentations of memory impairment (i.e., being amnestic of remote information but being able to recall specific recent instances of forgetting, and reporting profound memory impairment while still able to drive and maintain employment). Second, her response suggests several incentives for symptom exaggeration or feigning (i.e., she appears to desire leaving the workforce and might be considering disability, she appears to receive emotional support from her husband, and she seems to be excused from household duties because of her symptoms). Third, by spontaneously providing such an elaborated symptom report, she clearly sees her memory difficulties as a primary concern. Fourth, despite reporting such severe memory impairment, she appears to be well aware of the reason for the appointment (i.e., evaluation of memory) and, potentially, how it might be benefit her (i.e., assisting her in leaving the workforce). Fifth, the majority of her examples of memory impairment relate to forgetting her childhood or key family events, which can be common in individuals with histories of trauma, psychological dysfunction, and/or conflicting feelings toward family relationships. Finally, she also reports impairment due to fatigue and chronic pain. Thus, her response provides some insight into factors (e.g., psychological distress, needs for nurturance or understanding from family members, pain, and fatigue) that might underlie her desire to leave the workforce and receive more assistance and nurturance and possibly be excused from responsibilities at home.

Starting the clinical interview in this open and nonleading manner can also sometimes illuminate personality characteristics and possible negative expectations/biases that could affect rapport if not recognized and appropriately handled by the clinician. For example, consider a patient who responds, "Dr. Smith referred me because he's an idiot who doesn't know how to deal with me and doesn't understand neuro-Lyme disease and just likes to blame debilitating problems on mental health. I can't even remember who my own children are, and I am in bed crying all day, and he won't sign off on my disability paperwork and is just telling me to go see some shrink." From this response, the clinician has again gained an understanding of the patient's symptoms, the nature and perceived salience of factors to which the symptoms are being attributed, and the patient's goals for the evaluation (i.e., validation that she has severe symptoms attributed to neuro-Lyme disease, and pursuit of disability). Importantly, the clinician is also now aware that the patient perhaps takes a cautious stance toward health care providers and is likely vigilantly observing for any signs of skepticism or inferences that her "neurological" symptoms are related to psychiatric factors.

Detailed Account of the Presenting Problem

After addressing the reason for referral and informed consent, we often move on to asking the patient about more detail regarding the presenting problem. Since there is typically a collateral informant involved in our clinical interviews, we usually start by making a statement similar to the following "I'd like to ask you (the patient) more questions about that (the issue driving the referral). After I hear your thoughts and experiences, I'd then like to talk to your wife (or other collateral informant) to get her thoughts and perspectives. Is that okay with both of you?" This further helps to form rapport with the patient, as it makes it clear to the patient that we want his or her perspective above and beyond anything else. This also helps the collateral informant understand that we do not want that person to interrupt the patient; the collateral informant will get a chance to provide any information that he or she wants to provide after the patient is done talking.

Next, we proceed by making a statement along the lines of "So when did you first start noticing the problems with your memory (or whatever else is identified as being the reason for referral)?" We ask about the onset of all reported symptoms including the time frame for when the symptoms started. In cases of accidents or injury, we ask if the injury that caused the symptoms to emerge was related to their own doing (although not in those specific words; for example, "Oh no; I'm sorry to hear that. It sounds like you were the individual blamed for this accident too?") or due to another individual's actions, which could suggest the possibility of a lawsuit. We also ask about the progression of symptoms, examples of symptoms (for example, we might ask "Can you provide me with an example of how your memory problems affect you?"), the degree of posttraumatic amnesia that is present (if pertinent), whether there are any other co-occurring symptoms (e.g., other cognitive difficulties, psychological changes or stressors, or physical issues), the functional impact that the symptoms have on the patient, and so on. During this line of questioning, it is recommended that questions initially be open ended and that they largely *follow* the patient's story *as opposed to primarily directing* the patient's line of thinking. Furthermore, if the patient starts looking to the collateral informant to address questions, we often provide a statement such as "I agree, I'd like your wife's input but for right now, I'd really like to get just your perspective on what you've noticed. It is helpful to get both perspectives." Finally, it is important to note that interest in hearing the patient's responses should be clear to the patient and genuine even when there are strong suspicions that the patient's report is not factual. Having a clear and genuine interest helps to build rapport, which will be critical at the time of feedback; it reduces the likelihood that the patient will feel misunderstood or disregarded; and it increases the likelihood that the clinician will continue to provide a professional service even when there might be challenging patients.

When seeking to understand the onset and course of symptoms, it is also important to investigate for any physical, emotional, or psychosocial factors that might have contributed. As a caveat, however, such factors require careful questioning in some patients, especially those who are strongly enmeshed with the idea that their symptoms are due to a particular injury/illness or who are pursuing an external incentive related to a particular injury/illness. For example, consider a patient who denies experiencing any mental health symptoms prior to sustaining a concussion that reportedly caused persisting and debilitating symptoms. Upon further inquiry, this patient discloses that less than 1 year before the concussion, she lost her fiancé to cancer, relocated to an entirely different part of the country, and began a new job. If these factors are discussed in the context of being potential contributors to the alleged postconcussive symptoms, the patient might be more likely to discount their significance. Conversely, if the clinician queries about these topics later in the clinical interview and without suggesting an agenda of uncovering alternative causes of the patient's symptoms, a more forthright discussion might ensue. Therefore, although it is essential to inquire about other factors that potentially contribute to the patient's symptoms, whether to ask about such factors while discussing symptom onset or elsewhere in the interview is often a matter of clinical judgment.

After giving the patient the chance to present his or her narrative in an open-ended format, we give the collateral informant the same opportunity and we might clarify with the informant any unclear or atypical details that the patient presented. By interviewing the patient and family members individually (although they are in the same room at the same time), the clinician can assess the convergence between data sources and, in cases of implausible symptom report, assess the degree to which the family member has agreed with or bought into the patient's narrative. Understanding the latter can sometimes be helpful in appreciating their level of insight into the patient's symptom claims, the extent to which they might be complicit in the patient's external incentive goals, and/or the extent to which their reaction to the patient's symptoms (e.g., taking over home responsibilities, providing emotional nurturance) might be internally or externally incentivizing to the patient.

If there is no collateral informant available for the clinical interview, we have found that it can be helpful to ask, "If your spouse were here, what do you think he (or she) would say about your (reported symptoms)?" In some cases, the patient says that his or her spouse has noticed the same thing. In a number of other cases, though, the response is "He (or she) hasn't noticed anything." This statement is sometimes then followed up by the patient with "but he's not very observant" or something similar. Even if this type of follow-up statement is provided, it could still suggest that the patient's issues are so mild (or nonexistent), that the person with the most knowledge of the patient is not aware of issues.

After talking with the collateral informant (or asking the patient what a collateral informant would likely say), we often return to asking the patient questions. However, we now ask if the patient has experienced any of a number of symptoms that were not initially described during the open-ended questions. For example, if the patient only reported having memory issues during open-ended questioning of their symptoms, we might ask if they have also experienced any issues with attention, thinking/processing speed, word-finding, planning, problem-solving, and so on (providing each option in a checklist-like fashion). It is important to wait to use the checklist-like options until after the open-ended questions have ceased, as it is important not to prime the patient with examples of issues that might potentially be endorsed. In an accurately reporting patient, priming the individual with these symptoms might skew their own report of their perception of issues, and, in invalidly reporting patients, it might prompt them to endorse having symptoms that they wouldn't have otherwise thought about reporting on their own.

Clearly, this line of questioning is essential for understanding the patient's complaints and perspectives, whether the complaints and perspectives are valid or not. With regard to validity assessment, in particular, examples of patient reporting styles that could potentially suggest inaccurate symptom report (whether due to malingering or other causes) include the examples below.

- Reporting having cognitive dysfunction but being unable to spontaneously provide clear examples of that dysfunction, or, conversely, describing examples that seem to contradict the symptom that is being reported (e.g., reporting severe memory problems but then describing each instance of forgetting with detailed clarity)
- Reporting having severe psychological symptomatology (e.g., extreme depression or posttraumatic stress) but not demonstrating any behaviors consistent with the disturbances (e.g., not appearing to have a depressed affect or showing emotionality when detailing traumatic events)

- Reporting significant cognitive dysfunction in a younger individual, with no clear injury history or medical explanation for the onset of cognitive dysfunction
- Reporting having significant memory issues due to an incident despite being able to clearly recall all details surrounding that incident
- Reporting having significant word-finding problems despite quickly and fluently describing history
- Reporting few symptoms during the open-ended line of questioning but endorsing numerous symptoms during the close-ended checklist-like line of questioning
- Reporting primarily vague symptoms using nonspecific terms such as "brain fog" or "in a cloud"
- Reporting symptoms that do not make neurological sense (e.g., significant cognitive impairment a year after a concussion or reporting right-sided motor dysfunction after striking the right side of one's head)
- Reporting having significant cognitive dysfunction despite performing normally on previously administered cognitive screening tests
- Reporting cognitive dysfunction that is disproportional to level of independence and success in daily functioning, as described next

Daily Functioning

Assessing the patient's daily functioning and ability to perform instrumental activities of daily living (ADLs) is an important aspect of the clinical interview when trying to determine whether invalidity and/or inaccurate self-report may be present. The style of questioning in this area should be similar to that which was used when obtaining an account of the patient's presenting problem. That being said, the clinician should start by asking open-ended questions and then move on to close-ended questions. An open-ended question might be "Could you walk me through a typical day? I'd like to understand what a day looks like for you." After the patient describes their day, the clinician might probe for additional information and ask more close-ended questions to try to more precisely determine what the patient can and cannot do.

Within the context of validity assessment, asking about ADL functioning can help to draw out discrepancies within the patient's narrative. For example, a patient might report that his "memory is shot," and he has trouble doing "everything." When asked about his typical day, however, he might describe waking up, making a simple breakfast, driving to work, and then running errands after work, which seems to contradict his reported significant cognitive dysfunction.

When asking about symptom impact on specific ADLs, it can be helpful to ask questions that go beyond overall success versus failure in daily activities as some patients might initially describe dysfunction in activities but then struggle to provide clear indications of failure when queried. For example, consider a patient that states that they believe that they are no longer able to work because of memory difficulties. However, upon inquiry they note that their debilitating memory symptoms have been present for 12 months and that, during that time frame, they have never experienced adverse consequences at work (e.g., negative performance evaluations, reprimands by supervisor, loss of clients, customer complaints, or unmet deadlines) as a result of their cognitive symptoms. Similarly, a patient might state that they get lost while driving, but, upon clarification, it might become apparent that "getting lost" entails milder difficulties, such as missing turns in unfamiliar areas, isolated issues of difficulty finding new places, or increased usage of GPS prompted only by subjective concerns of getting lost.

In addition to examining for the severity of difficulty in daily activities as described above, it is important to ask follow-up questions that determine the frequency of such difficulties. This is particularly important when patients are hyperbolic in their descriptions, something that can occur with intentional exaggeration, but also when individuals have a lot of anxiety about their symptoms. For example, consider a patient who states, "I've lived in this city my entire life, but now I can't even remember the major streets and highways." This could reflect significant cognitive dysfunction raising concern about driving safety. However, if the clinician were to ask for clarification and/or examples, the patient might then discuss a single instance where they could not remember the name of a major highway they regularly drive successfully, and then they proceed to name that highway to the clinician. If this is the only concern raised regarding driving, the clinician has both avoided overestimating the severity of driving difficulty and now understands that the patient's report might be either exaggerated or dramatized.

It is also important to investigate to what degree reported difficulties in daily functioning represent a change. In some cases, patients might discuss difficulties in daily functioning and then, upon inquiry, acknowledge that they have always had these issues. For example, a patient might discuss overdrawing their checking account since a head injury but then admit that this was happening even prior to their injury. Of course, patients who are seeking an external incentive related to a particular injury might not admit to having preexisting issues. Even absent of intentional exaggeration, patients enmeshed in the idea that their current difficulties are attributable to a particular event or injury will commonly describe their previous functioning in unrealistically positive terms, a phenomenon sometimes referred to the "good ol' days" bias. Because of this, when investigating change from prior functioning, the clinician should ask questions regarding more objective markers of preexisting difficulties (e.g., "had you ever been written up/caused an accident/forgotten to pay your bills before your injury"). Even then, however, patients might not always admit to such previous failings, especially when motivated to demonstrate that their dysfunction is directly related to a specific injury. For this reason, in addition to seeking more objective documentation, clinicians sometimes must ask more broadly or covertly about historical functioning. For example, consider a patient who initially denies problems at work prior to their accident, but then describes a checkered employment history and admits that they have never held a job for more than 2 years. The clinician could then ask about each job and why they moved on in each instance, being alert to trends or explanations that minimize potential working difficulties (e.g., my boss just had it out for me from day one, he was always scrutinizing my work, or he was a real jerk).

Another reason why assessing daily functioning, and specifically functioning in ADLs, is important is because, when realistically reported, this information can help to determine which performance validity tests might be most appropriate to administer (e.g., Word Choice Test or Coin-in-the-Hand Test) and/or which cutoff scores should be utilized. As described in Schroeder and Martin (2022c), false-positive rates on some traditional performance validity tests can be unacceptably high in patients with dementia/major neurocognitive disorders. Consequently, incorporating knowledge of realistically reported ADL functioning with other information (e.g., base rates of dementia given known factors such as patient age, convergence of reported symptoms to known dementia syndrome stereotypes, having a medical history and/or neuroimaging findings raising concern for the possibility of severe cognitive dysfunction) can help to determine whether there is a reasonable possibility that a patient *might* have a major neurocognitive disorder which would then help with choosing appropriate validity tests and/or cutoffs to maximize sensitivity while minimizing the likelihood for false-positive errors.

Medical and Psychiatric History

It is important to ask patients about their medical and psychiatric history, along with treatment compliance related to any potentially pertinent diagnosed conditions, as many medical and psychiatric conditions can negatively impact cognitive functioning particularly if the conditions are not well controlled. In validly presenting patients, obtaining this information (along with pertinent family medical and psychiatric history) will be crucial in narrowing down a differential diagnosis. Even in invalidly performing patients, though, this information could potentially lead to recommendations during the feedback session. Take, for example, an invalidly performing patient who has a history of obstructive sleep apnea and reports during the clinical interview that he does not use his CPAP machine, and he is chronically fatigued. Despite invalidating testing, a reasonable recommendation for the patient during the feedback session would be to utilize his CPAP, as untreated sleep apnea could cause fatigue, current cognitive concerns, and increased risk for stroke.

While obtaining medical history is necessary, it is, again, important to point out that patients who tie their pursuit of external incentives to cognitive symptoms might resist attempts to acknowledge the impact of noncognitive factors on their functioning. For this reason, the clinician should be careful to avoid implying that they believe there is an association between a medical or psychiatric condition and the patient's cognitive complaints. Sometimes it can be helpful to disassociate questions about factors such as sleep, pain, and mood from questions about cognitive and daily functioning. For example, one might segue into such topics by saying "Okay, now we are going to switch gears . . . " or by saying something like "There are a few other areas that we also need to cover, how is . . . ?"

In addition to obtaining medical history for differential diagnosis and treatment planning purposes, it can be informative to understand what patients know and are able to recall about their medical history. For example, sometimes patients who ultimately invalidate testing and seem to be malingering report having difficulty remembering information about their history but, when asked about their medical history surrounding an accident, they are able to easily recall information, providing an exceptionally detailed amount of material. As another example, patients with somatic symptom disorder might report having or suspecting a wide variety of medical conditions, including medical conditions with which most laypeople and even some health care providers might not be familiar. They might also report having a history of medically unexplained symptoms and being sensitive to most all medications, which result in an inability to tolerate nearly all medications including psychotropic medications (although, coincidently or not, in our experience, benzodiazepines seem to be an exception that is noted by many of these individuals). Additionally, some individuals with somatic symptom disorders report that they have seen a large number of health care professionals looking for help, have undergone many diagnostic tests without clear findings, and/or have gone to highly respected clinics (e.g., Mayo Clinic) only to be told that nobody knows what is causing the symptoms or that they have been "dismissed" and "inaccurately told that everything is in my head just because they (health care providers) don't know what's going on."

Finally, in addition to medical history, it is important to address psychiatric and psychological history. It can be very helpful to identify an abuse history (especially a childhood abuse history) and/or longstanding problematic personality factors, as these are issues that can often co-occur with somatic symptom disorders. It is also helpful to identify any history of psychosocial stressors, especially those that occurred within close proximity to an onset or exacerbation of cognitive issues, as stressors are strongly linked to somatic symptom presentations and some individuals with somatic symptom disorders struggle to connect psychosocial stressors as being related to the onset of their symptoms. As previously noted, querying for psychosocial stressors is also important for patients who may be intentionally exaggerating or feigning symptoms, as identifying realistic stressors and recommending interventions for them during feedback can be a way to address distress in these patients.

Educational and Work History

Obtaining information about educational and occupational history is important, as educational and occupational attainment have been linked to premorbid functioning and neuropsychological test performance. Thus, knowing about occupational attainment (including knowledge of the highest level of attainment and the job that represented the longest period of time employed) and educational attainment (including whether there were specific subjects that were strengths or weaknesses) will help to predict premorbid cognitive functioning when a clinician might not be able to use performance-based premorbid estimates, such as those derived from word reading performances, due to patients performing invalidly during testing (Martin et al., 2018). It is important to keep in mind, though, that some people experience barriers in elevating occupational attainment, and other individuals might be promoted despite not having the skill set typically necessary of that job. Likewise, when it comes to education, education quality within regions of the United States can differ, and education quality from within and outside of the United States can also differ. Furthermore, educational performance can be inaccurately reported by patients. Empirical literature indicates that adults are often poor reporters of their previously obtained GPAs (Kuncel, Credé, & Thomas, 2005). Somewhat relatedly, we have evaluated a number of patients who reported having obtained IQ scores well above the 99th percentile (e.g., "my IQ was tested at 160") while their highest level of educational attainment, occupational attainment, current presentation, and current IQ scores very strongly suggest that the patient's reported IQ score is not accurate. Because of these potential limitations, it is important to obtain a good history of both occupational and educational attainment to try to draw the most accurate conclusions about premorbid function as possible.

In addition to obtaining information about scholastic history to help estimate premorbid functioning, it is important to determine whether those individuals who are currently in school are seeking accommodations, which could be an external incentive for producing invalid testing. If students report struggling with their scholastic performances but they do not spontaneously report trying to obtain scholastic accommodations, we tend to first ask if they are fearful of failing their courses. We then gently ask if they have talked or plan to talk with anyone at their school about trying to obtain accommodations. This is a casual way to gauge their interest in obtaining academic accommodations, which may lead to a discussion of this potential external incentive.

Similarly, there should be a discussion of occupational functioning in all working-age patients, as occupational injuries could result in Workers' Compensation claims (which increase the risk of invalidity occurring), and occupational issues and/or dissatisfaction with current jobs could lead to an external incentive of disability. While an evaluation secondary to a Workers' Compensation claim should typically be clear since Workers' Compensation frequently pays for these evaluations, evaluations where patients are pursuing disability may be less clear. For example, while some patients might readily emphasize that they can no longer work due to their cognitive or psychiatric symptoms and inform their clinician that they are seeking the evaluation to support a disability claim, other patients who are pursuing disability might (1) not mention pursuing disability and/or (2) deny having an intention to file for disability or insist that they desire to continue working (although perhaps state that they, unfortunately, feel incapable of doing so).

Because some patients are not forthcoming with their desire to pursue disability (see for example, Schroeder et al., 2022), we have found that directly asking about this pursuit is not always productive. Instead, we tend to ask about a variety of instrumental ADLs, with work functioning being the last query in this series of activities. We ask whether the patient has noticed any work-related issues, whether others in the workplace have mentioned any issues to them, and whether there have been any reprimands for issues that have occurred. After this, we ask if the patient is fearful that they might be fired or let go from work or if they are considering leaving their job. If the answer is yes, this allows for a smooth and casual transition into asking what the patient would plan to do if they did not have their job and whether they have thought about pursuing disability. Personally, we have found this line of questioning to elicit disability pursuit discussions more frequently than abruptly asking if patients are pursuing disability.

In cases where a patient reports that they are in the process of pursuing disability, follow-up questions should include what symptoms their disability claim is linked to (e.g., "What symptoms are you noting that contributes to the disability?") and what step they are in within the process (e.g., "Have you submitted paperwork for disability yet?"). In many cases, the disability claim will be associated with the symptoms (cognitive or psychological) being evaluated by the neuropsychologist, but, in some cases, the claim might involve unrelated medical conditions or physical symptoms. Additionally, some patients will report that they are awaiting the results of the evaluation to file a disability claim, and, at the other extreme, some patients will report their disability claim as been denied multiple times over. As previously described, the fact that a patient is pursuing disability does not, in and of itself, preclude the neuropsychologist from conducting a clinical evaluation and having the evaluation legitimately reimbursed by medical insurance; however, for the purpose of informed consent, it is important that the patient be aware that the neuropsychologist does not determine whether disability is awarded and will not provide an opinion on whether the patient is employable (these are decisions to be made by Disability Determination Services).

Military History and Current Involvement with the VA (if a Veteran)

Illnesses and injuries incurred or aggravated during military service can potentially result in disability-related financial compensation through the VA. Furthermore, veterans' clinical records can be accessed and reviewed when they are initially applying for service-connected disability or for an increase in their already approved service-connected disability, so having documentation of impairment in medical records could result in compensation. It is likely for this reason that Shura et al. (2022a) have documented relatively high rates of invalidity for veterans in clinical settings, with Horner, Denning, and Cool (2023) reporting the highest rates of invalidity for veterans who endorsed that they were either applying for or already receiving VA service-connected disability for psychiatric or neurological conditions.

When talking to veterans during the clinical interview, it can be helpful to ask a series of questions to see what the veteran's attitude is toward the military and subsequent follow-up care, and if there are possibilities that the veteran might be pursuing service-connected disability. Questioning could start by benignly asking what branch of the military the veteran served in and when the veteran served. The veteran could then be asked what his or her occupation/duties were, and if he or she was deployed overseas at any time. After that, the veteran could be asked what he or she thought of his or her service time. Next, questions about whether the veteran sustained any injuries or medical conditions as a result of being in the military could be discussed. After that, veterans could casually be asked if they are service-connected through the VA for any of those reported injuries/conditions, whether they are looking for service connection through the VA, and/or whether they feel that the service connection rating that they currently have is appropriate (or if they are trying to increase that rating). Endorsement of some of these items could be cues that invalidity is more likely to occur as research has indicated that both veterans who already receive service-connected disability for psychiatric or neurological conditions and veterans who report applying for service-connected disability for psychiatric or neurological conditions are nearly two times more likely to invalidate neuropsychological testing than those who are not service connected for related conditions or are not attempting to become service connected for related conditions (Horner et al., 2022).

Social and Cultural Functioning

Many topics can (and do) fall under the broad heading of social and cultural functioning. These topics include areas such as childhood development, legal history, and language and cultural history. Information regarding childhood development is important to obtain, as it could give clues as to whether there is an abuse history that might increase the likelihood for a somatic symptom disorder or personality disorder, and whether there were any problems in development that might lead to low premorbid functioning. With regard to legal history, the clinician should establish whether the patient has had encounters with the law, either previously or currently. Clearly, having ongoing criminal issues can lead to the patient having external incentives to invalidate testing.

Information on language and cultural history is also important to obtain. The clinician should ask about the patient's primary language (including how often the patient speaks that language versus other languages), how many languages are fluently spoken, and which language was the first that was learned. This is particularly pertinent, as language history and language proficiency can sometimes impact certain tests assessing premorbid functioning, cognitive functioning, and performance and symptom validity. In addition to queries about language use, the clinician should ask questions regarding where the patient was born, raised, and educated, while addressing other pertinent aspects of cultural background and functioning that may be relevant for the evaluation. Acculturation, education quality, test wiseness, exposure to technology, and other factors can potentially influence the outcome of an evaluation (see Strutt & Stinson, 2022). Clearly, knowledge of, and training in, cultural diversity is essential to adequately address this topic and ensure that patients receive a valid, evidence-based evaluation.

Concluding Questions and Statement

After obtaining all pertinent information, we conclude the clinical interview with the following five points. First, we find it helpful to provide a brief review of the "high points" presented by the patient and his or her collateral informant to ensure that the takeaway points accurately capture the patient's narrative. This also reinforces that the clinician is thorough and cares about the patient's perspective. Second, we find it useful to ask if the patient or collateral informant can think of any other pertinent information or if all pertinent information has been discussed. This can help to reduce the likelihood that pertinent information was missed, and it can further help to give the patient confidence that the clinician is considering all important information. Third, we recommend asking the patient and his or her collateral informant what they think might be contributing to the presenting problem. Their responses might be accurate or inaccurate but knowing their responses can help the clinician address those issues during the feedback session. Fourth, we find it useful to summarize the previously stated goals of the evaluation and then ask if there are any additional questions, concerns, or goals that the patient and his or her collateral informant hope can be addressed by the evaluation. In this regard, we usually state something along the lines of "So our goal is to understand what all is contributing to these memory difficulties and then, hopefully, find ways to try to address the issue if we can. To make sure that I'm being as helpful as I can and that I'm not overlooking anything, though, I want to ask if you have any other specific questions or concerns that you hope will be addressed by this evaluation." If questions related to disability or litigation emerge based on this question, discussion of that topic and informed consent surrounding that topic should be provided (see Chapter 2). Additionally, if the patient states that he or she has a goal that might not be able to be achieved by the evaluation (e.g., wanting a certain diagnosis), the clinician should acknowledge that as one of the patient's goals but also state that obtaining the outcome (in this case, a specific diagnosis) will depend on the evaluation findings. Furthermore, the patient should be informed of any goals with which the clinician is unable to directly help (e.g., awarding them SSDI benefits, which can only be awarded by Disability Determination Services). Fifth, we provide a brief description of testing and a brief discussion of the need for testing to be valid so that appropriate conclusions can be made and so that the patient's concerns and questions can hopefully be addressed by the evaluation findings. In this regard, we often make a statement similar to the following:

> "Alright, we're about ready to shift gears and move into doing the testing. I want to let you know before we get started that some of the test items will be very easy for you, some of the items will be very challenging, and others will be in between those two extremes. You won't be able to get all items on all tests correct, nobody does; even a genius completing these tests wouldn't be able to get all items correct. They are designed that way so that we can identify where your abilities stop, as all of us have abilities that stop at some point. This method of testing helps to ensure that we are able to identify even mild difficulties that a person might be experiencing with thinking. So, your job is simply to do your best, regardless of whether test items are easy or challenging. By doing your best, we can get an accurate and valid pattern of results. Conversely, and I tell everyone this, if a person were to underperform or not do their best on tests to try to show areas of weakness, that will only muddy the pattern of results that we obtain, and it will make it less likely that a diagnosis of a clinical condition could be made. So, again, it is very important for you to do your best on all tests regardless of whether they are easy or challenging. Do you have any questions about this?"

While we have no empirical data to support the utility of this type of statement; observationally, we have found that rates of invalidity in our clinical practices seemed to have declined since incorporating the statement.

THE CLINICAL INTERVIEW AS THE FOUNDATION FOR EFFECTIVE FEEDBACK

As important as the clinical interview is for assessing the validity of a patient's presentation (as described throughout this chapter), we argue that the clinical interview is just as crucial for setting the stage for later management of noncredible symptomatology. This is because:

1. It is typically within the clinical interview that the clinician has the greatest opportunity to develop rapport and build trust with the patient and collateral informant, which will be carried into the feedback session to help facilitate patient and collateral informant receptiveness to feedback.
2. The clinical interview is a time to establish that *both* the clinician and the patient (along with the collateral informant) are active collaborators in understanding and addressing the patient's presenting problem. Thus, if either individual is not fully engaged and forthcoming with open and honest discussions, accurate findings are less likely to occur.
3. The clinical interview provides an opportunity to understand how the patient presents his or her first-hand account and perspective regarding his or herself,

his or her symptoms, and his or her functioning. Even if the reported account of history is not accurate or medically justifiable (whether due to malingering, a somatic symptom presentation, or other cause), it reveals the narrative threads holding together the patient's understanding or portrayal of what happened, how symptoms evolved, what casual attributions the patient has (or hasn't) made, what issues are most troubling to the patient, and how all of these factors fit into his or her biographical context (Fink, 2017). In this regard, information from the clinical interview sometimes even sheds light on factors that might be driving the pursuit of external incentives (e.g., job distress resulting in a desire to quit work and obtain disability), which can be addressed during the feedback session even if testing is invalid.

4. Other problematic health behaviors can sometimes be identified through the clinical interview, which can be targets for intervention that might help the patient to function better even if not the cause of his or her reported complaints.
5. The clinical interview provides the clinician with the opportunity to explore if patients or collateral informants might have defenses about potential problems or diagnoses that are being considered, and to gently foreshadow possible outcomes of the evaluation.

For all of these reasons, conducting a thorough and strategic clinical interview is imperative for helping to orchestrate a successful feedback session when symptom and/or performance invalidity is identified as being present.

THE NEED TO CONSIDER VARIOUS TYPES OF BIASES

No chapter on clinical interviews would be complete without acknowledging the need for considering inaccurate reporting and potential biases. Throughout this chapter, it has been discussed that patients can inaccurately report their own symptoms due to attempting to obtain an external incentive (within the context of malingering) or due to having an internal need or desire for symptom relief or psychosocial assistance (within the context of a somatic symptom or related disorder). It is important to additionally note, though, that a collateral informant might be emotionally or financially invested in the outcome of the evaluation as well. Consequently, the collateral informant might also present distorted or inaccurate information. Indeed, empirical research has indicated that collateral informants sometimes invalidate symptom response scales addressing the patient's behaviors, albeit less often than the patient's themselves (Marshall et al., 2010). Follow-up research on this topic has indicated that, as a group, informants of examinees who invalidate cognitive testing report worse functioning in the examinee than informants of examinees who complete cognitive testing validly (Webber et al., 2022). Importantly, this is not due to having a higher degree of caregiver burden, suggesting that some informants may report skewed information in an attempt to help the examinee present a noncredible narrative.

While the accuracy of patient and informant report must be considered in all clinical interviews, it is equally important to consider whether our own countertransference and biases may be influencing the way that we look at and characterize information provided by the patient. Some clinicians have strong countertransference toward individuals who they believe are feigning, which could skew their clinical interpretations. Even outside of countertransference, though, clinicians sometimes subconsciously engage in cognitive biases, which can influence the way that they look at and interpret information. While describing all potential biases is well beyond the scope of this chapter (for additional discussion, please see Fink, 2017; Strutt & Stinson, 2022; and Sweet & Klipfel, 2021), Table 3.1 presents some biases that are important to consider in clinical practice.

Finally, it must be stated that although some of the factors described in this chapter are associated with an increased likelihood for invalidity, they do not necessarily mean that a patient will present invalidly. Even in the case of medically unexplained symptoms, atypical or yet unexplained symptoms sometimes do not, by themselves, rule out a potential medical explanation. It is helpful for clinicians to develop a differential diagnosis and to formulate certain hypotheses throughout the evaluation; however, it is also essential that clinicians (1) adjust their formulations as new data become available during the clinical interview and testing and (2) make active efforts to avoid confirmation bias.

CLOSING REMARKS

In summary, the clinical interview is important for simultaneously assessing for the veracity of possible diagnostic issues and for setting the stage to facilitate a successful feedback session. Table 3.2 summarizes goals of the clinical interview when considering validity assessment and management. Table 3.3 summarizes the structure of the clinical interview that could help to achieve those goals set out in Table 3.2.

TABLE 3.1. Potential Biases That Can Emerge during and after a Clinical Interview

Bias	Definition	Example
Anchoring effect	Relying on information obtained early in the decision-making process while failing to adjust that impression in light of later information	Concluding an outcome based on information obtained during the clinical interview while disregarding test results that are obtained later
Availability heuristic	Overestimating a probability of an outcome because examples are easy to recall	After hearing multiple media reports that brain injury can cause chronic traumatic encephalopathy (CTE), which leads to suicidal ideation, the clinician begins diagnosing CTE frequently when there is a history of concussion and suicidal ideation despite the base rate of CTE being relatively low
Base rate neglect	Ignoring the base rate of a condition in favor of individuating information	Ignoring the base rate of cognitive dysfunction after concussion due to the patient presenting a seemingly reasonable history of cognitive issues after concussion
Confirmation bias	Selectively considering only information that supports one's expectation of what is occurring	Ignoring or explaining away some information obtained during the clinical interview while focusing on other information that supports the clinician's expectation of what is causing symptoms
Diagnosis momentum	Accepting a previously made diagnosis without identifying the accuracy of the diagnosis	Accepting that a patient has posttraumatic stress disorder (PTSD) because the patient reports having been diagnosed with it by other providers
Framing effect	Drawing conclusions based on how information is presented	Concluding that symptoms are noncredible because, during the clinical interview, a patient behaviorally demonstrates atypical symptoms
Halo effect	Generalizing a positive trait that an individual has to all traits of that individual	Forming a belief that an individual's self-report during clinical interview must be accurate because they describe a history of engaging in significant positive community service
Inattentional blindness	Missing information due to attending to different stimuli	When talking to a patient's spouse, failing to observe that the patient is expressing emotional distress upon hearing details of an accident that the spouse discusses
Overconfidence bias	Overestimating your ability to determine an outcome due to having excessive certainty in your belief	Determining that a symptom presentation is credible because you are confident of that after the clinical interview
Premature closure	Determining a diagnosis is accurate before it has been verified	Determining a diagnosis from clinical interview data without verifying it by other means (e.g., testing)
Self-report bias	Relying too heavily on self-reported information rather than more objectively information	Relying on self-reported information, allowing that information to skew later interpretation of test data

TABLE 3.2. Goals of the Clinical Interview When Considering Validity Assessment and Management

1. Develop rapport and build trust to facilitate patient receptiveness to feedback.
2. Establish that *both* the clinician and patient are active collaborators in addressing the presenting problem.
3. Determine if there are true medical, neurological, or psychiatric conditions present which might be directly or indirectly contributing to the presenting problem.
4. Identify problematic health behaviors that can be addressed during feedback even if testing is invalid.
5. Assess for atypical or inconsistent symptomatology that might indicate noncredible issues.
6. Understand the patient's first-hand account and perspective, including what the patient reportedly thinks is occurring and which causal attributions the patient has and hasn't made.
7. Explore whether patients have defenses surrounding potential issues or diagnoses being considered.
8. Gently foreshadow information, as appropriate, regarding possible outcomes of the evaluation.
9. Determine whether external incentives exist, which increase the likelihood of there being noncredible findings.
10. If external incentives are possibly or clearly present, identify factors that might be driving pursuits of the external incentives, which can be addressed during feedback.
11. Determine the patient's ability to engage in daily activities, especially instrumental activities of daily living.
12. Identify if the patient's behavioral interactions during the clinical interview are consistent with reported functioning.
13. Determine if there are social or cultural factors that might impact validity test performance.
14. Identify the patient's goals for the evaluation.
15. Encourage patients to perform testing validly.
16. Address informed consent if necessary.

TABLE 3.3. Structure of the Clinical Interview

1. Review history questionnaire to help anticipate and direct discussion during the clinical interview.
2. Inform the patient that you reviewed records, but you want to understand his/her reason for the evaluation.
3. Discuss informed consent issues if necessary.
4. Indicate that you will start by discussing the patient's concerns and then you will turn to the collateral informant's concerns.
5. Obtain the patient's account of the presenting problem in an open-ended manner.
6. Obtain the collateral informant's account of the presenting problem in an open-ended manner.
7. Obtain additional detail from the patient by directly asking about symptoms and functioning.
8. Obtain additional detail from the collateral informant by directly asking about symptoms and functioning.
9. Fill in gaps regarding daily functioning, medical and psychiatric history, education and work history, and social and cultural functioning.
10. Ask if the patient and collateral can think of other pertinent information that has not been discussed.
11. Briefly review the "high points" of the information presented by the patient and collateral informant.
12. Ask the patient and collateral informant what they think might be contributing to the presenting problem.
13. Ask what questions or concerns the patient and collateral informant hope can be addressed by the evaluation.
14. Discuss informed consent issues if necessary.
15. Provide a brief discussion of the need for testing to be valid so that valid conclusions can be drawn.

APPENDIX 3.1

Neuropsychology History Questionnaire

Please complete this questionnaire **prior to your first neuropsychology appointment.** This information will help your clinician gain an understanding of the problems for which you were referred.			
Full Name	Date of Birth	Age	Sex
Who referred you to this clinic?		Today's Date	Race
What cognitive, emotional, or behavioral symptoms are you currently experiencing?			
How long have these been a problem?			
Have you ever had a neuropsychological or psychological evaluation?		☐ No ☐ Yes (Describe below)	
If yes, by whom?	Date of evaluation:		

Please send copies of any previous evaluations to your clinician prior to your first appointment.

EDUCATION & EMPLOYMENT	
Highest grade or degree completed:	Technical or trade school: ☐ No ☐ Yes
Field of study:	College or post-graduate school: ☐ No ☐ Yes
Are you currently working? ☐ No ☐ Yes	Year you retired or last worked: ☐ No ☐ Yes
Are you currently on disability? ☐ No ☐ Yes	Do you plan to apply for disability? ☐ No ☐ Yes
What is/was your occupation?	
How long did you hold your longest job?	
Did you serve in the military? ☐ No ☐ Yes	Branch:
Highest rank:	Type of discharge:

(continued)

LEGAL INVOLVEMENT

Are you currently engaged in any lawsuits or other legal proceedings? ☐ No ☐ Yes

Are you considering any lawsuits or legal proceedings in the near future? ☐ No ☐ Yes

If yes, please describe:

MEDICAL HISTORY

Please list any medications you are taking **currently**, for any reason:

Name of Medication	Dose/Time of Day	Side Effects

(continued)

Please check if you have ever experienced any of the following:		
☐ Memory problems	☐ Stroke	☐ Brain injury
☐ Concussion	☐ Seizures	☐ Staring spells
☐ Dizziness	☐ Frequent falls	☐ Clumsiness
☐ Numbness	☐ Headaches	☐ Blackouts/fainting
☐ High blood pressure	☐ High cholesterol	☐ Heart problems
☐ Speech problems	☐ Handwriting problems	☐ Episodes of confusion
☐ Hearing problems	☐ Vision problems	☐ Difficulty walking
☐ Sleep problems	☐ Sleep walking	☐ Major accident or injury
☐ Unusual childhood illnesses	☐ Hallucinations	☐ Depression
☐ Anxiety	☐ Obsessive/compulsive behavior	☐ Aggressive behavior
☐ Attention problems/ADHD	☐ Learning problems	☐ Skin problems
☐ Weight changes	☐ Digestive/GI problems	☐ Other
Please list any surgeries and the year they took place:		

MENTAL HEALTH HISTORY			
How many alcoholic beverages do you drink in an average week?			
What other substances do you use?			
Have you ever attempted suicide?		☐ No ☐ Yes	
Are you at high risk of attempting suicide in the near future?		☐ No ☐ Yes	
Have you received mental health treatment?		☐ No ☐ Yes (See next page)	
Date	Clinician/facility name	Type of treatment (medication, therapy, hospitalization)	Was it effective?

(continued)

Neuropsychology History Questionnaire *(page 4 of 4)*

FAMILY HISTORY			
Please note any family history (mother, father, sister, brother, daughter, son) of the following disorders:			
Condition	**Family Member**	**Condition**	**Family Member**
Stroke		Depression	
Alzheimer's disease		Anxiety	
Parkinson's disease		Bipolar disorder	
Dementia		Schizophrenia	
Seizures		Heart disease	
Huntington's disease		Learning problems	
Cancer		Other:	

DEVELOPMENTAL HISTORY

Where were you born and raised?

As a child or adolescent, did you experience any of the following?

Physical abuse ☐ No ☐ Yes

Sexual abuse ☐ No ☐ Yes

Other trauma ☐ No ☐ Yes

Indicate any problems experienced during childhood or adolescence:

☐ Delayed speech

☐ Delayed motor development

☐ Excessive shyness

☐ Excessive aggression

☐ Hyperactivity

☐ Learning problems

☐ Illegal behavior

☐ Poor peer relationships

☐ Drug abuse

☐ Excessive alcohol use

☐ Depression

☐ School failure/dropout

☐ Runaway behavior

☐ Other:

APPENDIX 3.2

Neuropsychological Evaluations within the Context of Current or Upcoming Lawsuits

Please read this document carefully, especially if you have a current or potential upcoming lawsuit. This document broadly outlines distinctions among neuropsychological evaluations when provided within the context of routine health care versus when provided as part of a possible legal proceeding. Please discuss questions and/or concerns with your neuropsychologist.

Within a health care setting, information obtained from a neuropsychological evaluation is used for diagnostic and/or treatment needs. The purpose of the neuropsychological evaluation is to provide information to assist in improving your care and/or quality of life. These health care-related evaluations are typically billed to health insurance.

When a lawsuit is occurring or expected to occur, neuropsychological evaluations are sometimes recommended. Within this legal setting, the purpose of the evaluation often differs from that of the health care-related evaluation. Lawsuits can be adversarial in nature, and an opposing side's attorney may scrutinize submitted records, looking for reasons to dismiss those records from the lawsuit. Consequently, when evaluations are conducted for legal reasons, it is often necessary for the neuropsychologist to comprehensively review full medical records along with other records such as scholastic and accident records. Additional neuropsychological testing may also be necessary, such as completing testing of academic abilities. These activities may be necessary to legally justify that cognitive or psychological issues resulted directly from the injury in question. These activities also increase the time necessary to complete an evaluation when compared to the standard evaluation for health care purposes, and health insurance does not cover the cost of this type of evaluation. If one were to bill health insurance for this type of evaluation, it could potentially constitute health insurance fraud.

To conclude, evaluations performed for health care purposes differ from those evaluations performed for litigation purposes. To protect our patients and ensure that they get the evaluation that they need, we ask that our patients indicate the reason for pursuing this evaluation. Each evaluation is considered *either* health care related *or* legal related, not both.

I understand the information in this document, I will discuss any questions or concerns with my neuropsychologist, and I am documenting that I am pursuing the following type of evaluation.

______ Neuropsychological evaluation related to health care needs

______ Neuropsychological evaluation related to a legal proceeding

____ _________________________

Printed Name Date

____

Signature

CHAPTER 4

Using Stand-Alone Performance Validity Tests

Clinical Guidance and Cutoffs

Information from the clinical interview should generate a number of thoughts about which validity tests to select for administration. These thoughts should often include:

- Does the patient seem to be emphasizing specific cognitive difficulties (e.g., attention issues within the context of an evaluation for ADHD or memory issues within the context of an evaluation for a brain injury)? If so, the clinician will likely want to ensure that validity tests associated with those specific cognitive difficulties are selected.
- Does the patient seem to be exaggerating psychological or somatic symptoms? If so, it would be wise to ensure that symptom validity scales focusing on those types of symptoms are included in the test battery.
- Is it known (or is there evidence to realistically suggest) that the patient might have a clinical condition (e.g., dementia, intellectual disability, large left cerebrovascular accident) that could cause false-positive findings on certain performance validity tests (PVTs)? If so, I should probably avoid those PVTs in which false positives commonly occur for these conditions and, instead, pick different ones.

After considering how these patient-related factors might influence choice of validity test administration, the clinician should think about the feasibility of using specific validity tests within his or her setting. In this regard, a recent survey of neuropsychologists indicates that the primary consideration, outside of patient-related factors, that impacts choice of validity test administration in clinical settings is time (Martin et al., 2024). Specifically, just over one-third of neuropsychologists working in clinical settings reported that evaluation time limits imposed by health insurance guidelines have caused them to use fewer validity tests than they would have otherwise chosen to use. For this reason, much of the rest of the chapter (and the following chapter, which discusses embedded PVTs) focuses on discussing common validity tests and how patient-related and time-related factors might impact the choice to administer the test. First, though, we will briefly discuss core validity test concepts that are essential to understand when selecting and administering validity tests.

CORE CONCEPTS UNDERLYING PERFORMANCE VALIDITY TESTS

Two Broad Types of PVTs

A PVT is a type of test used to identify whether an examinee's test-taking responses are so atypical in pattern or degree that the responses are unlikely to represent the individual's true ability (Sweet et al., 2021). There are two primary forms of PVTs, *stand-alone PVTs* (sometimes referred to as freestanding PVTs) and *embedded PVTs* (sometimes referred to as embedded validity indicators). A stand-alone PVT is a test that was created typically for the sole purpose of identifying validity status. This test appears as though it is measuring cognitive ability but, instead, it is usually solely used to identify whether testing is completed in a valid or invalid manner. There are multiple stand-alone PVTs, with the Test of Memory Malingering (TOMM) being the most frequently used one (Martin et al., 2024). An embedded PVT is a validity measure that is embedded within a test that is designed to measure cognitive ability. There are multiple embedded PVTs, with Reliable Digit Span (RDS) from the Wechsler Adult Intelligence Scale—4th Edition (WAIS-IV) Digit Span subtest being the most frequently used one (Martin et al., 2024). The WAIS-IV Digit Span subtest measures attention and working memory but, when calculated in a specific, nonscaled score fashion, it can help to identify whether test-taking behavior was so atypical that it is unlikely to be valid.

Sensitivity and Specificity

The accuracy of PVTs is typically explained using the concepts of sensitivity and specificity (collectively referred to as classification accuracy rates). *Sensitivity* of a validity test refers to the accuracy of the test in identifying invalid test-taking behavior. *Specificity* of a validity test refers to the accuracy of the test in identifying valid test-taking behavior. So, if a PVT has a sensitivity rate of 69% and a specificity rate of 90%, this means that it accurately identifies 69% of invalid test takers as being invalid while also accurately identifying 90% of valid test takers as being valid.

Each PVT has its own classification accuracy rates (i.e., sensitivity and specificity rates). Furthermore, as a general rule of thumb, stand-alone PVTs often have higher classification accuracy rates than embedded PVTs, which is not surprising when considering that stand-alone PVTs were developed specifically to assess validity status. As an example of this, compare the most common stand-alone PVT, the TOMM, against the most common embedded PVT, RDS. Meta-analytic data indicate that the TOMM has a sensitivity rate of 61% and a specificity rate of 98% when using the traditional cutoff values for Trial 2 and Retention (Martin et al., 2020). RDS, however, has been found to have a sensitivity rate of 30% and a specificity rate of 96% when using the common cutoff score of six or less (Schroeder, Twumasi-Ankrah, Baade, & Marshall, 2012c).

The astute reader will recognize that both the TOMM and RDS have high specificity rates with lower sensitivity rates. Similarly, while both tests have accuracy rates well above chance performance, neither test has a perfect accuracy rate (i.e., 100% sensitivity and 100% specificity). This is typically the case with all diagnostic tests, whether PVTs, cognitive tests, or even medical diagnostic tests. Sensitivity and specificity are inversely related, meaning that as sensitivity goes up, specificity goes down (and vice versa). Within neuropsychology, it is typically considered worse to have low specificity (i.e., misclassifying individuals who are validly performing as invalidly performing) than it is to have low sensitivity (i.e., misclassifying individuals who are invalidly performing as validly performing), so *the standard in the field of neuropsychology is to use PVT cutoffs that maintain specificity at 90% or higher* (Sweet et al., 2021).

While high specificity rates are necessary within clinical practice, it is ideal to have the highest possible sensitivity rates as well. The most common way to achieve the goal of increasing sensitivity while maintaining high specificity is to utilize multiple PVTs in an evaluation. Because PVTs (unlike most cognitive tests) do not follow a normal distribution and because cutoffs are skewed toward limiting false-positive errors, it is known that utilizing multiple PVTs in combination can notably increase sensitivity rates while minimally affecting specificity rates. For example, Victor et al. (2009) found that sensitivity was 84% and specificity was 94% when four validity tests were administered and failure of two or more validity tests was the criterion for identifying invalidity. Similarly, Larrabee (2003) found that sensitivity was 88% and specificity was 94% when five validity tests were administered and failure of two or more validity tests was the criterion for identifying invalidity. Larrabee (2014) expanded upon this work and found that sensitivity was 98% and specificity was 89% when seven validity tests were administered and failure of two or more validity tests was the criterion for identifying invalidity. Thus, to increase classification accuracy rates, it is imperative that multiple performance validity tests be administered within the full neuropsychological test battery. Table 4.1 shows a summary of this discussion, demonstrating that sensitivity rates notably increase with relatively minimal impact on specificity rates when multiple PVTs are utilized.

TABLE 4.1. Sensitivity and Specificity Rates When Using One PVT versus Multiple PVTs

	Sensitivity	Specificity	Citation
Use of one PVT			
Test of Memory Malingering	61%	98%	Martin et al. (2020)
Reliable Digit Span	30%	96%	Schroeder et al. (2012c)
Use of multiple PVTs			
Failure of 2+ PVTs when four tests were administered	84%	94%	Victor et al. (2009)
Failure of 2+ PVTs when five tests were administered	88%	94%	Larrabee (2003)
Failure of 2+ PVTs when seven tests were administered	98%	89%	Larrabee (2014)

Positive and Negative Predictive Power

Other important statistics to be aware of regarding diagnostic accuracy are positive predictive power (PPP) and negative predictive power (NPP). Whereas sensitivity and specificity refer to the *accuracy of a test* in identifying those with and without a condition of interest (in the case of validity tests, the "condition of interest" is invalid responding), PPP and NPP speak to the *accuracy of the test finding in the individual patient*. Sensitivity and NPP are related as both address the likelihood of true positive findings. Specificity and PPP are related as both address the likelihood of false-positive findings.

Again, sensitivity and specificity relate to the accuracy of the test itself, while PPP and NPP relate to the accuracy of the test finding when applied to a specific patient. Specificity is a static variable, but PPP varies according to the prevalence (or base rate) of the condition (i.e., invalidity) that is being measured by the test in the population to which the patient belongs. PPP is, therefore, a function of both specificity and base rates. As either or both specificity of the test and/or the base rate of invalidity increases so does PPP. That is, the likelihood that a positive finding on a validity test is a true positive (i.e., PPP) will be higher when using a test with a high specificity value and/or when the patient comes from a clinical population with relatively high base rates of invalidity (e.g., patients applying for disability as opposed to patients without an external incentive). This means that, even when using multiple PVTs associated with ~90% specificity, the confidence allowed by a positive finding (as conveyed by PPP) will be lower in certain patient groups that have low base rates for invalidity (e.g., patients with no known external incentives).

Let's walk through an example of this using a predictive power calculator such as the one found at *http://vassarsttats.net/clin2.html*. If we know that a PVT has a sensitivity rate of 33% and a specificity rate of 90% but the base rate of invalid responding in the patient's setting is only 10%, we can calculate PPP. In the calculator, we enter sensitivity as .33 and specificity at .90. The prevalence is our base rate of invalid responding in the setting, which is .10. After we hit "calculate" on the calculator, we see that PPP is .268. This would indicate that there is about a 27% chance that the failure in our low base-rate setting was truly due to the examinee performing invalidly. Conversely, if we use the same PVT in a setting where base rates of invalidity are higher (e.g., 40%), we can recalculate PPP (i.e., replace the .10 figure with .40) and see that the PPP finding noticeably increases to .688. This would indicate that there is about a 69% chance that the failure in our higher base-rate setting is truly due to the examinee performing invalidly.

Based on the previous example, one might think that clinicians should not administer many PVTs to patients when base rates of invalidity are low since the PPP outcome is relatively low. While, on the surface, this would seem reasonable, it is actually an incorrect assumption. In settings with low base rates of invalidity, there is a need for multiple PVTs to be administered. This is because the more PVTs that are administered, the more PVTs there are available to be failed. As demonstrated by Victor et al. (2009), Larrabee (2003), and Larrabee (2014), the more PVTs failed, the higher the specificity of the PVT battery. Since specificity is positively associated with PPP, as the number of failures increases so does the PPP, and the higher the PPP, the more confidence the clinician can have that validity test failures are indeed indicative of invalidity. As an example of this, let's imagine that seven PVTs are administered and three are failed. Per Larrabee (2014), this would result in a sensitivity rate around 88% and a specificity rate around 96%. At a base rate of .10, the PPP would be .709 (as compared to .268 when 1 of 1 PVT was failed in the 10% base-rate setting). Let's now assume that four of the seven PVTs were failed. Per Larrabee (2014), this would result in a sensitivity rate around 63% and a specificity rate of 100%. At the base rate of .10, the PPP would be 1.00, indicating that there is essentially a 100% probability that the PVT failures were due to invalidity even in this low base-rate setting.

In summary, administering a multiple PVT battery in clinical settings (even when base rates of invalidity are thought to be low) is important (1) to maintain an approach that is adequately sensitive to invalidity, and (2) to ensure that sufficient evidence of invalidity is gathered so that we can have confidence that PVT failures do not reflect false-positive errors even in populations where base rates of invalidity are low.

False-Positive Errors

A final core concept underlying PVTs that needs to be discussed in this chapter is the topic of false-positive errors. A false-positive error, as applied to PVTs, occurs when the test is "failed" (i.e., "positive"), indicating an invalid performance when the patient actually performed validly. Therefore, it is an inaccurate, or "false," "positive" PVT finding.

Empirical research indicates that an examinee's background and/or clinical condition can sometimes lead to relatively high rates of false-positive PVT findings. In general, the more that an examinee's background and/or clinical condition deviates from the test's normative sample, the more likely it is that a false-positive error could possibly occur. For example, if a verbally based PVT is normed with primary English-speaking individuals but the test is administered to someone who speaks English as a second language, the likelihood for a false-positive error could potentially increase.

As related to language and cultural factors, surveyed North American neuropsychologists and validity testing experts indicate that they are likely to make adjustments to their PVT approach in examinees tested in a language other than English, and they will "sometimes" make adjustments in (1) non-native English speakers tested in English and (2) examinees born outside of the United States (Martin et al., 2024). Surveyed neuropsychologists also discussed factors likely to lead to decisions to alter their validity testing approach, which included (in order of frequency) language factors, (un)availability of appropriate norms or research, cultural factors such as level of acculturation, and educational factors (e.g., level, quality, or presence of very low education). With that in mind, most surveyed neuropsychologists indicated that they still tend to assess validity in most examinees in some fashion, regardless of language and cultural factors. Strutt and Stinson (2022) also discuss evaluating culturally diverse individuals and non-native English speakers. In brief, they highlight the potential impacts that premorbid level of functioning, education/literacy, cultural beliefs and behaviors, language, and exposure to technology could have on validity testing. They also discuss the topics of explicit bias, implicit bias, and stereotype threat, and they provide a summary of research findings pertaining to specific PVTs conducted with diverse populations.

Outside of an individual's spoken language and/or cultural background, an individual's clinical condition can potentially increase risk for false-positive findings on some PVTs. Because PVTs are developed to identify whether a patient's test-taking responses are so atypical in pattern *or degree* that the responses are unlikely to represent the individual's true ability, individuals with a clinical condition that causes a *significant* degree of neurocognitive dysfunction could be at risk for producing false-positive errors on some PVTs. Clinical conditions that have been identified as potentially resulting in false-positive errors are dementia/dementia-level impairment, intellectual disability, large and clearly identifiable stroke, and epileptic seizures occurring in close proximity of neuropsychological testing (Schroeder & Martin, 2022a). Conversely, when an individual's clinical condition results in minimal to no neurocognitive dysfunction, the risk of false-positive errors decreases. As an example of this, research fairly consistently indicates that specificity rates are higher when PVTs are administered to individuals with a history of concussion/mild traumatic brain injury than when administered to individuals with a history of moderate or severe traumatic brain injury (e.g., Greve, Bianchini, & Doane, 2006; Heinly, Greve, Bianchini, Love, & Brennan, 2005). This and other core concepts discussed above are summarized in Table 4.2.

TABLE 4.2. Summary of Core Concepts Regarding PVTs

1. A performance validity test is a type of test used to identify whether a patient's test-taking responses are so atypical in pattern or degree that the responses are unlikely to represent the individual's true ability.
2. There are multiple freestanding and embedded performance validity tests, and each validity test will have its own sensitivity and specificity rate.
3. Sensitivity and specificity are inversely related. Sensitivity refers to the accuracy of the test in identifying invalid test-taking behavior while specificity refers to the accuracy of the test in identifying valid test-taking behavior.
4. The standard in the field of neuropsychology is to use performance validity test cutoffs that maintain specificity at 90% or higher even though this reduces the sensitivity of the test.
5. Sensitivity can increase while maintaining high specificity by utilizing multiple performance validity tests in an evaluation.
6. When using PVTs in settings where base rates of invalidity are low, positive predictive power will be lower. This does not mean that PVTs shouldn't be administered in these settings; instead, multiple PVTs are necessary to ensure that multiple failures occur (which would increase positive predictive power via increasing specificity).
7. An individual's language and cultural background can sometimes cause false-positive errors to increase on some tests so it is important to be aware of this research.
8. An individual's clinical condition can sometimes cause false-positive errors to increase or decrease.

STAND-ALONE PVTs

In this section of the chapter, we present information on stand-alone PVTs. Table 4.3 provides a list of commonly used cutoff scores for a number of stand-alone PVTs. In addition to this table, though, we have highlighted below seven of the most frequently used stand-alone PVTs. We provide an overview of each of these PVTs including typical administration time, strengths and weaknesses, and commonly utilized cutoffs and associated classification accuracy rates. We then discuss research, when available, on examinees whose background and/or clinical condition might increase the risk of false-positive PVT findings. This information is written in a "user friendly" manner, with the goal of ensuring that the reader has a basic understanding of each PVT with information that he or she can start applying in clinical practice. With that said, it is important to emphasize that clinicians should always be aware of the samples from which their PVTs and associated cutoff values have been validated. If the test and/or cutoff has been validated on a sample that significantly differs from the individual that is being seen, classification accuracy errors are more likely to occur. Thus, for additional information on each PVT, we recommend consulting the individual PVT articles.

TABLE 4.3. Common Stand-Alone PVTs

PVT	Common cutoff
Visual memory	
Test of Memory Malingering (Original Validity Indices)	<45 on Trial 2 or Retention (Tombaugh, 1996)
Test of Memory Malingering (Trial 1 Validity Indices)	≥2 errors on TOMMe10 (Denning, 2012); <42 on Trial 1 (Martin et al., 2020)
Test of Memory Malingering (Consistency Validity Indices)	≥10 inconsistent responses on ACI (Gunner, Miele, Lynch, & McCaffrey, 2012); ≥3 inconsistent responses on IFFI (Buddin et al., 2014)
Nonverbal Medical Symptom Validity Test (Option 1)	≤90% mean on IR, DR, CNS, DRA, DRV, and PA; if GMIP criteria are met, the test is not "failed" (Green, 2008)
Nonverbal Medical Symptom Validity Test (Option 2)	≤88% mean on DR, CNS, DRA, & DRV; if GMIP criteria are met, the test is not "failed" (Green, 2008)
Rey 15-Item	<9 total score (Reznek, 2005)
Rey 15-Item with Recognition	<20 total combined score (Boone, Salazar, Lu, Warner-Chacon, & Razani, 2002b)
Coin-in-the-Hand Test	≤8 correct responses (Schroeder, Peck, Buddin, Heinrichs, & Baade, 2012a)
Verbal memory	
Word Memory Test	≤82.5% on IR, DR, or CNS; if GMIP criteria are met, the test is not "failed" (Green, 2003)
Medical Symptom Validity Test	≤85% on IR, DR, or CNS; if GMIP criteria are met, the test is not "failed" (Green, 2004)
Word Choice Test	≤42 total score (Bernstein, Resch, Oysiew, & Soble, 2021)
Warrington Recognition Memory Test—Words	≤41 total score (Erdodi et al., 2017)
Digit based	
Victoria Symptom Validity Test	≤22 on Easy items or ≤15 on Hard items (Resch et al., 2021)
Computerized Assessment of Response Bias	<90% total score (Condor et al., 1992)
Portland Digit Recognition Test	≤18 on Easy items, ≤17 on Hard items, or ≤38 on all items (Binder, 1993)
Other formats	
Dot Counting Test	17+ on E-score (Boone et al., 2002b)
b Test	≥155 E-score (Boone et al., 2002b)
Validity Indicator Profile	Invalid finding on the Verbal or Nonverbal subtests (Frederick (1997)

Note. TOMMe10 = first 10 items of Trial 1; ACI = Albany Consistency Index; IFFI = Invalid Forgetting Frequency Index; IR = immediate recognition; DR = delayed recognition; CNS = consistency score; DRA = delayed recognition archetypes; DRV = delayed recognition variations; PA = paired associates; GMIP = genuine memory impairment profile.

Test of Memory Malingering

Table 4.4 provides an overview of the TOMM. The TOMM is a stand-alone PVT which is based on a visual memory paradigm. The TOMM is the most well-validated and commonly utilized stand-alone PVT in clinical practice (Martin et al., 2024; Schroeder & Martin, 2021). Over time, a significant amount of research has accumulated on the TOMM, and this research has resulted in modifications to the way that the test may be used. Consequently, we will provide an overview of the test's original and updated usage patterns.

The TOMM has three trials: Trial 1, Trial 2, and Retention. Originally, the test publisher did not consider Trial 1 as a validity index, Trial 2 was designated as being the primary validity index, and the Retention trial was considered an optional validity index (Tombaugh, 1996). As research on the test accumulated, though, there were findings that using both Trial 2 and Retention in conjunction increased sensitivity of the test while still yielding high specificity rates. Consequently, it was suggested that the Retention trial not be considered optional any longer (Greve & Bianchini, 2006).

TABLE 4.4. Test of Memory Malingering

Overview of the test

- The most commonly used and well-validated stand-alone performance validity test
- Full administration takes 15 to 20 minutes
- Trial 1 can be used as a stand-alone PVT without Trial 2 or Retention; administration time of Trial 1 takes 5 to 10 minutes
- Standard Trial 2 and Retention cutoffs have high specificity rates with somewhat low sensitivity rates, but cutoffs can be modified for some clinical samples (e.g., chronic pain and mild traumatic brain injury patients) to increase sensitivity rates
- The test is copyrighted; test and forms must be purchased from the publisher

Common cutoffs with classification accuracy rates

Trial	Cutoff	Sensitivity	Specificity
TOMMe10	≥2 errors	34–82%	89–93%
Trial 1	<42	63–69%	91–95%
Trial 2	<45	46–56%	96–98%
Retention	<45	50–56%	96–99%
Albany Consistency Index	≥10 IR	57–77%	85–92%
Invalid Forgetting Frequency Index	≥3 IR	63–76%	92–94%

Caution with . . .

Dementia, Moderate to severe intellectual disability, Non-native English speakers who have extremely limited educational attainment

Note. IR = Inconsistent Responses; Classification accuracy rates are from Martin et al. (2020) and Soble, Webber, and Bailey (2022).

Per the TOMM test manual, original cutoffs for both Trial 2 and Retention are <45 (Tombaugh, 1996), but subsequent research has found that this cutoff results in very high specificity rates (e.g., 96–98%) and moderate sensitivity rates (e.g., 46–55%). Because specificity rates were higher than necessary and sensitivity rates were only moderate, the point was made that Trial 2 and Retention cutoffs could likely be adjusted to maximize sensitivity rates while still maintaining adequate specificity. Reflective of this, a recent TOMM meta-analysis indicated that cutoff scores for both Trial 2 and Retention could be increased to as high as <49 when the test is used with certain populations, particularly those where minimal to no neurocognitive impairment is expected (e.g., healthy controls, chronic pain patients, and individuals with mild traumatic brain injury; Martin et al., 2020).

Although the TOMM test manual provided cutoffs for only Trial 2 and Retention, Trial 1 has since been examined and supported as an additional validity index (Denning, 2012). In their meta-analysis, Martin and colleagues (2020) indicated that a cutoff of <42 for Trial 1 maximized sensitivity rates while maintaining adequate specificity rates across clinical samples.

To increase the sensitivity of the TOMM even further, clinicians can analyze one of the two more common consistency indices that have been developed for the TOMM: the Albany Consistency Index (ACI; Gunner et al., 2012) and the Invalid Forgetting Frequency Index (IFFI; Buddin et al., 2014). The ACI examines whether there are inconsistent responses to TOMM items across all three trials of the TOMM (i.e., getting the item correct on at least one trial but incorrect on at least one other trial). Ten or more inconsistent responses on the ACI suggests invalidity (Gunner et al., 2012). Like the ACI, the IFFI examines whether there are inconsistent responses to TOMM items across all three trials of the TOMM. Unlike the ACI, though, the IFFI corrects for true learning patterns. For example, if an individual misses an item on Trial 1 but proceeds to get that item correct on both Trial 2 and Retention, the ACI would count this pattern of responses as an inconsistent response whereas the IFFI would not count this pattern as an inconsistent response because it conforms to a true learning pattern. Conversely, if an individual gets the item correct on Trial 1 but then misses the item on Trial 2 and/or Retention, that response pattern does not conform to a true learning pattern, and the pattern of responses would be considered inconsistent on both the ACI and IFFI. In total, three or more inconsistent responses on the IFFI suggests invalidity (Buddin et al., 2014). A calculator for these consistency indices can be obtained by emailing Dr. Howard Buddin (howard.buddin@gmail.com) or Dr. Ryan Schroeder (ryan.w.schroeder.psyd@hotmail.com); for test security purposes, the calculator will only be provided to licensed psychologists.

The final validity index that can be examined is a short form of the TOMM, named the TOMMe10 (Denning, 2012). This short form is comprised of only the first 10 items on Trial 1. A cutoff score of two or more errors on the first 10 items is suggestive of invalidity. While suggestive of invalidity, we recommend that the test generally not be discontinued after item 10; the examiner should continue with the remainder of Trial 1. We suggest this because stopping after item 10 might "tip off" a savvy patient that they performed so poorly that the remaining 40 items from Trial 1 could be discontinued. They might then adjust their response style so that they are still performing invalidly but less obviously so (thereby making the invalidity more challenging to detect with additional PVTs).

With the addition of new validity scales within the TOMM, a clinician might ask if all of the scales can be examined concurrently. To our knowledge, only two studies to date have examined this question. Kulas, Axelrod, and Rinaldi (2014) found that specificity of the TOMM was 89% when examining TOMMe10 (cutoff of 3 or more errors), Trial 1 (cutoff of 40 or less), Trial 2 (cutoff of 44 or less), Retention (cutoff of 44 or less), and ACI (cutoff of 10 or more inconsistent responses) concurrently. Using this method, sensitivity of the TOMM was 75%. Likewise, Schroeder, Olsen, and Martin (2019c) found that specificity of the TOMM was 90% when examining Trial 1 (cutoff of 41 or less), Trial 2 (cutoff of 44 or less), Retention (cutoff of 44 or less), and ACI (cutoff of 10 or more inconsistent responses). Associated sensitivity, using this method, was 67%. Because specificity rates are maintained near 90%, these scales can be concurrently utilized when the same cutoffs as those noted in the studies are used.

Using only Trial 1 of the TOMM

In clinical, nonforensic, evaluations, one might administer only Trial 1 of the TOMM in order to save test administration time. One might wonder if administering only Trial 1, as opposed to the full TOMM, reduces sensitivity rates. Per data from Kulas et al. (2014), Trial 1 of the TOMM (cutoff of 40 or less) was associated with a sensitivity rate of 67% and a specificity rate of 92%. When adding findings from the full TOMM (i.e., Trial 1, Trial 2, Retention, and ACI), sensitivity increased by only eight points beyond what was identified by Trial 1 alone. Similarly, Schroeder et al. (2019c) found that Trial 1 (cutoff of 41 or less) was associated with a sensitivity rate of 57% and a specificity rate of 93%. When adding findings from the full TOMM (i.e., Trial 1, Trial 2, Retention, and ACI), sensitivity increased by 10 points beyond what was identified by Trial 1 alone. Finally, previously presented (i.e., Schroeder, 2022) but currently unpublished data from our clinical database was examined when using a Trial 1 cutoff of 42 or less. It was found that only 1.4% of invalidly performing individuals (identified as invalidly performing based on other PVTs) passed Trial 1 but failed Trial 2, Retention, or the IFFI. In sum, this research indicates that there is some loss of sensitivity by using only Trial 1 of the TOMM, but the loss in sensitivity is so small, especially when using a cutoff of 42 or less, that using only Trial 1 in clinical, nonforensic settings would be warranted especially when there are limits on test administration time.

Clinical Groups that Might Cause False-Positive Findings

In their extensive review of the TOMM literature, Martin and colleagues (2020) found that the TOMM generally results in low false-positive rates but there are a few groups of patients for whom high false-positive rates might occur. The patient group that appears most at risk for false-positive findings is individuals with dementia. Martin and colleagues found that specificity was consistently below 90% for all TOMM trials when the test was administered to patients with dementia.

Individuals with a mild intellectual disability typically produced adequate specificity rates when administered the traditional TOMM indices (with traditional cutoffs) with specificity rates often near 90% (Martin et al., 2020). Unfortunately, no literature was available on how individuals with moderate or severe intellectual disabilities perform on the TOMM. Given, though, that examinees with mild intellectual disabilities often produce specificity rates near 90%, it would be reasonable to suggest caution when using the TOMM with individuals who have a moderate or severe intellectual disability as higher false-positive rates with these individuals are conceivable.

Finally, Martin and colleagues (2020) found that *select* examinee groups whose primary language was not English performed poorly on the TOMM. The authors examined 19 studies on this topic, which were published on both individuals residing within and outside of the United States and when the TOMM was administered in various different languages. Specificity was 90% or better in 16 of the 19 samples, suggesting that the TOMM is appropriate for use across most samples of examinees whose primary language is not English. It was indicated that it is generally cohort-specific factors uniquely associated with increased age or very low education (e.g., a primary level of education) that could cause false-positive rates to elevate in some non-English speaking samples.

Dot Counting Test

Table 4.5 provides an overview of the Dot Counting Test (DCT). The DCT is a stand-alone PVT, which is based on an attention and mental processing speed paradigm. It is the second most commonly used stand-alone PVT, and it is the most commonly used stand-alone PVT that is not based on a memory paradigm (Martin et al., 2024). Of note, this is a brief PVT, which takes only about 2 to 5 minutes to administer (Soble et al., 2021).

The DCT was developed as a PVT by André Rey (1941), but the test gained more widespread popularity when its procedures were further advanced by Boone, Lu, and Herzberg (2002a). Specifically, Boone and colleagues developed an index for this test, called the E-score, which is based on both the patient's time to completion and accuracy. Boone and colleagues then validated the E-score in multiple patient groups. While E-score cutoffs can vary based on clinical populations, the general cutoff reported in the test manual for a mixed clinical sample is 17 or above (Boone et al., 2002a). Since publication of the test manual, this cutoff has been found to maintain adequate specificity in other studies that have used mixed clinical samples (e.g., McCaul et al., 2018; Soble et al., 2018).

A strength of the DCT is that, in addition to being validated with adult samples, it has been validated in older adult samples, and it also has some cross-cultural

TABLE 4.5. Dot Counting Test

Overview of the test

- The second most frequently used stand-alone performance validity test
- One of few stand-alone PVTs that is not based on a memory paradigm
- Full administration takes 2 to 5 minutes
- Alternate cutoffs are available for various clinical conditions
- Can be used with patients who have dementia (at different cutoffs)
- The test is copyrighted; the test and forms must be purchased

Common cutoffs with classification accuracy rates

Trial	Cutoff	Sensitivity	Specificity
E-score	≥17	53–55%	91–97%

Caution with . . .

Individuals with dementia when not adjusting the cutoff score

Note. Classification accuracy rates are from Soble et al. (2021)

research support. Martin, Schroeder, and Olsen (2022a) found that DCT specificity rates remained adequate (i.e., 90% or better) at a cutoff of ≥15 for older adults with no cognitive impairment, ≥17 for older adults with mild cognitive impairment, ≥22 for older adults with mild dementia, and ≥40 for older adults with moderate dementia. With regard to cross-cultural research, Strutt and Stinson (2022) reviewed the DCT literature and discussed its empirical support in various Spanish-speaking populations, including those with low acculturation and education levels.

Word Memory Test

Table 4.6 provides an overview of the Word Memory Test (WMT). The WMT was developed by neuropsychologist, Paul Green. It is the third most frequently used stand-alone PVT (Martin et al., 2024), and it is based on a verbal memory paradigm. The test is comprised of three "easy" validity indices and multiple "hard" subtests which allow for a calculation of a genuine memory impairment profile (GMIP) to help protect against false-positive errors. There have been a number of research studies on the easy validity indices from the WMT, with simulation designs, differential prevalence designs, and case series designs generally producing positive results. Conversely, in the few studies that have utilized known-groups designs, specificity rates have been suboptimal with regard to the easy validity indices.

As reported by Schroeder and Martin (2022c), three of five published articles with known-groups designs highlighted lower than desired specificity rates for the WMT. In a study by Alverson, O'Rourke, and Soble (2019), WMT specificity was only 66% in a sample of veterans who passed other validity tests. A study by Greve, Ord, Curtis, Bianchini, and Brennan (2008) found that the WMT had a specificity rate of 90% in a pain sample, but specificity was only 70% in a TBI sample.

Furthermore, Fazio, Sanders, and Denney (2015) found a specificity rate of 68% in a mixed criminal sample unless the GMIP was utilized. While these studies show similar trends of high false-positive findings, Green, Flaro, and Courtney (2009) argued that the WMT does not have a high false-positive rate regardless of any studies demonstrating lower than optimal specificity. Their primary contention was that children who are developmentally disabled can pass the WMT cutoffs so adults with less significant cognitive dysfunction should also be able to pass the test. Thus, there is still some disagreement regarding the degree of false-positive errors on the WMT easy validity indicators.

Given the concern expressed about the easy validity indicators, the GMIP, which can help to control for false-positive errors, should certainly be discussed. A GMIP is a profile where at least one easy validity index is failed, no scores are below chance level performance, and the mean of the easy WMT indices is 30 points or more above the mean of the WMT hard indices. When this pattern is present, it could suggest that failure on the easy WMT validity indices was due to genuine memory impairment as opposed to invalidity. Because individuals can potentially feign a GMIP profile, it was originally recommended that this profile only be examined when there is concern about major neurocognitive impairment being present. Research, however, has shown that individuals with mild cognitive impairment fail the easy validity indicators at high rates and the GMIP is useful when assessing these individuals (Green, Montijo, & Brockhaus, 2011). Research has also shown that individuals with brain injuries, intractable epilepsy, other clinical conditions, and non-native English speakers can fail the easy validity indicators and the GMIP can be useful when assessing

TABLE 4.6. Word Memory Test

Overview of the test

- The third most frequently used stand-alone performance validity test
- Full administration takes 15 to 20 minutes
- Cutoffs have high sensitivity but concern has been raised about low specificity in some samples
- The test can be used with patients with amnestic forms of dementia when using the GMIP
- The test is copyrighted; the test/computer administrations must be purchased

Common cutoffs with classification accuracy rates

Trial	Cutoff	Sensitivity	Specificity
Failure of IR, DR, or CNS	≥82.5% on Any Trial	57–95%	66–90%
GMIP	≥30% point difference	—	91–95%

Caution with . . .

Major neurocognitive disorder/dementia when not using the GMIP, Major neurocognitive disorder/dementia with significant language and comprehension issues even when using the GMIP, Individuals with less than a third-grade reading level (if administered computer version)

Note. Classification accuracy rates are from Soble et al. (2021); IR = immediate recognition; DR = delayed recognition; CNS = consistency score; GMIP = Genuine memory impairment profile.

these individuals (Alverson et al., 2019; Hampson, Kemp, Coughlan, Moulan, & Bhakta, 2014; Strutt & Stinson, 2022). In conclusion, to avoid false-positive findings of invalidity, Schroeder and Martin (2022c) have suggested that the GMIP be examined when there is a suspicion of dementia, mild cognitive impairment, or other neurological condition that could produce organic cognitive impairment. Similarly, Strutt and Stinson (2022) have suggested that the GMIP be examined any time that a non-native English speaker or culturally diverse individual is evaluated, particularly when patients have suspected cognitive impairment or low educational attainment.

Clinical Groups that Might Cause False-Positive Findings Even When Using the GMIP

While the GMIP can help to protect against false-positive errors, there might be cases where an unacceptable number of false-positive errors could occur even when utilizing the GMIP. For example, in the WMT manual (Green, 2003), it is noted that children with a third-grade reading level have been found to perform well on the test. Conversely, there is no information on how individuals who have a reading level below the third grade might perform on the test and it is conceivable that they could potentially fail the test due to reading issues. Additionally, Howe, Anderson, Kaufman, Sachs, and Loring (2007) found that the GMIP from the MSVT (which is conceptually similar to the GMIP from the WMT) controlled for most false-positive errors in their dementia sample, but individuals with significant language and comprehension issues were not identified by the GMIP as being false-positive errors. Thus, it appears possible that individuals with exceptionally low reading levels or those with significant language issues could produce false-positive findings on the WMT even when the GMIP is utilized.

Medical Symptom Validity Test

Table 4.7 provides an overview of the Medical Symptom Validity Test (MSVT). The MSVT is the fourth most commonly used stand-alone PVT (Martin et al., 2024). This is another PVT developed by Paul Green, and it is constructed very similarly to the WMT although it is shorter and easier (Green, 2004). The test is comprised of three "easy" validity indices and two "hard" subtests which allow for a calculation of a GMIP to help protect against false-positive errors. While fewer research studies have been published on the MSVT than the WMT, there are fewer concerns about false-positive errors with this test (Schroeder & Martin, 2022c).

Multiple differential prevalence and case series designs have shown the MSVT to be relatively resilient to cognitive dysfunction (for a thorough review see Schroeder & Martin, 2022c). In one of the few studies that utilized external criteria for classifying patients as performing validly or invalidly, Suesse, Wong, Stampler, Carpenter, and Scott (2015) found that the MSVT had around 90% specificity when administered via standard guidelines, which included use of the GMIP when major

TABLE 4.7. Medical Symptom Validity Test			
Overview of the test			
• The fourth most frequently used stand-alone performance validity test • Similar to, but briefer than, the WMT • Full administration takes 5 to 10 minutes • Can be used with patients who have Alzheimer's dementia (when using the GMIP) • The test is copyrighted; the test/computer administrations must be purchased			
Common cutoffs with classification accuracy rates			
Trial	**Cutoff**	**Sensitivity**	**Specificity**
Failure of IR, DR, or CNS	≤85% on Any Trial	55–75%	87–93%
GMIP	≥20% point difference	—	89–100%
Caution with GMIP			
Major neurocognitive disorder/dementia when not using the GMIP, Major neurocognitive disorder/dementia with significant language and comprehension issues even when using the GMIP, Individuals with less than a third-grade reading level (if administered computer version)			
Note. Classification accuracy rates are from Soble et al. (2021); IR = immediate recognition; DR = delayed recognition; CNS = consistency score; GMIP = Genuine memory impairment profile.			

neurocognitive dysfunction was present. Likewise, in a known groups design, Resch, Rhoads, Osview, and Soble (2022) found specificity of the easy MSVT validity indices to be 90% in their sample that excluded individuals with a major neurocognitive disorder. When examining individuals with a major neurocognitive disorder, only 46% of patients passed the easy validity indices but all of those individuals who failed the MSVT, except for one, met GMIP criteria.

As suggested by the literature cited above, when individuals have dementia or dementia-level cognitive impairment, false-positive error rates can increase to an inappropriate level if the GMIP is not utilized. When the GMIP is utilized, though, false-positive rates are generally low. As indicated in Table 4.7,, specificity rates have been found to range from 89 to 100% when using the GMIP. Consequently, the GMIP should be examined whenever major neurocognitive impairment is suspected as realistically being possible.

Clinical Groups That Might Cause False-Positive Findings Even When Using the GMIP

This section of text largely corresponds to the text written about the WMT. Specifically, while the GMIP will be important for protecting against false-positive errors when a major neurocognitive disorder is possible, there might be cases where an unacceptable number of false-positive errors could occur even when utilizing the GMIP. In the MSVT manual (Green, 2004), it is noted that children with a third-grade reading level have been found to perform well on the WMT "and a grade three level is probably also sufficient to perform the MSVT" (p. 14). It is reasonable to assume, though, that individuals who have a reading level below the third grade might not perform well on the test given reading limitations. Additionally, as previously described, Howe and colleagues (2007) found that the GMIP from the MSVT controlled for most false-positive errors in their dementia sample, but individuals with significant language and comprehension issues were not identified by the GMIP as being false-positive errors.

Word Choice Test

Table 4.8 provides an overview of the Word Choice Test (WCT). The WCT is a stand-alone PVT, which is based on a verbal memory paradigm. It was developed by the test publishing company Pearson, and it is available as part of the Advanced Clinical Solutions package for the WAIS-IV and WMS-IV (Pearson, 2009). The test is the fifth most commonly used stand-alone PVT (Martin et al., 2024).

The Advanced Clinical Solutions (ACS) manual provides specificity rates for the test at various cutoff scores for multiple clinical groups (e.g., traumatic brain injury, temporal lobectomy, schizophrenia, intellectual disability). In addition, the manual provides specificity rates for a combined clinical sample group at various cutoffs. The cutoff score associated with 90% specificity in the combined clinical sample group was ≤43. Since publication of the WCT (and test manual), performance of the WCT has been examined across various samples. A meta-analysis, based on eight research studies, found that a slightly more conservative cutoff (i.e., ≤42) could maintain at least 90% specificity (Bernstein et al., 2021). Given this, we recommended a cutoff of ≤42, which resulted in a sensitivity rate of 54% and a specificity rate of 93% across studies.

TABLE 4.8. Word Choice Test

Overview of the test			
• The fifth most commonly used stand-alone performance validity test • Full administration takes 5 to 10 minutes • Alternate cutoffs are available for various clinical conditions • The test is copyrighted; the test and forms must be purchased			
Common cutoffs with classification accuracy rates			
Trial	**Cutoff**	**Sensitivity**	**Specificity**
Total Score	≥42	54%	93%
Caution with . . .			
Individuals with intellectual disability when not adjusting the cutoff, Individuals with dementia, Possibly culturally diverse individuals and non-native English speakers			
Note. Classification accuracy rates are from Bernstein et al. (2021).			

Clinical Groups that Might Cause False-Positive Findings

High false-positive rates were seen in the ACS intellectual disability special group, whether using a cutoff score of ≤42 or ≤43. With that said, the ACS data suggest that the WCT cutoff score can be adjusted to ≤35 to maintain adequate specificity in individuals with a mild intellectual disability. Furthermore, individuals with dementia might be at increased risk for producing high false-positive rates on the WCT. While data on this is not reported in the Advanced Clinical Solutions manual, independently conducted research suggests this to be the case (e.g., Bain & Soble, 2019; Bernstein et al., 2021; Tyson et al., 2023). Finally, it should be noted that we are not aware of research examining WCT performance in culturally diverse individuals or non-native English speakers. That said, it makes conceptual sense that some non-native English speaking groups and individuals from certain non-U.S. backgrounds might be disadvantaged by and more likely to perform worse on the test, especially given that the test is verbally mediated and likely influenced by words and concepts that are not uniformly familiar across languages and cultures.

Rey 15-Item Test with Recognition Trial

Table 4.9 provides an overview of the Rey 15-Item Test with Recognition Trial. The Rey 15-Item Test is an older stand-alone PVT (Rey, 1964) that is based on a visual memory paradigm. Strengths of the original Rey 15-Item Test are that it takes only about 2 minutes to administer, and the test is within the public domain making it free to use (for a copy of the test, see Lezak, Howieson, Bigler, & Tranel, 2012, or Strauss, Sherman, & Spreen, 2006). A weakness of the original test, however, is that sensitivity rates are relatively modest when adjusting the cutoff score (often, a cutoff of <9) to maintain adequate specificity rates (Reznek, 2005). Because of this, Boone and colleagues (2002b) developed a recognition trial to add to the original Rey-15 Item Test (see Boone et al., 2002b). When combining a free recall score with a combination recognition score (i.e., free recall + [recognition true positives – recognition false positives]), it was found that a cutoff of <20 resulted in adequate specificity while increasing sensitivity by 24% above the free recall score alone. Use of the Rey 15-Item Test with Recognition Trial generally takes 5 minutes or less to administer, and it is the sixth most commonly used stand-alone PVT (Martin et al., 2024).

Cross-validation studies of the Rey 15-Item Test with Recognition Trial have generally found the cutoff of <20 to result in adequate specificity rates (Soble, Webber, & Bailey, 2021). In fact, some studies have even suggested that cutoff scores can be adjusted slightly higher while still resulting in specificity rates slightly above 90% (e.g., Ashendorf, Clark, & Humphreys, 2021; Morse, Douglas-Newman, Mandel, & Swirsky-Sacchetti, 2013; Poynter et al., 2019). With that said, specificity rates decline when adults age 50+, individuals with IQ <80, and individuals with significant cognitive impairment such as dementia are administered the test (Poynter et al., 2019).

TABLE 4.9. Rey 15-Item Test with Recognition Trial

Overview of the test

- The sixth most commonly used stand-alone performance validity test
- Full administration generally takes 5 minutes or less
- Alternate cutoffs are available for various clinical conditions
- The test (including the recognition component) is in the public domain and can be used without purchase

Common cutoffs with classification accuracy rates

Trial	Cutoff	Sensitivity	Specificity
Rey 15-Item Free Recall (without the recognition trial)	<9	36%	90%
Combination score (which includes the recognition trial)	<20	47–71%	92–98%

Caution with . . .

Individuals age 50+, Individuals with IQ <80, Individuals with major neurocognitive disorder/dementia

Note. Classification accuracy rates are from Reznek (2005) and Soble et al. (2021).

Coin-in-the-Hand Test

Table 4.10 provides an overview of the Coin-in-the-Hand Test. The Coin-in-the-Hand Test is based on a visual memory paradigm. It was developed by Narinder Kapur to be a simple and brief performance validity test (Kapur, 1994). Schroeder and colleagues (2012a) further advanced the test by creating and validating standardized instructions and a response protocol (see Appendix 4.1 at the end of this chapter). While this PVT is the tenth most commonly used stand-alone PVT, we decided to include it in this chapter because it is the second most popular stand-alone PVT in the public domain (Martin et al., 2024) and it is a useful PVT when individuals have significant cognitive impairment, including dementia (Schroeder & Martin, 2022d).

As just indicated, a strength of the Coin-in-the-Hand Test is that it has been validated with clinical samples that have significant cognitive impairment. For example, Kapur (1994) found that a sample of five patients who had herpes simplex encephalitis that resulted in "dense amnesia" (p. 385) scored perfectly on the test. Additionally, Rudman, Oyebode, Jones, and Bentham (2011) found that no individual with mild dementia made more than a single error. Furthermore, Schroeder and colleagues (2012a) found that 89% of inpatients with dementia made no more than one error on the test. Consequently, a cutoff score of 2+ errors (or ≤8 correct responses) was proposed as a cutoff score.

In what appears to be the most comprehensive study on the Coin-in-the-Hand Test to date, Martin et al. (2022a) examined the specificity of the PVT in an older adult sample of patients referred for dementia workups. They found that all patients without cognitive impairment obtained a perfect score, and 97% of patients with mild cognitive impairment also obtained a perfect score. For individuals with mild dementia, a score of ≤8 (i.e., 2+ errors) resulted in 90% specificity. Finally, for individuals with moderate dementia, a score of ≤6 errors (i.e., 4+ errors) resulted in 90% specificity.

Another strength of the Coin-in-the-Hand test is that it has positive cross-cultural research support. Yeh and colleagues (2019), for example, found that a cutoff of ≤9 resulted in a 100% specificity rate in a healthy sample of Taiwanese older adults, and a cutoff of ≤8 resulted in 88% specificity in a clinical sample of Taiwanese individuals with dementia (average Mini-Mental Status Examination, or MMSE, score was 17.7). Daugherty and colleagues (2021) found that performance on a modified "extended version" of the Coin-in-the-Hand Test was not significantly different across samples of individuals from four countries (i.e., Colombia, Spain, Portugal, and the United States). Ferreira and colleagues (2022) also examined the extended version of the Coin-in-the-Hand Test; their sample included healthy Portuguese adults and Portuguese adults with dementia. The researchers found that the test was insensitive to sociodemographic variables and cognitive dysfunction, and the test also demonstrated good convergent validity with other PVTs.

A weakness of the Coin-in-the-Hand Test is that sensitivity rates have only been evaluated via simulators. While sensitivity rates for the test are high when simulators feign cognitive impairment (e.g., Hanley, Baker, & Ledson, 1999; Kelly, Baker, van den Broek, Jackson, & Humphries, 2005), it is unclear how high (or low) sensitivity rates are when evaluating real clinical patients who are invalidating testing in the neuropsychology clinic.

TABLE 4.10. Coin-in-the-Hand Test

Overview of the test

- The tenth most commonly used stand-alone performance validity test
- The second most commonly used stand-alone performance validity test that is within the public domain
- The test can be used without purchase
- Full administration takes approximately 5 minutes
- Can be used with patients who have dementia
- The cutoff can be increased to ≤9 when patients have less impairment than dementia

Common cutoffs with classification accuracy rates

Trial	Cutoff	Sensitivity	Specificity
Total score	≤8	Unclear	89%

Caution with . . .

Individuals with moderate dementia when using the standard cutoff

Note. Classification accuracy rates are from Schroeder et al. (2012a).

CLOSING REMARKS

It is generally recommended that clinicians include stand-alone PVTs in each test battery (Sweet et al., 2021). This is partly because stand-alone PVTs often have better classification accuracy rates than embedded PVTs. The median number of stand-alone PVTs typically included in nongeriatric adult clinical cases is two, and the median number of stand-alone PVTs typically included in geriatric adult clinical cases is one (for neuropsychologists at large) to two (for validity assessment experts; Martin et al., 2024). Which stand-alone PVTs are chosen will likely depend on the clinician's access to the tests, the amount of time that the clinician has for testing, whether the patient seems to be potentially exaggerating any specific cognitive function (e.g., attention or memory), and whether patient characteristics are likely to increase the possibility of false-positive findings on specific PVTs.

APPENDIX 4.1

Coin-in-the-Hand Test Protocol

Instructions: People often forget things easily when they are distracted, so this next test will measure how easily you can remember even after a distraction. I will put a coin in one hand **[hold both hands out so that palms are facing up, then put a coin in one hand]**, and then I will close both my hands. I will then ask you to close your eyes and distract yourself by counting backward from 10 to 1, counting aloud so I can hear you. After you reach 1, open your eyes, try to remember which hand the coin was in, and point to that hand. The coin will always be in the same hand it was in before you closed your eyes. We will do this memory task 10 times even though it might be challenging at times. Are you ready for the first time? **[Explain again if the patient does not understand.]**

[After each time the patient chooses a hand, open both hands and say either "That's right" or "That's wrong," depending on the patient's response. Continue this task 10 times. Show which hand the coin is in for approximately 2 seconds before closing the hands. Use a United States nickel as the coin.]

______ Right hand

______ Left hand

______ Left hand

______ Right hand

______ Right hand

______ Left hand

______ Right hand

______ Left hand

______ Right hand

______ Left hand

Total score: ______

Note. Originally published in Schroeder et al. (2012a).

CHAPTER 5

Employing Embedded Performance Validity Tests

Clinical Guidance and Cutoffs

Although embedded performance validity tests (PVTs) generally have lower classification accuracy rates than stand-alone PVTs, there are multiple advantages to using these tests. First, they are time efficient, since they are built into or derived from standard cognitive tests that are already being administered and, therefore, typically do not require extra time to be added to the test battery. Second, because they are built into/derived from cognitive tests, they can easily be interspersed throughout the test battery, allowing the neuropsychologist to continuously monitor the validity of the examinee's test performance. Third, embedded validity tests are less likely to be identified as validity tests by test takers who have researched or been coached on how to feign cognitive impairment while evading detection during a neuropsychological evaluation. Fourth, given that embedded validity tests are available across neuropsychological domains and tests, they easily allow for the detection of underperformance even when nuanced or domain-specific feigning occurs.

In this section of the chapter, we present information on embedded PVTs. Table 5.1 provides a listing of commonly used cutoff scores for a number of popular (Martin et al., 2015; Martin et al., 2024) and well-validated embedded PVTs within each cognitive domain. As can be seen, the majority of embedded PVTs are within the memory domain. Conversely, relatively few are in the processing speed and executive functioning domains as cognitive abilities in these domains are frequently affected by neurological disorders, often making PVTs in these domains challenging to establish (e.g., Nelson, Lee, & Sweet, 2021). In addition to this summary table, we have highlighted below seven of the most frequently used embedded PVTs regardless of cognitive domain. We provide an overview of each of these PVTs, including typical administration time, strengths and weaknesses, and commonly utilized cutoffs and

TABLE 5.1. Common Embedded PVTs Grouped by Neuropsychological Domain

PVT	Parent test	Common cutoff
	Batteries	
RBANS Effort Index	RBANS	≥3 (Goette & Goette, 2019; Shura et al., 2018)
Excessive Decline from Premorbid Functioning FSIQ	WAIS-IV and Test of Premorbid Functioning	≥18 (Martin et al., 2017)
	Attention/working memory	
Reliable Digit Span	Wechsler Adult Intelligence Scale	≤6 (Schroeder et al., 2012b)
Reliable Digit Span—Revised	Wechsler Adult Intelligence Scale	≤10 (Soble et al., 2021b)
Digit Span Scaled Score	Wechsler Adult Intelligence Scale	≤5 (Sobel, Babikian, & Boone, 2021a)
Summed T-scores: Omi+Com+HRTSD+HRTISIC	Conners' CPT-3	>256 (Ord et al., 2021a; Scimeca et al., 2021)
	Mental processing speed	
TMT-A Demographically Adjusted T-score	Trail Making Test	≤30 (Peak, Marceaux, Chicota-Carroll, & Soble, 2024)
	Language	
Sentence Repetition Test Raw Score	Sentence Repetition Test	≤10 (Schroeder & Marshall, 2010)
COWAT Age and Education Corrected T-score	Controlled Oral Word Association Test	<30 (Martin & Schroeder, 2021b)
Token Test Total Score	Token Test	≤150 (Meyers, Galinsky, & Volbrecht, 1999)
	Visuospatial	
Judgment of Line Orientation Raw Score	Judgment of Line Orientation	≤18 (Whiteside, Walde, & Busse, 2011)
Hooper Visual Organization Test Total Score	Hooper Visual Organization Test	≤20.5 (Whiteside et al., 2011)
Rey Complex Figure Raw Score	Rey Complex Figure	≤24.5 (Whiteside et al., 2011)
	Memory	
CVLT Forced Choice Recognition	California Verbal Learning Test	≤14 (Schwartz et al., 2016)
Logical Memory Recognition	Wechsler Memory Scale–4	≤17 (Pearson, 2009)
Visual Reproduction Recognition	Wechsler Memory Scale–4	≤3 (Pearson, 2009)

(continued)

TABLE 5.1. *(continued)*

PVT	Parent test	Common cutoff
	Memory *(continued)*	
Verbal Paired Associates Recognition	Wechsler Memory Scale–4	≤31 (Pearson, 2009)
Rey Combination Score Equation	Rey Complex Figure with Recognition Trial	≤47 (Lu, Boone, Cozolino, & Mitchell, 2003)
BVMT-R Recognition Discrimination	Brief Visuospatial Memory Test—Revised	≤4 (Soble et al., 2021b)
BVMT-R Recognition Hits	Brief Visuospatial Memory Test—Revised	≤4 (Soble et al., 2021b)
RAVLT Combination Score	Rey Auditory Verbal Learning Test	≤10 (Boone et al., 2022a)
RAVLT Recognition Total 50 Item	Rey Auditory Verbal Learning Test	≤9 (Boone et al., 2022a)
HVLT-R Recognition Discrimination	Hopkins Verbal Learning Test—Revised	≤5 (Soble et al., 2021b)
HVLT-R Forced Choice Recognition	Hopkins Verbal Learning Test—Revised	≤11 (Abeare et al., 2021)
	Executive functioning	
Failure to Maintain Set Raw Score	Wisconsin Card Sorting Test	≥3 or ≥4 (Greve, Heinly, Bianchini, & Love, 2009; Larrabee, 2003)
Color–Word Conditions 1–4 Summed Scaled Scores	Delis–Kaplan Executive Function System	≤18 (Eglit et al., 2020)
	Motor	
Finger Tapping Dominant Hand (3-trial mean raw)	Finger Tapping Test	≤35 (males) ≤28 (females) (Arnold et al., 2005)
GPB Dominant Hand Demo Adjusted T-score	Grooved Pegboard	≤29 (Erdodi et al., 2017; Erdodi, Kirsch, Sabelli, & Abeare, 2018b)

Note. RBANS = Repeatable Battery for the Assessment of Neuropsychological Status; WAIS-IV = Wechsler Adult Intelligence Scale—4th Edition, Omi+Com+ HRTSD+HRTISIC = Omissions+Comissions+HRT SD+HRT ISI Change; TMT-A = Trail Making Test part A; COWAT = Controlled Oral Word Association Test; CVLT = California Verbal Learning Test (most research applied to the second version, but limited research suggests similar findings for the third version); BVMT-R = Brief Visuospatial Memory Test—Revised; RAVLT = Rey Auditory Verbal Learning Test; HVLT-R = Hopkins Verbal Learning Test—Revised; GPB = Grooved Pegboard.

associated classification accuracy rates. We then discuss research, when available, on examinees whose background and/or clinical condition might increase the risk of false-positive PVT findings. As with the stand-alone PVTs in Chapter 4, this information is written in a "user friendly" manner, with the goal of ensuring that the reader has a basic understanding of each PVT with information that he or she can start applying in clinical practice.

Finally, before presenting additional information, we want to again (as first noted in Chapter 4) highlight that, in addition to knowing what cutoffs are commonly used, it is important to be aware of the samples from which the PVTs and associated cutoff values have been validated. This is likely of even greater importance when examining embedded PVTs (as compared to stand-alone PVTs), as some embedded PVT cutoffs are derived from only a handful of samples and the diagnostic and demographic characteristics of those samples might not readily generalize to the patient that the clinician is evaluating. In cases where embedded PVT cutoffs are based only on the performance of samples comprised primarily of nonpathological or presumably cognitively unimpaired patients (e.g., samples predominately comprised of patients with mTBI, anxiety or depressive disorders, or healthy controls), caution is emphasized, particularly if scores are at or just below the recommended cutoff.

When examining embedded PVTs, we also encourage clinicians to consider the normality/abnormality of the performance relative to the normative sample. Within the embedded PVT literature, there are (generally infrequent) instances where performances that are relatively common in the normative sample are found to be uncommon in certain samples used to validate an embedded PVT. This can occur when the validation sample is largely comprised of individuals without cognitive impairment and/or with individuals who have higher educational levels and premorbid intellectual abilities than the normal population. In these instances, a score that is, for example, a low average standard score (e.g., SS = 7; 16th percentile) might be determined as evidence for invalidity because it was found to occur in less than 10% of validly performing individuals in the research sample (thus meeting the 90% specificity threshold). We would strongly caution against applying such a liberal cutoff in many clinical cases and would encourage the clinician to, instead, examine for more robust evidence of invalidity.

EMBEDDED PVTs

Reliable Digit Span

Table 5.2 provides an overview of Reliable Digit Span (RDS), which is the most well researched and frequently used embedded PVT in neuropsychological practice (Martin et al., 2024; Schroeder et al., 2012b). This PVT is embedded within the Digit Span subtest from the fourth edition of the Wechsler Adult Intelligence Scale (WAIS-IV); and previous WAIS editions. RDS is calculated by "summing the longest string of

TABLE 5.2. Reliable Digit Span

Overview of the test			
• The most frequently used and well researched embedded performance validity test • Embedded within the Digit Span subtest of the WAIS-IV (and previous WAIS editions) • Takes no additional time to administer if already administering Digit Span			
Common cutoffs with classification accuracy rates			
Trial	**Cutoff**	**Sensitivity**	**Specificity**
RDS score	≤6	30–35%	96–97%
RDS-R score	≤10	25–43%	89–98%
Caution with . . .			
Individuals with CVAs, Significant memory disorders, Dementia, Intellectual disability, Borderline intellectual functioning, English as a second language, Hispanic individuals, especially when low educational attainment is present			

Note. WAIS-IV = Wechsler Adult Intelligence Scale–4th Edition; WAIS = Wechsler Adult Intelligence Scale; RDS = Reliable Digit Span; RDS-R = Reliable Digit Span–Revised; CVAs = Cerebrovascular accidents; Classification accuracy rates are from Schroeder et al. (2012b) and Soble et al. (2021b).

digits repeated without error over two trials under both forward and backward conditions" (Greiffenstein, Baker, & Gola, 1994, pp. 219–220). Thus, the administration of this PVT does not add any additional time to the administration of the Digit Span subtest.

Numerous studies have investigated RDS since its development in 1994. Results from a systematic review and meta-analysis (Schroeder et al., 2012b) indicate that a cutoff score of ≤6 maintains adequate specificity while optimizing sensitivity. In addition to performing the meta-analysis, Schroeder et al. (2012b) conducted a large cross-validation study, which, when combined with findings from the meta-analysis, indicated that there are some clinical groups that are at risk for high false-positive errors, even when a ≤6 cutoff is used. These groups include individuals with cerebrovascular accidents, significant memory disorders, dementia, intellectual disabilities, borderline intellectual functioning, and English as a second language. It has also been suggested that Spanish-speaking individuals, specifically, might be at risk for elevated false-positive rates on RDS and other Digit Span-based validity indicators, especially when low educational attainment is present (Salazar, Lu, Wen, & Boone, 2007; Schroeder et al., 2012b; Strutt et al., 2011). Even when Digit Span is translated into an examinee's native language, caution should be exercised in generalizing English-administered norms to other languages given the potential differences in test complexity secondary to language differences. For example, most digits 1–9 are monosyllabic when spoken in English, whereas 6 digits 1–9 contain more than one syllable when spoken in Spanish. To this point, Hall et al. (2018) found that bilingual Americans performed similarly on all subtests of the RBANS regardless of whether testing was administered in Spanish or English, with the sole exception of Digit Span.

On Digit Span, bilingual individuals completing the test in Spanish performed lower than bilingual individuals completing the test in English.

Finally, it should be noted that there is a sequencing component added to the Digit Span subtest on the fourth edition of the WAIS, which was not present on Digit Span subtests from previous WAIS editions. A revised RDS (RDS-R) score is now available, incorporating performance on the sequencing trial with performance on Digit Span forward and backward. RDS-R can be calculated by summing the longest string of digits repeated without error over both trials with regard to the forward, backward, and sequencing trials. A cutoff score of ≤10 has been proposed, with adequate classification accuracy rates supporting its usage (Soble et al., 2021b). RDS-R is currently used less frequently than RDS, though, potentially because research on RDS-R is more limited than research on RDS.

California Verbal Learning Test – II: Forced Choice Recognition

Table 5.3 provides an overview of the California Verbal Learning Test–II (CVLT-II) forced choice (FC) recognition validity index, which is the second most frequently used embedded PVT (Martin et al., 2024). This PVT is added as an optional subtest at the end of the CVLT-II. In this regard, it takes an additional 2–5 minutes to administer if one is already administering the CVLT-II. This embedded PVT has also been added as an optional subtest for the third edition of the CVLT (CVLT-3) with relatively minor changes (changes to 8 of 16 foil words). While research suggests that CVLT-3 FC performs similarly to CVLT-II FC (Donders & Vos, 2023), the current discussion focuses on the CVLT-II version given that it has been more extensively studied at the time of the writing of this chapter.

Schwartz and colleagues (2016) note that the authors of the CVLT-II FC recognition PVT found that most healthy individuals in the CVLT-II normative sample

TABLE 5.3. California Verbal Learning Test–II: Forced Choice Recognition

Overview of the test			
• The second most frequently used embedded performance validity test • Embedded within the CVLT-II and CVLT-3 • Takes approximately 2–5 additional minutes to administer the embedded validity index • A cutoff of ≤15 can likely be appropriately used with mild traumatic brain injury patients			
Common cutoffs with classification accuracy rates			
Trial	**Cutoff**	**Sensitivity**	**Specificity**
Raw score	≤14	50%	93%
Caution with . . .			
Individuals with dementia			

Note. CVLT = California Verbal Learning Test; Classification accuracy rates are from Schwartz et al. (2016).

obtained a perfect score (16/16) on the embedded PVT although a small number of individuals scored lower. Based on these data, the authors of the test suggested that a score of ≤14 may suggest invalid performance. Since that time, additional studies have been conducted on CVLT-II FC, including studies of individuals with neuropsychological conditions. In a systematic review of the literature, Schwartz and colleagues (2016) found that the average base rate of test failure across studies of clinical patients (excluding individuals with dementia or intellectual disability) was 6.8% at the ≤14 cutoff (translating into a 93% specificity rate).

In individuals with minimal to no cognitive impairment, research supports a more liberal cutoff. For example, Erdodi and colleagues (2018a) examined the CVLT-II FC recognition PVT in a sample primarily consisting of patients evaluated following a mild TBI. In this sample, they found that the cutoff score could be raised to ≤15 while still maintaining adequate specificity rates. Axelrod, Miller, and LaBuda (2021) write that "these findings of adequate specificity at a cutoff of ≤15 likely reflect the fact that the sample was primarily mTBI, and such patients are expected to recover entirely, certainly by 3 months postinjury; this population performs most similarly to normal controls, who achieve 100% specificity at an FCR cutoff of 14. Thus, the argument can reasonably be made that in the differential of actual versus feigned mTBI, a cutoff of ≤15 is appropriate." (p. 135).

A few studies have examined the CVLT-II FC recognition PVT with individuals who have significant cognitive impairment. Clark and colleagues (2012) found that most individuals with mild cognitive impairment passed CVLT-II at a cutoff of ≤14, but 12.5% of validly performing individuals with mild Alzheimer's disease and 71.4% of individuals with moderate Alzheimer's disease performed below this cutoff. Thus, based on their study, it appears that dementia is a condition in which false-positive rates are unacceptably high on CVLT-II FC recognition PVT when using typical cutoffs. Interestingly, though, Marshall and Happe (2007) found that nearly 90% (specifically, 89%) of individuals with mild to moderate intellectual disabilities passed CVLT-II FC. This latter study suggests that individuals with mild to moderate intellectual disabilities are likely to pass CVLT-II FC recognition.

Finally, regarding the cross-cultural generalizability of this PVT, Gasquoine, Weimer, and Orta (2019) found that all of their non-clinical, Mexican American, bilingual individuals passed FC recognition from the CVLT-3 at a cutoff of ≤14; data which are comparable to findings in healthy monolingual, English speakers. However, the accuracy of CVLT FC tests in patients who are non-English speaking, of other cultural backgrounds, and originate from outside of the United States has not yet been sufficiently studied, and more cross-cultural research is needed.

Repeatable Battery for the Assessment of Neuropsychological Status: Effort Index

Table 5.4 provides an overview of the Repeatable Battery for the Assessment of Neuropsychological Status (RBANS) Effort Index, which is the third most frequently used

TABLE 5.4. Repeatable Battery for the Assessment of Neuropsychological Status: Effort Index			
Overview of the test			
• The third most frequently used embedded performance validity test • Embedded within the Repeatable Battery for the Assessment of Neuropsychological Status • Takes no additional time to administer if already administering the test			
Common cutoffs with classification accuracy rates			
Trial	**Cutoff**	**Sensitivity**	**Specificity**
Weighted score	≥3	48%	93%
Caution with . . .			
Individuals with dementia when using the original cutoff scores, Possibly culturally diverse individuals and non-native English speakers			
Note. Classification accuracy rates are from Shura et al. (2018).			

embedded PVT (Martin et al., 2024). This PVT is embedded within the RBANS, and it is calculated using scores from the Digit Span and List Recognition subtests. Digit Span raw scores need to be converted to Digit Span weighted scores using the following conversion system:

- Digit Span raw scores of 0–4 = weighted score of 6
- Digit Span raw score of 5 = weighted score of 5
- Digit Span raw score of 6 = weighted score of 3
- Digit Span raw score of 7 = weighted score of 2
- Digit Span raw scores of 8–16 = weighted score of 0

Similarly, List Recognition raw scores need to be converted to List Recognition weighted scores using the following conversion system:

- List Recognition raw scores of 0–9 = weighted score of 6
- List Recognition raw score of 10 = weighted score of 5
- List Recognition raw scores of 11–12 = weighted score of 4
- List Recognition raw scores of 13–14 = weighted score of 3
- List Recognition raw scores of 15–16 = weighted score of 2
- List Recognition raw score of 17 = weighted score of 1
- List Recognition raw scores of 18–20 = weighted score of 0

The Digit Span and List Recognition weighted scores are then summed to obtain a final summed weighted score.

Two meta-analyses, published in very close proximity, have examined cutoff scores for the RBANS Effort Index. In one meta-analysis (i.e., Goette & Goette, 2019), the authors aggregated cutoff scores and reported that an "optimal" cutoff would be 3.11. Using a multiple threshold analysis, the estimated sensitivity and specificity rates associated with the cutoff were 44% and 90%, respectively. Shura et al. (2018) arrived at a similar conclusion in their meta-analysis, finding that a cutoff of ≥3 achieves a sensitivity rate of 48% and a specificity rate of 93%.

Results from both meta-analyses suggest that significant cognitive impairment and dementia may be risk factors for increased false-positive rates. In fact, the Goette and Goette (2019) meta-analysis estimated specificity to be 75.77% at the cutoff of 3.11 in dementia samples. To more thoroughly explore this topic, Martin et al. (2022a) examined the RBANS Effort Index in older adult clinical samples. They found that the cutoff of ≥3 resulted in 92% specificity for older adults who had cognitive concerns but who did not have cognitive impairment. The same cutoff resulted in a specificity rate of 91% for older adults with mild cognitive impairment. The cutoff had to be adjusted to ≥6 and ≥9, however, to maintain 90+% specificity rates in samples of older adults with mild dementia and moderate dementia, respectively.

Finally, it should be noted that there is limited data on how culturally diverse individuals and non-native English speakers perform on the RBANS Effort Index. While it is possible that individuals from some non-U.S., non-native English-speaking groups might perform fairly well on the PVT (as suggested by Aguilar, Bailey, Karyadi, Kinney, & Nitch, 2023), it is also conceivable that adjusted cutoff scores might be needed for some patient groups given research showing lower performance on WAIS-based Digit Span PVTs. Further research on this topic is needed.

Wechsler Memory Scale—Fourth Edition: Logical Memory Forced Choice Recognition

Table 5.5 provides an overview of the *Wechsler Memory Scale—Fourth Edition* (WMS-IV) Logical Memory Forced Choice Recognition embedded PVT, which is the fourth most frequently used embedded PVT (Martin et al., 2024). This PVT is derived by simply counting the number of correct responses on the WMS-IV Logical Memory Forced Choice Recognition subtest. Thus, the administration of this PVT does not add any additional time to the administration of the Logical Memory subtest.

The ACS manual (Pearson, 2009) provides specificity rates for Logical Memory Recognition at various cutoff scores for multiple clinical groups (e.g., traumatic brain injury, temporal lobectomy, schizophrenia, intellectual disability). In addition, the manual provides specificity rates for a combined clinical sample group. The cutoff score associated with 90% specificity in the combined clinical sample group is reported to be ≤17. Interestingly, cutoff scores that maintain 90+% specificity are generally near or above the ≤17 score for most clinical groups, including a temporal lobectomy group (cutoff score of ≤16). The only clinical group in the ACS manual that required a significant adjustment to the cutoff score was the mild intellectual

TABLE 5.5.	Wechsler Memory Scale—Fourth Edition: Logical Memory Forced Choice Recognition		
Overview of the test			
• The fourth most frequently used embedded performance validity test • Embedded within the Wechsler Memory Scale – Fourth Edition Logical Memory subtest • Takes no additional time to administer if already administering Logical Memory			
Common cutoffs with classification accuracy rates			
Trial	**Cutoff**	**Sensitivity**	**Specificity**
Raw score	≤17	15–22%	90–100%
Caution with . . .			
Individuals with intellectual disability or dementia			
Note. Classification accuracy rates are from Tyson et al. (2023).			

disability group (a cutoff score of ≤12 is required for specificity rates to reach 90% in this clinical group).

In examining additional literature, it can be seen that researchers often find that the cutoff score of ≤17 results in specificity rates of 90+% (e.g., Pliskin et al., 2021; Tyson et al., 2023) unless individuals with dementia are included in the sample (e.g., Soble et al., 2019). Given that a more conservative cutoff would be required for individuals with dementia, which would likely result in prohibitively low sensitivity, use of this validity index in patients with dementia is unlikely to be very useful.

Wechsler Memory Scale—Fourth Edition: Visual Reproduction Forced Choice Recognition

Table 5.6 provides an overview of the WMS-IV Visual Reproduction Forced Choice Recognition embedded PVT, which is the seventh most frequently used embedded PVT (Martin et al., 2024). This PVT is derived by counting the number of correct responses on the WMS-IV Visual Reproduction Recognition subtest. Thus, the administration of this PVT does not add any additional time to the administration of the Visual Reproduction subtest.

The ACS manual (Pearson, 2009) provides specificity rates for Visual Reproduction Recognition at various cutoff scores for multiple clinical groups (e.g., traumatic brain injury, temporal lobectomy, schizophrenia, intellectual disability). In addition, the manual provides specificity rates for a combined clinical sample group. The cutoff score associated with 90% specificity in the combined clinical sample group is reported to be ≤3. Interestingly, cutoff scores that maintain 90+% specificity are generally at or near the ≤3 score for most clinical groups including a temporal lobectomy group (cutoff score of ≤3). The only clinical group in the ACS manual that required a significant adjustment to the cutoff score was the mild intellectual disability group

TABLE 5.6. Wechsler Memory Scale—Fourth Edition: Visual Reproduction Forced Choice Recognition

Overview of the test			
• The seventh most frequently used embedded performance validity test • Embedded within the Wechsler Memory Scale –Fourth Edition Visual Reproduction subtest • Takes no additional time to administer if already administering Visual Reproduction			
Common cutoffs with classification accuracy rates			
Trial	**Cutoff**	**Sensitivity**	**Specificity**
Raw score	≤3	33–50%	95–98%
Caution with . . .			
Individuals with intellectual disability or dementia			

Note. Classification accuracy rates are from Tyson et al. (2023).

(a cutoff score of ≤1 is required for specificity rates to reach 90% in this clinical group). In cross-validation research, Tyson and colleagues (2023) found the ≤3 cutoff to result in sensitivity rates ranging from 33 to 50% and specificity rates ranging from 95 to 98%. Finally, while minimal data are currently available on how individuals with dementia perform on this PVT, it would appear likely that high false-positive rates would emerge in this population given that patients with dementia are known to perform somewhat poorly on other forced choice visual memory recognition tests (e.g., TOMM).

Wisconsin Card Sorting Test: Failure to Maintain Set

Table 5.7 provides an overview of the Wisconsin Card Sorting Test (WCST) Failure to Maintain Set (FMS) embedded PVT. Embedded PVTs within the Wisconsin Card Sorting Text (WCST) are the fifth most commonly used embedded PVTs, with the FMS embedded PVT being the most popular (Martin et al., 2015; Martin et al., 2024). This PVT is derived by summing the number of times an individual fails to maintain set on the test. Because this calculation is a standard part of the test, it does not add any additional time to the administration of the test.

A variety of cutoffs for WCST FMS have been proposed. There are likely multiple reasons for this, a primary one being that scores on WCST FMS appear to vary as a function of degree of cognitive dysfunction in validly performing individuals. Greve and colleagues (2009c), for example, found that specificity rates at a cutoff of ≥2 were 82% for a mild TBI sample, 73% for a moderate to severe TBI sample, and 69% for a severe TBI sample. At a cutoff of ≥3, specificity improved to 89% in both the mild TBI sample and the moderate to severe TBI sample, but specificity was only 82% in the severe TBI sample. When increasing the cutoff to ≥4, specificity achieved 90% or better in all TBI samples, and specificity was also 90% or better in cerebrovascular

TABLE 5.7.	**Wisconsin Card Sorting Test: Failure to Maintain Set**		
Overview of the test			
• The fifth most frequently used embedded performance validity test • Embedded within the Wisconsin Card Sorting Test • Takes no additional time to administer if already administering the test			
Common cutoffs with classification accuracy rates			
Trial	**Cutoff**	**Sensitivity**	**Specificity**
Raw score	≥3	24–29%	89–96%
Caution with . . .			
Individuals with relatively severe cognitive dysfunction (e.g., severe brain injury, large cerebrovascular accidents, severe memory impairment/dementia); Perhaps some individuals of culturally diverse backgrounds			
Note. Classification accuracy rates are from Soble et al. (2021b).			

accident, memory disorder, and psychiatric (predominantly depression and anxiety) samples. This increase in specificity was associated with an expected reduction in sensitivity, though, with sensitivity dropping to 18% when using a cutoff of ≥4. Other research has supported cutoffs of ≥3 and ≥4 as well. Larrabee (2003), for example, reported that an FMS cutoff of ≥3 resulted in 96% specificity in a valid sample of individuals with moderate to severe TBIs (sensitivity was 20%). When the cutoff was increased to ≥4, specificity increased to 100% for the moderate to severe TBI sample (sensitivity fell to 12%).

In sum, there is support for use of the ≥3 cutoff, particularly when injuries/illnesses are relatively mild. When an individual has more significant cognitive impairment, as might be seen within the context of a severe brain injury, cerebrovascular accident, or severe memory impairment, the cutoff would need to increase to ≥4. This increase in cutoff does, however, lower sensitivity rates. Finally, it should be noted that it is unknown how individuals with intellectual disabilities and individuals of culturally diverse backgrounds (especially when limited education, low acculturation, and/or low test wiseness are present) might perform on WCST FMS, so use with those populations is cautioned.

Rey Complex Figure Test and Recognition Trial: Combination Score Equation

Table 5.8 provides an overview of the Rey Complex Figure Test and Recognition Trial: Combination Score equation (sometimes also referred to as the Effort Equation) embedded PVT. There are multiple embedded PVTs within the Rey Complex Figure Test and Recognition Trial and, when combined, these PVTs are the sixth most commonly embedded PVTs (Martin et al., 2024). For a comprehensive review

TABLE 5.8. Rey Complex Figure Test and Recognition Trial: Combination Score Equation

Overview of the test			
• The sixth most frequently used embedded performance validity test • Embedded within the Rey Complex Figure Test and Recognition Trial • Takes no additional time to administer if already administering the test			
Common cutoffs with classification accuracy rates			
Trial	**Cutoff**	**Sensitivity**	**Specificity**
Combination Score	47	43–76%	91–100%
Combination Score	50	12–80%	90–96%
Caution with . . .			
Individuals with intellectual disability, Dementia, Significant visuospatial deficits, or Significant visuospatial memory deficits			

Note. Classification accuracy rates are from Lu et al. (2003); Reedy et al. (2013); Shura, Miskey, Rowland, Yoash-Gantz, and Dennings (2016); and Ashendorf (2019). The specificity rate range for the ≤47 cutoff does not include the visual memory impairment group from Lu et al. (2003).

of all Rey Complex Figure Test and Recognition Trial embedded PVTs, we refer the reader to Boone (2021). Our focus in this chapter is on the Combination Score equation embedded PVT, as it is the most popular Rey Complex Figure Test and Recognition Trial PVT (Martin et al., 2015).

The Rey Complex Figure Test and Recognition Trial: Combination Score equation was developed by Lu and colleagues (2003), and it is based on scores obtained when using the Meyers and Meyers (1995) scoring system for the Rey Complex Figure Test and Recognition Trial. The test data that are needed to calculate the PVT are the Meyers and Meyers (1) Copy Raw score, (2) Recognition True Positives raw score, and (3) eight atypically endorsed items from the Recognition False Positives index. The eight atypically endorsed items from the Recognition False Positive index are items 1, 4, 6, 10, 11, 16, 18, and 21. Once that information is obtained, the embedded PVT can be calculated using the following equation:

$$\text{Combination Score} = \text{copy score} + [(\text{true positive recognition} - \text{atypical recognition errors}) \times 3]$$

Because this equation is based on scores that are obtained by administering the standard test, use of the PVT does not add any additional time to the administration of the test.

It should be noted that Lu and colleagues (2003) used a modified administration of the Meyers and Meyers (1995) Rey Complex Figure Test and Recognition Trial test when developing the embedded PVT. Typically, the test starts by having the examinee copy the stimuli on a piece of paper (this is the copy trial). After this, there is a 3-minute delay, and then the examinee is asked to recall and reproduce the figure from memory (this is the immediate recall trial). Then, 30 minutes after the copy trial of the test is completed, the examinee is again asked to recall and reproduce the figure from memory (this is the delayed recall trial). Immediately after the delayed recall trial is complete, the examinee is presented with a recognition trial, in which the individual is asked to indicate which pieces of the figure were actual parts of the original figure. When Lu and colleagues developed the Combination Score equation, though, they intentionally skipped administering the delayed recall trial, and they had the examinees complete the recognition trial immediately after completing the immediate recall portion of the test. Using this administration method, they found that a cutoff score of ≤47.0 resulted in a high sensitivity rate (i.e., 75.9%) and a good specificity rate (91.4%) in their total clinical sample. When examining patients with specific types of memory impairment, they found that a 93.3% specificity rate in patients without memory impairment, a 95.7% specificity rate in patients with verbal memory impairment, and an 82.4% specificity rate in patients with visual memory impairment. Decreasing the cutoff score to ≤45.0 increased the specificity rate to 88.2% in the group of individuals with visual memory impairment. Finally, the authors noted that no individuals with intellectual disability or dementia were included in their sample, so use of this embedded PVT with individuals who have those conditions is questionable. They also noted that the embedded PVT should be used cautiously when patients have significant visuospatial constructional deficits due to the PVT's heavy reliance on visuospatial ability.

Reedy and colleagues (2013) cross-validated the Combination Score PVT using the same administration procedure for the majority of their examinees. They found that the cutoff score of ≤47 resulted in a specificity rate of 96.0% and a sensitivity rate of 67.8%. Their analyses also indicated that the demographics of gender, education level, ethnicity/culture, and language characteristics did not appear to be risk factors for failure of the PVT. Conversely, older age, lower intelligence, and a history of learning problems in school (possibly due to lower intelligence) were thought to be possible risk factors for false-positive errors on the test. Finally, because specificity was so high, they suggested another potential cutoff score of ≤50, which resulted in 90.3% specificity in their sample.

Others have validated the embedded PVT using different test administration methods. For example, Ashendorf (2019) administered the Rey Complex Figure Test and Recognition Trial "using a landscape-oriented stimulus page for design copy, followed by immediate recall (i.e., not using a 3-minute delay) and then a 30-minute delayed recall condition . . . The Meyers and Meyers (1995) recognition trial . . . was administered immediately following the delayed recall trial" (p. 1391). Using this administration method, Ashendorf found that the cutoff of ≤47 resulted in 100% specificity and 43.2% sensitivity in his sample. A cutoff score of ≤50 resulted in 95.7% specificity and 48.6% sensitivity. Shura et al. (2016) used the full Meyers and Meyers (1995) administration method in their sample, which was a pure research sample (not a clinical sample). Using this administration method, they found that the cutoff of

≤50 resulted in 95% specificity and 12% sensitivity. The fact that the sensitivity rate was so low may have been due to the fact that the sample was recruited specifically for research purposes and, therefore, the noncredible sample likely did not include patients who were truly feigning impairment. Finally, Blaskewitz, Mertin, and Brockhaus (2009) also used the full Meyers and Meyers (1995) administration method. Their sample was a clinical sample of German speaking patients. The authors of the study only reported data for a cutoff score of ≤45, but using this cutoff, they found a specificity rate of 95% and a sensitivity rate of 52%.

In sum, the research appears to suggest that relatively minor variations in administration method have minimal impact on the use of the embedded Combination Score PVT. Regardless of administration method, a cutoff score of ≤47 should often maintain specificity rates around 90%. There are, of course, exceptions to this, which are discussed above and highlighted in Table 5.8.

CLOSING REMARKS

As stated earlier, there are multiple advantages to using embedded PVTs. Furthermore, at this point in time, there is a significant amount of literature on embedded PVTs, allowing clinicians to identify validity indices from many popular standard cognitive tests regardless of their chosen battery. Which embedded PVTs are chosen will likely depend on the clinician's access to the tests, whether the patient seems to be potentially exaggerating any specific cognitive function (e.g., attention or memory), and whether patient characteristics are likely to increase the possibility of false-positive findings on specific PVTs. At present, the median number of embedded PVTs typically included in nongeriatric adult clinical cases is three (for neuropsychologists at large) to five (for validity assessment experts; Martin et al., 2024). The median number of embedded PVTs typically included in geriatric adult clinical cases is two (for neuropsychologists at large) to three (for validity assessment experts).

CHAPTER 6

Interpreting Symptom Validity Tests

Clinical Guidance and Cutoffs

Whereas performance validity tests assess the credibility of performance-based cognitive tests, symptom validity tests (SVTs) assess the credibility of an examinee's symptom report. As is the case with PVTs, there are both stand-alone and embedded SVTs available. Stand-alone SVTs are typically used for the specific purpose of assessing the validity of symptom report. Embedded SVTs can be found on multipurpose psychological inventories, such as versions of the Minnesota Multiphasic Personality Inventory (MMPI) and the Personality Assessment Inventory (PAI). These embedded SVTs serve the dual purpose of assessing for the validity of symptom report and determining whether the results from the rest of the inventory are valid and interpretable. The vast majority of SVTs assess the veracity of psychological symptom report, but there are some SVTs that assess the veracity of cognitive and/or somatic symptom report.

SVTs are important to include within a neuropsychological exam because the veracity of self-reported symptoms is unknown when there are no validity checks. Accepting patients' symptom reports as accurate, without screening for indications of exaggeration or feigning, increases the risk for inaccurate diagnostic conclusions. When a patient fails SVTs, the clinician can have increased confidence that self-report symptoms are inaccurate. When a patient fails both PVTs and cognitively based SVTs, the clinician can be highly confident that the PVT failures were not false-positive findings (even when patients have genuine underlying neurological conditions) since there is evidence that the patient both underperformed on testing and actively overstated their symptoms. Conversely, when SVTs are passed, the clinician can have increased confidence that the patient is not overstating their symptoms. This can be particularly helpful for the clinician when PVTs are failed but psychiatrically focused SVTs are passed, as this might suggest that, although the patient is perhaps attempting to feign cognitive impairment, they are accurately reporting their psychiatric symptoms, which might then allow for the possibility of psychiatric diagnoses and treatment recommendations.

While it is important to include SVTs within most clinical evaluations, it is understood that there are reasons why it can sometimes be challenging to include them. For example, clinicians might not have enough clinical time to include standalone SVTs or long personality assessments with embedded SVTs, patients might not have strong reading skills to complete certain measures, and/or patients might have such profound cognitive impairment (such as in the case of significant dementia) that it could be challenging for them to complete some SVTs. These are potentially valid reasons for excluding SVTs in certain clinical cases, but the clinician must realize that the veracity of self-reported symptoms is limited in such cases, which then requires caution when making diagnostic conclusions based on the self-reported symptoms.

Finally, before discussing individual SVTs in detail, it is important to note that SVT cutoff score interpretation is sometimes similar to, but sometimes different from, PVT cutoff score interpretation. With PVTs, clinicians often have a single cutoff score that is generally applied (e.g., <45 for TOMM Trial 2) and/or is specifically applied to select examinee groups (e.g., <49 for TOMM Trial 2 when individuals have no neurocognitive impairment). When SVTs are condition/syndrome focused, such as when an SVT is specifically designed to assess for overreported PTSD symptomatology, individual cutoff scores (similar to those on PVTs) can be derived for the scale. This is because items on the SVT are selected because they are uncommonly endorsed by individuals who actually have the condition of interest (e.g., PTSD). Conversely, when SVTs are less condition/syndrome focused, such as when an SVT is designed to assess for a broad overreport of psychopathology, cutoff score ranges are often utilized instead of individual, specific cutoff scores. This is because some measures encourage the clinician to consider the likely severity of the patient's actual psychiatric symptoms when interpreting the SVT. For example, on most embedded SVTs of the MMPI-2-RF, several ranges are provided with guidance for considering whether scores in each range are due to overreporting or genuine psychopathology. Additionally, some clinical conditions have different and, often, more severe symptoms than others (e.g., people with schizophrenia versus people with adjustment disorders), which could impact the patient's endorsement of items on the broad-based SVT. Consequently, ranges of cutoff scores (when appropriately validated and applied to the patient) help to reduce both the risk that false-positive and false-negative findings are occurring based on the examinee's psychiatric history and/or suspected degree of psychopathology.

SVTs EMBEDDED WITHIN BROAD PSYCHOLOGICAL INVENTORIES

Minnesota Multiphasic Personality Inventory–2—Restructured Form

The most commonly utilized embedded SVTs in neuropsychological practice are those embedded within iterations of the MMPI (Martin et al., 2024). The MMPI family instruments are broadband psychological tests, as they provide an assessment of multiple clinically relevant variables. In addition to assessing for psychological symptoms, behavioral and interpersonal characteristics, and treatment-related factors, there are multiple validity scales embedded within these instruments. With regard to specific MMPI versions that are routinely administered, 61% of neuropsychologists commonly utilize SVTs within the MMPI-2-RF, 29% of neuropsychologists commonly utilize SVTs within the MMPI-3, and 18% of neuropsychologists commonly utilize SVTs within the MMPI-2 (Martin et al., 2024).

Because North American neuropsychologists most commonly utilize the MMPI-2-RF and other versions of the MMPI are used less frequently in the assessment of symptom validity (Martin et al., 2024), our discussion will focus on the MMPI-2-RF. The SVTs within the MMPI-2-RF include noncontent-based validity indices in addition to content-based validity scales. The noncontent-based validity scales are those validity indices that ensure items are responded to and/or consistently endorsed regardless of item content. These include the Cannot Say scale (CNS), the Variable Response Inconsistency scale (VRIN-r), and the True Response Inconsistency scale (TRIN-r). Per the MMPI-2-RF manual, "content non-responsiveness needs always to be considered first because its occurrence would compromise the interpreter's ability to evaluate the other two types of validity threats" (i.e., over-reporting and under-reporting validity threats; Ben-Porath & Tellegen, 2008, p. 22).

The CNS scale is simply a calculation of how many items could not be scored on the test. This could be due to the patient skipping items or marking an item as being both true and false. The premise behind this validity scale is that "unscorable responses artifactually lower scores on the MMPI-2-RF because the scoring method used (counting the number of items on a scale that the test taker answered in the keyed direction) treats these responses as though the test taker answered in the non-keyed direction, which he or she did not" (Ben-Porath & Tellegen, 2008, p. 23). Consequently, if CNS contains even just one point (i.e., one item on the test was not scorable), the clinician is to examine the rest of the MMPI-2-RF scales. Any scale that has less than 90% of the items from it unscored should typically be considered uninterpretable because that scale may underestimate the examinee's reported symptoms/problems. CNS scores of 1–14 could invalidate some shorter "specific problems" scales, while CNS scores of 15+ are more likely to invalidate longer scales (e.g., restructured clinical scales) in addition to those shorter scales.

The VRIN-r scale is comprised of pairs of items with similar content (e.g., "I am usually happy" and "I am usually in a positive mood"). If the pairs of items are marked inconsistently (e.g., marking true to one item and false to the other), this counts as a variable response. The number of variable responses is summed and converted to a *T*-score. The MMPI-2-RF manual indicates that *T*-scores of 30–38 indicate evidence of strongly consistent responding, and *T*-scores of 39–69 provide evidence of consistent responding. *T*-scores of 70–79 indicate some evidence of inconsistency (resulting in caution being taken when interpreting other scales), while *T*-scores of 80 or above indicate clear evidence of inconsistency which invalidates interpretation of the test (Ben-Porath & Tellegen, 2008).

The last content nonresponsiveness validity index is the TRIN-r scale. This index is comprised of pairs of items that should be keyed inconsistently. For example, one item might read "I enjoy being around people" while the other item reads "I don't like being around people." Thus, one item should be marked as true and the other marked as false. The number of false-false responses is subtracted from the number of true-true responses, and a *T*-score is generated. The test manual indicates that *T*-scores of 50–69 indicate no evidence of inconsistent responding, *T*-scores of 70–79 provide some evidence of inconsistent responding (resulting in caution being taken when interpreting other scales), and *T*-scores of 80+ provide clear evidence of excessively inconsistent responding that would cause the protocol to be uninterpretable (Ben-Porath & Tellegen, 2008).

If the content nonresponsiveness validity scales do not invalidate the rest of the protocol, the content-based validity scales can be analyzed (Ben-Porath & Tellegen, 2008). The content-based validity scales include overreporting validity scales and underreporting validity scales. The overreporting validity scales are Infrequent Responses (F-r), Infrequent Psychopathology Responses (Fp-r), Infrequent Somatic Responses (Fs), Symptom Validity (FBS-r), and Response Bias Scale (RBS). The underreporting validity scales include Uncommon Virtues (L-r) and Adjustment Validity (K-r).

The first overreporting scale is F-r. Items on this scale were rarely endorsed by the MMPI-2-RF *normative* sample (but not necessarily clinical sample; Ben-Porath & Tellegen, 2008). High scores on this index are said to be "associated with overreporting of a broad range of psychological, cognitive, and somatic symptoms. However, elevated scores can, up to a certain level, also be generated by individuals experiencing genuine difficulties" (p. 26).

The test manual provides ranges of scores for F-r interpretation. *T*-scores below 79 provide no evidence of overreporting (Ben-Porath & Tellegen, 2008). *T*-scores between 79 and 89 indicate possible overreporting of psychological dysfunction. Individuals who score in this range may be valid test takers with genuine psychological issues. If, however, the patient who scored in this range has no history or current evidence of psychological dysfunction, scores in this range likely indicate overreporting of symptoms. *T*-scores of 90 to 99 also indicate possible overreporting of psychological dysfunction. Patients who score in this range may be valid test takers with substantial psychological issues. If the individual does not have a history of or current evidence of substantial psychological issues, though, scores in this range are likely due to overreporting. *T*-scores in the range of 100–119 indicate possible overreporting of psychological dysfunction, as well. It is noted that "this level of infrequent responding may occur in individuals with genuine, severe psychological difficulties who report credible symptoms" (p. 26) but if no history of or current evidence of this level of dysfunction is present, scores very likely indicate overreporting. Finally, when *T*-scores reach 120, the test manual notes that this degree of an elevation is uncommon even for individuals with severe psychological dysfunction, and the psychological protocol should be considered invalid due to overreporting.

While the F-r score ranges are useful in interpreting scores, they leave some degree of ambiguity, especially when trying to interpret moderately elevated scores (e.g., what is the difference between substantial and severe psychological difficulties as defined in *T*-scores of 90–99 and 100–119, respectively?). For this reason, we find it helpful to utilize the professional literature when determining whether a patient's score is more likely to be related to valid or invalid responding. Originally provided in Hall and Ben-Porath (2022), data in Table 6.1 show mean scores (and standard deviations) obtained by individuals of various validly and invalidly endorsing groups.

The next overreporting scale is Fp-r. Items on this scale were infrequently endorsed by examinees with genuine, severe psychopathology, with items sometimes

TABLE 6.1. Mean Scores of Valid and Invalid Responders on the MMPI-2-RF F-r Scale

	Mean/*SD*	*n*
Valid group performances		
Sample; examinees with:		
Epilepsy[a]	61.2 (14.3)	50
Traumatic brain injury[a]	64.5 (17.8)	27
Mixed neuropsychological conditions[b]	65.3 (19.5)	220
Mixed neurologic conditions seen in a neuropsychology clinic[a]	68.9 (17.1)	28
Schizophrenia[c]	79.48 (27.91)	56
Severe psychopathology requiring hospitalization[d]	82.43 (22.27)	127
Posttraumatic stress disorder[c]	83.17 (26.61)	106
Mixed psychiatric conditions seen in a neuropsychology clinic[a]	83.5 (19.1)	21
Major depressive disorder[c]	85.66 (23.59)	75
Somatoform disorders[e]	89.36 (25.75)	69
Invalid group performances		
Sample; examinees with:		
Mixed neuropsychological conditions; failing 2 PVTs[b]	77.5 (22.1)	96
Mixed neuropsychological conditions; failing 3 PVTs[b]	87.5 (22.9)	60
Traumatic brain injury; malingering based on Slick et al. (1999) criteria[c]	87.5 (24.8)	21
Feigned mental illness; coached simulators[d]	92.43 (22.80)	70
Posttraumatic stress disorder; naïve simulators[c]	106.65 (34.43)	67
Feigned mental illness; simulators not coached[d]	109.89 (16.87)	107
Major depressive disorder; naïve simulators[c]	110.39 (26.58)	67
Major depressive disorder; sophisticated simulators[c]	110.75 (26.70)	30
Posttraumatic stress disorder; sophisticated simulators[c]	118.99 (36.41)	30
Schizophrenia; sophisticated simulators[c]	122.23 (29.38)	30
Schizophrenia; naive simulators[c]	142.90 (36.07)	67

Note. MMPI-2-RF = Minnesota Multiphasic Personality Inventory–2—Restructured Form; *SD* = Standard deviation; PVTs = performance validity tests.
[a]Schroeder et al. (2012a).
[b]Jones, Ingram, and Ben-Porath (2012).
[c]Marion, Selborn, and Bagby (2011).
[d]Sellbom and Bagby (2010).
[e]Sellbom, Wygant, and Bagby (2012).

representing uncommon psychotic symptomatology (Ben-Porath & Tellegen, 2008). Consequently, examining "scores on Fp-r can be particularly helpful when a test taker produces a substantially elevated score on F-r and the interpreter needs to determine whether this reflects over-reporting or genuine dysfunction" (p. 27). With that said, the clinician should keep in mind that some patients who overreport emotional, somatic, or cognitive dysfunction but do not overreport psychotic symptoms might produce high scores on F-r but have an Fp-r score in the normal range. In other words, it is helpful to use F-r and Fp-r to reduce false-positive determinations of invalidity, but there will still be times where the MMPI-2-RF is considered invalid because of an elevated F-r score despite a normal Fp-r score.

Similar to F-r, the MMPI-2-RF test manual provides ranges of scores for interpretation of Fp-r. *T*-scores below 70 provide no evidence of overreporting (Ben-Porath & Tellegen, 2008). *T*-scores between 70 and 79 indicate possible overreporting of psychopathology. Patients who score in this range may be valid test takers with severe psychological issues. If the individual does not have a history or current evidence of severe psychological issues, though, scores in this range are likely due to overreporting. *T*-scores of 80–99 are even more suggestive of overreporting of psychopathology as they are uncommon even for individuals with severe psychopathology. In many cases, scores in this range will reflect overreporting, but validly reporting individuals with very severe psychopathology and/or thought dysfunction could potentially score in this range. Finally, when *T*-scores reach 100 or above, the psychological protocol should be considered invalid as scores in this range are very uncommonly obtained by genuine test takers even when severe psychopathology is present. Table 6.2 shows data originally published in Hall and Ben-Porath (2022) on mean scores obtained by individuals in various validly and invalidly endorsing groups to help with validity status determination.

Unlike F-r and Fp-r, which both assess for overreporting of psychopathology, Fs assesses for overreporting of somatic dysfunction. The items on this scale have been found to be infrequently endorsed by medical patients with various physical conditions (Ben-Porath & Tellegen, 2008). Per the MMPI-2-RF test manual, *T*-scores below 80 provide no evidence of overreporting (Ben-Porath & Tellegen, 2008). *T*-scores between 80 and 99 indicate possible overreporting of somatic symptoms. The test manual notes that "this level and type of infrequent responding may occur in individuals with substantial medical conditions who report credible symptoms, but it could also reflect exaggeration. In individuals with no history of corroborating evidence of physical health problems, this probably indicates non-credible reporting of somatic symptoms" (p. 28). *T*-scores of 100 or greater indicate that somatic complaints may be invalid as this degree of symptom endorsement is very uncommon for examinees with significant medical problems. Originally published in Hall and Ben-Porath (2022), Table 6.3 shows data on mean scores obtained by individuals in various validly and invalidly endorsing groups to help differentiate whether examinee scores in the moderate elevation range are more likely to be valid or invalid representations of functioning.

TABLE 6.2. Mean Scores of Valid and Invalid Responders on the MMPI-2-RF Fp-r Scale

	Mean/*SD*	*n*
Valid group performances		
Sample; examinees with:		
Mixed neurologic conditions seen in a neuropsychology clinic[a]	51.6 (10.9)	28
Traumatic brain injury[a]	52.0 (12.1)	27
Epilepsy[a]	53.1 (12.2)	50
Mixed neuropsychological conditions; military setting[b]	54.9 (15.0)	220
Mixed psychiatric conditions seen in a neuropsychology clinic[a]	59.4 (21.5)	21
Major depressive disorder[c]	60.13 (15.99)	75
Somatoform disorders[d]	61.30 (16.49)	69
Severe psychopathology requiring hospitalization[e]	63.02 (17.20)	127
Posttraumatic stress disorder[c]	67.10 (17.28)	106
Schizophrenia[c]	79.48 (27.91)	56
Invalid group performances		
Sample; examinees with:		
Traumatic brain injury; malingering based on Slick et al. (1999) criteria[a]	61.0 (19.4)	21
Mixed neuropsychological conditions; failing 2 PVTs; military setting[b]	62.2 (15.9)	96
Mixed neuropsychological conditions; failing 3 PVTs; military setting[b]	69.7 (19.6)	60
Major depressive disorder; sophisticated simulators[c]	85.06 (28.89)	30
Feigned mental illness; coached simulators[e]	90.16 (24.22)	70
Posttraumatic stress disorder; naïve simulators[c]	94.17 (37.86)	67
Major depressive disorder; naïve simulators[c]	103.54 (25.98)	67
Posttraumatic stress disorder; sophisticated simulators[c]	104.36 (43.02)	30
Feigned mental illness; simulators not coached[e]	106.50 (20.78)	107
Schizophrenia; sophisticated simulators[c]	111.50 (32.10)	30
Schizophrenia; naive simulators[c]	153.66 (44.08)	67

Note. MMPI-2-RF = Minnesota Multiphasic Personality Inventory–2—Restructured Form; *SD* = Standard deviation; PVTs = performance validity tests.
[a]Schroeder et al. (2012a).
[b]Jones, Ingram, and Ben-Porath (2012).
[c]Marion et al. (2011).
[d]Sellbom et al. (2012).
[e]Sellbom and Bagby (2010).

FBS-r was developed to identify examinees engaged in civil litigation who were found to be noncredibly presenting symptoms (Ben-Porath & Tellegen, 2008). As noted in the test manual, this particular validity scale has been highly studied and frequently used in neuropsychological settings. *T*-scores below 80 are said to provide no evidence of overreporting. It is noted that *T*-scores between 80 and 99 may be seen in validly reporting examinees with substantial medical problems, but scores in this range may also reflect exaggeration of somatic and/or cognitive complaints. *T*-scores of 100 or greater indicate likely overreporting as these scores are very uncommon in validly reporting examinees. Data originally published in Hall and Ben-Porath

(2022) are presented in Table 6.4. Again, this data can be helpful in differentiating valid from invalid scores that fall in a moderately elevated range.

RBS was created to "detect negative response bias in forensic neuropsychological or disability assessment settings" (Gervais, Ben-Porath, Wygant, & Green, 2007, p. 196). More specifically, a multiple regression was utilized to identify items that differentiated examinees who passed and failed PVTs. While RBS is said to be "associated with non-credible memory complaints" (Ben-Porath & Tellegen, 2011, p. 4),

TABLE 6.3. Mean Scores of Valid and Invalid Responders on the MMPI-2-RF Fs Scale

	Mean/*SD*	*n*
Valid group performances		
Sample; examinees with:		
Chronic pain[a]	54.0 (13.0)	45
Medical conditions; outpatients[b]	57.3 (12.2)	44
Medical conditions; outpatients[c]	59.29 (18.70)	74
Traumatic brain injury[d]	59.9 (16.7)	27
Mixed neuropsychological conditions; military setting[e]	60.7 (17.3)	220
Mixed neurologic conditions seen in a neuropsychology clinic[d]	62.0 (13.8)	28
Mixed psychiatric conditions seen in a neuropsychology clinic[d]	64.9 (18.2)	21
Epilepsy[d]	67.8 (12.7)	50
Schizophrenia[f]	68.38 (21.38)	56
Major depressive disorder[f]	70.90 (19.15)	75
Posttraumatic stress disorder[f]	75.45 (22.35)	106
Somatoform disorders[c]	75.67 (24.34)	69
Invalid group performances		
Sample; examinees with:		
Mixed neuropsychological conditions; failing 2 PVTs[e]	71.8 (19.4)	96
Chronic pain; malingering based on MPRD criteria[a]	78.4 (20.1)	174
Mixed neuropsychological conditions; failing 3 PVTs[e]	80.3 (22.4)	60
Traumatic brain injury; malingering based on Slick et al. (1999) criteria[d]	81.1 (21.7)	21
Schizophrenia; sophisticated simulators[f]	84.84 (25.22)	30
Major depressive disorder; sophisticated simulators[ff]	86.44 (24.47)	30
Physical health problems; simulators[c]	94.93 (27.52)	114
Major depressive disorder; naïve simulators[f]	95.29 (26.67)	67
Posttraumatic stress disorder; naïve simulators[f]	105.32 (34.52)	67
Posttraumatic stress disorder; sophisticated simulators[f]	107.83 (38.41)	30
Medical conditions; outpatients exaggerating dysfunction[b]	109.9 (38.7)	32
Schizophrenia; naive simulators[f]	123.39 (39.87)	67

Note. MMPI-2-RF = Minnesota Multiphasic Personality Inventory–2—Restructured Form; *SD* = Standard deviation; PVTs = Performance validity tests; MPRD = Malingered Pain-Related Disability.
[a]Bianchini et al. (2018).
[b]Wygant et al. (2009).
[c]Sellbom et al. (2012).
[d]Schroeder et al. (2012a).
[e]Jones, Ingram, and Ben-Porath (2012).
[f]Marion et al. (2011).

TABLE 6.4. Mean Scores of Valid and Invalid Responders on the MMPI-2-RF FBS-r Scale

	Mean/*SD*	*n*
Valid group performances		
Sample; examinees with:		
Medical conditions; outpatients[a]	53.07 (12.82)	74
Medical conditions; outpatients[b]	53.4 (12.5)	32
Epilepsy[c]	59.5 (13.1)	50
Mixed neuropsychological conditions; military setting[d]	60.9 (14.3)	220
Chronic pain[e]	62.0 (10.1)	45
Mixed neurologic conditions seen in a neuropsychology clinic[c]	62.7 (12.4)	28
Schizophrenia[f]	63.43 (12.91)	56
Traumatic brain injury[c]	67.1 (14.0)	27
Mixed psychiatric conditions seen in a neuropsychology clinic[c]	67.5 (13.9)	21
Cognitive disorders[g]	71.01 (12.37)	21
Low IQ (<85)[g]	73.43 (11.80)	24
Major depressive disorder[f]	78.43 (13.90)	75
Posttraumatic stress disorder[f]	81.74 (16.62)	106
Somatoform disorders[a]	85.89 (14.15)	69
Invalid group performances		
Sample; examinees with:		
Schizophrenia; sophisticated simulators[f]	69.98 (13.41)	30
Mixed neuropsychological conditions; failing 2 PVTs[d]	73.4 (12.5)	96
Physical health problems; simulators[a]	78.01 (13.26)	114
Mixed neuropsychological conditions; failing 3 PVTs[d]	80.3 (15.1)	60
Major depressive disorder; naïve simulators[f]	80.54 (13.74)	67
Schizophrenia; naive simulators[f]	81.75 (18.41)	67
Chronic pain; malingering based on MPRD criteria[e]	83.7 (13.7)	174
Major depressive disorder; sophisticated simulators[f]	87.56 (13.32)	30
Traumatic brain injury; malingering based on Slick et al. (1999) criteria[c]	89.0 (16.3)	21
Posttraumatic stress disorder; naïve simulators[f]	89.73 (15.06)	67
Below chance performance on a PVT[g]	91.57 (10.31)	42
Posttraumatic stress disorder; sophisticated simulators[f]	92.96 (17.25)	30
Medical conditions; outpatients exaggerating dysfunction[b]	109.9 (38.7)	44

Note. MMPI-2-RF = Minnesota Multiphasic Personality Inventory–2—Restructured Form; *SD* = Standard deviation; PVTs = performance validity tests; MPRD = Malingered Pain-Related Disability.
[a]Sellbom et al. (2012).
[b]Wygant et al. (2009).
[c]Schroeder et al. (2012a).
[d]Jones, Ingram, and Ben-Porath (2012).
[e]Bianchini et al. (2018).
[f]Marion et al. (2011).
[g]Rogers, Gillard, Berry, and Granacher (2011).

it should be noted that only roughly 40% of the items from the scale reflect cognitively based content (Hall & Ben-Porath, 2022). Other items reflect somatic dysfunction, denial of antisocial acts, and mistrustful beliefs. Per the MMPI-2-RF manual, *T*-scores below 80 are said to provide no evidence of overreporting (Ben-Porath & Tellegen, 2011). *T*-scores between 80 and 99 can occur in patients who have substantial emotional disturbances, but scores in this range could reflect invalid test taking. *T*-scores of 100 or more indicate that the patient's responses are likely invalid as this degree of symptom endorsement is very atypical even for individuals with substantial

TABLE 6.5. Mean Scores of Valid and Invalid Responders on the MMPI-2-RF RBS Scale

	Mean/*SD*	*n*
Valid group performances		
Sample; examinees with:		
Medical conditions; outpatients[a]	55.91 (15.37)	74
Epilepsy[b]	63.1 (13.9)	50
Mixed neuropsychological conditions; military setting[c]	64.9 (17.0)	220
Mixed neurologic conditions seen in a neuropsychology clinic[b]	69.1 (14.4)	28
Traumatic brain injury[b]	69.1 (15.8)	27
Medicolegal evaluations; no evidence of invalidity[d]	72.78 (16.77)	103
Posttraumatic stress disorder[e]	76.23 (14.42)	18
Neurologic problems[f]	76.48 (20.17)	40
Mixed axis I disorders[e]	77.02 (17.66)	136
Cognitive disorders[e]	77.74 (14.22)	21
Low IQ (<85)[e]	78.34 (16.30)	24
Mixed psychiatric conditions seen in a neuropsychology clinic[b]	79.4 (20.1)	21
Major depressive disorder[e]	81.22 (17.19)	120
Somatoform disorders[a]	83.91 (19.90)	69
Invalid group performances		
Sample; examinees with:		
Physical health problems; simulators[a]	76.90 (17.99)	114
Mixed neuropsychological conditions; failing 2 PVTs[c]	85.9 (16.4)	96
Neurologic problems; malingering based on Slick et al. (1999) criteria[f]	86.60 (17.49)	30
Mixed neuropsychological conditions; failing 3 PVTs[c]	93.1 (15.5)	60
Traumatic brain injury; malingering based on Slick et al. criteria[b]	93.3 (14.2)	21
Medicolegal evaluation; evidence of invalidity[d]	97.64 (15.27)	91
Below chance performance on a PVT[e]	103.36 (13.44)	42
Feigned mental disorders[e]	111.92 (20.50)	32

Note. MMPI-2-RF = Minnesota Multiphasic Personality Inventory–2—Restructured Form; *SD* = Standard deviation; PVTs = performance validity tests.
[a]Sellbom et al. (2012).
[b]Schroeder et al. (2012a).
[c]Jones, Ingram, and Ben-Porath (2012).
[d]Wygant et al. (2011).
[e]Rogers et al. (2011).
[f]Nguyen, Green, and Barr (2015).

emotional disturbances. Hall and Ben-Porath's (2022) review data are provided in Table 6.5.

The first of the two underreporting scales on the MMPI-2-RF is L-r. High scores on this index indicate that the examinee denied minor faults/shortcoming and presented himself or herself in a particularly favorable light (Ben-Porath & Tellegen, 2008). The MMPI-2-RF manual indicates that *T*-scores below 65 indicate no evidence of underreporting symptoms. *T*-scores between 65 and 69, as well as *T*-scores between 70 and 79, indicate the possible presence of underreporting symptoms. However, individuals with traditional virtuous backgrounds may score somewhere within these ranges. *T*-scores of 80 or more indicate that the protocol is likely invalid, and absences of substantive scale elevations are uninterpretable. Data, originally published in Hall and Ben-Porath (2022), on this scale are provided in Table 6.6.

The final validity scale within the MMPI-2-RF is K-r. High scores on this index reflect an examinee presenting himself or herself as being particularly well adjusted. Per the MMPI-2-RF manual (Ben-Porath & Tellegen, 2008), *T*-scores less than 60

TABLE 6.6. Mean Scores of Valid and Invalid Responders on the MMPI-2-RF L-r Scale

	Mean/*SD*	***n***
Valid group performances		
Sample; examinees with:		
Mixed psychiatric conditions seen in a neuropsychology clinic[a]	48.1 (9.2)	21
College students[b]	49.71 (9.57)	46
Schizophrenia[b]	51.67 (10.78)	43
Mixed neurologic conditions seen in a neuropsychology clinic[a]	52.7 (9.4)	28
Cognitive disorders[c]	53.49 (8.55)	21
Mixed neuropsychological conditions; military setting[d]	56.5 (10.4)	220
Traumatic brain injury[a]	57.3 (11.3)	27
Low IQ (<85)[c]	57.52 (9.94)	24
Epilepsy[a]	58.5 (13.1)	50
Invalid group performances		
Sample; examinees with:		
Mixed neuropsychological conditions; failing 3 PVTs[d]	56.8 (10.0)	60
College students trying to be symptom-free[b]	57.92 (15.11)	48
Mixed neuropsychological conditions; failing 2 PVTs[d]	58.5 (9.4)	96
Child custody and access evaluations[b]	59.69 (12.11)	109
Traumatic brain injury; malingering based on Slick et al. (1999) criteria[a]	60.4 (12.9)	21
Individuals failing PVTs[c]	63.04 (12.60)	42
Schizophrenia trying to produce a symptom free profile[b]	63.66 (14.75)	44

Note. MMPI-2-RF = Minnesota Multiphasic Personality Inventory–2—Restructured Form; *SD* = Standard deviation; PVTs = performance validity tests.
[a]Schroeder et al. (2012a).
[b]Sellbom and Bagby (2008).
[c]Rogers et al. (2011).
[d]Jones, Ingram, and Ben-Porath (2012).

indicate no evidence of underreporting. *T*-scores of 60–65 could reflect an individual with good psychological adjustment but, for individuals who are not well adjusted, scores in this range likely reflect an underendorsement of symptoms and problems. *T*-scores of 66–69, could reflect an examinee with very strong psychological adjustment but, for individuals who are not particularly well adjusted, scores in this range very likely reflect an underendorsement of symptoms and problems. Finally, *T*-scores of 70 or above are extremely uncommon in accurately reporting individuals, and scores in this range should be considered as reflecting an underreporting of symptoms and problems. Like with L-r, when there is evidence of underreporting, an absence of substantiative scale elevation is not interpretable. Mean scores of various valid and invalid examinee groups, originally presented in Hall and Ben-Porath (2022), are presented in Table 6.7.

The previous discussion and presentation of data should help clinicians make more nuanced determinations of validity status when interpreting an MMPI-2-RF, particularly in neuropsychological settings. If additional information is desired on

TABLE 6.7. Mean Scores of Valid and Invalid Responders on the MMPI-2-RF K-r Scale

	Mean/*SD*	*n*
Valid group performances		
Sample; examinees with:		
Low IQ (<85)[a]	41.44 (9.03)	24
Cognitive disorders[a]	41.74 (8.99)	21
Mixed psychiatric conditions seen in a neuropsychology clinic[b]	46.4 (11.5)	21
College students[c]	46.54 (9.68)	46
Schizophrenia[c]	46.60 (8.79)	43
Mixed neuropsychological conditions; military setting[d]	48.7 (11.1)	220
Epilepsy[b]	49.5 (8.41)	50
Mixed neurologic conditions seen in a neuropsychology clinic[b]	50.6 (10.3)	28
Traumatic brain *injury*[b]	54.6 (11.3)	27
Invalid group performances		
Sample; examinees with:		
Individuals failing PVTs[a]	41.34 (8.73)	42
Mixed neuropsychological conditions; failing 3 PVTs[d]	41.6 (9.9)	60
Mixed neuropsychological conditions; failing 2 PVTs[d]	45.1 (9.8)	96
Traumatic brain injury; malingering based on Slick et al. (1999) criteria[b]	47.6 (12.3)	21
Child custody and access evaluations[c]	56.12 (10.66)	109
Schizophrenia trying to produce a symptom free profile[c]	57.81 (9.97)	44
College students trying to be symptom free[c]	59.42 (8.23)	48

Note. MMPI-2-RF = Minnesota Multiphasic Personality Inventory–2—Restructured Form; *SD* = Standard deviation; PVTs = performance validity tests.
[a]Rogers et al. (2011).
[b]Schroeder et al. (2012a).
[c]Sellbom and Bagby (2008).
[d]Jones, Ingram, and Ben-Porath (2012).

the MMPI-2-RF validity scales, though, we would recommend reading Ben-Porath and Tellegen (2011), Ben-Porath (2012), Hall and Ben-Porath (2022), and Schroeder et al. (2012a).

Personality Assessment Inventory

Embedded SVTs within the Personality Assessment Inventory (PAI) are the second most commonly used embedded SVTs in neuropsychological practice, frequently used by 47% of neuropsychologists (Martin et al., 2024). Like the MMPI-2-RF, the PAI is a broadband psychological test that assesses multiple clinically relevant variables, including psychological symptoms, behavioral and interpersonal characteristics, and treatment-related factors. Response options are [1] false, not at all true; [2] slightly true; [3] mainly true; or [4] very true (as opposed to the MMPI-2-RF format of providing only options of [1] true or [2] false). Also, like the MMPI-2-RF, there are validity scales embedded within the PAI that include both noncontent-based validity indices and content-based validity indices. It is noted, though, that there are fewer standard validity indices in the PAI than the MMPI-2-RF, and the PAI does not have standard validity indices specific to the overreport of somatic symptoms or symptoms within the context of neuropsychological settings.

In interpreting the PAI, the first step is to ensure that most items have been appropriately responded to by the patient (i.e., there is not an excessive number of items skipped or endorsed in a nonscorable manner). While there is not a formal scale for this first step (such as there is with the CNS on the MMPI-2-RF), the PAI test manual clearly indicates that the test should not be interpreted if 5% of the items (i.e., 17 items) or more were not endorsed with scorable responses (Morey, 2007). Furthermore, if 20% or more of items comprising any scale (regardless of the number of items that were answered on the full inventory) are omitted, that scale should not be interpreted.

After ensuring that an appropriate number of items were endorsed, the clinician should examine the four standard validity scales. The first validity index is the inconsistency (ICN) index. This scale contains pairs of items with similar content to ensure that consistent responding occurred. The test manual notes that "ICN elevations are probably not the result of efforts at impression management . . . if someone is consciously trying to distort the truth in a given direction, ICN often does not elevate at all. Rather, ICN is more likely to reflect carelessness or confusion in responding" (Morey, 2007, p. 27). In terms of interpretation of scores, the test manual indicates that low scores on the scale (i.e., *T*-scores less than 64) suggest attentive and consistent responding. Moderately elevated scores (i.e., *T*-scores of 64–72) indicate some degree of inconsistent responding that should result in the clinician taking caution when examining the PAI test protocol. High scores (i.e., *T*-scores of 73 or above) indicate that the patient was inconsistent in responding to items and the test protocol should be considered invalid.

The second standard PAI validity scale is the infrequency (INF) scale. This scale is said to primarily assesses for careless responding (Morey, 2007). The items that make up this scale are nonbizarre items but items that would be answered with a very low base rate by both clinical or nonclinical examinees. As an example, an item might read "My two favorite dancers are Ryan Schroeder and Phillip Martin." By answering true to this item, the patient clearly is not responding in a careful and accurate manner. The PAI manual indicates that low scores (i.e., *T*-scores below 60) suggest that the patient appropriately attended to item content. Moderately elevated scores (i.e., *T*-scores of 60–74) indicate some degree of atypical responding, which should cause the clinician to review the remainder of the test protocol with caution. Highly elevated scores (i.e., *T*-scores of 75 or above) invalidate the test profile.

The primary overreporting validity scale on the PAI is the negative impression (NIM) scale. This scale "contains items that present an exaggerated unfavorable impression or represent extremely bizarre and unlikely symptoms. The scale was designed to alert the interpreter to the possibility that the results of the test may portray a more negative impression of the individual than might otherwise be merited" (Morey, 2007, p. 29). While items on the scale have low base rates of endorsement in both healthy and clinical samples, clinical samples do score higher than normal samples.

Per the PAI test manual, low scores on NIM (i.e., *T*-scores below 73) do not suggest negative distortions of symptoms (Morey, 2007). Moderate elevations are defined as being *T*-scores between 73 and 83, and scores in this range suggest some degree of symptom exaggeration. *T*-scores between 84 and 91 indicate an even higher likelihood of negative symptom distortion. At a *T*-score of 92 or above, the risk of symptom distortion is particularly high. Per the test manual, at this point, the clinician should suspect that the patient has responded carelessly, with an exceptionally negative self-presentation, or in a manner that may reflect malingering. Regardless of cause, the PAI test protocol should typically be considered invalid at a *T*-score of 92 or above.

The ranges of scores reported in the previous paragraph appear to align with additional data reported in the PAI test manual. Specifically, it is noted that, in the original PAI clinical standardization sample (comprised primarily of individuals with substance use disorders and affective disorders), a NIM *T*-score of 84 is associated with the commonly sought 90% specificity mark (Morey, 2007). A *T*-score of 92 represents the cutoff which is two standard deviations above the mean of the clinical standardization sample; this resulted in a 94% specificity rate for that sample. When reviewing literature outside of the PAI clinical standardization sample, Boccaccini and Hart (2018) identified similar findings. Specifically, when reviewing and combining results from the peer-reviewed literature ($k = 8$), they found that a cutoff of 84 or above resulted in an average (median) specificity rate of 89% (58% sensitivity associated). Furthermore, a cutoff of 92 or above ($k = 20$) resulted in an average (median) specificity rate of 91% (50% sensitivity associated). While all of these data are helpful in understanding that a *T*-score cutoff near 84 may result in specificity rates of about 90%, the specificity rate at this cutoff could change based on the clinical population. Indeed, this would appear to be true when looking at individual studies published in the literature, as demonstrated by Table 6.8. A striking finding is that many individuals likely to be seen within a neuropsychological clinic (regardless of whether they are validly or invalidly endorsing symptoms) will produce *T*-scores below the *T*-score cutoff of 84.

The primary underreporting validity scale on the PAI is the positive impression (PIM) scale. This scale was derived by comparing distributions of scores from healthy individuals, clinical patients, and research respondents asked to respond in an overly favorable manner (Morey, 2007). Low scores on PIM (i.e., *T*-scores below 44) are

TABLE 6.8. Mean Scores of Valid and Invalid Responders on the PAI NIM Scale

	Mean/*SD*	*n*
Valid group performances		
Sample; examinees with:		
Severe Traumatic Brain Injury[a]	50.3 (9.7)	35
Mild Traumatic Brain Injury[a]	52.2 (10.5)	87
Generalized anxiety disorder[b]	53.46 (—)	40
Mixed clinical neuropsychology clinic referrals[c]	56.21 (13.88)	257
Pain patients[d]	58.40 (12.10)	317
PTSD; community samples not seeking treatment[e]	62.78 (18.01)	46
Major depressive disorder[b]	64.93 (—)	136
Schizophrenia[b]	68.10 (—)	45
PTSD; psychiatric inpatients[f]	78.07 (19.07)	26
Inpatient psychiatric inmates; passed SIRS[g]	81.08 (19.06)	25
Invalid group performances		
Sample; examinees with:		
Generalized anxiety disorder; sophisticated simulators[b]	54.84 (—)	19
Mixed clinical neuropsychology clinic referrals[c]	64.86 (19.39)	49
Mild traumatic brain injury[a]	65.0 (18.4)	21
Major depressive disorder; sophisticated simulators[b]	68.57 (—)	21
Pain; coached simulators[d]	74.11 (23.33)	77
Generalized anxiety disorder; naïve simulators[b]	75.74 (—)	38
Pain; naïve simulators[d]	77.10 (24.83)	75
Schizophrenia; sophisticated simulators[b]	82.32 (—)	20
Major depressive disorder; naïve simulators[b]	85.97 (—)	39
PTSD; coached simulators[e]	88.12 (29.09)	79
Schizophrenia; naive simulators	89.02 (—)	39
PTSD; psychiatric inpatients exaggerating[f]	98.16 (19.98)	26
PTSD; naïve simulators[e]	98.21 (28.65)	77
Inpatient psychiatric inmates; failing SIRS[g]	100.53 (17.43)	15

Note. PAI = Personality Assessment Inventory; NIM = Negative Impression Management; *SD* = Standard deviation; PTSD = Posttraumatic Stress Disorder; SIRS = Structured Interview of Reported Symptoms.
[a]Lange et al. (2012).
[b]Rogers, Gillard, Berry, and Granacher (1996).
[c]Gaasedelen, Whiteside, and Basso (2017).
[d]Hopwood, Orlando, and Clark (2010).
[e]Thomas et al. (2012).
[f]Wooley and Rogers (2015).
[g]Wang et al. (1997).

said to suggest that the individual responded candidly. *T*-scores ranging from 44–56 "suggest that the respondent did not attempt to present an unrealistically favorable impression in completing the test, although scores in the upper end of this range tend to be unusual in clinical settings" (p. 31). Moderate scores on PIM (i.e., *T*-scores between 57 and 67) are said to suggest a denial of shortcomings which could be due to an overt or covert response style. High scores (i.e., *T*-scores of 68 or greater) indicate a significant denial of shortcomings and the validity of the test protocol needs to be considered quite suspect. Table 6.9 shows mean scores obtained on the PIM

TABLE 6.9. Mean Scores of Valid and Invalid Responders on the PAI PIM Scale

	Mean/*SD*	*n*
Valid group performances		
Sample; examinees with:		
Major depressive disorder[a]	40.18 (—)	136
Generalized anxiety disorder[a]	42.56 (—)	40
Substance abusing individuals honestly responding[b]	43.0 (11.2)	25
Schizophrenia[a]	46.07 (—)	45
Mixed clinical neuropsychology clinic referrals[c]	47.14 (11.43)	257
Controls (PAI in English)[d]	48.24 (10.24)	25
Controls (PAI in Spanish)[d]	49.88 (9.45)	25
Mild traumatic brain injury[e]	52.2 (9.9)	87
Controls[b]	52.3 (10.9)	25
Severe traumatic brain injury[e]	53.6 (8.9)	35
Invalid group performances		
Sample; examinees with:		
Major depressive disorder; naïve simulators overendorsing symptoms[a]	37.90 (—)	39
Generalized anxiety disorder; naïve simulators overendorsing symptoms[a]	39.00 (—)	38
Major depressive disorder; sophisticated simulators overendorsing symptoms[a]	40.95 (—)	21
Schizophrenia; naive simulators overendorsing symptoms[a]	44.71 (—)	39
Generalized anxiety disorder; sophisticated simulators overendorsing symptoms[a]	46.42 (—)	19
Mixed clinical neuropsychology clinic referrals failing PVTs[c]	47.78 (12.09)	49
Mild traumatic brain injury; fail PVTs[e]	49.3 (12.0)	21
Schizophrenia; sophisticated simulators[a]	49.95 (—)	20
Substance abusing individuals asked to respond defensively[b]	66.7 (10.1)	25
Controls simulating good impression for employment (English)[d]	67.39 (9.69)	23
Controls simulating good impression for employment (Spanish)[d]	67.83 (9.11)	23
Suspected substance abusing individuals referred by criminal justice system[b]	68.8 (11.7)	25

Note. PAI = Personality Assessment Inventory; PIM = Positive Impression Management; *SD* = Standard deviation; PVTs = performance validity tests.
[a]Rogers, Gillard, Berry, and Granacher (1996).
[b]Fals-Stewart and Lucente (1997).
[c]Gaasedelen et al. (2017).
[d]Fernandez, Boccaccini, and Noland (2008).
[e]Lange et al. (2012).

in various samples. In addition to documenting that individuals who underreport shortcomings score higher on PIM, the data seem to suggest that some individuals who overreport symptoms might at times produce low *T*-scores on the underreporting validity index.

In addition to the core validity scales described above, supplemental validity indicators have been derived. The two supplemental overreporting validity indicators that are included in the PAI manual and interpretative report are Rogers Discriminant Function (RDF) and the Malingering Index (MAL). RDF is a discriminant function which was created to help distinguish PAI profiles of individuals simulating psychiatric conditions from individuals who truly have psychiatric disorders (Morey, 2007). When discriminant function raw scores are higher than 0 (corresponding to a *T*-score of 59), invalid responding/malingering is said to be suggested. Conversely, when discriminant function raw scores are lower than 0, this suggests against the likelihood for invalid responding/malingering. While this is an intriguing validity index, demonstrated to function well in some simulation-based research designs, "real world" research with clinical and forensic examinees have frequently indicated that the RDF has limited to no clinical utility (Boccaccini & Hart, 2018; Fokas & Brovko, 2020; Sleep, Petty, & Wygant, 2015). In fact, Boccaccini and Hart note that "This is such a consistent finding that it is difficult to make recommendations for the use of RDF scores for detecting the feigning of severe impairment in real-world forensic evaluations . . . it may be that RDF just does not work as well in real-world settings, where the motivations to feign differ from those in simulation studies" (p. 289). We have observed similar results in our nonforensic clinical practice, and we tend to routinely disregard the findings from this scale as they frequently do not correlate with other validity markers. Given the lack of support for RDF in real-world settings, we will not summarize additional literature on the validity index here.

Unlike RDF, MAL has positive research supporting its utility in real-world clinical settings (Boccaccini & Hart, 2018). MAL is a validity index that is "composed of eight configural features of the PAI profile that tend to be observed much more frequently in the profiles of individuals simulating mental disorder (particularly severe mental disorders) than in actual clinical patients . . . The features of MAL range from basic elevations of the validity scales to particular (and peculiar) configural aspects of the clinical scales and subscales" (Morey, 2007, p. 31). Because elevations on MAL are rather specific to feigned impairment, the scale is said to be "relatively independent of psychopathology" (p. 31).

The PAI manual indicates that a MAL raw score of 3, which corresponding to a *T*-score of 84, is a score that is greater than two standard deviations above the mean score obtained by the original clinical standardization sample (Morey, 2007). Furthermore, this score was found to result in a 94% specificity rate in the clinical standardization sample. Consistent with these findings, an analysis of published data ($k = 23$) found that the raw score cutoff of 3 resulted in an average (median) specificity rate of 93% (sensitivity was 51%; Boccaccini & Hart, 2018). Table 6.10 shows mean scores on MAL which have been achieved by various validly and invalidly responding examinee samples. As can be seen, scores tend to increase the most when psychiatric

TABLE 6.10. Mean Scores of Valid and Invalid Responders on the PAI MAL Scale

	Mean/*SD*	*n*
Valid group performances		
Sample; examinees with:		
Pain patients[a]	49.55 (9.27)	317
Mixed clinical neuropsychology clinic referrals[b]	51.22 (11.18)	257
PTSD; community samples not seeking treatment[c]	55.19 (13.08)	46
PTSD; psychiatric inpatients[d]	60.96 (15.42)	26
Prisoners[e]	0.99^{raw}(1.12)	146
Inpatient psychiatric inmates; passed SIRS[f]	1.84^{raw}(1.25)	25
Invalid group performances		
Sample; examinees with:		
Mixed clinical neuropsychology clinic referrals[b]	56.12 (14.83)	49
Pain; naïve simulators[a]	61.82 (19.82)	75
Pain; coached simulators[a]	64.40 (20.16)	77
PTSD; coached simulators[e]	74.01 (23.31)	79
PTSD; psychiatric inpatients exaggerating[d]	77.72 (19.11)	26
PTSD; naïve simulators[c]	81.87 (24.62)	77
Prisoners simulating PTSD[e]	2.03^{raw}(1.25)	36
Prisoners simulating depression[e]	2.48^{raw}(1.44)	48
Prisoners simulating schizophrenia[e]	2.67^{raw}(1.79)	58
Inpatient psychiatric inmates; failing SIRS[f]	2.93^{raw}(2.05)	15

Note. PAI = Personality Assessment Inventory; MAL = Malingering Index; *SD* = Standard deviation; PTSD = Posttraumatic Stress Disorder; SIRS = Structured Interview of Reported Symptoms.
[a]Hopwood et al. (2010).
[b]Gaasedelen et al. (2017).
[c]Thomas et al. (2012).
[d]Wooley and Rogers (2015).
[e]Pignolo, Giromino, Ales, and Zennaro (2023).
[f]Wang et al. (1997).

(particularly severe psychiatric) issues are being feigned. Conversely, scores are not particularly high when neuropsychological conditions are being feigned, which suggests that MAL is likely less sensitive to overreporting of cognitive than psychiatric symptoms.

Finally, it should be acknowledged that there are a number of additional PAI validity scales that have been created since the inventory's development. Most of these additional validity scales have limited cross-validation data, which makes it challenging to recommend their usage at the present time. We do wish to highlight one scale, though, which has been named the Cognitive Bias Scale (CBS; Gaasedelen, Whiteside, Altmaier, Welch, & Basso, 2019). This validity index has accumulated multiple supportive research findings and will likely be helpful in neuropsychological settings particularly since NIM and MAL do not appear to readily identify invalid neuropsychological conditions.

CBS was specifically designed to differentiate neuropsychological examinees passing and failing PVTs (somewhat akin to RBS from the MMPI-2-RF). The scale contains 10 items (items 33, 72, 113, 166, 206, 209, 242, 252, 274, and 304) which were empirically identified as predicting PVT failure in a sample of neuropsychological outpatients with mixed neurological and psychiatric diagnoses. Two of the items on CBS come from the PAI Depression scale, two from the Anxiety scale, two from the Somatization scale, one from NIM, one from PIM, one from the Anxiety Related Disorders scale, and one from the Treatment Rejection scale.

At present, CBS is not considered by the test publisher to be a formal core or supplemental validity index, so it is not included on interpretative reports. Consequently, the scale needs to be calculated by hand. CBS is unit-weighted meaning that, for items 33, 72, 113, 166, 206, 209, and 274, a response of "False" yields 0 points, a response of "Somewhat True" yields 1 point, a response of "Mainly True" yields 2 points, and a response of "Very True" yields 3 points (Gaasedelen et al., 2019). For items 242, 252, and 304, reverse scoring is coded (e.g., a response of "False" yields 3 points). Item totals are summed, with the summed total representing the CBS total score.

Gaasedelen and colleagues (2019) found that CBS had good classification accuracy (area under the curve = .72) and a strong effect size (Cohen's d = – 0.96) when differentiating a sample of 306 mixed neuropsychological outpatients who passed or failed two or more PVTs. Furthermore, it outperformed other PAI validity scales in predicting PVT failure. At a cutoff of ≥16, specificity was 90% and sensitivity was 37%. While this cutoff met the commonly accepted specificity standard of 90%, the authors of the study also highlighted the cutoff of ≥19, which resulted in a specificity rate of 96% (sensitivity = 31%).

Since publication in 2019, there have been a handful of cross-validation studies. In 2020, Armistead-Jehle, Ingram, and Morris examined CBS in a sample of active-duty military personnel undergoing neuropsychological evaluations. Groups of examinees were identified as failing validity testing at various levels (e.g., failure of 1 PVT, failure of 2 to 3 PVTs) and, at the CBS cutoff of ≥16, specificity ranged from 92 to 95% (with sensitivity ranging from 20 to 55%). In 2021, Tylicki, Rai, Arends, Gervais and Ben-Porath examined CBS in a sample of civil disability claimants presenting with psychiatric or pain conditions. They noted that CBS correlated well (.72) with the MMPI-2-RF scale RBS, and CBS produced the strongest effect size (d = 1.03) of any PAI validity index when differentiating individuals failing PVTs and meeting criteria for malingering from individuals providing valid performance. With that said, the CBS cutoff required adjustment upward to ≥20 in order to achieve 90% specificity (specificity = 92%, sensitivity = 32%). In 2022, Boress et al. examined CBS in an outpatient neuropsychological clinic. At the cutoff of ≥16, specificity was 86% (sensitivity was 38%). To achieve 90% specificity, the cutoff required adjustment to ≥18 (specificity = 90%, sensitivity = 35%). In 2023, Shura and colleagues examined CBS in a nonclinical research veteran sample (Shura, Ingram, et al., 2023). When comparing participants classified as valid or invalid according to their performance on the WMT, a cutoff of ≥18 achieved 90% specificity and 25% sensitivity. When classifying participants according to their responses to the Miller Forensic Assessment of Symptoms Test (M-FAST), the cutoff of ≥18 resulted in 89% specificity and 41% sensitivity, whereas a CBS score of ≥19 resulted in 93% specificity and 41% sensitivity.

When summarizing the results of all CBS studies, CBS does appear to be a useful SVT within neuropsychological settings. Cutoffs have varied to some degree, but a cutoff of ≥19 has maintained 90% specificity or better across all analyses except for one, which suggested a cutoff of ≥20 may be needed (it is of note that this was in a forensic psychiatric and pain sample; Tylicki et al., 2021). Thus, at present, a score of ≥19 would appear to be the most supported cutoff when looking to maintain specificity at 90% or higher in clinical settings.

Trauma Symptom Inventory–2

The third most frequently used set of embedded SVTs within neuropsychological practice (endorsed as being used by approximately 15% of neuropsychologists; Martin et al., 2024) are those from the Trauma Symptom Inventory–2 (TSI-2). The TSI-2 is a psychological inventory that assesses trauma-related symptoms and behaviors (Briere, 2011). On this test, the examinee is asked to indicate the frequency at which certain statements apply to them on a scale ranging from 0 ("Never") to 3 ("Often"). There are two formal validity scales embedded within this inventory, one that assesses for an underreporting of symptoms (Response Level; RL) and a second that assesses for an overreporting of trauma-related symptoms (Atypical Response; ATR). Additionally, while not a formal validity scale, the test manual indicates that "if there are more than two blank items within any scale or more than one blank item within any subscale, the score for that scale or subscale should not be calculated" (p. 8).

RL is a scale that is comprised of items which were infrequently endorsed at a "0" response in the normative sample. The scale is thought to "reflect the extent to which the individual denies behaviors, thoughts, or feelings that most other respondents would report" (p. 13, Briere, 2011). Per the test manual, testing should be considered invalid when *T*-scores reach 75 or above, a finding that occurred in less than 5% of the standardization sample. This cutoff appears to be the most consistently used cutoff for the scale; limited independent research has been conducted to suggest otherwise.

ATR is a scale that is described in the TSI-2 manual as evaluating "the tendency of the respondent to overendorse trauma-related symptoms" (p. 14, Briere, 2011). Regarding item content, Nussbaum, Ales, Giromini, Watsom, and Erdodi (2023) indicated that "a review of the ATR's item content reveals a mixture of different detection mechanisms: rare symptom endorsement combined with neurologically (global amnesia) or physiologically (inability to meet basic needs for prolonged periods of time) implausible level of impairments. At face value, reporting a high frequency of these symptoms seems incompatible with genuine distress, unless the associated psychopathology is correlated with severe cognitive deficits that interfere with the examinees' ability to objectively evaluate their level of functioning (i.e., clinically significant impairments in reality testing) . . . In other words, there are no salient, face-valid a priori reasons to justify the need for a highly conservative cutoff" (p. 353).

Regarding an ATR cutoff, the test manual indicates that a raw score of 15 equates to a *T*-score of 110 for individuals under age 55 (Briere, 2011). This cutoff also represents a score that is almost two standard deviations above the overall clinical sample's obtained mean score. Based on these findings, the test publisher recommended the raw score of 15 as the cutoff point as indicating invalid responding in clinical and forensic settings.

While the TSI-2 test manual recommends a clinical cutoff score of 15, other research has noted that the cutoff is "prohibitively conservative" (Nussbaum et al., 2023, p. 363), and lower cutoff scores have been found to be appropriate for individuals with PTSD. Gray, Elhai, and Briere (2010), for example, found that a cutoff score of 8 resulted in 83% specificity in college students who had both a trauma history and clinically significant PTSD Checklist scores (44 or above) while achieving 65% sensitivity (in simulated malingerers). The raw score of 8 would translate to a *T*-score of 79 in younger adults and ≥100 in older adults, per the TSI-2 test manual (Briere, 2011).

Henry and Gornbein (2022) examined ATR in a sample of personal injury litigants and disability claimants with PTSD. At a raw score cutoff of 7, specificity was found to be 90% and sensitivity was found to be 45%. At the cutoff of 8, specificity was still observed to be 90% but sensitivity fell to 32%. In addition to reporting on ATR, the authors reported that a high TRAUMA Factor index score on the TSI-2 (i.e., a *T*-score ≥75) was associated with a specificity rate of 90% and a sensitivity rate of 39% in their sample.

Pachet et al. (2022) examined ATR in a sample of disability and compensation-seeking claimants (primarily Workers' Compensation claimants) with suspected PTSD. Approximately 90% of examinees spoke English as their first language; interpreters were used in a minority of cases if necessary. It was found that ATR scores did not significantly correlate with Word Memory Test (WMT), Victoria Symptom Validity Test (VSVT), or some MMPI-2-RF scores (i.e., TRIN-r, VRIN-r, and Fp-r); however, ATR scores did significantly correlate with MMPI-2-RF F-r scores. When examining ATR scores in predicting F-r scores, it was found that an ATR cutoff of 15 resulted in very high specificity (97%) and very low sensitivity (12%). At a cutoff of 7, specificity was 73% and sensitivity was 77%, and, at a cutoff of 8, specificity was 77% and sensitivity was 47%. It was not until the cutoff reached 11 that specificity approximated 90% (89%); sensitivity was low to moderate (24%) at this cutoff.

Nussbaum and colleagues (2023) conducted analyses on a group of individuals undergoing medicolegal neuropsychological evaluations related to motor vehicle collisions. Most individuals in the sample had claimed brain injuries (predominantly mild brain injuries) and 43% of the sample also reported having clinically significant

PTSD symptomatology. Regardless of how the criterion groups were formed in the study, a cutoff score of ≥9 resulted in 90% or higher specificity (90 to 95%) and associated sensitivity rates ranged from 26 to 53%.

In addition to the studies discussed above, it should be noted that Weiss and Rosenfeld (2017) examined the TSI-2 ATR in a trauma-exposed sample of African immigrants who had been granted asylum. No external validity indices were used in the study to ensure valid responding by examinees, and the TSI-2 was translated to French for some of the examinees. Results are reported for ATR, but the cutoff that was utilized was never explicitly noted (presumably 15 but this is unclear), and some of the results of the study were atypical. For example, individuals with subclinical symptoms of PTSD performed worse on certain validity tests (i.e., Dot Counting Test and Test of Memory Malingering) than individuals with clinically significant symptoms of PTSD. Additionally, results from other studies on PTSD have found specificity rates to be nearly two times greater than those found in the Weiss and Rosenfeld study (Detullio, Messer, Kennedy, & Millen, 2019). Because there were no external validity indicators to ensure that responses were valid, atypical results raise concern about study findings, the sample was comprised exclusively of African immigrants who had been granted asylum, and some of the examinations were conducted with a translated TSI-2, there should be extreme caution in trying to generalize these findings to other samples.

Filone and DeMatteo (2017) also examined the TSI-2 ATR in a nonconsecutively seen trauma-exposed sample of immigrants. This sample was culturally diverse; examinees were from 46 different countries; 80% of TSI-2 examinations were completed in English and 20% were completed in Spanish. All evaluations were administered during court evaluations related to asylum, extreme hardship waiver, or other relief proceeding issues. The authors reported that the mean ATR raw score was 5.98 (SD = 5.17) and 6.2% of examinees scored at or above the ATR raw score cutoff of 15. The authors appropriately added, though, "it is important to note that this study did not independently assess for feigning, and therefore it is not known whether the invalidated profiles reflected true overreporting of symptoms" (p. 704). Thus, this study has a similar notable limitation as the Weiss and Rosenfeld (2017) study, which significantly limits interpretation of results and generalization of findings.

Finally, Palermo and Brand (2019) examined the TSI-2 ATR in a sample of inpatients with diagnoses of dissociative identity disorder. No external validity indices were utilized in this study; all patients were presumed to be responding honestly. Specificity rates were low at all examined ATR cutoffs: 49% at the cutoff of 7, 51% at the cutoff at 8, and 77% at the cutoff of 15. It is not entirely clear why specificity rates were this low. It is possible that not all examinees were responding honestly as the study authors assumed, it is possible that the TSI-2 ATR might not have high specificity rates in samples with dissociative identity disorder, and it is possible that there are other unknown reasons. Regardless, results of this study (which also has notable limitations) might raise some preliminary caution in using the TSI-2 with individuals with dissociative identity disorder.

In conclusion, the TSI-2 ATR cutoff that was originally recommended for use in clinical and forensic settings is 15 (raw). Independent research, however, has indicated that this cutoff is far too conservative, especially for evaluations of individuals with suspected PTSD seen within outpatient neuropsychological settings (i.e., Henry & Gornbein, 2022; Nussbaum et al., 2023; Pachet et al., 2022). Lower cutoff scores ranging from 7 to 11 have been associated with specificity rates around 90% in these settings. Based on the study findings, a clinician might consider a score of ≥7 as possibly reflecting overreporting (based on Henry & Gornbein, 2022), a score of ≥9 as likely reflecting overreporting (based on Henry & Gornbein, 2022 and Nussbaum et al., 2023), and a score of ≥11 as very likely reflecting overreporting of PTSD-related symptomatology (based on Henry & Gornbein, 2022; Nussbaum et al., 2023; and Pachet et al., 2022). With that said, studies of lower methodological rigor suggest possible caution in applying these cutoffs to culturally and language diverse immigrants and inpatients with diagnoses of dissociative identity disorder (based on Filone & DeMatteo, 2017; Palermo & Brand, 2019; Weiss & Rosenfeld, 2017).

SVTs EMBEDDED WITHIN BRIEF SYMPTOM-FOCUSED INVENTORIES

More recently, embedded SVTs have been developed for two commonly used brief symptom-focused psychological inventories, the PTSD Checklist for DSM-5 (PCL-5) and the Beck Depression Inventory-2 (BDI-2).

PTSD Checklist for DSM-5

The PCL-5 is one of the most frequently used PTSD assessment scales in clinical practice (Blevins, Weathers, Davis, Witte, & Domino, 2015). For this checklist, patients are asked to rate the severity of distress they have felt for each of the 20 DSM-5 symptoms of PTSD (i.e., Criteria B, C, D, and E) over the last month. Item ratings range from 0 (Not at all) to 4 (Extremely). Total scores can range from 0 to 80 with cutoff scores of 31 to 33 typically used to suggest clinically significant PTSD symptomatology (National Center for PTSD, n.d.). The checklist takes approximately 5 minutes to complete.

Shura and colleagues (Shura, Rowland, et al., 2023) were the first to publish embedded SVTs derived from the PCL-5 checklist items. In their study, the authors used two samples of veterans and military service members recruited specifically for research purposes. The first embedded SVT, the PCL-5 Symptom Severity scale (PSS), was developed as a measure of overreported PTSD symptomatology. The PSS can be calculated by simply summing the PCL-5 total score. When applied to their research samples, it was found that a raw score cutoff of 56 or above resulted in 90% specificity or better, with sensitivity being as high as 52%.

The second embedded SVT created by Shura and colleagues (2023), the PCL-5 Rare Items scale (PRI), was developed to detect atypical or rare PCL-5 item reporting.

The items that comprise the PRI were items that were infrequently endorsed by their samples of veterans and military service members, including individuals who had been diagnosed with PTSD. In calculating the PRI, one point is given when each of the following items are endorsed at the specified cutoff: Item 3 endorsed at "4," Item 9 endorsed at "4," Item 10 endorsed at "4," Item 15 endorsed at "4," Item 8 endorsed at "3" or "4," and Item 16 endorsed at "3" or "4." Because the PRI is comprised of six items and each item can result in a point toward the PRI score, scores can range from zero to six on this scale. In applying this SVT to their research samples, Shura et al. (2023) reported that a cutoff of two or more points resulted in specificity of 90% or better, and associated sensitivity rates were as high as 49%.

Schroeder and Bieu (2024) cross-validated the PSS and PRI in their clinical sample of veterans undergoing neuropsychological evaluations. A PSS score of 56 resulted in strong sensitivity (57%) but lower than desired specificity in both the full valid sample (specificity = 86%) and in a valid PTSD subsample (specificity = 72%). Schroeder and Bieu found that a PSS cutoff score of 64 or above was required to achieve 90% specificity or better all of their samples. Specifically, a cutoff of ≥64 resulted in 95% specificity in the full sample of validly reporting veterans, 100% specificity in a subsample of veterans without PTSD diagnoses, 100% specificity in a subsample of veterans with historical diagnoses of PTSD, and 90% specificity in a subsample of veterans with active PTSD.

In addition to reporting the aforementioned findings on the PSS, Schroeder and Bieu (2024) addressed potential concerns that might be raised in using DSM-5 symptoms of PTSD as a validity indicator. First, they noted that the validity index cutoff of ≥64 is very high, as it essentially doubles the clinical cutoffs for PTSD (i.e., 31 to 33). They then showed that a score of ≥64, which equates to endorsing 80% of the maximum obtainable PCL-5 score, represents a profound degree of pathology that is uncommonly experienced by outpatients reporting true PTSD symptomatology. Specifically, Schroeder and Bieu reviewed published research studies that examined PCL-5 scores in individuals with PTSD who did not have external incentives to over-report symptoms. When combining all studies, the collective sample size of individuals with PTSD was 1,668. The mean PCL-5 score was 46.43, and a score of 64.86 was found to be 1.3 standard deviations above the mean (i.e., only approximately 10% of individuals in the published studies produced a score this high). Thus, the Schroeder and Bieu study results and other empirical research findings align and indicate that scores of 64 or above are very uncommon (specificity = 90%) in validly reporting individuals with PTSD.

In addition to examining the PSS, Schroeder and Bieu (2024) examined the PRI in their study. The PRI performed less well, resulting in specificity as low as 72% at the cutoff of 2 or more. The PRI cutoff required an increase to 4 or higher to achieve 90% specificity or above across all validly reporting groups of patients. At the cutoff of 4 or above, specificity was 96% in the full sample, 100% in the non-PTSD subsample, 100% in the subsample of patients with historical diagnoses of PTSD, and

92% in the subsample of patients with active PTSD. Unfortunately, sensitivity rates fell to 13% at this cutoff, which suggests limited clinical utility.

In addition to examining the PSS and PRI, Schroeder and Bieu (2024) created and validated a new PCL-5 validity index, the PCL-5 Extreme Symptom scale (PES). "This index was based on the premise that individuals who exaggerate or feign PTSD might endorse a greater number of immoderate scores as compared to individuals with genuine PTSD. Consequently, this . . . validity index was based on the number of PCL-5 items that were endorsed at the most extreme responses (i.e., a score of 3 or 4)" (p. 4). At a cutoff of 17 or above, specificity was 95% in the full valid sample, 100% in the non-PTSD subsample, 100% in the subsample of patients with historical diagnoses of PTSD, and 90% in the subsample of patients with active PTSD. The associated sensitivity rate was 39%.

Like with the PSS, Schroeder and Bieu (2024) addressed potential critiques of using PES as a validity scale given that it is derived from true PTSD symptomatology. They noted that the PES score of 17 is quite high, meaning that 85% of all PCL-5 items (i.e., 17 of 20 items) must be endorsed at the extreme ratings of 3 or 4 for the cutoff to be reached. Especially for outpatients with PTSD, this seems unlikely to occur, as it would indicate that these individuals are "highly and essentially equally distressed by nearly every possible symptom listed in the DSM-5" (p. 7). Supporting this, published research indicates that validly responding individuals do not endorse such an extreme symptom profile. Bovin and colleagues (2016), for example, found that veterans, on average, rated 12 of the 20 PCL-5 items as a 1 (i.e., "a little bit" distress), and the remaining 8 items were rated, on average, at a 2 (i.e., "moderately" distressing). Further bolstering this, the Schroeder and Bieu (2024) data indicated that PES scores of 17 or higher were "more likely than not to be associated with invalid findings on the PAI symptom validity indices" (p. 7).

A third study, unpublished at the time of this writing (Schroeder, Spector, Snodgrass, & Bieu, 2025) examined the PSS, PRI, and PES in a cross-cultural sample of 79 examinees who underwent forensic evaluations related to pursuit of federal Workers' Compensation claims for PTSD. For the PSS, when using the Inventory of Problems–29 (IOP-29) as the criterion validity measure, a PSS cutoff of 63 or above resulted in specificity of 90% and sensitivity of 47%. For the PES, a cutoff score of ≥17 resulted in 92% specificity and 33% sensitivity. For the PRI, the optimal cutoff score was 3 or more. At this cutoff, specificity was 94% and sensitivity was 43%. Finally, additional analyses indicate that there were not statistically significant relationships between any of the PCL-5 SVTs and the number of traumatic events encountered by the examines in the valid or invalid groups.

In summary, when combining the data from the aforementioned studies, certain conclusions can be made regarding PCL-5 SVT cutoff scores. First, a PSS cutoff of 64 or above achieved adequate specificity rates in all samples from all studies; thus, this cutoff is likely appropriate for use in outpatient PTSD evaluations. Second, a PES cutoff of 17 or above achieved adequate specificity in all samples. Consequently, this cutoff will likely be appropriate in clinical practice. Third, research findings have been less consistent regarding PRI cutoff scores to date, which makes it harder to recommend a single cutoff value. The most conservative cutoff would be a score of 4 or above as this resulted in 90% or better specificity across all studies. At this cutoff, however, sensitivity rates are quite low. A more liberal cutoff score of 3 or above was found to maintain adequate specificity rates in two of three studies; at this cutoff, sensitivity rates improved. If using the PRI, the clinician will have to use clinical judgment as to whether a cutoff score of 3 or 4 should be considered invalid. Lastly, at the cutoff scores described above, research indicates that positive findings are unlikely to be due to true PTSD reporting in outpatient samples even though the items comprising the SVTs are derived from DSM-5 PTSD symptoms.

Beck Depression Inventory-2

The BDI-2 is a frequently utilized depression inventory in neuropsychological settings (Rabin, Paolillo, & Barr, 2016). For this test, patients are to rate statements regarding depressive symptoms on a scale ranging from 0 (no symptoms) to 3 (the most severe symptoms). There are 21 items and the summed final score from these items can range from 0 to 63. According to the BDI-2 manual, scores of 0 to 13 indicate minimal depressive symptoms, scores of 14 to 19 indicate mild depressive symptoms, scores of 20 to 28 indicate moderate depressive symptoms, and scores of 29 or above indicate severe depressive symptoms (Beck, Steer, & Brown, 1996). Completion of this inventory takes approximately 10 minutes.

In the first study touching on the potential utility of the BDI-2 as an SVT, Merten, Kaminski, and Pfeiffer (2020) found a relationship between elevated BDI-2 scores and invalidity as determined by two stand-alone SVTs, the Structured Inventory of Malingered Symptomatology and the Self-Report Symptom Inventory. The researchers documented that 84% of the patients who scored above 40 on the BDI-2 failed at least one of aforementioned SVTs. Conversely, 98% of individuals who passed both SVTs scored 40 or lower on the BDI-2.

Fuermaier, Dandachi-Fitzgerald, and Lehrner (2023) later formally assessed whether an embedded SVT could be derived from the BDI-2. In their study, examinees were forensic claimants pursuing early retirement due to reports of cognitive dysfunction; approximately one-third of examinees had depressive disorder diagnoses. The authors found that BDI-2 total scores of 38 or above successfully differentiated valid from invalid test takers (90% specificity and 58% sensitivity). The authors noted, though, that the cutoff score could potentially vary slightly based on examinee vocabulary skill and/or education level.

In a follow-up study, Boucher, Giromini, Roth, and Erdodi (2024) examined the BDI-2 total score as an embedded SVT within a sample of 74 clinical patients. Approximately 60% of the patients had major depressive disorder, and the average BDI-2 score was 18.7 (mild depressive symptoms range). The authors found that the

BDI-2 scores were not significantly correlated with education, reading level, IQ, age, or gender. People who failed the BDI-2 SVT had lower IQ, but it is unclear whether this was due to them invalidating the cognitive test (thus, resulting in a lower IQ) or whether they truly were of lower intelligence.

When conducting additional analyses, Boucher et al. (2024) found that the previously proposed BDI-2 cutoff score of ≥38 resulted in specificity rates ranging from 95 to 96% with sensitivity rates ranging from 33 to 50%. They also found that a more liberal BDI-2 cutoff of ≥33 resulted in specificity rates of 89 to 90% and sensitivity rates ranged from 44 to 67%. The authors then reported that various clinical factors did not relate to failing the BDI-II SVT. Specifically, having a psychiatric disorder diagnosis, a major depressive disorder diagnosis, or a history of suicidal ideation or history of psychiatric hospitalization were not associated with elevated BDI-2 SVT failure rates. Somewhat oddly, though, the presence of external incentives was also not associated with elevated BDI-2 SVT failure rates.

A third study has been conducted by Shura, Schroeder, and colleagues (Shura et al., 2024). In this study, the BDI-2 total score was examined as an SVT (termed the BDI-2 Symptom Severity Scale; BSS) in both a research sample of veterans and a clinical sample of veterans (total N = 603). Additionally, the authors created and validated a BDI-2 Extreme Symptom scale (BES) and a BDI-2 Rare Items scale (BRI). The BES is calculated by summing the number of BDI-2 items that are endorsed at the most extreme "3" response. The BRI is comprised of item responses endorsed by less than 15% of validly reporting individuals with active depressive disorders but 15% or more of invalidly reporting individuals. To calculate the BRI, one point is awarded every time any of the following items are endorsed at a "3" response: Items 1, 3, 4, 5, 8, and 19; BRI scores can range from 0 to 6.

Analyses in the Shura, Schroeder, and colleagues (2024) study were conducted using the total research sample, the total clinical sample, and various subsamples, including subsamples of examinees with current depressive disorders. For the BSS, at a cutoff of ≥33, specificity rates were often poor in our subsamples of examinees with active and lifetime psychiatric disorders. Specificity rates were typically adequate at a cutoff of ≥38 when applied to examinees without active depressive disorders, but a higher cutoff was needed to maintain adequate specificity rates in our samples with active depressive disorders. Specifically, a cutoff of ≥42 was required in these active depressive disorder subsamples. This cutoff score resulted in specificity rates of 89% or better in all of our samples/subsamples regardless of patient diagnoses. Sensitivity rates at this cutoff ranged from 15 to 30%.

In considering the BSS findings, the need for a cutoff score of ≥42 was very likely due to the fact that the valid group was comprised solely of individuals who *all* have active depressive disorders. By contrast, in the analyses conducted by Boucher et al. (2024) and Fuermaier et al. (2023) only about 60% and 33% of the valid samples, respectively, were individuals with active depressive disorders. We argue that it is important to apply cutoffs to a sample of patients comprised exclusively of the condition of interest when validating an SVT derived from real symptomatology because the question in clinical practice will be "Does the patient's elevated BDI-2 score point to exaggerated/feigned depression or a current depressive disorder?" This is a question that can only be addressed by comparing the patient's score to scores obtained by a group of patients who all have depressive disorders (as opposed to a group of patients where only some of the individuals have depressive disorders). By using a cutoff of ≥42, a clinician can be confident that the elevated score is not likely due to an active depressive disorder.

In addition to noting that a BSS cutoff of ≥42 is highly specific in all of the subsamples, including subsamples of examinees with active depressive disorders, it is noted that this score is nearly 4 standard deviations above the mean for individuals with mild major depressive disorder, 1.5 standard deviations above the mean for individuals with moderate major depressive disorder, and 1 standard deviation above the mean for individuals with severe major depressive disorder (per Beck et al., 1996). Moreover, analyses with the clinical patient data show that a score of 42 is almost three times more likely to be due to invalid than valid responding even when examinees with active depression are endorsing symptoms (LR+ = 2.73). Therefore, while the BES validity scale is comprised of real symptoms of depression, scores of 42 or above are unlikely to be due to true depression especially if the examinee is not observably demonstrating signs of severe depression.

In addition to expanding findings related to BSS, the authors conducted analyses on BES and BRI. For the BES, specificity rates were 90% or higher in all samples/subsamples, including the active depression subsample, at a cutoff of ≥8 (sensitivity rates ranged from 15 to 35%). Congruently, data from the BDI-2 manual suggests that extreme item endorsement is uncommon; mean ratings for items in an outpatient sample ranged from .47 to 1.47. Finally, for the BRI, specificity rates were 90% or higher in all samples/subsamples at a cutoff of ≥3 (sensitivity rates ranged from 15 to 22%). The fact that this finding holds true across both real clinical patients and well-categorized research examinees increases confidence that the items comprising the scale truly are rarely endorsed by valid test takers.

In summary, the BDI-2 SVT with the most empirical support behind its usage is BSS (the BDI-2 total score). Suggested scores have been ≥33, ≥38, and ≥42. As detailed above, we believe that the cutoff of ≥42 is most appropriate for clinical settings. Not only does this cutoff maintain adequate specificity rates in all of Shura et al.'s (2024) analyses, but it also maintains >90% specificity rates in the Boucher et al. (2024) and Fuermaier et al. (2023) samples. BES and BRI show clear promise as well, but cross-validation of these SVTs would still be useful.

STAND-ALONE SVTs

Stand-alone SVTs appear to be less commonly used in neuropsychological practice than well-established embedded SVTs (Martin et al., 2024; Rabin et al., 2016).

The most commonly utilized stand-alone SVT in neuropsychological practice is the Structured Inventory of Malingered Symptomatology (SIMS), which is only used by approximately one-fourth of neuropsychologists (Martin et al., 2024). Comparatively, as previously noted, validity indices within the MMPI-2-RF are used by 61% of neuropsychologists and SVTs within the PAI are used by 47% of neuropsychologists. Conceivably, the less frequent use of stand-alone SVTs may be due to the fact that (1) research often indicates that SVTs within the MMPI family instruments and PAI have stronger classification accuracy rates than many of the available stand-alone SVTs, (2) stand-alone SVTs take additional time to administer while not simultaneously collecting information on true psychopathology, and (3) including stand-alone SVTs within test batteries adds to the cost of the test battery. With that said, given the relatively limited number of embedded SVTs that are available, an awareness of stand-alone SVTs will likely be beneficial for the practicing clinician.

Structured Inventory of Malingered Symptomatology

As just noted, the SIMS is the most commonly utilized stand-alone SVT in neuropsychological practice, and is used by approximately one-fourth of neuropsychologists (Martin et al., 2024). The SIMS is a 75-item true/false *screening* inventory that takes approximately 15 minutes to complete. The SIMS is said to assess for feigning of symptoms across the following five content areas: neurological impairment, amnestic disorders, low intelligence, affective disorders, and psychosis.

Per the SIMS test manual, the proposed cutoff score for invalidity is a Total score of >14 (Widows & Smith, 2005). This score achieved impressive classification accuracy rates (sensitivity = 94.63%, specificity = 87.88%) in a sample of college students that were instructed to respond honestly or feign symptoms. The SIMS manual also identifies cutoff scores for each subscale: neurological impairment >2, amnestic disorders >2, low intelligence >2, affective disorders >5, and psychosis >1.

In 2022, Shura, Ord, and Worthen (2022b) produced a comprehensive literature review on the SIMS. They described research creating short forms of the inventory, the derivation of alternative scales, and translation to other languages, while noting that the short forms, alternative scales, and translations have limited cross-validation research. Shura and colleagues (2022b) additionally summarized SIMS cutoff score-based classification accuracy rates that have been published in the professional literature, noting the following. In simulation studies, which generally have limitations in generalizability to clinical settings, the most commonly examined Total score cutoffs were >14 and >16. At the cutoff of >14, simulation study specificity rates ranged from 28 to 100% (most studies, though, ranged from 79 to 100%) and sensitivity rates ranged from 52 to 98%. At a cutoff of >16, specificity rates ranged from 23 to 100% (most studies had specificity rates ranging from 83 to 100% though) and sensitivity rates ranged from 36 to 98%. In real-world clinical and forensic studies, the SIMS Total score of >14 was often found to produce high sensitivity rates (e.g., above 75%) but low specificity rates (e.g., below 75%). Finally, with regard to SIMS subscale cutoff scores, Shura et al. (2022b) indicated that sensitivity rates are moderate to high (e.g., 35 to 92%) but specificity rates are low (e.g., 52 to 91%, with most below 90%).

Based on the available known groups research studies, Shura and colleagues (2022b) provide interpretative recommendations for the SIMS. One recommendation is that the cutoff of >14 should typically be avoided as it results in low specificity rates across most contexts. This recommendation is similar to that which Boone (2013) has previously provided: "available data from real-world samples indicate that the recommended SIMS cutoff of >14 results in unacceptable specificity. The test authors (Widows & Smith, 2005) argue that they intended the measure as a 'screen,' and thus they wanted to err on the side of capturing the majority of potential malingerers, with more comprehensive testing in positive cases to rule out false positives. However, it can be argued that use of a cutoff that has a false-positive rate approaching 40% is irresponsible and harmful to credible patients, who will have an indication of possible malingering memorialized in their records" (p. 103).

Another recommendation that Shura and colleagues (2022b) make is to consider "a graded approach for interpreting SIMS scores" (p. 11), which is noted below (along with typical specificity rates associated with each cutoff score).

- Scores of >16 are *possibly invalid.* This cutoff appears to result in specificity rates around 60–70% in real-world examinees (Alwes et al., 2008; Benge et al., 2012; Lewis et al., 2002).
- Scores of >19 are *probably invalid.* This cutoff appears to result in specificity rates around 85% in real-world examinees (Benge et al., 2012).
- Scores of >23 are *very likely invalid.* This cutoff appears to result in specificity rates between 90% and 100% in real-world examinees (Benge et al., 2012; Wisdom et al., 2010).

In addition to proposing the graded cutoff approach, Shura and colleagues (2022b) make recommendations regarding cutoffs when using the SIMS in screening settings and nonscreening clinical/forensic settings. In screening settings, they recommend using a cutoff of >19; individuals who score at this level would then undergo more comprehensive validity assessment. Conversely, when using the SIMS in nonscreening clinical/forensic settings, they recommend utilizing a cutoff score of >23, which will result in a low number of false-positive errors (note that this cutoff score of >23 is also suggested by Boone (2013) in her review of the SIMS literature). Finally, Shura et al. (2022b) note "caution is warranted when considering elevated subscales, given lack of research on subscale classification accuracy. Invalid subscale scores based on manual cutoffs might be best for explaining what types of exaggerated symptoms are driving an elevated Total score, rather than being used in isolation or when the total score is not elevated" (p. 11).

Shura and colleagues (2022b) conclude their comprehensive review of the SIMS by noting that the test has strengths such as being an efficient, relatively low-cost

SVT that can be used with different types of examinees. Additionally, it is available in multiple administration modalities (e.g., paper and pencil or electronic), it has been written in several languages, and it has been validated with examinees of various cultural groups from the United States and Europe. Regarding weaknesses, Shura et al. (2022b) note that the test has incremental value when comparing cutoff-derived validity determinations to clinical judgment, but the SIMS does not demonstrate incremental value beyond validity scales on more commonly utilized tests such as the MMPI-2-RF and PAI. Additionally, the authors describe "the most notable limitation to the SIMS" as being that some of the test items are not atypical or extreme. "For example, two items describe trouble sleeping in general and middle insomnia specifically, neither of which are worded as extreme or severe. . . . In other words, many SIMS items represent quasi-rare symptoms (Rogers, 2018), as opposed to bizarre ones" (p. 12). Likely for this reason, research findings indicate that relatively high cutoff scores (as discussed above) are needed to maintain adequate specificity rates.

Miller Forensic Assessment of Symptoms Test

The second most utilized stand-alone SVT in neuropsychological practice is the Miller Forensic Assessment of Symptoms Test (M-FAST), which is frequently used by 10% of neuropsychologists (Martin et al., 2024). The M-FAST is a 25-item structured *screening* interview that can be administered in approximately 5 to 10 minutes. The M-FAST focuses on assessing malingered psychiatric illness and it provides scores for seven feigning symptoms/strategies: endorsement of unusual hallucinations, endorsement of rare combinations of symptoms, endorsement of extreme symptomatology, discrepancies between reported and observed behaviors, assessment of negative self-image, report of unusual symptom course, and suggestibility. Scores from these items are summed (ranging from 0 to 17), and a cutoff of ≥6 has been recommended (Miller, 2001). Per the test manual, this cutoff resulted in a sensitivity rate of 93% and a specificity rate of 83% in clinical samples.

As expected, given that the M-FAST focuses on malingered psychiatric illness, most of the clinical research that has been conducted on the structured interview has been done with psychiatric patients in psychiatric settings (Detullio et al., 2019). Per Detullio and colleagues' meta-analysis of the M-FAST, sensitivity values have been found to range from 25 to 100%, and specificity values have been found to range from 37 to 100% when using the ≥6 cutoff. A random-effects analysis was performed to combine all published data, and it found an average sensitivity rate of 83% and an average specificity rate of 85%. However, when a second random-effects analysis was performed based only on research with clinical comparison groups, the average sensitivity rate was found to be 87% and the average specificity rate was 80% (at the test manual suggested cutoff of ≥6). Unfortunately, a cutoff score associated with 90% specificity was not reported.

Relatively limited additional research on the M-FAST has been published since the Detullio et al. (2019) meta-analysis, and, at present, there does not appear to be a consensus cutoff score for achieving specificity rates of 90% or better. Boone (2013) has previously opined that the cutoff score "should probably be raised to at least 7" (p. 92); while we agree that this statement seems reasonable, this cutoff has not been empirically validated. Given the cutoff score limitations, a recommendation by Shura et al. (2023) seems fitting: " . . . Conceptually, the M-FAST may be best used as an adjunct SVT in cases where more sensitive SVTs are already employed. This could provide a quick means to sample other types of detection methods when the primary measures rely solely on rarely or quasi-rarely endorsed symptoms. For example, if an MMPI-3 is already administered, with SVTs mainly addressing quasi/rarely endorsed psychological symptoms (F, Fp, etc.), adding the M-FAST allows a more thorough evaluation of symptom validity by sampling such strategies as rare symptom combinations or unusual course" (pp. 178–179).

Memory Complaints Inventory

The third most commonly utilized stand-alone SVT in neuropsychological practice is the Memory Complaints Inventory (MCI), which was developed by Paul Green, who also developed the Word Memory Test, Medical Symptom Validity Test, and other tests. The MCI is a 58-item computer-administered questionnaire that assesses for exaggerated or feigned memory complaints. Examinees are to read all 58 items and rate each one on a scale of 0 (Not at all) to 4 (Extremely). In total, the questionnaire takes approximately 10 minutes to complete. It is available in six languages (English, Spanish, French, German, Dutch, and Portuguese) but there has not yet been any research published on the non-English versions (Armistead-Jehle & Shura, 2022). The test is being utilized by 8% of neuropsychologists (Martin et al., 2024).

The MCI is comprised of nine rationally designed scales (Green, 2019). Six of the scales involve domains of plausible memory complaints assessing the following: general memory problems, numeric information problems, visuospatial memory problems, verbal memory problems, pain interferes with memory, and memory interferes with work. The remaining three scales involve implausible memory complaints assessing the following: impairment of remote memory, amnesia for complex behavior, and amnesia for antisocial behavior. These latter three scales are believed to be implausible for the majority of individuals with memory complaints due to organic etiologies but common for individuals with memory complaints due to psychiatric etiologies or individuals who are exaggerating memory complaints.

Data from the MCI test manual are well summarized in four points by Armistead-Jehle and Shura (2022):

1. The authors highlight that the MCI scales (including the plausible scales) are not substantially elevated by individuals with neurological conditions. Conversely, individuals with psychiatric conditions (notably depressive disorders) elevate MCI scales. Armistead-Jehle and Shura note that "This reflects the

trend where individuals with psychiatric conditions present with more memory complaints than those diagnosed with neurological disease and severe TBI (Rohling, Green, Allen, & Iverson, 2002; Smith, Petersen, Ivnik, Malec, & Tangalos, 1996)." (p. 2).

2. Armistead-Jehle and Shura (2022) note that the scores on the MCI are not related to scores on the California Verbal Learning Test, which further indicates that the MCI does not measure true memory function/dysfunction.
3. A moderate negative correlation was found between memory-based PVT scores and MCI scores. To demonstrate this, it was reported that individuals who produced scores of 91 to 100% on the Word Memory Test (clearly passing of the test) scored 25%, on average, on the MCI. Conversely, for individuals who produced scores of 60% or lower on the Word Memory Test, the average MCI score was much higher at 55%.
4. MCI scores correlate with other memory-related SVTs. Specifically, when examining correlations with MMPI-2-RF validity scales, it was found that MCI scores correlated most strongly with RBS.

Data, as summarized above, indicate that the MCI is indeed an SVT. Per the test manual, after an examinee completes the MCI, various reports become available to the clinician. Traditionally, scores from the nine scales are compared to clinical groups, and a "best-fit" analysis is conducted by the computer program to show groups of patients who had mean scores that are similar to the examinee's scores (e.g., individuals who failed the Word Memory Test). The clinician then uses this information to determine whether memory complaint exaggeration is likely.

A limitation to the traditional interpretative approach is that classification accuracy rates associated with the examinee's scores are not known. In addressing this limitation, subsequently published research has sought to develop cutoff scores for the MCI. The most common score that is interpreted is the mean MCI score from all subscales. Green (2019) reported that a cutoff score of 52% was associated with 33% sensitivity and 90% specificity in a sample of mixed clinical outpatients. In a sample of civil forensic outpatients, a cutoff of 47% was associated with 37% sensitivity and 90% specificity. Armistead-Jehle, Grills, Bieu, and Kulas (2016) found that a cutoff of 50% resulted in sensitivity rates of 16% and 23% (depending on the sample grouping criterion test used) with specificity rates of 93 to 96% in a sample of active-duty Army outpatients. Huber, Jones, Capps, and Buchanan (2022) found that a somewhat lower cutoff score of 40% resulted in a sensitivity rate of 65% and a specificity rate of 90% in a sample of mixed clinical outpatients.

When combining the empirical literature with a recommendation from the test developer (i.e., mean MCI scores over 30% should cause the clinician to suspect either symptom exaggeration or emotional explanations for memory complaints), Armistead-Jehle and Shura (2022) propose an interpretive approach that can supplement the "best-fit" results from the computer printouts.

- A mean MCI score of ≥50% is suggestive of globally exaggerated memory complaints. As the mean score increases further above this point, the likelihood of invalidity continues to increase as well.
- When scores of ≥50% occur across the plausible memory complaint scales, this suggests exaggerated memory complaints. When scores of ≥30% occur across the implausible memory scales, this suggests fabricated memory complaints.
- When scores of ≥50% occur on any specific plausible memory scale, this suggests an exaggeration of that specific complaint (e.g., verbal memory). When scores of ≥30% occur on any specific implausible memory scale, this indicates fabrication of that specific complaint (e.g., remote memory).
- The *z*-score comparisons created by the computerized scoring software can help to contextualize results for those who are validly reporting symptoms, are neurologically impaired, and/or who are invalidly completing PVTs.

Overall, the MCI has strengths and weaknesses (Armistead-Jehle & Shura, 2022). A weakness is that there are still relatively few publications on the test, especially by authors outside of the test developer. Another weakness is that there are few empirical findings to define invalidity based on subtests of the MCI (as opposed to the total percentage of items endorsed). Conversely, a strength is that, of the literature that is available, a total score cutoff of 50% does indeed appear appropriate for identifying exaggerated or feigned memory complaints. Furthermore, in some cases, a failure on the test might be able to help to increase confidence that failed PVTs (especially when failed just at the cutoff) are indeed due to invalidity and are not false-positive findings. In other cases, it is possible that a failed MCI, within the context of passed PVTs, could be informative for understanding that a patient's subjective memory complaints are exaggerated despite performing validly on cognitive testing. Lastly, the MCI adds to the small number of memory-based SVTs that are available, and the test can be completed in only approximately 10 minutes. Therefore, the MCI is a stand-alone SVT that could add clinical value for neuropsychologists.

CLOSING REMARKS

As discussed throughout this chapter, it is important to include SVTs within neuropsychological batteries because the veracity of self-reported symptoms is unknown when there are no validity checks. Furthermore, the symptom validity literature has continued to expand in recent years, supporting new embedded and stand-alone symptom validity indicators and providing further empirically backed guidance. While various factors might impact the clinician's choice of which SVT(s) to use, utilizing measures with diverse validity scales (e.g., the MMPI-2-RF) and/or measures assessing specific patients reporting syndromes (e.g., the PCL-5 validity scales) will likely be ideal.

CHAPTER 7

Elevating Validity Administration Practices and Making Confident Validity Determinations

The previous chapters have discussed the rationale for assessing validity within the neuropsychological evaluation, outlined methods for managing consults, detailed strategies for approaching the clinical interview, and provided guidance for the use and interpretation of individual validity tests. Arriving at conclusions regarding validity status, however, does not rely on the interpretation of single data points; instead, it requires a multidimensional approach that incorporates data from all sources of information, filtered through the lens of the neuropsychologist's understanding of brain–behavior relationships, neuropathology, and psychometrics. Furthermore, assessment of validity can be a dynamic process as indications of invalidity can be present early in the evaluation, which can raise questions of how to proceed with the rest of the evaluation. The current chapter will discuss how to efficiently and effectively design a PVT battery, incorporate that battery into the testing session, proceed with the evaluation when testing is invalid, and interpret validity assessment results within the context of the full evaluation.

DESIGNING THE MULTIPLE PVT BATTERY

Nearly all surveyed neuropsychologists agree with the statement that an evaluation with multiple validity tests interspersed throughout testing is of higher quality than an evaluation with few or no validity tests included (Martin et al., 2024). Accordingly, of 445 surveyed neuropsychologists, 95% report that they standardly administer at least three PVTs in their nonforensic clinical evaluations of nongeriatric adults and >75% report that they administer at least four PVTs. Furthermore, the same survey data indicate that clinicians use an average (median) of five PVTs in clinical evaluations of nongeriatric adults and an average (median) of four PVTs when evaluating older adults. These data clearly indicate that it is a standard of practice to administer multiple PVTs even within a clinical nonforensic test battery.

As already discussed in other chapters, it is common to utilize a mixture of stand-alone and embedded PVTs. Embedded PVTs assist in evaluating validity in a variety of domains across the test battery without adding administration time; however, the clinician should keep in mind that embedded PVTs are generally less sensitive to invalidity than stand-alone PVTs (as discussed in Chapter 4). For this reason, we recommend that the clinician include *at least* one stand-alone PVT within their validity test battery, although including at least two stand-alone PVTs within the battery is generally even more ideal. Consistent with these recommendations, survey data indicate that over 90% of neuropsychologists typically include at least one stand-alone PVT within their clinical batteries, and almost 60% typically include at least two stand-alone PVTs (Martin et al., 2024). Moreover, the average (median) number of stand-alone PVTs used in clinical settings by neuropsychologists is two, a finding that is consistent with the average (median) number used by validity testing experts.

As noted in Chapter 4, there are a variety of stand-alone PVTs from which to choose, and many of the most commonly used stand-alone PVTs conform to a recognition memory paradigm. When selecting stand-alone PVTs for one's battery, it is often advisable to include at least one memory-based PVT because memory is a frequently feigned cognitive domain (Tan, Slick, Strauss, & Hultsch, 2002). Of memory based PVTs, the Test of Memory Malingering (TOMM) is clearly the most popular among neuropsychologists. Nearly 90% of both neuropsychologists and validity test experts report frequently administering the TOMM, which is approximately twice the number of neuropsychologists and experts who use the next most popular memory-based PVT (i.e., Word Memory Test; Martin et al., 2024). While the TOMM is the most popular memory-based PVT, there are other good memory-based stand-alone PVTs from which to choose as well (see Chapter 4).

If administering a second stand-alone PVT, one might choose to use another memory-based one. Conversely, clinicians may choose to use a validity test that appears to measure a different cognitive domain. One of the primary rationales for choosing a different type of stand-alone PVT is that, by using PVTs that seem to assess different cognitive domains, the clinician may be more likely to identify feigning if the patient is attempting to feign only a single cognitive ability (e.g., feigning only attention issues). Survey data indicate that the most commonly administered nonmemory-based stand-alone PVT is the Dot Counting Test (Martin et al., 2024). Thus, this brief attention and processing speed-based PVT could be a logical choice for a second stand-alone PVT although other options are also available.

Regardless of whether a second stand-alone PVT is used, the domain diversity of the PVT battery can be further expanded with planful selection of embedded PVTs. For example, a domain diverse PVT battery could include the TOMM (appearing to assess visual memory), an embedded Hopkins Verbal Learning Test—Revised validity index (appearing to assess verbal memory), Dot Counting Test (appearing to assess attention and mental processing speed), the Sentence Repetition Test embedded validity index (appearing to assess verbal ability), and a Wisconsin Card Sorting Test embedded validity index (appearing to assess executive functioning). Again, a rational for including PVTs that appear to assess a variety of cognitive domains is that some patients might feign specific cognitive domains, so having validity tests related to multiple cognitive domains theoretically increases the likelihood that invalidity will be identified in underperforming patients.

Although noted in other chapters, it is worth reemphasizing that all PVTs selected for use in a battery should be appropriate for the patient being evaluated in order to both reduce false-positive findings and maximize sensitivity rates. With regard to reducing false-positive findings, PVTs (and PVT cutoffs) that are selected for inclusion in the PVT battery should have adequate normative data for the population being evaluated. For example, it will likely be inappropriate to administer an embedded PVT to someone with dementia if that embedded PVT only has cutoffs validated for use with individuals with mild traumatic brain injuries. Likewise, it will likely be inappropriate to administer some verbally based PVTs to individuals with very limited English proficiency unless there is research validating that PVT in a similar sample. With regard to maximizing sensitivity rates, PVTs with high sensitivity rates in general are ideal if they are adequately validated with individuals similar to the patient being evaluated. Additionally, if evaluating someone who is likely to feign a specific cognitive domain (e.g., feigning of attention deficits in a workup for attention-deficit/hyperactivity disorder), it will be wise to include at least one PVT that appears to assess that cognitive domain.

When placing the selected PVTs within the broader neuropsychological test battery, at least one stand-alone PVT should typically be administered toward the beginning of the battery (Lippa, 2021). This is because some patients who intend to feign cognitive impairment may be more likely to fail validity tests when administered at the beginning of testing, potentially because they do not yet understand how easy the validity tests are compared to true cognitive tests. Along these same lines, it is recommended that stand-alone PVTs be administered before actual neurocognitive tests that appear to assess the same cognitive domains (e.g., administering the TOMM prior to a test of genuine memory such as the Brief Visuospatial Memory Test—Revised). Using this strategy helps to reduce the likelihood that the patient will identify the very easy PVT as a validity test by comparing it to much more challenging neurocognitive tests.

While it is recommended to administer a stand-alone PVT toward the beginning of the test battery, additional PVTs (stand-alone and/or embedded) should be spread throughout the test battery. This is because motivation and engagement can potentially fluctuate across the evaluation. Interspersing the validity tests throughout the battery may help to identify invalidity that occurs sporadically or in one section of the evaluation (e.g., toward the end of the evaluation). Furthermore, if testing were to occur across multiple days, validity tests should be administered each day that testing occurs, as invalidity could occur during any part of the testing process.

Finally, for convenience, Table 7.1 summarizes previously discussed key points for selecting PVTs and incorporating them into the neuropsychological test battery. Additionally, as time efficiency has become an increasingly important consideration for neuropsychologists in constructing their clinical test batteries, Tables 7.2 through 7.4 provide examples of PVT batteries that would consume no more than roughly 10 minutes of test-taking time. Table 7.2 shows a PVT battery that could easily be incorporated into a neuropsychological workup of a younger adult. Table 7.3 shows a battery that could easily be utilized in older adult evaluations. Note that this battery is appropriate for most all older adults, as it has been validated in older adults with no cognitive impairment, mild cognitive impairment, mild dementia, and moderate

TABLE 7.1. Considerations When Selecting PVTs and Incorporating Them into the Test Battery

1. Select multiple PVTs (median usage in clinical evaluations = 5).
2. Administer at least 1 stand-alone PVT (more ideally 2).
3. Typically include at least one memory-based PVT.
4. Select PVTs that reduce risk for false-positive findings while simultaneously maximizing sensitivity rates.
5. Select PVTs that appear to assess multiple cognitive domains.
6. Place at least one stand-alone PVT toward the beginning of the test battery.
7. Place stand-alone PVTs that appear to assess specific cognitive domains (e.g., memory) before cognitive tests that actually assess that domain.
8. Spread PVTs throughout the neuropsychological test battery.
9. If testing occurs across multiple days, administer validity testing each day.

TABLE 7.2. Example PVT Battery: Younger Adult Workup

Test	Administration time
1. Test of Memory Malingering (Trial 1)	5–10 minutes
2. Dot Counting Test	2–5 minutes
3. WMS-IV Logical Memory Recognition	0 additional minutes
4. WMS-IV Visual Reproduction Recognition	0 additional minutes
5. Reliable Digit Span	0 additional minutes
6. WCST Failure to Maintain Set	0 additional minutes

Note. WMS-IV = Wechsler Memory Scale—4th Edition; WCST = Wisconsin Card Sorting Test.

TABLE 7.3. Example PVT Battery: Older Adult/Dementia Workup

Test	Administration time
1. Coin in the Hand Test	5 minutes
2. Dot Counting Test	2–5 minutes
3. Sentence Repetition Test	0 additional minutes
4. WAIS-IV (Digit Span Forward Scaled Score)	0 additional minutes

dementia (see Martin et al., 2022a). Table 7.4 demonstrates how a PVT battery might be constructed for individuals being evaluated for specific conditions where feigning of a specific cognitive domain might be more likely. In this specific example, feigning of attention and/or memory impairment might be more likely, so multiple PVTs that appear to assess attention are included in the battery (but not at the exclusion of other PVTs). Lastly, Table 7.5 demonstrates how multiple PVTs might be incorporated within the context of a full neuropsychological test battery.

CONSIDERATIONS WITHIN THE TESTING SESSION

In Chapter 3, we discussed talking with the patient at the end of the clinical interview about the importance of doing one's best. If you are doing testing yourself and start testing immediately after the clinical interview, there is likely not a need to repeat that information. If, however, you administer testing on a different day, you have a technician administer the testing (regardless of whether the testing is on the same or a different day as the clinical interview), or you take a break before administering testing, we recommend reemphasizing the importance of doing one's best. With that said, we do not recommend disclosing that the patient will be administered validity tests, as disclosure of this fact could encourage a savvier approach to feigning, making it

TABLE 7.4. Example PVT Battery: ADHD Workup

Test	Administration time
1. Medical Symptom Validity Test	5–10 minutes
2. Dot Counting Test	2–5 minutes
3. Conners CPT-3 Embedded	0 additional minutes
4. Reliable Digit Span	0 additional minutes
5. Logical Memory (Recognition Hits)	0 additional minutes
6. Visual Reproduction (Recognition Hits)	0 additional minutes

Note. ADHD = attention-deficit/hyperactivity disorder; CPT = Continuous Performance Test.

TABLE 7.5. Example of Test Battery with PVTs Interspersed Throughout

Test	Type of test	Rationale for battery placement
TOMM (Trial 1)	Validity test	PVT at the beginning of the evaluation and before memory tests
Logical Memory I	Neurocognitive test	
Dot Counting Test	Validity test	PVT interspersed throughout the battery and before processing speed and attention tests
Tower	Neurocognitive test	
Logical Memory II & Recognition	Neurocognitive Test & Embedded PVT	PVT interspersed throughout the battery
Visual Reproduction I	Neurocognitive Test	
D-KEFS Verbal Fluency and Color Word	Neurocognitive Tests & Embedded PVT	PVT interspersed throughout the battery
WAIS Digit Span & Vocabulary	Neurocognitive Tests & Embedded PVT	PVT interspersed throughout the battery
Visual Reproduction II & Recognition	Neurocognitive Test & Embedded PVT	PVT interspersed throughout the battery
HVLT-R	Neurocognitive Test	
Digit Vigilance Test	Neurocognitive Test	
WAIS Coding & Block Design	Neurocognitive Tests	
HVLT-R Recall & Recognition	Neurocognitive Test & Embedded PVT	PVT interspersed throughout the battery
BVMT-R	Neurocognitive Test	
Sentence Repetition Test	Neurocognitive Test & Embedded PVT	PVT interspersed throughout the battery
Test of Premorbid Functioning	Neurocognitive Test	
Trail Making Test	Neurocognitive Test	
BVMT-R Recall & Recognition	Neurocognitive Test & Embedded PVT	PVT interspersed throughout the battery
Rey Complex Figure (Copy)	Neurocognitive Test	
MMPI-2-RF	Psychological Testing	SVT included

Note. PVT = Performance validity test; TOMM = Test of Memory Malingering; D-KEFS = Delis–Kaplan Executive Function System; WAIS = Wechsler Adult Intelligence Scale; HVLT-R = Hopkins Verbal Learning Test—Revised; BVMT-R = Brief Visuospatial Memory Test—Revised; MMPI-2-RF = Minnesota Multiphasic Personality Inventory–2-Restructured Form; SVT = Symptom Validity Test.

more difficult to detect underperformance if present (Suhr & Gunstad, 2007; Youngjohn, Lees-Haley, & Binder, 1999). Additionally, we recommend only emphasizing the need for valid performance before testing starts, as doing so during testing could have potential negative consequences. For example, in invalidly performing patients, providing a "reminder" that one needs to do their best suggests that you are aware that they are not doing their best. This could create a problem if the patient were to then improve their performance to the point that they are not identified by subsequent validity tests. Although one might consider it positive that the examinee has improved their performance in such a scenario, the clinician cannot be confident that subsequent data are valid just because the patient does not fail any further PVTs as the patient has now demonstrated the behavior of noncredible performance within the evaluation. Although it is possible that such a patient began to provide their "best effort" after the examiner's intervention, it is also possible that the patient improved their performance only to the point that they were not identified by further validity tests but not to a degree representative of their true capabilities. The clinician can never be certain (Youngjohn et al., 1999).

Encouragement to provide one's best after testing has commenced could have a negative impact when one is already providing their best performance as well. That is, if providing the "reminder" to perform at ones' best in the middle of testing to a validly participating patient, it might suggest to them that you think they are not doing their best and/or believe that they are doing poorly. This could lead to increased doubt in the test taker's mind, which might potentially impact the rapport or performance throughout the remainder of the evaluation.

While administering the test battery, a clinician can easily score many validity tests on the fly. As such, examiners will often know that validity tests are being failed within the test session, itself. When this occurs, one might wonder, "Do I continue administering testing or do I stop administering testing since it is invalid?" This is a good question regarding a topic for which practices and beliefs vary. Of neuropsychologists surveyed in 2015, 41% of respondents indicated that they often/always terminate the examination earlier than planned when invalidity is suspected, whereas a slight majority (i.e., 59%) indicated that they would rarely/never do so (Martin et al., 2015).

Although perspectives vary on the topic, our recommendation is to proceed with your planned test battery even after evidence of invalidity is provided by the patient. One reason to continue with the test battery even after performance validity indicators are failed is that some patients providing invalid performance will sometimes perform near or within normal ranges on some tests of genuine cognitive ability. In such cases, certain test results can *sometimes* help to answer referral questions, rule out certain cognitive impairments, and/or rule out certain diagnostic conditions despite the data, overall, being invalid.

There are several potential explanations as to why an individual who fails validity testing early in the evaluation might then provide normal or near-normal cognitive test performances. First, some clinical patients who invalidate testing might realize that it will take longer or require more mental effort to underperform throughout the entirety of the test battery and then revert to a performance that is less suppressed as the evaluation proceeds. For example, consider the examinee who comes up with the correct answer to items, suppresses that correct answer, and generates an incorrect answer that still seems believable, all while attempting to be consistent in their underperformance and feigned behaviors (e.g., frustrated facial expressions and statements such as "Doctor, I just don't remember seeing either item."). This is a lot of information to mentally juggle, especially over a sustained multihour period of time. As a result, *some* clinical patients will do better on testing as the evaluation progresses due to getting tired of expending significant effort to look impaired and/or wanting to finish testing more quickly. In some instances, we have seen patients flagrantly fail validity testing and then start performing within an average or higher range of functioning as testing continues. In addition to periodically (although somewhat uncommonly) seeing this in our clinical practice, research demonstrates that it occurs. For example, in a neuropsychological study where university students were asked to feign a brain injury, 68% of students reported that they found it difficult to maintain their feigning strategy throughout testing, and 48% reported altering their strategy at some point within the exam (Tan et al., 2002). The most frequently reported reasons were difficulty in maintaining concentration, trouble with maintaining consistent responses, issues with inhibiting wrong responses, and feeling embarrassed about giving incorrect responses. Thus, if a patient starts performing well as testing goes on, the results—while still invalid and still potentially an underestimate of their true ability—could, nonetheless, help to demonstrate that the patient is capable of performing within normal limits in those cognitive domains in which they do well, and the results could further help to rule out certain diagnostic conditions.

Another explanation for why some patients fail validity testing but score within or near normal ranges on testing of cognitive ability is the "point shaving" phenomenon. *Point shaving* is a term used to describe a sports player who is incentivized to underperform in a game, often because they are betting (or colluding with someone who is betting) against their own team. The sports player must perform just poorly enough that they throw the game in the direction of the wager but not so poorly that it is evident to others that they are intentionally "tanking" their performance.

In the same vein, a savvy examinee who is attempting to feign or exaggerate impairment might realize that, if they perform too poorly, their performance will not seem credible. Consequently, they might shave points in an effort to underperform just enough to demonstrate impairment with the aim of avoiding detection. Unfortunately for that examinee, a strength of many well-validated validity tests is that they are sensitive to even subtle attempts to underperform. For example, consider an examinee that approaches testing by thinking "I'll just try to be about 80% as accurate as what I'm capable." To the examinee, that 80% might still be a B–, which to the naïve test taker might not seem like a flagrant underperformance. With this reasoning, perhaps the examinee figures a B– on testing is just enough to show impairment but not enough to be identified as noncredible. What the examinee doesn't know, however, is that a B– on the TOMM (and other well-validated validity tests) would still provide a clear indication of invalidity (i.e., a score of 40). If the examinee applies the same B– approach to tests of genuine ability, such as Logical Memory of the Wechsler Memory Scale, their performance might still be near their expected "normal," which, again, would be helpful data in ruling out significant memory impairment even in the context of invalid data.

The possibility of such a phenomenon is demonstrated by a study by Martinez et al. (2021) in which individuals simulating malingering of traumatic brain injury were instructed to underperform on testing to a point that demonstrated impairment but not to such an extent that might alert the examiner to their deceptive performance. Although the simulators performed significantly worse than honestly performing controls on the TOMM and CVLT-II Forced Choice, they performed similarly on most subtests of the CVLT-II assessing genuine memory ability. In fact, of the simulators, 36% scored no worse than average and 73% scored no worse than low average on any of the examined CVLT-II indices. Such findings highlight that individuals who intentionally underperform but attempt to do so in a subtle manner to avoid detection might often produce average or near-average performance on some cognitive tests, supporting the "point shaving" phenomenon and, in our opinion, providing reason to administer the remainder of the test battery even when validity tests are failed.

Another advantage of completing the planned test battery, even after evidence of invalid performance is presented, is that further testing can often be helpful in identifying variability in performance. For example, it is not uncommon to see an invalidly performing clinical patient score within an exceptionally low range on some cognitive tests but within a low average range on other tests measuring the same cognitive ability. In this instance, the clinician might be able to use the variability in the performances to discuss the very low likelihood that the scores are due to a neurologically based condition. For example, consider a patient with a claimed mild traumatic brain injury. During feedback, the neuropsychologist could discuss that research indicates that individuals with a single uncomplicated concussion should not have significant persisting neurologically based cognitive impairment, reinforce that the patient's neuroimaging does not show findings of brain damage, discuss that significant variability in performance on tests measuring similar abilities is not consistent with genuine cognitive dysfunction, and then discuss that non-neurologic factors are likely at play. In another instance, consider that one is attempting to interpret PVT failures while also considering the possibility of dementia. Even if many scores are low, there might be instances of higher scores that assist in ruling out certain etiologies of dementia or even dementia altogether. Thus, even when testing is determined to be invalid early in the evaluation, data from the remainder of the test battery can sometimes be helpful in supporting diagnostic conclusions, ruling out conditions or significant impairment in certain domains, and communicating conclusions about the invalid nature of the data.

Finally, administering the entire test battery can often yield useful behavioral data. In some instances, behavioral observations might indicate why testing was invalid. For example, we have evaluated individuals who fell asleep during testing and, unsurprisingly, performed poorly and invalidly due to not being awake during the presentation of some stimuli. In other instances, though, behavioral observations might suggest that feigning occurred. Clinically, we have found that some patients who feign impairment state that easy tests (including PVTs) are very challenging, and/or somewhat dramatically report struggling to remember information or know the answers. Additionally, a number of individuals who feign impairment have been found to take an excessive amount of time to complete tests, including PVTs, whereas individuals who validly complete testing efficiently complete easy tasks. Consistent with our observations, Denning (2021) showed that excessive TOMM administration time predicted PVT performance. Relatedly, Tan and colleagues (2002) found that individuals instructed to malinger reported that feigning memory loss and performing slowly were the most frequently reported strategies. At the same time, other strategies were also reported (i.e., feigning poor concentration, confusion, nervousness, dyslexia, and lack of comprehension) and yet other individuals who were instructed to malinger did not use any particular strategy.

IDENTIFYING INVALIDITY

After neuropsychological testing has been completed, the clinician will have to come to a formal conclusion about whether the obtained test data provide an accurate picture of the examinee's functioning. In doing so, the clinician should look at a number of validity test-related outcomes. In addition to examining validity test outcomes, though, the clinician should also consider whether the findings are consistent with expectations that are relevant to the case. Furthermore, the clinician should consider whether any behavioral observations help to explain any of the findings. All of these topics are discussed in detail below.

Examining Validity Tests

Examining for Symptom Validity Test Failure

If SVTs were included within the neuropsychological evaluation, the SVTs should be examined. As noted in Chapter 6, various SVTs are available to help ensure that self-report of psychiatric, cognitive, and somatic symptoms is accurate. Typically, failure of any single SVT would warrant a conclusion of invalidity regarding the specific type of self-reported symptoms that the SVT measures (Sherman et al., 2020). For example, if an individual performed beyond appropriate cutoffs on an SVT assessing overreporting of psychiatric symptoms, the reported psychiatric symptoms should be considered invalid and exaggerated or feigned. If SVTs measuring other constructs (e.g., cognitive or somatic issues) are passed though, clinicians can generally interpret the obtained symptom report from those other constructs as being validly endorsed unless PVT data or extra test data suggest otherwise.

Two or More Performance Validity Test Failures as Criteria for Invalidity

As emphasized throughout this book, clinicians should administer multiple PVTs within the neuropsychological test battery. Practice trends indicate that it is not uncommon for North American neuropsychologists to utilize four to seven validity tests in clinical settings, and it is not uncommon for validity testing experts to utilize five to nine validity tests (Martin et al., 2024). If three or fewer PVTs are administered (which is not typical in North American practice and generally not recommended), failure of one of them could potentially signal that the test battery is invalid (Silk-Eglit, Stenclik, Miele, Lynch, & McCaffrey, 2015; Denning, 2023). If four to nine PVTs are administered, though, research indicates that failure of only one validity test could potentially be a false-positive finding (Davis & Millis, 2014; Larrabee, 2014; Schroeder, Martin, Heinrichs, & Baade, 2019; Silk-Eglit et al., 2015; Victor et al., 2009). For this reason, the cutoff for invalidity is *usually* defined as being failure of two or more PVTs when four to nine validity tests are administered (Victor et al., 2009; Davis & Millis, 2014; Larrabee, 2014). Preliminary research indicates that a cutoff of three PVT failures might be needed if 10 or more PVTs are administered and interpreted though (Larrabee, Rohling, & Meyers, 2019; Leese et al., in press).

Table 7.6 shows specificity rates based on the number of PVTs that are failed versus the number of PVTs that are administered, as reported in a study by Silk-Eglit et al. (2015). As demonstrated by these data, as the number of PVT failures increases, the associated specificity rate increases. Silk-Eglit and colleagues (2015), for example, found that when seven PVTs were administered to their sample of examinees, failure of one PVT resulted in a 63% specificity rate but failure of two PVTs resulted in a 92% specificity rate. It is important to note, though, that the data in Table 7.6 are from a single study, and the exact specificity rate findings are likely to vary to some degree based on the specificity rates of the individual PVTs that are utilized in clinical practice. That said, related research has demonstrated that specificity rates

TABLE 7.6. Specificity Rates Based on the Number of PVTs That Are Failed versus Administered

Number of PVTs administered	Failure of 1+	Failure of 2+	Failure of 3+	Failure of 4+	Failure of 5+	Failure of 6+	Failure of 7+
1	92%	—	—	—	—	—	—
2	92%	100%	—	—	—	—	—
3	92%	100%	100%	—	—	—	—
4	83%	100%	100%	100%	—	—	—
5	83%	96%	100%	100%	100%	—	—
6	79%	96%	96%	100%	100%	100%	—
7	63%	92%	96%	100%	100%	100%	100%

Note. Data from Silk-Eglit et al. (2015); similar specificity rates have been found in other publications (e.g., Davis & Millis, 2014; Larrabee, 2014; Pearson, 2009).

typically exceed 90% once two or more PVTs are failed within a multi-PVT battery (e.g., Davis & Millis, 2014; Larrabee, 2015; Victor et al., 2009). As previously noted, 90+% specificity is the recommended benchmark for setting cutoff values for individual PVTs, and the same benchmark can often be applied when determining invalidity in a multi-PVT battery (Sweet et al., 2021).

Increasing Confidence in PVT Findings and Minimizing False Positives

Clinicians should keep in mind the concept of positive predictive power (PPP) when interpreting validity test failures. As discussed in Chapter 4, PPP is influenced by both specificity and the suspected base rate of invalidity in the patient's population (e.g., clinical patients pursuing disability), and it refers to the likelihood that a determination of invalidity for the individual patient is accurate (as opposed to speaking to the overall accuracy of the test, which specificity does). If specificity for the validity assessment is just at or near 90% in a patient from a population where invalidity base rates are low (e.g., clinical evaluation with very low suspicion of an external incentive), PPP can be underwhelming, which entails a higher risk of a false-positive determination of invalidity. That said, it will be very helpful to keep in mind that specificity in many cases of validity test failure well exceeds the recommended 90% threshold and, that by considering several factors that increase both specificity and PPP, the clinician can, in many cases, have high confidence in their validity test findings.

First, the clinician should consider the number of validity test failures beyond just making a dichotomous determination of whether there are less than two versus two or more PVT failures. As seen in Table 7.6, Silk-Eglit et al. found that, whereas 90% specificity was achieved with two or more failures in their sample, 100% specificity was seen once an examinee failed three PVTs when five PVTs were administered or failed four PVTs when seven PVTs were administered. Similarly, Larrabee (2003) found that 100% specificity was achieved once three of five PVTs were failed; Victor et al. (2009) found that 99% specificity was achieved once three of four PVTs were failed; and Larrabee (2014) found that 100% specificity was achieved once four of seven PVTs were failed. This principle holds true even in samples of individuals with more significant cognitive impairment (e.g., dementia), presuming that appropriate cutoffs are utilized for the individual PVTs (Martin et al., 2022a). Thus, extant research demonstrates that as the number of PVT failures increases, so does specificity, and specificity likely approximates 100% once three to four PVTs are failed (at very least in a battery of eight or fewer PVTs). As 100% specificity entails 100% PPP regardless of the base rate of invalidity in the examinee's population, failure of three to four PVTs (again, in a battery of eight or fewer PVTs) can be interpreted with high confidence that performance is invalid regardless of the clinical setting and presence or absence of an external incentive to underperform.

In addition to examining how many PVTs are failed, it is also wise to look at the degree of any PVT failures. This is because an egregious validity test failure can be associated with a very high specificity rate. This means that as the degree of validity test failure increases, confidence that testing is invalid increases even if an individual fails only a single PVT. Table 7.7 illustrates an example of the principal that specificity (and therefore PPP) increases based on an increasing degree of PVT failure. As described in Chapter 4, a common cutoff score for TOMM Trial 2 is ≤44. In their mild traumatic brain injury (mTBI) sample, though, Greve et al. (2006) found that this cutoff score was associated with a 98% specificity rate. While this is already a very high specificity rate, a 100% specificity rate was demonstrated in their mTBI sample at a cutoff of ≤43. Similar to instances where high numbers of PVTs are failed, when a patient scores at or beyond a PVT cutoff that is associated with 100% specificity for their background and clinical condition, the clinician can be exceedingly confident that the PVT failure was not a false-positive finding given that no validly performing patient with a similar background and/or clinical condition produced scores that poorly.

Another approach for examining degree of failure is to compare a patient's PVT performance to samples of individuals with more severe impairment than could be reasonably suspected for that patient. For example, as previously discussed in this book, traditional cutoffs for many PVTs, while appropriate across many clinical populations, are often not appropriate in individuals suspected of severe cognitive impairment, such as seen in those with dementia. With that said, the PVT literature base in dementia samples continues to expand, which means that modified cutoff points have been empirically validated for many PVTs in patients with dementia (see for example, Dean et al., 2009; Martin et al., 2020; Schroeder et al., 2012). If a patient without dementia fails a PVT at a traditional cutoff value and the score is so low that it is beyond thresholds for valid performance even in individuals with dementia, the clinician can have even greater confidence that the performance is non-credible.

TABLE 7.7. Demonstration of How Specificity Rates Increase as Degree of Validity Test Failure Increases

TOMM Trial 2 score ≤	Mild TBI
49	85
48	93
47	96
46	98
45	98
44	98
43	100
42	100
41	100
40	100

Note. Data based on TOMM Trial 2 findings from Greve et al. (2006).

Take for example a 37-year-old patient being evaluated following a mTBI with an otherwise unremarkable health history who scores a 24 on the Dot Counting Test and 5 on Reliable Digit Span. Both scores would be considered invalid when applying the traditional cutoffs of ≥17 and ≤6, respectively. The patient's scores, though, are so poor that they would also be considered invalid even for an individual with dementia when utilizing data from Martin et al. (2022), which found both scores (i.e., Dot Counting Test of 24 and Reliable Digit Span of 5) to be associated with greater than 90% specificity in individuals with mild dementia. As the patient should not be suspected of having mild dementia or cognitive dysfunction at the level of mild dementia, comparing the patient's PVT results to such findings would allow for an even greater degree of evidence that the data are invalid.

Finally, clinicians should examine for below chance performance on any two-alternative forced choice tests administered. Although below chance findings occur infrequently, when they do occur, they provide unequivocal evidence of invalid performance. Two-alternative forced choice PVTs are ones in which an examinee must pick the correct answer from two possible options (the TOMM, for example, is a two-alternative forced choice PVT). Because there are only two options from which to choose, pure random guessing would result in a performance of approximately 50% correct (e.g., scoring 25 out of 50 on the TOMM). Sometimes (although not commonly; Greve et al., 2009b), individuals who feign issues do so to such an extreme degree that they produce scores that are statistically worse than chance (e.g., scoring 12 out of 50). Statistically worse than chance performances demonstrate that the examinee had more incorrect answers than can be explained by random guessing, indicating that they must have known the correct answers but chose to provide incorrect answers instead. It is for this reason that below chance performance on a forced choice PVT has been referred to as "the smoking gun of intent" (Binder & Chafetz, 2018; Pankratz & Erickson, 1990). When this degree of PVT failure occurs, the clinician can know without any degree of doubt that neuropsychological testing is invalid and that the invalid performance was produced intentionally.

When calculating below chance performance, it is important to do so correctly. Below chance performance is not simply a score that is less than 50% correct, as guessing can sometimes result in a performance that is slightly lower (or higher) than exactly ½ correct. For example, an individual could flip a coin 100 times and the coin might land on heads 46 times, 50 times, 54 times, etc. Because chance performance is not always exactly 50%, it is important to use statistical calculations to indicate when performances are so far below chance that they did not occur randomly, which typically involves calculating a binomial probability. Likely the easiest way to calculate below chance performance using binomial probabilities is to use a binomial calculator. There are multiple binomial calculators freely available online, such as one at VassarStats (*www.vassarstats.net/binomialX.html*).

For easy calculation, we will walk through using a binomial calculator (Table 7.8). This type of calculator will ask the clinician to enter the number of opportunities that were present (sometimes denoted by the lower case letter "n"). If using a test

TABLE 7.8. Example of a Binomial Calculator

Number of opportunities (*n*)	Number of successes (*k*)	Probability of success (*p*)
50	17	0.50
One-tailed outcome: 0.02 (rounded to the nearest hundredth)		
Two-tailed outcome: 0.03 (rounded to the nearest hundredth)		

such as TOMM Trial 1, the clinician would enter "50" because there were 50 items or opportunities for success on TOMM Trial 1. The clinician will also be asked to enter the number of times success was observed (sometimes denoted by the lower case letter "k"). If the examinee scored 17 items correct on TOMM Trial 1, the number 17 would be entered. Finally, the clinician will be asked for the probability of success (sometimes denoted by the lower case letter "p"). Because there is a 50% chance of getting each item correct, the value that would be entered would be 0.50 (i.e., 50%). The clinician can then have the calculator run the analysis.

The outcome of interest is the probability level (or p level) of the score occurring. In many early works discussing below chance PVT performance (e.g., Slick et al., 1999), a cutoff value of $p < .05$ was recommended for determining that a performance was statistically below chance, as this is the cutoff typically applied when testing a hypothesis and determining statistical significance in scientific research. However, Binder, Larrabee, and Millis (2014) argue that a cutoff of $p < .05$ is unnecessarily conservative for testing the hypothesis that a standardized forced-choice test score is below chance. They, instead, recommend using a p value of < .20, supporting this cutoff with empirical data showing that validly performing individuals do not perform at this level. Additionally, Binder et al. (2014) recommend that a one-tailed test of significance be examined when testing for below-chance performance on a forced-choice PVT because we are only interested in one tail of the distribution (i.e., examining whether the score is *below* chance).

Depending on the calculator that is used, a probability level for a one-tailed analysis, two-tailed analysis, or both one-tailed and two-tailed analyses will be displayed. In our example of a patient who scored 17/50 on a forced choice PVT (see Table 7.8), we would focus upon the one-tailed p level outcome which, in this case, is .02. The probability of .02 is well below .20, so the score of 17/50 would be considered statistically below-chance performance when using the .20 p level cutoff (and also if using the .05 level cutoff).

Considering the Potential for False-Positive Findings on PVTs

As noted at various points throughout this book, when considering PVT outcomes, the clinician must consider whether any PVT failure could be a false-positive finding. The process of minimizing the likelihood for false positives should begin when choosing which PVTs to utilize with the examinee (e.g., not administering a language-based

PVT when there is clearly a large left frontal stroke identified on imaging or not administering a PVT to someone with significant cognitive impairment when the PVT has only been validated with people who have minimal to no cognitive impairment). Considering false positives, though, is worth considering again when examining PVT findings. As previously noted in this book, conditions that have been linked to false-positive errors on some PVTs include dementia, intellectual disability, significant stroke, and frequent epileptic seizures with seizure activity occurring in close proximity of testing. Language and cultural factors have also been linked to false-positive findings on some PVTs. If a false-positive finding is believed to be present, that finding should not be counted as evidence of exaggerated or feigned symptomatology.

Examining for Consistency

While PVTs are necessary in determining whether cognitive testing is valid, each individual validity test typically emphasizes specificity over sensitivity (i.e., specificity rates are typically 90% or higher while sensitivity rates are often somewhere between only 20% and 70%). Because of this emphasis, a false-negative PVT finding (i.e., the PVT is passed in a patient providing invalid performance) is generally more likely to occur than a false-positive finding (i.e., the PVT is failed in a patient providing valid performance). Even when using multiple PVTs within the test battery, sensitivity is not 100% and negative predictive power (as mentioned in Chapter 4) can sometimes still be low. Therefore, it is possible that an individual who passes validity tests could still be invalidly completing testing, and this becomes even more likely if only a small number of validity tests is utilized and/or when an individual presents with circumstances that increase pretest odds (or base rates) for invalidity (e.g., the patient has an external incentive) due to the impact of base rates on negative predictive power. To help protect against the possibility of a false-negative finding, it is important to examine for data outside of PVTs (in addition to PVT data) such as consistencies within and between test results. Larrabee (1990, 2012a, 2022) has described a four-part model for analysis of consistency, which we will briefly review here.

One area of consistency analysis that Larrabee (2022) describes is termed *consistency of performance with behavior.* In short, a patient's cognitive test performances should not be discrepant with observed behaviors and abilities. Larrabee gives an example of an individual who can describe events from an accident, doctors, previous findings, and diagnoses, but that individual performs below the 5th percentile on all memory tests.

A second area of consistency analysis is termed *consistency of performance within and between domains of ability.* As an example of a "within domain" discrepancy, Larrabee (2022) discusses that individuals with true upper motor neuron findings typically perform worse on more challenging motor tests such as Grooved Pegboard than on easier motor tests such as Finger Tapping. When the opposite pattern emerges, this could potentially be due to an invalid test-taking performance. As an example of a "between domain" discrepancy, Larrabee discusses that individuals with true posttraumatic sequelae following significant brain injuries are likely to have worse memory functioning than attention functioning, and the opposite pattern might be seen in someone feigning a brain injury.

The third and fourth areas of consistency analysis described by Larrabee (2022) are similar in some ways. The third area is termed *consistency with established patterns for known disorders such as amnesia or dementia.* As an example of this, clinicians should not typically expect someone with dementia or a severe brain injury to perform above average on complex tasks that would be expected to be impacted by the neurologic disease or injury. The fourth area is termed *inconsistency between performance and injury severity (violation of the dose-response expectancy).* As an example of this, clinicians should not expect someone with a mild injury (e.g., mild traumatic brain injury) to perform at a similar or worse level than an individual with a more severe injury (e.g., severe traumatic brain injury).

If inconsistency emerges in one or more of the aforementioned areas, the validity of the examinee's presentation should be questioned even if PVTs and/or SVTs are passed. Survey data appear to reinforce this point, indicating that neuropsychologists appreciate that, in some cases, data cannot be viewed as credible even when validity tests are passed. Although findings from our recent survey (Martin et al., 2024) indicate that PVT results supersede clinical impressions in the majority of cases, both neuropsychologists and validity testing experts reported that they will conclude the examinee's presentation as noncredible in about 25% of cases where the examinee passes validity testing but the neuropsychologist's impressions are that the examinee otherwise presents noncredibly. This was a much greater percentage when compared to the inverse scenario (i.e., determinations of valid performance when the examinee fails validity testing when impressions are otherwise of a credible presentation).

Considering Behavioral Observations

Behavioral observations should not be used *in isolation* for determining whether testing is valid or invalid. This is because clinicians' predictions and judgments of validity status are more likely to be inaccurate when validity test outcomes are not considered (Dandachi-FitzGerald et al., 2015). Sometimes examinees can *appear* cooperative and/or motivated during testing yet still perform invalidly, and sometimes examinees might *appear* uncooperative and/or unmotivated during testing yet still might perform validly. At the same time, behavioral observations can *sometimes* be helpful when considering validity-related issues. For example, behavioral observations can periodically help to indicate why specific tests or the battery of tests are invalid despite the examinee passing validity tests. In other instances, behavioral observations might help to generate hypotheses as to why validity tests were failed. Thus, behavioral observations are an important factor to consider when determining validity status even if they should not be solely relied upon for making validity status conclusions.

Sometimes, examinees pass formal validity indicators but perform invalidly on one or two cognitive tests. This type of situation could occur for a variety of reasons. For one example, external stimuli might cause the examinee to lose focus on a task. External stimuli causing distractions could include things like a patient's cell phone ringing and/or vibrating in the middle of a test or loud noises occurring in the hallway outside of the exam room. As a second example, we have seen patients experience internal stimuli that cause them to lose focus of a task. Internal stimuli could include sudden onset shooting pains, distraction from needing to immediately use the restroom, or even sneezing (for example, in the middle of Digit Span being read). Furthermore, an examinee's physical issues might interfere with their ability to adequately perform some tests. Although such issues are ideally identified prior to testing, there can be instances where issues are not known when putting together the testing battery. An example of this could be when the examinee does not appear to have any physical ailments but, during testing, the individual makes a remark that manipulating the pencil, a finger tapper, or other test supply is challenging due to an old finger or hand injury. Regardless of the source of the issue, anytime that an external stimulus, internal stimulus, or other factor negatively impacts an individual's ability to perform a neuropsychological test in a manner that accurately reflects their cognitive capabilities, that specific test performance should be considered invalid and not interpreted (although not necessarily considered as evidence that the patient is, overall, approaching testing from a noncredible perspective).

As opposed to not performing to their best ability on one or two tests, examinees might sometimes pass validity tests, but they might not be performing to their best ability during the entirety of the test battery. This could occur due to the examinee experiencing issues during testing that prevent him or her from performing at his or her typical peak ability. For example, an individual could express that they are not functioning at their peak ability because they are exceptionally tired due to sleeping poorly or minimally the night before or due to experiencing substance withdrawal symptoms. Behavioral opposition could also negatively impact testing. As an example, an individual might perform testing adequately until tests become challenging. At that point, the examinee might refuse to try to complete the rest of the test. Comments such as "It's too hard, I don't even want to try." could signal this occurrence (although, of note, similar comments are sometimes provided by impaired individual who are unable to perform any additional test items).

Finally, patients might fail validity testing, and behavioral observations can sometimes help to explain why validity testing was failed. For example, an individual falling asleep during testing is an observation that would explain invalidity. Likewise, an individual refusing to actively engage in testing would be an explanation as to why testing was invalid. Furthermore, an individual who is actively attempting to portray himself as struggling to recall information when it is clear that he knows the information (e.g., as demonstrated by performing below chance) would strongly suggest that the individual is feigning cognitive impairment. Regardless of the scenario and PVT outcome, it is important to document behavioral observations and consider these observations when determining if an individual performed testing to the best of his or her ability.

Arriving at a Conclusion about Validity Status

After the testing session has been completed, the clinician will need to determine whether to ultimately deem testing valid or invalid. In doing so, the clinician should consider all of the data points discussed above. The neuropsychologist should examine PVT results to determine whether performance on cognitive testing can be considered valid. SVT results should be examined to determine whether findings from psychological testing, as well the patient's symptom self-report, are valid or biased by overreport, exaggeration, or underreport. Additionally, SVTs can sometimes provide context to cognitive test findings. As one example of this, failure of cognitively based SVTs should alert the clinician to carefully consider the patient's cognitive test performance given that such a finding would indicate that the patient is exaggerating or fabricating their reported cognitive symptoms. As another example, if a patient fails both PVTs and cognitively focused SVTs, it is highly likely that the patient's underperformance on cognitive testing was intentional as the examinee is *both* demonstrating invalidity during testing (as evidenced by the PVT failures) and reporting exaggerated or feigned cognitive symptoms via self-report (as evidenced by the SVT failures). With that said, not all individuals who exaggerate, feign, or malinger cognitive symptoms fail both PVTs and SVTs (De Boer et al., 2023; Ord et al., 2021; Van Dyke, Millis, Axelrod, & Hanks, 2013), so failure of both types of validity tests should not be considered necessary for concluding that testing is invalid (Sweet et al., 2021).

Table 7.9 provides a summary of points that have been discussed in relation to determining if cognitive testing is valid, with information written in the form of questions that a clinician could ask oneself. If *any* of the first three questions are answered "yes," testing should typically be considered invalid unless there are strong reasons to believe that the validity test failure(s) is/are a false-positive finding (see Question 4). In addition to asking the first four questions, Questions 5 and 6 should also be considered. If testing is already deemed invalid, positive responses to either of these latter questions can potentially provide additional qualitative evidence of invalidity and possibly even assist in conceptualizing the invalidity. If validity testing is considered "passed," yet significant atypical inconsistencies and/or behavioral observations strongly suggestive of invalidity are present, the clinician should consider the degree and level of clinical confidence in such qualitative findings. In some cases, significant inconsistencies and observations might necessitate a more cautious approach to interpreting the test data or even be sufficient to consider the test data invalid. That said, since research indicates that objective validity tests are more accurate than a clinician's subjective appraisal of observations and cognitive test results (Dandachi-FitzGerald et al., 2017; Faust et al., 1988; Heaton et al., 1978), such inconsistencies and observations will need to be starkly compelling to determine data invalid in cases where formal validity testing is passed.

TABLE 7.9. Questions to Consider When Determining If Cognitive Testing Is Invalid

Information from PVTs:
1. Is there failure of at least two PVTs when four to nine are administered (and appropriate cutoffs are used)?
2. If there is failure of only one PVT, is that failure so extreme that there is a 100% specificity rate for individuals with similar clinical conditions?
3. Are any PVTs failed at below chance level?
PVT failure rule-out question:
4. Are there any strong reasons to believe that the validity test failure(s) is/are a false-positive finding?
Information from sources outside of validity tests:
5. Are there significant atypical inconsistencies that strongly suggest cognitive test invalidity?
6. Are there significant behavioral observations that strongly suggest cognitive test invalidity?

CLOSING REMARKS

It is now clear that multiple validity tests should be interspersed throughout the neuropsychological test battery. Neuropsychologists report that they, on average, administer five PVTs in their clinical evaluations of nongeriatric adults. This includes a mixture of both stand-alone and embedded validity tests. Multiple recommendations for choosing validity tests and building the test battery have been provided. At the beginning of the testing session, it is typically recommended that clinicians re-emphasize the importance of the patient performing to his or her best ability. It is not recommended that the clinician provide additional information beyond this, as doing so is not often beneficial, and can even be harmful. If a patient fails validity testing, the clinician could choose to abbreviate the rest of the test battery; however, there are benefits in continuing with the battery largely as originally planned. After testing is completed, the clinician should consider validity test performances, examine for consistency, and consider behavioral observations when arriving at a formal conclusion regarding validity status. Cognitive test results should also be reviewed but, when validity testing is failed, the clinician must keep in mind that any and/or all scores might underrepresent the patient's true capability.

CHAPTER 8

Accurately Interpreting and Conceptualizing Noncredible Findings

As neuropsychologists, we are typically tasked not only with administering and interpreting tests but also relating these results to a human condition. When testing reveals cognitive impairment, we ask, "What is the cause of the cognitive impairment?" When a patient endorses significant depression, we ask, "What diagnostic condition best explains the report of depression?" or, "What personality, medical, historical, or psychosocial issues might be contributing to the depression?" Similarly, when testing is determined to be invalid, a logical follow-up is to ask, "Why are the data invalid?"

Sometimes when testing is invalid, the cause of the invalidity is unknown and will remain unknown. In other cases, however, the cause of invalidity might be suspected, strongly suspected, or even seemingly obvious. In these latter cases, some neuropsychologists might communicate the suspected cause of invalidity to the patient and/or referring providers. Conversely, other neuropsychologists might choose to refrain from communicating the suspected cause of invalidity to others.

There are several reasons why a clinician might refrain from drawing and communicating conclusions about the cause of the invalidity.

1. Although validity testing can provide objective and, in many cases, unequivocal evidence that data are invalid, validity test findings do not, in and of themselves, reveal the cause of invalidity. Determining the cause of invalidity requires some degree of inference on part of the clinician, and, even when the cause appears apparent and its determination follows well-crafted decision rules (e.g., criteria from Sherman et al. [2020]), speaking to cause could potentially result in others viewing the determination of invalidity as being less objective and empirically determined than is the case.
2. Most often, the person in the evaluation who has the most accurate

understanding of why the testing was invalid is the patient. However, patient explanations of why testing was invalid should not be relied upon given that failed validity testing implies the possibility that the patient is being deceptive. Therefore, asking patients why performance or symptom report was noncredible often cannot lead to confident conclusions.

3. In many cases, labeling the suspected cause of invalidity is unlikely to yield much benefit above and beyond simply stating that testing is invalid.
4. Discussing suspected causes of the invalidity is more likely to interfere with further treatment efforts and lead to negative outcomes.

For the aforementioned reasons, we typically refrain from overtly communicating a cause of invalidity to patients and referring clinical providers. Nonetheless, we believe that it is important for neuropsychologists to conceptualize invalid findings in their patients in a manner that is evidence based. Therefore, clinicians need to be aware of factors that increase risk for invalidity as well as explanations that should be avoided because of their lack of scientific support. In a recent survey, we asked both neuropsychologists and validity testing experts how often invalid test findings were due to various factors within clinical settings (survey takers were asked to use a 7-pont Likert scale ranging from "never" to "always"; Martin et al., 2024). As seen in Tables 8.1 and 8.2, differences emerged between the perspective of neuropsychologists and validity testing experts, both with regard to the rank of mean response as well as the median response. In the following sections, we discuss findings from the neuropsychological literature base, which indicates that some of the explanations of invalidity that neuropsychologists use are well supported, whereas other explanations are not. We have broken down these explanations as being "credible" and "noncredible" ones.

TABLE 8.1. Neuropsychologists' Perceptions of How Frequently Various Factors Cause Invalidity in Clinical Settings

	Rank	Median
Somatization	1	Somewhat frequent
Attitude toward testing	2	Somewhat frequent
Depression/anxiety	3	Somewhat frequent
Cry for help	4	Somewhat frequent
Physical factors	5	Somewhat frequent
Malingering	6	Infrequent
Conversion disorder	7	Infrequent
Factitious disorder	8	Infrequent

Note. Survey data from Martin et al. (2024).

TABLE 8.2. Experts' Perceptions of How Frequently Various Factors Cause Invalidity in Clinical Settings

	Rank	Median
Malingering	1	Frequent
Somatization	2	Somewhat frequent
Attitude Toward Testing	3	Somewhat frequent
Factitious Disorder	4	Infrequent
Depression/Anxiety	6	Very infrequent
Physical Factors	5	Very infrequent
Conversion Disorder	7	Infrequent
Cry for Help	8	Never

Note. Survey data from Martin et al. (2024).

NONCREDIBLE EXPLANATIONS OF INVALIDITY

In this section, we discuss several posited explanations for invalidity that are not supported by empirical literature but are used by some clinicians in clinical practice. It is our suspicion that some clinicians use these explanations because they are unaware of the literature that indicates that the explanations are noncredible ones, and the explanations *seem* logical in some cases. In other instances, though, some of these explanations might be used because they provide a more palatable explanation of invalidity for patients and clinicians as they directly attribute invalidity to clinical conditions or sympathetic circumstances of the patient. Regardless, the reader should be aware of the literature (discussed below) that suggests that these particular explanations are not credible ones for the vast majority of invalid test takers.

Depression and Anxiety

As patients referred for clinical neuropsychological evaluations typically present with symptoms of cognitive and/or psychological disorders, clinician's might be tempted to explain invalid performance as being the result of either cognitive or psychological dysfunction. As discussed throughout the book, although significant cognitive impairment (as seen in dementia) can cause individuals to perform beyond traditional cutoffs on some performance validity tests, the same is generally not true for most psychiatric presentations, particularly depression and anxiety. Nonetheless, some neuropsychologists appear to attribute invalid performance to depression and anxiety with some regularity. As seen in Table 8.1, surveyed neuropsychologists, overall, rank depression and anxiety as being the third most frequent cause of invalidity in clinical settings, and, on average, believe depression and anxiety to "somewhat frequently" be the cause of invalid test performance. By comparison, surveyed validity assessment experts, on average, report depression and anxiety to "very infrequently" be the cause of invalidity in clinical settings (Table 8.2).

The discrepancy in perspective between neuropsychologists and validity testing experts perhaps relates to differing degrees of knowledge regarding validity testing literature, which falls on the side of expert opinion, consistently demonstrating that depression and anxiety do not cause invalid test performance. It has been discussed throughout this book that the foundational premise of many PVTs is that they are easy enough to be passed by individuals in most clinical contexts, except by those with significant cognitive dysfunction. Green and Merten (2013) make the point that research indicates that individuals with depression and anxiety who are screened for valid performance do not demonstrate significant cognitive dysfunction and, therefore, such patients are not expected to fail performance validity tests for these conditions. Beyond this logical assertion, however, the most robust evidence that PVTs should not be failed because of depression and anxiety comes from a large body of empirical research showing that PVT specificity values in depression and anxiety patient samples are consistently above 90% and generally in line with findings from healthy controls. Marshall and Schroeder (2022) provide an extensive review, including 18 studies of individuals with depression and anxiety who were administered a wide variety of both stand-alone and embedded PVTs. All samples performed above traditional PVT cutoffs at >90% specificity, including samples of individuals with significant depression. This included, for example, a sample of psychiatric inpatients with severe major depression (Guilmette, Hart, Giuliano, & Leininger, 1994) and a sample of inpatients with moderate to severe depression (average hospital stay was 6 weeks) in which nearly 40% had a history of electroconvulsive therapy (Rees, Tombaugh, & Boulay, 2001).

With that literature summarized, it should be noted that some neuropsychologists might have noticed in clinical practice that patients with psychiatric disorders fail validity testing more often than other patients, such as those with clear organic disorders. Given this observation, clinicians might make the assumption that it is the psychiatric condition that is responsible for the invalid performance and, therefore second guess the research findings or feel that their patients are exceptions to the research findings. While such an association between psychiatric conditions and invalidity may be true in some clinical settings, we caution the clinician from making inferences about cause and effect (i.e., correlation is not causation). Invalidity, when seen in someone with a psychiatric condition, is much more likely to be due to other "credible" explanations such as a hidden external incentive linked to malingering, conversion or somatoform issues, factitious features, or an oppositional attitude toward testing. In any case, except for special instances where an individual is observably so markedly distraught, anxious, or profoundly depressed that they can't maintain engagement with testing, clinicians should avoid using depression or anxiety as explanations of invalidity given that it is not evidence based and, on the contrary, stands in the face of extant neuropsychological research.

Cry for Help

The cry for help explanation of invalidity and symptom exaggeration was initially proposed as an explanation for elevations on the F scale of the Minnesota Multiphasic Personality Inventory (Dahlstrom, Welsch, & Dahlstrom, 1972). The theory was that some patients exaggerate symptoms simply because they are in distress and want to ensure that the distress is recognized by the clinician so that they receive treatment for their symptoms. The cry for help theory, however, is not currently perceived as a valid explanation for invalidity by validity testing experts: surveyed experts, on average, view a cry for help as "never" being the cause for invalidity (Table 8.2). According to the same survey data, general clinicians, however, appear to view the cry for help explanation as being relatively more plausible in clinical settings. Although surveyed neuropsychologists, on average, regarded invalid testing as being due to a cry for help "somewhat infrequently," a not insignificant minority noted invalidity being due to a cry for help either "somewhat frequently" or "frequently" (Table 8.1).

If it were true that individuals who present noncredibly do so in an attempt to optimize their likelihood to receive treatment or some other form of clinical assistance, one would expect individuals who fail validity testing to be particularly engaged in treatment following their evaluations. Yet, research shows the opposite to be true. Greene (1988) found that patients overreporting on the MMPI stayed in treatment for significantly less time than patients responding validly and that one-third to one-half of invalid patients stayed in treatment for only a single session. Moore et al. (2013) found that individuals with schizophrenia who performed poorly on a validity index embedded within the Repeatable Battery for the Assessment of Neuropsychological Status had poorer treatment adherence than individuals who performed well on the validity index. Finally, Goedendorp, van der Werf, Bleijenberg, Tummers, and Knoop (2013) found that patients with chronic fatigue who failed the Amsterdam Short-Term Memory Test dropped out of a study on cognitive behavioral therapy at higher rates than those who passed. These studies do not support the theory that patients invalidate testing as a cry for help in order to receive treatment. Instead, the opposite appears to be the case: those that fail validity are less likely to have a genuine interest in treatment than those who present credibly.

While research does not support the theory of a cry for help as a valid explanation for invalidity within a treatment seeking context, Young (2019) argued that the concept for cry for help should be extended beyond one's efforts to secure placement in psychotherapy. He stated that "the cry for help in the assessment and testing context might not be to get psychotherapy, but just to get attention, and be heard." He also argued that "the cry for help is part and parcel of the reaction to trauma, pain, and related disorders, potentially leading to its expression in the psychiatric forensic disability evaluation and related context." Also, within this article, Dr. Young presented a six-item scale to measure cry for help, which includes items such as "the situation is unbearable and is worsening how I feel" and "no one is giving me the help I need or cares, and I'm getting worse because of it."

Dandachi-FitzGerald, Merckelback, and Merten (2022) provided a three-pronged argument against Dr. Young's expanded conceptualization of the cry for help explanation, though. First, they noted that the "cry for help is a metaphor with no explanatory depth," and they illustrated that in many cases of malingering or factitious disorder one could make the argument that exaggeration or feigning overlaps with a cry for help explanation. Second, they demonstrated that a cry for help explanation is difficult to operationalize. The authors conducted a study using the cry for help rating scale proposed by Dr. Young. They found that when applied to two different vignettes, one describing a case of malingering and a second being a vignette proposed as depicting a cry for help, psychologists' and trainees' ratings on Dr. Young's cry for help scale did not vary between the vignettes. Finally, they noted that the cry for help explanation is nonscientific as it is nonfalsifiable and could theoretically be stamped on any case of invalidity.

Like Dandachi-FitzGerald et al. (2022), it is our perspective that clinicians should avoid attributing an invalid presentation to being a cry for help because the theory is not evidence based and, when applied, often ignores more plausible, direct, diagnostically sound, and research-supported explanations. It can be tempting to explain away noncredibility using the cry for help framework particularly when patients present with sympathetic circumstances or when they appear to present with true emotional distress; however, as discussed by Dandachi-FitzGerald et al. (2022) such factors do not obviate the presence of causal factors that are empirically supported and coded by the *Diagnostic and Statistical Manual of Mental Disorders, 5th Edition* (DSM-5) (e.g., malingering, factitious disorder). In reference to Young's (2019) expanded definition of a cry for help and resultant clinical scale, factors suggesting a cry for help overlap considerably with Rogers' adaptational model of malingering (1990), which Rogers found to be the most prototypical explanation of malingering in clinical settings (Rogers, Salekin, Sewell, Goldstein, & Leonard, 1998). Components of Rogers' adaptational model of malingering include a cost-benefit analysis and the presence of adversarial circumstances, the latter including the subcomponents of "coping with a bad situation" and "trying to meet needs in an unsympathetic situation," which are nearly identical to items on Dr. Young's cry for help scale.

As Roger's (1990) model demonstrates, an individual who volitionally invalidates testing in the presence of true suffering, which they then hope to alleviate by obtaining an award of an external incentive is, nonetheless, malingering. Take for example, an individual who finds regular employment to be untenable and the cause of genuinely appreciated pain (emotional or physical), who then feigns cognitive impairment with the goal of being awarded SSDI benefits. Such an individual is crying for help, perhaps seeking the support of their society because they believe that working is too difficult for them. Although such individuals may have sympathetic reasons for exaggerating their symptoms, the behavior is best conceptualized as malingering as the individual is exaggerating or feigning symptoms in their pursuit of an external incentive. Similarly, individuals with factitious disorder can be said to be making a cry for help as they are exaggerating their symptoms to receive attention and/or support from their doctors or loved ones; however, many individuals who seek attention and support from their clinical providers and loved ones do not exaggerate or falsify their symptoms. Thus, it is the falsification of symptoms that defines the test performance, not the desire for help, which makes the cry for help theory a poor explanation for invalidity.

Physical Factors

Various physical factors such as pain, fatigue, and medication effects have been proposed as possible causes of invalidity. Once again, surveyed validity testing experts view such explanations as noncredible in most cases, rating these physical factors as being "very infrequent" causes of invalidity (Table 8.2). Conversely, a general sample of neuropsychologists rated pain, fatigue, and medication effects as being relatively more plausible causes of invalidity in clinical evaluations, noting that, on average, physical factors are a "somewhat frequent" cause of invalidity (Table 8.1).

The extant literature, however, does not support the belief that physical factors can commonly lead to invalid test performance. For example, research indicates that pain is not related to high PVT failure rates so long as incentives to underperform are not present. Gervais et al. (2001) found that 35% of examinees with fibromyalgia failed validity testing when external incentives were present but only 4% failed when external incentives were absent. Likewise, Greve, Bianchini, Etherton, Ord, and Curtis (2009) found that once malingering is excluded, chronic pain patients demonstrate low false-positive PVT failure rates. In studies by Etherton, Bianchini, Greve, and Ciota (2005b) and Etherton, Bianchini, Ciota, and Greve (2005a), research volunteers subjected to acute pain passed both stand-alone or embedded PVTs at rates typical of other validly performing clinical and healthy control samples. These studies provide compelling evidence that pain should typically not cause one to invalidate testing. Likely the only exception would be if a patient is in such severe pain that it is obvious that they are not well engaged in the testing process.

The hypothesis that medication effects (or side effects) might lead to invalidity was initially supported by a study by Loring and colleagues (2011), which reported that 21% of healthy adults who were administered 2 mg of lorazepam failed the Word Memory Test (WMT). Green and Merten (2013) disagreed with the conclusion that lorazepam administration caused WMT failure, though. They, instead, argued that the most likely explanation for the findings was poor motivation to do well by research participants. They arrived at this conclusion by noting that (1) two individuals in the study failed the WMT validity indices when administered a placebo and one individual later dropped out of the study, and (2) three individuals who failed the WMT did not produce a genuine memory impairment profile, suggesting cognitive dysfunction from lorazepam was not the reason for the PVT failure. Providing further support that participants in the Loring et al. study (2011) failed validity testing due to low motivation as opposed to medication side effects, Rohling (2013) reanalyzed the original Loring et al. dataset examining additional validity indicators, including those that were administered at baseline (before lorazepam was administered). He found that almost 40% of participants in the study failed validity indicators even when not administered lorazepam.

Other literature further suggests that sedating medications, such as antipsychotics and opioid medications, generally do not cause invalid performance. In a study by Schroeder and Marshall (2011), only 7% of patients with psychotic disorders (most of whom were on antipsychotic medications) failed two or more out of seven PVTs. Similarly, in a meta-analysis of PVT performance in individuals with psychotic disorders, Ruiz, Raugh, Bartolomeo, and Strauss (2020) found that the use of antipsychotic medications was not a significant moderating variable for PVT failure. Finally, Dorociak, Schulze, Piper, Molokie, and Janacek (2018) examined PVT performance in a sample of patients with sickle cell disease in which 94% of patients were taking at least one opioid pain medication and 33% took an opioid pain medication on the day of the neuropsychological evaluation. Despite the high use of opioid medications in the sample, high false-positive rates were not seen on embedded or stand-alone PVTs. Thus, when considering this research, collectively, medication effects do not appear to be a likely cause of invalidity. Anecdotally, this is in agreement with what we generally see clinically (obvious exceptions are when patients are so sedated by medication that they cannot meaningfully engage in the evaluation). That is, although we commonly evaluate patients taking narcotic, anxiolytic, or other sedating medications, such patients do not appear to fail PVTs at elevated rates so long as other factors associated with a high degree of PVT failure are not present.

Finally, while few carefully conducted validity assessment studies on fatigue and sleepiness have been conducted, research suggests that invalid performance should not be expected in cases of fatigue or sleepiness (assuming that obvious sleepiness, such as a patient falling asleep during testing, is not present). For example, in the aforementioned study by Dorociak et al. (2018), one-third of the sample reported significant daytime sleepiness. Yet, 98% of the sample passed Test of Memory Malingering (TOMM) Trial 2 at a cutoff of 45 and PVT performance did not correlate with scores on the Epworth Sleepiness Scale. Similarly, in a sample of patients with fibromyalgia who were administered the TOMM, Kaflon, Gal, Shorer, and Ablin (2016) found that TOMM scores were not correlated with fatigue, pain, or depression, and that patients failing the TOMM did not differ from those who passed the TOMM on ratings of fatigue, pain, or depression.

Apathy

While the North American neuropsychologist survey (Martin et al., 2024) did not ask about apathy as an explanation for invalid test performance (hence it is not listed in Tables 8.1 or 8.2), a brief discussion about apathy is warranted. Bigler (2015) has argued that individuals with apathy might fail performance validity tests due to being unable to invest effort or interest into testing. Paul et al. (2005) did not directly assess this question, but they did conduct a study that relates to it. They found that apathy scores did not differentiate individuals with human immunodeficiency virus who passed versus failed Trial 1 of the TOMM. In another study, Martínez-Horta, Pagonabarraga, De Bobadilla, Garcia-Sanchez, and Kulisevsky (2013) found that there were no differences on Trial 1 of the TOMM between Parkinson's disease patients with and without apathy. Finally, Dandachi-FitzGerald, Duits, Leentjens, Verhey, and Ponds (2020) found that PVT failure was associated with cognitive impairment in a sample of individuals with Parkinson's disease, mild cognitive impairment, or dementia, but PVT failure was not associated with degree of apathy. These studies all suggest that apathy should not typically cause PVT failures to occur.

AACN Validity Assessment Consensus Statement Conclusions Regarding Noncredible Explanations

Despite some neuropsychologists' perspective that factors such as depression, anxiety, pain, medication effects, fatigue, and the voicing of a cry for help can be plausible causes of invalidity in clinical settings, the empirical literature indicates otherwise. Surveyed validity assessment experts also tend to view such factors as generally poor explanations for invalid performance, and the American Academy of Clinical Neuropsychology (AACN) consensus statement on validity assessment agrees. Specifically, within the AACN consensus statement, it is stated that "Empirical research currently does not support interpretation of multiple PVT failures as due to depression, anxiety, pain, fatigue, medication effects, or other putative conditions that might inaccurately be used to minimize or explain away PVT findings" (Sweet et al., 2021, p. 1069).

CREDIBLE EXPLANATIONS FOR INVALIDITY

The following section discusses explanations for validity test failure for which there is more robust research support. Thus, these possible explanations for invalid performance are considered to be credible and empirically supported.

Severe Cognitive Dysfunction

As discussed throughout this book, individuals with severe cognitive dysfunction can perform beyond traditional cutoffs on various PVTs, not due to invalid performance, but due to their significant cognitive impairments. In this vein, it can be said that severe cognitive dysfunction can be a credible cause of failure on some PVTs, but this does not necessarily mean that it is accurate to say that significant cognitive dysfunction causes invalidity. Determinations of invalidity should be made only after considering whether validity test findings are false-positive ones, which presupposes that the PVTs and PVT cutoffs used have been deemed appropriate in light of the patient's clinical condition and possibility of severe cognitive impairment (as well as other important factors, such as language proficiency for some PVTs). When performance on traditional PVTs and PVT cutoffs are beyond customary thresholds for valid performance, the clinician should double check to ensure that the failures are not due to severe cognitive impairment (having first considered this when composing the PVT battery).

Attitude toward Testing

In some cases, individuals might provide less than their best effort, but this might not be for the explicit purpose of exaggerating or feigning symptoms. For example, an individual might simply provide poor effort because he or she does not want to be present at the evaluation. Alternatively, an individual might be uncooperative, oppositional, or even hostile during testing due to factors such as poor self-control. Additionally, a patient might willfully exaggerate or feign their symptoms, but do so to "play," outsmart, or harass his or her doctor. In such cases, assuming that other conditions such as factitious disorder or malingering are ruled out, it could very well be that the invalidity is due to the examinee's attitude toward testing.

When it comes to empirical evidence for attitude toward testing as a cause of invalidity, possibly the greatest evidence comes from studies with healthy research volunteers where there is (1) little incentive to perform well and (2) incentive to finish testing as quickly as possible. In a study of 120 undergraduate students administered seven PVTs over a 2-hour battery, An, Kaploun, Erdodi, and Abeare (2017) found that 10% failed one or more stand-alone PVTs, 31% failed one or more embedded PVTs, and 7% failed two or more PVTs (all PVT cutoffs were using liberal cutoffs). In a similar study, aptly titled "I just want my research credit: Frequency of suboptimal effort in a non-clinical healthy undergraduate sample," DeRight and Jorgensen (2015) found that 10% of the sample demonstrated poor effort, and students who were tested in the morning were more likely to fail validity indicators than those tested in the afternoon. Given that these samples were comprised of healthy controls without external or internal incentives, such PVT failures cannot be attributed to significant cognitive dysfunction, malingering, or other factors outside of attitude toward testing. Finally, as noted in Tables 8.1 and 8.2, surveyed neuropsychologists and validity assessment experts agree that attitude toward testing is a "somewhat frequent" cause of invalidity in clinical settings, ranking it as the second and third most likely cause, respectively.

Somatization and Conversion Disorder

Both North American neuropsychologists and validity testing experts rated somatization as being a "somewhat frequent" cause of invalidity in clinical evaluations, whereas conversion disorder was rated as being an "infrequent" cause by both neuropsychologists and experts (Tables 8.1 and 8.2). In a separate survey of North American neuropsychologists (Martin & Schroeder, 2020), we asked providers how often they believe "patients with somatoform disorder, conversion disorder, or medically unexplained symptoms" invalidate testing in clinical contexts. The median result was an estimated base rate of 50%, which was even higher than base rates associated with individuals who had possible external incentives. These data suggest that clinicians fairly frequently believe that individuals with various somatic symptom and related disorders (SSRD) invalidate testing in clinical settings.

With regard to this topic, Graver and Boone (2022) note that "clinical experience indicates that patients with SSRD, as a group, report an excessive number of symptoms, including cognitive symptoms on interview, despite their often relatively normal neuropsychological testing (Boone, 2017). . . . However, a subset of patients with SSRD, particularly those with diagnoses of conversion disorder, obtain lowered scores on neuropsychological testing, raising questions as to whether they are in fact performing to true ability" (pp. 360–361). In addition to noting their clinical experience, Graver and Boone comprehensively reviewed the empirical literature. In brief, they note that the literature indicates a subset of credibly performing individuals with SSRD fail select PVTs. Specifically, they report that credibly performing individuals with SSRD fail processing speed PVTs (e.g., b Test and Dot Counting Test) at high rates, although they tend to only score mildly beyond standard cutoffs. Additionally, motor speed, motor strength, and/or tactile sensory-based PVTs (e.g., Finger Tapping Test embedded PVT) might be failed at high rates by non-malingering individuals with SSRD.

Interestingly, when Graver and Boone (2022) reviewed the empirical literature on memory-based PVTs, they found that individuals with somatoform/pain (e.g., fibromyalgia) tend to fail these PVTs at high rates (24 to 56%) when evaluated within the context of external incentives, but they fail these PVTs at much lower rates (~10%) when external incentives are not present. Thus, it is possible that some individuals with SSRD who fail PVTs (particularly processing speed, motor, or sensory-based PVTs) may be doing so secondary to self-deception related to their clinical condition (Boone, 2017) but others who fail PVTs (particularly if the failures are well beyond PVT cutoffs and/or are on memory-based PVTs) may be consciously exaggerating or feigning impairment in addition to having an SSRD. Put another way, while individuals with an SSRD might fail validity testing at high rates in some instances, this does not rule out the possibility that other factors, including malingering, might also be at play when validity testing is failed in some contexts.

Factitious Disorder

Individuals who meet criteria for factitious disorder, by definition, intentionally attempt to deceive their health care providers, not for the purpose of an external incentive as would indicate malingering, but for the purpose of an internal incentive, typically related to obtaining nontangible benefits linked to assuming a sick role (American Psychiatric Association, 2000; American Psychiatric Association, 2022). The research on base rates and validity test performance in individuals with factitious disorder is quite limited. Nonetheless, given that factitious disorder entails a volitional attempt to exaggerate or feign symptoms, the impact on PVT performance in individuals purporting cognitive symptoms would presumably be similar to that of malingering. That is, although the motivation for exaggeration or feigning is different in individuals who are malingering than those with factitious disorder, both are at risk for underperforming on neuropsychological testing in an attempt to demonstrate that their cognitive functioning is worse than is actually the case (Chafetz, Bauer, & Haley, 2020). To this point, Rogers, Bagby, and Vincent (1994a) found that individuals with factitious disorder responded similarly to individuals who were malingering, with both groups of individuals producing an elevated rate of scores suggestive of invalidity. Although surveyed neuropsychologists and validity testing experts viewed factitious disorder as being an "infrequent" cause of invalidity in clinical settings (Tables 8.1 and 8.2), this perhaps relates to suspected base rates of factitious disorder being quite low. Nonetheless, as factitious disorder can involve the deliberate manipulation of clinical data for the purpose of deceiving health care providers, it is a credible explanation of invalidity that should be considered, especially when no external incentives are present and/or the patient appears to be seeking undue attention, care, and/or nurturance for their symptoms.

Malingering

Many of the early performance validity tests were developed for the purpose of detecting malingering, and much of the initial PVT research examined the ability of PVTs to distinguish between suspected malingerers and nonmalingerers. With time, though, it became appreciated that examinees can fail PVTs for reasons other than malingering and that PVT failure, while indicative of noncredible performance, does not reveal the motivation behind the noncredible performance. With this understanding, as well as the increasing utilization of PVTs in nonforensic evaluations, there has been an effort to dissociate the concepts of PVT failure and malingering (Sweet et al., 2021). Despite this important evolution in the conceptualization of invalid neuropsychological test performance, malingering does occur, certainly in forensic evaluations, but also in clinical evaluations. Although surveyed neuropsychologists, overall, perceive malingering as being an "infrequent" cause of invalidity in nonforensic clinical settings, the same perspective is not true of surveyed validity testing experts who view malingering as being (1) a "frequent" cause of invalidity in nonforensic clinical evaluations and (2) the *most* frequent cause of invalidity in clinical settings, overall (Tables 8.1 and 8.2).

As discussed elsewhere in this book, both empirical studies and survey research indicate that the likelihood for invalidity within clinical settings is typically greatest when external incentives are present (Martin & Schroeder, 2020; Schroeder, Clark, & Martin, 2022; Shura et al., 2022a; Sweet et al., 2021). Even when external incentives are not known to be present, though, malingering can still occur as research indicates that external incentives are not always disclosed to the examiner (Chafetz et al., 2011; Schroeder et al., 2022; Van Egmond et al., 2005). Thus, although malingering is typically viewed as a topic of salience in forensic evaluations, it is also an important topic of consideration in clinical evaluations, especially when patients present with external incentives and/or when validity testing is failed. Because malingering is a realistic factor that can cause invalidity in clinical settings, because experts note that it is the most frequently suspected cause of invalidity in clinical settings, and because malingering can sometimes be a controversial conclusion, the following section is devoted to discussing nuances of malingering within clinical settings.

MORE ON MALINGERING

Malingering: What It Is and What It Isn't

Malingering has been defined in various sources. The *Diagnostic and Statistical Manual of Mental Disorders, 5th Edition, Text Revision* (DSM-5-TR; American Psychiatric Association, 2022) states that "The essential feature of malingering is the intentional production of false or grossly exaggerated physical or psychological symptoms, motivated by external incentives" (p. 835). More specific to neuropsychology, neurocognitive malingering was defined in a seminal paper by Slick et al. (1999) as "the volitional exaggeration or fabrication of cognitive dysfunction for the purpose of obtaining substantial material gain, or avoiding or escaping formal duty or responsibility" (p. 552). In 2020, Sherman et al. published an update to their 1999 article and expanded their definition of malingering to include neurocognitive, somatic, and psychiatric malingering. In doing so, the definition of malingering was described as "the volitional feigning or exaggeration of neurocognitive, somatic, or psychiatric symptoms for the purpose of obtaining material gain and services or avoiding formal duty, responsibility, or undesirable outcome" (p. 739).

As can be seen by the previous definitions of malingering, malingering (1) is an intentional and deliberate exaggeration or fabrication of symptoms that (2) is motivated by an external incentive, which can be an effort to obtain items/resources and/or avoid negatively perceived responsibilities/punishment. DSM-5-TR descriptions (American Psychiatric Association, 2022), criteria set out by Slick et al. (1999), and criteria set out by Sherman et al. (2020) collectively provide the following examples of items and resources that would constitute an external incentive: money, financial compensation, disability payment, wage replacement, social assistance, services or accommodations in the community (e.g., social service eligibility), services or accommodations in academic settings, services or accommodations in work settings, drugs, prescription medication, and various goods. Likewise, there are a number of potential responsibilities and punishments that might be avoided through malingering, including: work responsibilities, work punishments (e.g., probation or termination), military duty, public service, legal proceedings (e.g., competency to stand trial), criminal prosecution, prison, home responsibilities, school responsibilities, school punishments (e.g., suspension or expulsion), child-support payments, and other financial obligations. Finally, descriptions of malingering also note that malingering is not just criminological or pathogenic, but it can be adaptive for an individual as well. Examples of adaptive malingering include feigning illness to be released in a hostage situation or to avoid being returned to an abusive situation.

As important as defining what malingering is, it is just as important to explicitly define what malingering is *not* so that the term is not misused. First, a patient who is uncooperative, deceitful, exaggerating symptoms, or faking symptoms is not necessarily malingering. Patients can be uncooperative and deceitful for a number of reasons, some of which are not related to pursuit of an external incentive (e.g., having an oppositional attitude toward testing).

Second, malingering should not be confused with factitious disorder. While individuals who malinger and individuals with factitious disorder both intentionally exaggerate or feign impairment, an individual who is malingering does so for the purpose of obtaining an external incentive. Conversely, as already noted, individuals with factitious disorder have historically been thought to exaggerate or feign impairment for an internal incentive (e.g., receiving nurturance or attention). Indeed, the DSM-5-TR states "Definite evidence of feigning (such as clear evidence that loss of function is present during the examination but not at home) would suggest a diagnosis of factitious disorder if the individual's apparent aim is to assume the sick role, or malingering if it is to obtain an incentive, such as money" (American Psychiatric Association, 2022, p. 835). It should be noted, though, that factitious disorder and malingering are not mutually exclusive. For example, an individual with a factitious disorder may start by feigning symptoms for attention from family members. The individual might later feel the need to malinger to pursue disability to maintain the facade that he or she is ill.

Third, malingering should be differentiated from somatic symptom disorders. Individuals who malinger and individuals who have somatic symptom disorders can both present with excessive complaints and/or symptoms that are not accounted for by neurological or medical conditions or are even incompatible with neurological or medical conditions. The difference between these two presentations, however, is that individuals with somatic symptom disorders are not complaining of or producing symptoms with the goal of obtaining an external incentive. Additionally, as previously discussed, the complaints and symptoms produced by individuals with somatic symptom disorders are not intentionally produced for the purpose of deceiving others (American Psychiatric Association, 2022). It should be noted, though, that somatic symptom disorder and malingering (like factitious disorder and malingering) are not mutually exclusive. For example, consider a case where an individual with a somatic symptom disorder experiences occupational issues due to his or her symptoms and applies for disability. Then, in an attempt to ensure that disability is awarded, the individual exaggerates their symptoms (i.e., malingering).

As a final note, we want to point out that reaching a conclusion of malingering is possible and, in some instances, can be made with a very high degree of confidence (Sweet et al., 2021). In other cases, though, one's confidence might not be as high.

This is normal and understandable depending on the circumstances of the case. To reach a conclusion of malingering, the clinician must know that the symptoms were exaggerated or feigned. The clinician must also know, or more likely infer, that the symptoms were intentionally produced, therefore, ruling out somatic symptom disorders. Additionally, the clinician must know or infer that the symptoms were motivated by pursuit of an external incentive, therefore, ruling out factitious disorder and noncooperative behaviors. Given that individuals who feign symptoms are doing so in a deceitful manner and given that information must be inferred in most cases, confidence in determining whether the invalidity was due to malingering can vary on a case-by-case basis.

Proposed Criteria for Determining Neurocognitive Malingering

Psychologists and neuropsychologists often look to the DSM for diagnostic criteria. The DSM defines malingering and discusses it as a problem that may be a focus of clinical attention, but the DSM does not provide diagnostic criteria for malingering. Likely partly because of this, Slick et al. (1999) proposed diagnostic criteria for malingered neurocognitive dysfunction. Under their proposed framework, an individual could be categorized as meeting criteria for definite malingering of neurocognitive dysfunction (see Table 8.3), probable malingering of neurocognitive dysfunction (see Table 8.4), or possible malingering of neurocognitive dysfunction (see Table 8.5). While these criteria were originally published in 1999, they are still commonly utilized by neuropsychologists nearly 25 years later (Martin et al., 2024).

In 2020, Sherman and colleagues published an update to their 1999 article and expanded their definition of malingering to include neurocognitive, somatic, and psychiatric malingering. In addition to expanding their definition, they provided criteria for malingering of each of these conditions. Their 2020 criteria have dropped the definite, probable, and possible designations and are now simply dichotomous diagnoses (i.e., malingering is or is not present). Their new diagnostic criteria are presented in Tables 8.6, 8.7, and 8.8. Of note, in addition to proposing criteria for neurocognitive, somatic, and psychiatric malingering, there is a fourth criteria set forth for mixed symptom presentation, which occurs when examinees meet criteria in two or three domains (e.g., meeting criteria for both neurocognitive and somatic malingering).

TABLE 8.3. Summary of Slick et al. (1999) Criteria for Definite Malingering of Neurocognitive Dysfunction
1. Presence of a significant external incentive
2. Below chance performance on at least one forced-choice test (defined by $p < .05$)
3. Criteria are not fully accounted for by psychiatric, neurological, or developmental factors
Note. Survey data from Slick et al. (1999).

TABLE 8.4. Summary of Slick et al. (1999) Criteria for Probable Malingering of Neurocognitive Dysfunction

1. Presence of a significant external incentive
2. Either 2a or 2b
   2a. Two or more types of evidence of exaggeration or feigning from neuropsychological testing as demonstrated by:
   - Invalid performance on one or more well-validated performance validity tests
   - Discrepancy between test data and known patterns of brain functioning
   - Discrepancy between test data and observed behavior
   - Discrepancy between test data and reliable collateral reports
   - Discrepancy between test data and documented background history

   2b. One type of evidence from 2a and one or more types of evidence of exaggeration or feigning from self-report as demonstrated by:
   - Discrepancy between self-reported history and documented history
   - Discrepancy between self-reported symptoms and known patterns of brain functioning
   - Discrepancy between self-reported symptoms and behavioral observations
   - Discrepancy between self-reported symptoms and information from collateral informants
   - Evidence of exaggerated or feigned psychological symptoms as indicated by symptom validity test results *or* contradiction between self-reported symptoms and behavioral observations or reliable collateral information
3. Criteria are not fully accounted for by psychiatric, neurological, or developmental factors

Note. Survey data from Slick et al. (1999).

TABLE 8.5. Summary of Slick et al. (1999) Criteria for Possible Malingering of Neurocognitive Dysfunction

1. Presence of a significant external incentive
2. One type of evidence of exaggeration or feigning from self-report as documented by:
   - Discrepancy between self-reported history and documented history
   - Discrepancy between self-reported symptoms and known patterns of brain functioning
   - Discrepancy between self-reported symptoms and behavioral observations
   - Discrepancy between self-reported symptoms and information from collateral informants
   - Evidence of exaggerated or feigned psychological symptoms as indicated by symptom validity test results or contradiction between self-reported symptoms and behavioral observations or reliable collateral information
3. Either 3a or 3b
   3a. Criteria are not fully accounted for by psychiatric, neurological, or developmental factors
   3b. Criteria for definite or probable malingering of neurocognitive dysfunction are met except for being unable to rule out psychiatric, neurological, or developmental etiologies as being cause

Note. Survey data from Slick et al. (1999).

TABLE 8.6. Summary of Sherman et al. (2020) Criteria for Malingering of Neurocognitive Dysfunction

1. Presence of a significant external incentive
2. At least one of the following is present:
   - At least one compelling inconsistency related to cognitive symptoms or deficits observed during the evaluation
   - Invalid cognitive performance based on PVT failure (using two or more PVTs)
   - Invalid cognitive symptom report based on at least one SVT failure
3. At least one *marked discrepancy* between test data/symptom report and any of the following:
   - Natural history and pathogenesis of the condition
   - Records or other media
   - Reliable collateral informant report
4. Criteria are not fully accounted for by psychiatric, medical, or developmental factors

Note. Compelling inconsistencies are "*observations during the examination* that indicate definitive evidence of feigning or exaggeration." For example, the examinee demonstrating a disputed capacity when thinking he or she is not observed. Marked discrepancies are discrepancies between test data or symptom report and *sources of information from outside of the assessment setting* (e.g., information about a condition, records or other media, and collateral reports). From Sherman et al. (2020). The quoted text is from page 739.

TABLE 8.7. Summary of Sherman et al. (2020) Criteria for Malingering of Somatic Symptom Presentation

1. Presence of a significant external incentive
2. At least one of the following is present:
   - At least one compelling inconsistency pertaining to somatic symptoms observed or documented during the evaluation
   - Invalid somatic symptom report based on at least one SVT failure
3. At least one *marked discrepancy* between test data/symptom report and any of the following:
   - Natural history and pathogenesis of the condition
   - Records or other media
   - Reliable collateral informant report
4. Criteria are not fully accounted for by psychiatric, medical, or developmental factors

Note. Compelling inconsistencies are "*observations during the examination* that indicate definitive evidence of feigning or exaggeration." For example, the examinee demonstrating a disputed capacity when thinking he or she is not observed. Marked discrepancies are discrepancies between test data or symptom report and *sources of information from outside of the assessment setting* (e.g., information about a condition, records or other media, and collateral reports). From Sherman et al. (2020). The quoted text is from page 739.

TABLE 8.8. Summary of Sherman et al. (2020) Criteria for Malingering of Psychiatric Symptom Presentation

1. Presence of a significant external incentive
2. At least one of the following is present:
   - At least one compelling inconsistency pertaining to psychiatric symptoms observed or documented during the evaluation
   - Invalid psychiatric symptom report based on at least one SVT failure
3. At least one *marked discrepancy* between test data/symptom report and any of the following:
   - Natural history and pathogenesis of the condition
   - Records or other media
   - Reliable collateral informant report
4. Criteria are not fully accounted for by psychiatric, medical, or developmental factors

Note. Compelling inconsistencies are *"observations during the examination* that indicate definitive evidence of feigning or exaggeration." For example, the examinee demonstrating a disputed capacity when thinking he or she is not observed. Marked discrepancies are discrepancies between test data or symptom report and *sources of information from outside of the assessment setting* (e.g., information about a condition, records or other media, and collateral reports). From Sherman et al. (2020). The quoted text is from page 739.

Whether to Conclude Malingering as the Cause When Suspected

There have been differing thoughts on whether a conclusion of malingering should be made in clinical evaluations even when the clinician is confident in the conclusion. In Martin et al. (2024), we asked both North American neuropsychologists and validity assessment experts how often they use the term malingering when it is suspected in clinical cases. Just under 10% of both North American neuropsychologists and validity assessment experts reported often or always using the term when malingering is suspected in their clinical evaluations. Rationales for making determinations of malingering by the survey respondents who do so included adhering to diagnostic criteria (such as the Sherman et al. criteria described above), benefiting patient care (e.g., clarifying issues and/or avoiding unnecessary procedures), and communicating the most accurate explanation for the invalidity. Conversely, just over 90% of both North American neuropsychologists and validity assessment experts reported rarely or never using the term in clinical practice. There were many explanations provided for avoiding the term in clinical practice, including:

1. It is difficult to know and/or prove the cause, motivation, or intention behind invalid test performances.
2. Use of the term can interfere with the clinical/therapeutic relationship.
3. Use of the term can be harmful to the examinee and his or her future care.
4. Malingering can be a pejorative or controversial term.
5. It can be difficult to identify an external incentive.
6. Use of the term provides no incremental benefit.
7. There can be risks to the examiner for using the term (e.g., being sued, being

subject to board complaints, and receiving negative reactions from other providers).

We, personally, see pros and cons of using and not using the term in clinical nonforensic practice, but we choose to not use the term for many of the reasons that were just described. Instead of using the term malingering, we typically describe that testing was invalid and results are inconsistent with expectations from the examinee's claimed injury or illness.

CONCEPTUALIZING FACTORS ASSOCIATED WITH INCREASED RISK FOR INVALIDITY

Regardless of what is stated about the patient's noncredible presentation and whether or not an impression of malingering is communicated, we believe that it is important for the neuropsychologist to attempt to be as accurate as possible when conceptualizing the patient. In the event of invalidity, this includes engaging in thoughtful considerations of factors surrounding the patient's noncredible presentation. As we have noted, we do not communicate impressions of malingering in our report when suspected in clinical evaluations. Nonetheless, we find that realizing that a clinical patient is likely malingering (or not) can be helpful in determining approaches for further management and clinical interactions. Furthermore, thinking through factors that are likely to be relevant to the patient's invalidity can help to guide treatment recommendations. In this final section of the chapter, we discuss various patient characteristics and historical factors associated with increased risk of invalidity, which clinicians should consider when conceptualizing patients who present noncredibly in clinical settings.

Mild Traumatic Brain Injury

Up to 20–25% of clinical patients with persistent complaints of cognitive dysfunction after a mild traumatic brain injury (mTBI) are thought to invalidate testing even when no litigation is known to be present (Galioto, Dhima, Berenholz, & Busch, 2020; Martin & Schroeder, 2020). While the exact cause of this might be unknown in the individual patient, there are conceivable possibilities as to why individuals with mTBI are at relatively high risk for invalidating testing. As one example, one of the strongest factors predicting persistent symptoms after mTBI is psychological factors, including pre-injury psychological factors (Kashluba, Paniak, & Casey, 2008; Stulemeijer, Vos, Bleijenberg, & van der Werf, 2007). Psychological factors can include depression, anxiety, personality disorder, and also somatoform symptoms (Larrabee, 2012b). Individuals with mTBI can be at risk for misattributing symptoms related to other causes (e.g., underlying psychological conditions) to their injury, and this misattribution can even be reinforced by other well-meaning clinicians. This iatrogenesis can worsen symptoms, exacerbate underlying somatoform features, and result in the patient engaging in a noncredible manner (Mittenberg, DiGiulio, Perrin, & Bass, 1992; Slick & Sherman, 2013). As another example, an mTBI is, by definition, the result of an injury, the blame of which can sometimes by placed on others, meaning that mTBI can be associated with an increased risk for litigation pursuit. Additionally, because patients reporting cognitive symptoms due to mTBI are often younger and of working age, such patients are at greater risk for considering disability. With such patients, it is important to understand that external incentives are not always disclosed to the clinician. Regardless of cause of invalidity, though, clinicians should be aware that individuals with mTBI are thought to be at greater risk for noncredible presentation even when external incentives are not reported.

Evaluation for Attention-Deficit/Hyperactivity Disorder (ADHD)

Patients presenting for assessment of ADHD are at increased risk for invalid testing, with base rates of invalidity approximating 20% (Marshall et al., 2010; Martin & Schroeder, 2020; Suhr et al., 2022). Adults pursuing ADHD evaluation often present with a potential external incentive in the form of obtaining academic accommodations (e.g., extended time to complete scholastic activities, use of others' notes, etc.). Another potential external incentive is to obtain stimulant medications. These medications are drugs of potential abuse, and these medications can also have cognitively enhancing effects even in students without ADHD (Suhr et al., 2022). Thus, some individuals pursuing ADHD evaluations underperform on testing and overreport their symptoms for the purpose of being awarded one or both external incentives. Although these incentives are nonfinancial, it is helpful to keep in mind that because they are, nonetheless, external incentives, producing invalid data in such contexts could still constitute malingering.

Problems at School

Regardless of ADHD status or diagnostic pursuit, individuals might have incentives to exaggerate or feign symptoms if they are experiencing problems at school. Obtaining a neuropsychological diagnosis could allow an individual to obtain accommodations at school and, in some instances, might even allow them to maintain a scholarship which pays for their schooling while no longer being required to meet certain criteria for that scholarship. Some students also experience significant parental pressure to perform well in school and, if they are not performing well, they may look to obtain an excuse for their poor performance (e.g., trying to obtain a diagnosis of a learning disability). Additionally, as previously noted, some individuals might exaggerate or feign attention impairments in an attempt to obtain stimulant medications, which they can use as cognitive enhancements for studying. Consequently, whenever school-related problems are present, there should be consideration of the potential for test invalidity.

Problems with Work, Pursuit of Disability, or Worker's Compensation Involvement

Within the United States, SSDI is a program that was enacted to help support individuals who are disabled from working. While the program has successfully helped many individuals who are truly in need, malingering to obtain financial benefits through the program also occurs (Chafetz, 2008; Chafetz, 2010). Given that most individuals who are of working age could potentially obtain financial benefits from the program, a clinician should understand that working-age individuals, especially those who report struggling at work or being out of work, may pursue SSDI benefits. Research indicates that nearly 45% of clinical patients who report pursuing disability invalidate testing and almost 40% of clinical patients who report that they are not committed to pursuing disability but are open to it invalidate neuropsychological testing (Schroeder, Clark, & Martin, 2022). Furthermore, patient-related survey research indicates that some patients pursue psychological services for help in obtaining disability and a number of those patients never disclose the external incentive to their clinicians (Van Egmond & Kummeling, 2002; Van Egmond et al., 2005). Consequently, any time that a working-age patient is evaluated, especially if issues with work are reported (regardless of whether the patient states that they are pursuing disability), considerations of work-related external incentives should be considered.

Workers' Compensation is a public program intended to provide medical benefits and salary replacement/compensation for individuals who have work-related injuries which delay or prevent them from returning to work (Peck & Oakes, 2022). Thus, any time that a work-related injury occurs, Workers' Compensation could be involved and could be a motivating factor for patients to invalidate testing. While medical benefits and salary compensation could be obtained from Workers' Compensation, research has also shown that factors such as pre-injury job strain and work stress can contribute to ongoing work-related disability (Canivet et al., 2013). When looking at empirical data, it has been found that 37% of Workers' Compensation claimants fail at least one performance validity test (Bianchini, Curtis, & Greve, 2006), and North American neuropsychologists estimate that base rates of invalidity are 33.5% when clinical patients have Workers' Compensation involved in their case (Martin & Schroeder, 2020).

Veteran Status

Professional surveys indicate that veterans within the VA system are more likely to produce invalid neuropsychological test data than civilians in clinical settings (Martin & Schroeder, 2020; Young, Roper, & Arentsen, 2016). Furthermore, empirical research indicates that approximately one-half of veterans undergoing VA disability evaluations fail validity testing, and approximately one-third of veterans in clinical settings fail validity testing (Shura et al., 2022a). This latter finding may be due to the fact that clinical evaluations of veterans can potentially be used, not only for clinical care, but also to obtain or increase a VA-based disability claim which could result in financial compensation. As discussed in Chapter 3, illnesses and injuries incurred or aggravated during military service can potentially result in disability-related financial compensation through the VA (U.S. Department of Veterans Affairs, 2019). Furthermore, veterans' clinical records can be accessed and reviewed when veterans are initially applying for service-connected disability or for an increase in their already approved service-connected disability. Consequently, having documentation of impairment in medical records could result in compensation. As a result of this, there may be a possibility for an financial external incentive any time a veteran is seen within a clinical context, especially if the pursued diagnosis can be linked to their military service (e.g., traumatic brain injury from military-related explosion, Parkinson's disease due to agent orange exposure, posttraumatic stress disorder from stressful incidents, or exacerbation of preexisting major depression due to various experiences during military service).

Mention of Accidents

It has been stated that, in the litigious society in which we live, almost any clinical matter can become a forensic matter. We have evaluated clinical patients with questions of dementia that later emerged into testamentary capacity cases, clinical patients with questions of cognitive deficits that later emerged into medical malpractice cases, and clinical patients with questions of brain injury that later emerged into civil litigation cases. In particular, patients reporting cognitive and psychological symptoms attributed to an accident, especially a motor vehicle accident, have a clear potential for filing a lawsuit. Consequently, when there are accidents that lead to neurological or psychiatric issues for which the patient is being referred, and when the accidents could arguably be attributed to another individual's wrongdoing, the possibility for invalidity to be present during the evaluation should be considered.

Criminal Issues or Charges

Individuals with criminal charges may be seen in forensic settings for reasons such as pretrial and presentencing issues. At the same time, individuals with similar issues can be seen in nonforensic settings for a variety of reasons. While it is unclear how often clinical patients with criminal issues invalidate testing, research indicates that forensically evaluated criminal defendants referred for neuropsychological evaluation invalidate testing up to 50% or more of the time (Ardolf et al., 2007). Given these high base rates in criminal forensic settings, one might expect that clinical patients that have anticipated or ongoing legal issues will likely invalidate testing more frequently than clinical patients with no such issues. Even if the clinical cases are seemingly unrelated to clear forensically based issues, such as determining competency to stand trial, obtaining clinical documentation stating that one has a psychiatric and/or neurological disorder could potentially be seen as being favorable in helping to mitigate or escape criminal punishment that is anticipated or ongoing.

Severe Cognitive Complaints in Younger Adults Who Do Not Have Medical Conditions Expected to Cause Cognitive Dysfunction

In adults, and younger adults especially, where (1) neurodegenerative diseases are less common and (2) certain external incentives are more likely to be present (pursuit of disability, pursuit of academic accommodations, etc.), severe cognitive complaints within the context of unremarkable neurodevelopmental and medical histories are thought to be associated with increased risk for noncredible test findings. As Larrabee (2022) has stated, in determining validity of evaluation findings, "everything must make sense, clinically and statistically" (p. 207). In cases that don't make sense, there should be consideration of why the cases don't make sense and whether noncredible symptomatology might be present. If there are potential external incentives (e.g., financial incentives, avoiding punishment or responsibilities, academic incentives, or medication incentives) that might motivate an individual to present noncredibly, malingering should be considered as a possibility. If there are potential internal incentives (e.g., somatoform presentations, attention-seeking behavior) that might motivate one to present noncredibly, disorders that fall into the DSM-5 category of somatic symptom and related disorders should be considered. If validity testing indicates that there are no concerns regarding invalid test taking and clinical testing indicates no significant cognitive dysfunction but significant psychopathology, there should be consideration that psychological factors (e.g., poor day-to-day attention secondary to a major depressive episode) may be the reason for the complaint of significant cognitive deficits.

CLOSING REMARKS

In conclusion, there are noncredible explanations for invalid test findings which include depression and anxiety, a cry for help, physical factors, and apathy. Research does not support these factors as typically causing PVT failures. Conversely, there are credible explanations for invalid test findings which include attitude toward testing, somatization and conversion disorder, factitious disorder, and malingering. Factors that are thought to be associated with increased risk for invalidity are having an mTBI with residual symptom complaints after recovery, pursuit of an adult ADHD evaluation, having school or work problems, pursuing disability or Workers' Compensation, pursuing service-connected disability through the VA, being involved in accidents that are another person's fault, having pending or active criminal issues, or having severe unexpected cognitive complaints. Many of these factors are linked to malingering, and validity testing experts believe that malingering is the most common cause of invalidity in clinical settings. Even if malingering occurs in the individual patient, though, most clinicians do not make explicit statements about it. With that said, it is important for the clinician to consider which factors are likely causing the patient to perform invalidity in order to assist in case conceptualization and the rendering of justifiable and helpful conclusion.

CHAPTER 9

Providing Feedback When Testing Is Invalid

A Challenge Made Easy

Many of us can likely recall a personal clinical encounter, either in relation to our own health care or that of a family member, and being struck by the impression "I really liked that doctor." It is also likely that we have had the opposite experience, leaving a medical appointment, thinking "Well, that was not at all helpful." or "What awful bedside manner." or "I certainly won't be seeing that doctor again." In reflecting on these experiences, what characteristics might lead one to view a clinical interaction as being positive or negative? Similarly, from a patient's perspective, what makes a good doctor? This latter question was asked of patients in a recent qualitative survey (Davis, Carbone, Fredericks, Lujan, & Basdeo, 2021). Analysis of the patient responses found good communication to be the most commonly noted characteristic, with respondents most frequently citing listening (47%), acknowledging patient concerns (18%), and either asking questions or making the patient feel comfortable to ask questions (14%) as important qualities of a "good doctor." Following communication, other important characteristics included thoroughness (33%), explaining (15%), and "treating the whole patient" (13%). In addition to analyzing response themes, the authors of the study coded the frequency of descriptive words recurring across responses, the most common of which are noted in Table 9.1.

Notably, results from Davis et al. (2021) highlight that being perceived as a good clinician is based upon strong bidirectional communication as well as a clinician's ability to establish rapport via demonstration of both knowledge and compassion. Strong clinical communication and, relatedly, the conveying of both clinical expertise and interest in patient welfare, is as important in clinical neuropsychology as it is in other specialties. This integration of art and science forms the backbone of effective neuropsychological feedback sessions with patients. And, unsurprisingly, preliminary

TABLE 9.1. What Makes a Good Doctor?: Common Descriptive Words Used	
Caring	26%
Trustworthy	15%
Knowledgeable	12%
Honest	7%
Understanding	7%
Personable	4%
Empathetic	3%
Patient	3%
Respectful	3%
Unbiased	3%
Humble	2%
Relatable	2%

Note. Data from Davis et al. (2021).

research suggests that patients who receive feedback often report high levels of satisfaction with the feedback experience, with some studies reporting improvements in outcomes such as quality of life; understanding of one's condition; utilization of coping strategies; and the severity of psychiatric, cognitive, or postconcussive symptoms (Rosado et al., 2018; Westervelt, Brown, Tremont, Javorsky, & Stern, 2007; Lanca et al., 2020; Kirkwood, Peterson, Baker, & Connery, 2017).

Even neuropsychologists who are particularly skilled in providing feedback, however, might feel apprehensive when preparing to provide feedback to clinical patients who invalidate testing, and there are a variety of understandable reasons for this. Some neuropsychologists might feel that they are not being clinically helpful to their patients. Others might fear that upon hearing that results are invalid, patients could perceive that their time and efforts are wasted, their concerns are not understood, or the clinician is uncaring. Yet others might find the feedback session to be unfulfilling given that hours of time have been devoted to trying to help the patient and results are clinically limited due to the patient providing an invalid performance.

Beyond having concerns of being seen as nonunderstanding, uncompassionate, and/or unhelpful, there are likely also times when clinicians anticipate an angry or aggressive reaction from the patient. This may be particularly likely when patients hope that the evaluation findings will facilitate achievement of a personal goal and/or external incentive (e.g., obtaining disability). Beyond worrying about the possibility of having an argumentative patient in the office, clinicians might have concerns that patients will complain to the neuropsychologist's employer or licensing board, or even file a malpractice lawsuit.

While all potential concerns are natural and understandable, it is our clinical experience that by demonstrating a combination of compassion, thoroughness, objectivity, and commitment to clinical care, the risk of negative consequences can be minimized and, most importantly, the opportunity to provide help to the patient can be maximized. In this chapter, we provide a feedback model that aspires both to avoid negative patient interactions and/or retaliation and achieve goals of positive patient care common to other neuropsychological evaluations where data are valid. Furthermore, our approach seeks to manage invalid data in a manner consistent with best practices in neuropsychology, avoid improper facilitation of patients' possible surreptitious objectives, and allow for a feedback interaction in which the patient feels heard and cared for.

In Martin and Schroeder (2021a) we discuss several constructs that can be considered when distinguishing various approaches to feedback in the context of invalid testing. These include: (1) degree of adherence to the APA Ethics Code (American Psychological Association, 2017) principles regarding accurate and evidence-based assessment (Sections 2.04, 9.01a, and 9.02a), (2) degree to which a collaborative doctor–patient relationship is maintained, and (3) degree to which the aspirational guidelines of beneficence and fidelity (General Principles 1 and 2 from the APA Ethics Code) are applied to the patient versus general society. Regarding the last construct, the APA Ethics Code describes the manner in which psychologists should attempt to "do good" (beneficence) and act with responsibility (fidelity) to both the clinical patient and the broader community. As clinical deception often involves pitting a patient's personal goals (e.g., obtaining SSDI payments) against important social considerations (e.g., not inappropriately overburdening social welfare institutions), clinicians are often tasked with considering beneficence and fidelity as it applies to both patients and society.

In Martin and Schroeder (2022) we outline three theoretical approaches to feedback in cases of invalidity and describe how each approach varies across the above constructs. We describe:

1. An *advocating* approach, in which the clinician ignores or minimizes evidence of invalidity as they unconditionally advocate for the patient's personal goals in an "at all costs" attempt to maintain the doctor–patient collaborative relationship (Figure 9.1).
2. An *objective* approach, in which the clinician stringently adheres to the objective findings of the invalid data and intentionally avoids making any effort to either aid or restrict the patient's personal evaluation goals (Figure 9.2).
3. An *enforcing* approach, in which the clinician becomes a social enforcer (i.e., the primary goal becomes reducing the potential negative social consequences of the patient's deception) who perceives himself as no longer beholden to the expectations of providing clinical assistance or maintaining a traditional doctor–patient relationship (Figure 9.3).

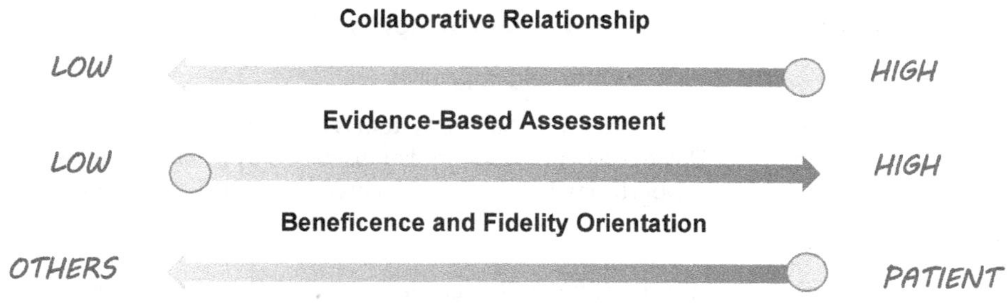

FIGURE 9.1. Advocating approach values emphasis.

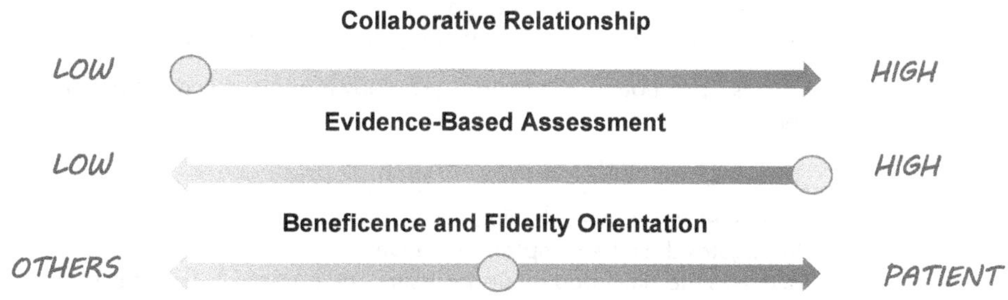

FIGURE 9.2. Objective approach values emphasis.

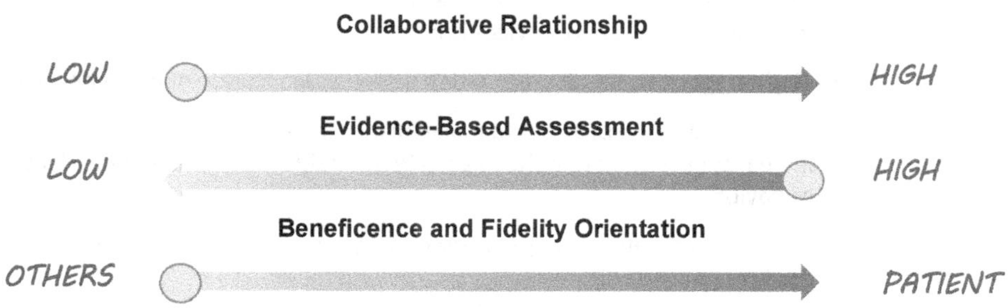

FIGURE 9.3. Enforcing approach values emphasis.

Although each of the three approaches has its rationales, each also has a very realistic potential for harm to the patient, society, and/or the neuropsychologist. Possible negative consequences of these approaches are listed in Table 9.2. To minimize the potential for such negative consequences and to increase the likelihood of a positive outcome, we recommend a *firm–beneficent* approach, a model first described in Martin and Schroeder (2022). The *firm–beneficent* approach places a strong emphasis on assessment accuracy, seeks to minimize harm and maximize good to both the patient and society, and aspires to maintain a strong collaborative relationship while being cognizant of the limitations imposed by the invalid data. Key assumptions and principles of the *firm-beneficent* approach are stated in Table 9.3.

TABLE 9.2. Potential Impact on Stakeholders by Approach

Enforcing approach	
Patient	• Reinforces the perception that the system is uncaring. • Increases likelihood of being ignored or dismissed by future clinicians. • Decreases opportunity for treatment for areas in need of clinical intervention.
Society	• N/A
Clinician	• Creates opportunity for unpleasant and/or unsatisfying interaction. • Increases likelihood of hostile/negative patient reaction and/or formal complaint. • Might negatively impact reputation or result in loss of referral source.
Referral source	• Reason for referral might have gone unaddressed. • Increases likelihood that the patient complains about being referred.
Neuropsychology	• Fosters a perception that neuropsychology is punitive and not patient centered.
Advocating approach	
Patient	• Reinforces deceptive behavior. • Propagates the false symptom narrative. • Increases the likelihood for unnecessary and potentially harmful intervention. • Misses the opportunity for discussion of factors actually in need of intervention.
Society	• Promotes the provision of unwarranted and costly resources and services. • Diverts services and resources away from those in greater need. • Increases financial and services burden.
Clinician	• Might negatively impact reputation if seen as inaccurate or easily deceived.
Referral source	• Might compel the provider to make further unnecessary referrals. • Increases likelihood that the referral feels unaided in managing the deceptive behavior.
Neuropsychology	• Fosters a perception that neuropsychological assessments are inaccurate or easily manipulated.
Objective approach	
Patient	• Causes dissatisfaction by lack of results despite time invested. • Reinforces the perception that the system is uncaring. • Decreases opportunity for treatment of areas in need of clinical intervention.
Society	• N/A
Clinician	• Could foster reputation of clinician as being unhelpful, uncaring, or detached.
Referral source	• If the evaluation was simply deemed invalid and no treatment plan was recommended, increases likelihood that the provider feels challenged in managing patient complaints.
Neuropsychology	• Misses an opportunity for neuropsychology to demonstrate its utility in managing a challenging patient type.

TABLE 9.3. Assumptions and Practices Related to the Firm–Beneficent Approach

- Invalidity prevents the interpretation of abnormal scores and precludes their use in informing diagnoses or recommendations. This is firmly communicated to the patient and referring provider.
- A quasi-collaborative relationship is sought in which the clinician can no longer collaborate with the patient in some aspects of the evaluation (e.g., understanding of cognitive deficits as informed by test results) but can collaborate in others (e.g., psychological or psychosocial factors related to invalidity).
- When appropriate, unimpaired scores might still be interpreted and behaviors inconsistent with impairment might still be discussed to demonstrate the patient's cognitive capabilities.
- Noncredible explanations of invalidity that pander to patient expectations are avoided, as are insinuations of intentionality that might reduce the potential for the clinician to positively effect change.
- Even in cases where invalidity is believed deliberate, the clinician maintains a compassionate perspective, realizing that suffering related to psychological or psychosocial stressors is likely present and might be motivating the efforts to deceive.

THE FIRM–BENEFICENT APPROACH: STEP-BY-STEP DESCRIPTION

Our model for feedback consists of four components: (1) Start with the clinical interview, (2) summarize the patient history during feedback, (3) communicate invalidity, and (4) move forward. Each of these components will be discussed in detail below.

Step 1: Start with the Clinical Interview

The first step in providing effective feedback to patients invalidating testing is to conduct a clinical interview that both establishes rapport and gathers information that promotes an understanding of the nature and potential motivating factors of the symptom distortion. Successfully developing rapport can potentially help to offset unwelcomed information provided at feedback, ideally facilitating the impression that although the clinician is providing undesirable news (e.g., testing is invalid and, therefore, results do not lend support to the patient's symptom claims), this does not mean that the clinician does not care about the patient's welfare. Likewise, the clinical interview can assist in unearthing information about factors that might motivate one to exaggerate/feign their symptoms or invalidate testing. Such information can help the clinician conceptualize factors contributing to invalidity and, perhaps of even greater importance in clinical evaluations, can provide a pathway for topics to be discussed during feedback, including potential interventions. For example, although knowing that a patient is planning to apply for SSDI benefits provides insight into an external incentive that might motivate invalid test performance, such information does little to inform potentially helpful interventions. However, if the clinician is aware that decisions to apply for disability are often associated with psychosocial, psychiatric, and/or job-related stress and then assesses for such possibilities during the clinical interview, specific targets for intervention can often be discovered. Notably, we do not imply that psychiatric, psychosocial, or job-related stress directly cause invalidity; however, these factors can sometimes underlie an individual's decision to exaggerate or feign their symptoms if they believe that doing so will allow them relief from a distressing situation. By understanding these factors, the neuropsychologist is not seeking excuses for an invalid presentation but is rather looking for the root of the desire to present invalidly so that he or she might be able to help direct future intervention.

Chapter 3 further expands on the clinical interview, but the following points are important goals to keep in mind for the clinical interview when it comes to providing feedback to patients who invalidate testing:

- Build rapport and convey an interest in conducting a thorough and practical evaluation that positively contributes to the patient's well-being.
- Communicate a desire to understand the patient's symptom experience and perspective.
- Observe for suggestions and evidence of symptom distortion.
- Learn about factors that might impact test engagement or motivate the patient to underperform, including potential external or internal incentives, as well as psychological, psychosocial, or other noncognitive symptoms that might motivate pursuit of such incentives.
- Inquire about the patient's evaluation goals.
- Communicate a desire to help the patient, but caution that the ability to assist with certain goals will depend on the evaluation findings.
- Inform the patient of any stated goals with which you are unable or might not be able to help them.
- Instruct the patient of the necessity of providing optimal performance.

Step 2: Summarize Patient History

At the beginning of the feedback session, we tend to start by providing a brief summary of the issues leading to the neuropsychological evaluation. The summary might incorporate information from records (e.g., neuroimaging findings) and other collateral sources (e.g., spouse's perspective of symptoms), although we typically highlight the information provided by the patient him/herself, and communicate the history in a manner that is likely to elicit agreement (i.e., agreement is most likely when the information that is summarized comes straight from the patient or consists of objectively documented facts). Providing this summary has several purposes, including:

- Communicating to the patient that the neuropsychologist thoroughly listened, comprehended, and considered the patient's perspective.
- Highlighting information that sets the stage for the clinician's impressions, diagnoses, and recommendations discussed later in the feedback session.
- Reminding the patient and family of the issues leading to the evaluation.
- Providing the patient an opportunity to clarify, correct, or add information regarding his or her self-report.
- Providing a cohesive narrative of the patient's symptoms.

To introduce the recapitulation of the symptom report, one can say something like:

> "How have you been since we last talked? Good. Well, we're here today to discuss your test results from last week. Before I get too far into the results, though, I'd like to briefly recap our conversation about what brought you in to see me. I'll hit upon key points but if I leave anything important out, if I state something incorrectly, or if you feel like something needs clarification, please let me know."

After the summary is completed, the neuropsychologist should ensure that it is accurate by saying something such as, "Is that similar to your understanding of things?" or, alternatively, "Did I hit all of the key points?"

If the neuropsychologist has been attentive and thorough in their clinical interview and note taking, patients should generally agree with the summary. It is not uncommon for patients to nod in agreement as they hear the summary. In some cases, patients respond very appreciatively, or make statements such as, "That was right on target. I couldn't have said it any better." In the less typical cases where the patient clarifies, corrects, or adds to the information provided, the clinician should communicate appreciation for the revision to the summary in a desire to "get it right." The clinician does not need to agree with the accuracy of the patient's perspective. Rather, the goal is for the clinician to accurately understand the patient's perspective and to ensure that such a goal is witnessed by the patient. By beginning the feedback session by discussing the patient's perspective, the clinician communicates that he or she cares about what the patient has to say and reinforces a message of patient–doctor collaboration. Starting the session from a point of mutual agreement can be particularly helpful in those cases where the clinician then must present divergent information from the patient's perspective, such as when discussing invalid test performance.

When presenting the symptom summary to patients who invalidate testing, it is important that the clinician communicate compassion, not skepticism. Important details that provide an alternative explanation or even contradict the patient's symptom report might be included, but not for the purpose of invalidating the patient's perspective. For example, consider a patient who reports implausible symptoms following a mild traumatic brain injury. The clinician might summarize:

"You were involved in motor vehicle accident 9 months ago during which you hit your head on the steering wheel. You remained conscious and, after you exited the vehicle, you called your wife who picked you up and later took you to the hospital. They did some testing at the ER, including a CT scan of your head, which was interpreted as normal, and you were diagnosed with a concussion. It sounds like you had a really awful headache, but at that time you were able communicate with the doctors and tell them what happened in the accident. You noted that you weren't aware of any memory problems initially, but about a week later you found yourself making some uncharacteristic mistakes at work, including a bookkeeping mistake that ended up being costly for your employer. Since you've noticed that, you feel like your memory has progressively worsened. You're noticing even more issues at work and you're also more frequently forgetting conversations with your wife, who has also become very concerned about your memory. It sounds like you are feeling very frustrated and concerned about your memory, and you're now wondering if you'll be able to continue working. On top of the accident and your memory difficulties, it sounds like this has just been a very difficult year for you. Right before the accident, you lost your son to cancer and you've had some run-ins with your new supervisor, whom you're not very fond of. You've been treated for depression off and on in the past and, recently, you've found yourself to be more depressed than you've ever been. It sounds like you don't perceive your depression as being the primary cause of your memory difficulties, but it also sounds like it doesn't make anything easier. Is that a pretty accurate picture of what we talked about last week?"

Most neuropsychologists reading the summary would agree that the patient's memory complaints are unlikely due to his concussion from 9 months ago, and any real memory concerns that might be noticed by the patient are much more likely accounted for by some combination of depression, grief, and/or stress. However, such conclusions can be reached by the content, not the tone, of the summary. The tone of the summary is generally neutral, erring on the side of compassion regarding the patient's potential suffering. Thus, the patient hearing the summary is likely to perceive it as validating, so long as it accurately captures his or her symptom report, avoids skepticism, and communicates interest in his or her well-being.

Although the information is merely a recapitulation of that provided by the patient and the tone does not convey bias, the framework of the information is strategic. It includes information regarding injury severity and symptom course that suggests that the injury is not likely the cause of cognitive symptoms as well as a discussion of psychosocial and psychological factors that are likely relevant to the patient's report of impairment. Once the patient agrees to the history, it becomes harder for the patient to refute the information when integrated by the neuropsychologist into his or her conceptualization later in the feedback session. Those neuropsychologists with forensic experience might think of the summary of symptom information as being analogous to an evidentiary hearing. Once the evidence is presented and accepted, it is fair game to be used in building one's case. In the vignette above, by agreeing with the historical summary, the patient cannot easily disagree when the neuropsychologist references other nonpathological findings (the normal neuroimaging), the patient's level of coherence following the accident which suggests a rather mild injury, or the severity of his depression when discussing other potential causes of the patient's dysfunction.

Another goal of providing a symptom summary is to subtly provide context to the patient's report. Patients are not always mindful of how their cognitive symptoms have developed over time or whether they have developed in concordance with other noncognitive factors. Such as in the example above, a patient might *separately* discuss markers of injury severity, a symptom history that is incompatible with the attributed cause, and a report of noncognitive issues that likely explain his or her symptoms. Patients might not, however, see the connection between these topics of discussion because they do not have expertise in brain disorders and because they do not always have the level or type of conceptualization skill to develop such a multifaceted framework. By weaving together such information into a contextual framework, the neuropsychologist helps the patient connect the dots in order to set the stage for adjusting an inaccurate symptom narrative or misattribution.

To recap, by summarizing the patient's history at the outset of the feedback session, the neuropsychologist should:

- Present information as understood and communicated by the patient.
- When possible, include information that can be referenced later in the feedback session to correct misattribution, revise the patient's symptom narrative, and recommend interventions.
- Convey information without skepticism and in a manner that conveys compassion for expressed suffering while demonstrating objectively and thoroughness.
- Demonstrate that you care about the patient's perspective.
- Invite the patient to clarify any perceived inconsistencies or add information not encapsulated by the summary.

Step 3: Communicate Invalidity

Once the patient's history has been summarized and agreed upon, the neuropsychologist should shift to the potentially daunting task of informing the patient that the test results are invalid. It is at this point that the spirit of unbridled patient–doctor collaboration can no longer be maintained as the neuropsychologist must note that the data provided by the patient cannot be relied upon as accurate. Except in very rare cases, the neuropsychologist should communicate explicitly and unambiguously that the data are "invalid." Since this statement will be included in the clinical report of patients who invalidate testing, not sharing such information with the patient raises the likelihood of a negative reaction should the patient later review the report and then wonder why the findings were not communicated directly during feedback. Furthermore, simply omitting a discussion of the test findings and, instead, talking about information from outside of testing (e.g., clinical interview information and neuroimaging reports) might cause the patient to feel confused as he or she might rightly assume that the neurocognitive testing, which likely required a time investment of several hours, constitutes a fundamental aspect of the evaluation.

After stating that the test results were invalid, what should be done next? As discussed earlier in this book, we advise against speculating with the patient why the data are invalid or directly asking the patient why testing is invalid. This is because when patients are asked why their testing was invalid, they often report that they tried their best on all tests despite validity testing indicating that this is not actually accurate. The clinician is then faced with the challenge of how to move forward. For example, the clinician might feel the need to accept the patient's false conclusion, challenge the patient to try to uncover the real reason for invalidity, offer alternative explanations hoping that the patient accepts one of them, etc.

We also advise against confronting and blaming the patient for the invalidity. Especially in those cases where a patient has obviously intentionally underperformed, confronting the patient about it can sometimes make the clinician feel like an accomplished sleuth ("Haha, I caught you!") but it is unlikely to yield any benefit to the patient's care. Accordingly, results from a recent survey indicate that such a tactic is much more likely to invoke an angry reaction by the patient (reported to occur in 50% of instances) than lead to admission of culpability (reported to occur in 5% of instances; Martin & Schroeder, 2020).

Another caution would be in attributing PVT failure to factors that research has found to rarely contribute to PVT failure (e.g., pain, depression, anxiety, or fatigue). Although attributing the PVT failure to these factors could potentially make for a smooth feedback session (e.g., "I know that you've been in a lot of pain, and I think your pain just got in the way of doing your best."), doing so is typically not evidence based. This, then, deviates from standards of the APA Ethics Code regarding assessment accuracy. Additionally, by communicating to the patient that these factors cause scores to be so poor that they cannot be accurately measured, a patient might understandably leave the feedback session with the thought that "Well even though the neuropsychologist said I don't have neurological-based impairment, he told me that my depression interferes with my memory so much that he can't even accurately measure my abilities."

Even though PVTs have previously been described as identifying poor, variable, or suboptimal "effort," we recommend avoiding such attributions in describing PVT failure. PVTs are generally designed to be quite easy with cutoffs empirically validated to yield low false-positive rates even in patients with rather notable cognitive impairment. PVTs are not designed to measure the construct of "effort" as even patients providing less than their best "effort" can pass PVTs (Larrabee, 2012c). Additionally, it has been noted that patients failing PVTs sometimes expend considerable "effort" in an attempt to look impaired (Boone, 2013). In addition to being potentially inaccurate when attributing PVT failure to low effort, such explanations open the possibility for disagreement. A patient might well respond "Well, no actually, I really did give my best effort." or perceive that the neuropsychologist is suggesting "You just did not try hard enough." Such exchanges have minimal opportunity for resolution or agreement. Conversely, if the neuropsychologist simply communicates that the test results are invalid (a statement which can be supported by empirical literature as opposed to insinuations regarding the patient's behavior and intentions), the patient cannot argue on the basis of their subjective experience and must accept the objective evidence of invalidity.

Another approach that we recommend avoiding is comparing patients' performances to those of low-functioning groups to demonstrate the absurdity of the test findings. Carone, Iverson, and Bush (2010) have recommended that patients providing invalid test performance be asked "if they would agree that they should perform better than a severely impaired clinical group, such as patients with Alzheimer's disease or children with mental retardation" (p. 766), followed by a demonstration that the patient did indeed perform below these groups. Despite overlap between our model and the Carone et al. feedback model, we recommend against comparing patients to those with dementia or intellectual disability for three primary reasons. First, we believe that some patients might find the conversation adversarial and, consequently, become less open to engaging in conversations about treatment recommendations. Second, some patients might consciously or subconsciously ignore or minimize the statement that testing is invalid and take from such feedback that they *are* more impaired than patients with Alzheimer's or children with mental retardation. Third, some patients might take offense to the question, perceive the clinician as uncaring and/or insulting, and, consequently, retaliate after the session by forming a complaint against the clinician.

Finally, we also recommend that neuropsychologists avoid explanations that might suggest that the neuropsychologist is at fault for the data being uninterpretable. For example, statements such as "I'm confused by the data." or "The results just don't make sense to me." or "This isn't what I typically see." all imply that the neuropsychologist is unable to make sense of the results due to his or her own shortcomings and that a neuropsychologist with better knowledge, skills, or experience might do better. Similarly, one would not want to suggest that the neuropsychological testing procedure was the cause of the invalidity. For example, we have heard of an approach for describing invalid test findings using the analogy of a contaminated lab draw, which could be taken by the patient to suggest that the neuropsychological data might have been useful had they been collected and managed more carefully by the service provider.

As the above cautions and examples demonstrate, we do not recommend discussing a cause of, or providing explanations for, invalidity with patients. Whereas determining that data are invalid is *objective and empirically based*, determining the *cause* of invalidity requires that *subjective impressions* be made by the clinician. There is the possibility that the clinician's inclinations for why testing is invalid are incorrect and, furthermore, even when the inclinations are correct, the subjective nature of the clinician's impression could take away from the objective nature of the validity test failure. Additionally, discussing causes of invalidity is unlikely to be helpful and might, instead, incite an argument or negative patient reaction, foster symptom misattribution, and/or detract from the neuropsychologist's ability to collaboratively address areas of intervention later in the feedback session. Instead of discussing causes of or explanations for invalidity, we recommend describing in layman's terms that the data are invalid (but in a manner that does not threaten trade secrets and test security). As described below, this could be done by using analogies, discussing inconsistencies and variability in scores, and/or simply providing context to the findings of invalidity.

Using A Motion Artifact Analogy

A potential method for describing that findings are invalid and that the results cannot be interpreted is to use a motion artifact analogy. This analogy relates the neuropsychologist's inability to interpret invalid neuropsychological test findings to a radiologist's inability to interpret a brain MRI containing significant motion artifact. The analogy has likely been used by neuropsychologists for some time and is also described as a method for communicating invalid test findings in the book, *Feedback that Sticks* (Postal & Armstrong, 2013). We sometimes use it given that many patients can easily understand the analogy and because the explanation neither implies that the patient intentionally did wrong nor provides an explanation for invalidity that is not scientifically based.

An example of applying this analogy is as follows:

> "Have you ever seen a picture before where someone appeared blurry because they were moving while the picture was being taken? Well, if someone gets an MRI of their brain, they are basically having a bunch of pictures taken of their brain. So, what happens if someone moves around or shakes their head while that MRI is being taken? As you can imagine, the MRI images will be blurry. And if the images are too blurry, then the radiologist can't interpret the findings because it would be hard to tell if something strange looking is the result of an issue such as a stroke or if it is just the result of all the blurriness. Similarly, when someone completes neuropsychological testing and there is too much variability for the scores to make neurological sense, the results cannot be interpreted because of all that blurriness. In your case, there are scores that don't make sense given your other test performances, which indicates that some of your performances do not reflect your actual capabilities. If one were to make conclusions on these scores, those conclusions could be incorrect and, potentially, harmful. Because there is

evidence that your cognitive test data are not a valid reflection of your cognitive abilities, the data cannot be interpreted."

Describing Invalidity as Variability Due to Non-Neurological Cause

Excluding certain neurological disorders that might cause marked fluctuations of attention or engagement (e.g., dementia with Lewy bodies, delirium, or poorly managed epilepsy), significant variability in performance across tests measuring a similar cognitive ability would be unexpected and neurologically unlikely. Likewise, if a patient fails a PVT, which is empirically demonstrated to be resilient to cognitive impairment except in those with profound cognitive dysfunction, but produces average or near-average performances on tests of genuine ability, such variability is unlikely to be due to a neurological cause and much more likely be due to an invalid test performance. In such cases, one could state the following:

"As you might recall, we had you complete a number of tests, and there were multiple tests looking at each thinking ability. For example, you didn't complete just one memory test, you completed four memory tests that were similar but slightly different from each other. If all of the memory test scores align, that indicates that the scores are consistent and likely accurate. If scores, however, significantly deviate, that indicates that we do not have a consistent or accurate measurement of that cognitive ability. This is important because we don't want to make a wrong diagnosis based on inaccurate information. In your case, when we looked at multiple tests within the same areas of functioning, we saw a lot of variability; that is, some scores were high, some were medium, and some were low. We also saw that you were able to do pretty well on some relatively challenging tasks but then were unable to correctly answer easier items. This tells me that your low scores on testing are not representative of your actual capabilities because your other scores demonstrate your capabilities to be higher. When people produce scores that are this low due to a neurological cause, they tend to perform low across the other tests in that same area of thinking because their brain is damaged and they cannot do better than the damaged brain allows. Given that this was not the case for you, the variability across your scores strongly suggests that your low scores are due to factors outside of neurologically based brain dysfunction."

Providing Context to Findings of Invalidity

In addition to noting that the test findings are invalid and describing the impact on interpretation of the results, it can sometimes be helpful to provide context to the results. In this regard, it can sometimes be useful to explain to the patient that a primary reason why the neuropsychologist must refrain from interpreting invalid data is that doing so could lead to improper diagnoses, treatments, or recommendations, which could ultimately be harmful. By doing this, the neuropsychologist communicates that his or her objective in assessing for validity is not to be difficult, punitive, or obstructive of the patient's goals, but rather to assure that the data are accurate in order to protect the patient.

In some cases, it can also be helpful to discuss the results within a "bad news–good news" framework (Carone et al., 2010). When appropriate, one can note that despite the bad news of the data being invalid or some test scores being low, the good news is that because the test results are not due to a stable neurocognitive deficit, there is opportunity for improvement in test performance and/or one's cognitive symptoms. It is highlighted that such news is certainly positive given that the neuropsychologist must often give bad news that deficits evidenced by testing are most likely permanent.

Keeping Step 3 Brief

While we have provided multiple potential example statements that could be used during Step 3 of our feedback model, it is important to note that any statements that we might choose to use on an individual basis are based on whether we believe that they will be helpful for the specific patient sitting in front of us. In some situations, none of the examples will be given and, instead, it will only be stated that testing was invalid. Regardless, after stating that testing is invalid and that the results are uninterpretable, we do not ask the patient if he or she has questions and we do not dwell on the topic of invalidity. Doing so is unlikely to yield clinical benefit and might, instead, increase the risk of damaging or losing patient rapport, making it more difficult to shift the discussion into a therapeutic direction. Additionally, in our experience, patients are generally satisfied by simply hearing that test results are invalid and uninterpretable using the approaches detailed previously. Overall, when determining the extent of time and emphasis allotted to discussing the invalid data, it can be helpful to ask oneself, "How will this be clinically helpful?" In that regard, we recommend that the clinician not devote much face-to-face clinic time to Step 3; we typically complete Step 3 in less than 5 minutes (and sometimes even less than 1 minute).

Summary

In summary, there are a variety of approaches one might take in discussing the invalid nature of the test findings. We recommend taking approaches that directly, efficiently, and objectively communicate that test findings are invalid and uninterpretable while avoiding discussion of cause of the invalid test findings because such discussions are more likely to result in a negative reaction, reinforce misattribution of symptoms, and be unlikely to be helpful to the patient. Approaches to potentially include and to avoid are summarized in Table 9.4.

TABLE 9.4. Recommended and Nonrecommended Approaches When Describing Invalidity
Recommended approaches
• Indicate that results are invalid and cannot be accurately interpreted
• Discuss invalidity in terms of variability
• When beneficial, interpret average or near-average range test scores
• If appropriate, use a good news–bad news approach
• Consider using an analogy (e.g., motion artifact analogy)
Approaches to avoid
• Discuss a cause for invalidity (in most cases)
• Use of confrontational or adversarial language
• Imply that the patient is lying, faking, or malingering
• Suggest underperformance is intentional
• Attribute invalidity to generally nonlegitimate explanations (e.g., fatigue, pain, depression, anxiety, medication effects) unless these factors were directly observed to obviously interfere with engagement
• Compare patients to low-functioning groups (e.g., dementia or intellectual disability)
• Describe results as being due to issues with effort unless behavioral observations clinical indicate this to be the cause
• Seek patient input regarding invalidity or explore their willingness to admit to poor effort
• Make statements that could suggest to the patient that it is the examiner's fault that interpretations of cognitive test data cannot be made
• Reveal information that would aide examinees in avoiding detection in future evaluations

Step 4: Move Forward (A Hard Shift)

As just noted, discussing suspected reasons behind invalid test findings with patients is unlikely to result in a clinically productive dialogue. Furthermore, because data are invalid, we cannot rely on the test data to inform conclusions and treatment recommendations. Because of this, after factually stating that testing is invalid (Step 3), we recommend making "a hard shift" in the focus of the feedback session.

The hard shift occurs because the clinician realizes that the invalid test findings led to a dead end with regard to providing feedback, and a new path for moving forward is required. Consequently, we (1) stop talking about the invalidity and (2) start discussing aspects of the patient's life that could realistically see benefit if some form of intervention were to occur. In our clinical experience, there is almost always at least one factor, if not multiple factors, that can be addressed in patients who invalidate testing. By shifting the feedback session in this manner, there is the potential to reestablish a quasi-collaborative patient–doctor relationship and continue to provide clinical care, even in the context of test invalidity. For this reason, Step 4 of the feedback model is generally the most time-intensive component of the feedback session, often comprising somewhere between 50 to 90% of the face-to-face feedback time with the patient.

So, what aspects of the patient's life should be addressed following this hard shift? The broad answer is any and all issues that are believed to negatively impact the patient's health and/or well-being. This could include addressing negative interpersonal relationships, job-related stress, substance abuse, poorly managed chronic pain, unmanaged depression or anxiety, untreated sleep apnea, uncontrolled vascular health issues, poor diet and a lack of physical activity, and other factors. When addressing these factors, though, it is strongly recommended that the provision of any therapeutic goals occur separately from, and not be conflated with, the discussion of invalidity (again, all discussion of invalidity stopped prior to the hard shift). For example, a patient might produce noncredible test data while validly appearing to have significant depression. In this case, the patient's depression can be a point of discussion regarding future intervention; however, the neuropsychologist should be mindful not to suggest that the patient's depression caused the noncredible performances during testing.

In some instances, negative psychological, psychosocial, medical, or physical issues that were discovered during the clinical interview (and are now being addressed during feedback), might have contributed to the patient's suffering and led the patient to decide to exaggerate or feign his or her symptoms. In support of this view, several studies by Rogers (Rogers, 1990; Rogers et al., 1998; Rogers, Sewell, & Goldstein, 1994b) suggest that malingering is often adaptational, not simply an antisocial act by a bad person. In other words, as a maladaptive coping strategy, a patient might malinger and invalidity perform during testing for the purpose of dealing with or avoiding an adverse situation. If this is believed to be the case, the neuropsychologist should (1) avoid implying that a patient's suffering has directly caused the invalid test performance and (2) be mindful that intervening on the negative psychological, psychosocial, medical, or physical issues might lead to improved quality of life for the patient and possibly a reduced desire to malinger to escape the issue that initially prompted the patient to malinger (see Figure 9.4).

Exactly how the described hard shift and subsequent recommendations are discussed can vary on a case-by-case basis. In a number of instances, though, it could be appropriate to make statements such as, "While the testing is invalid and cannot be interpreted, we've discussed issues going on in your life that could be improved to reduce stress and increase your quality of life, and I want to address those with you." If psychological testing is valid despite cognitive testing being invalid, it could be stated, "While the cognitive testing is invalid, the psychological testing is valid. It

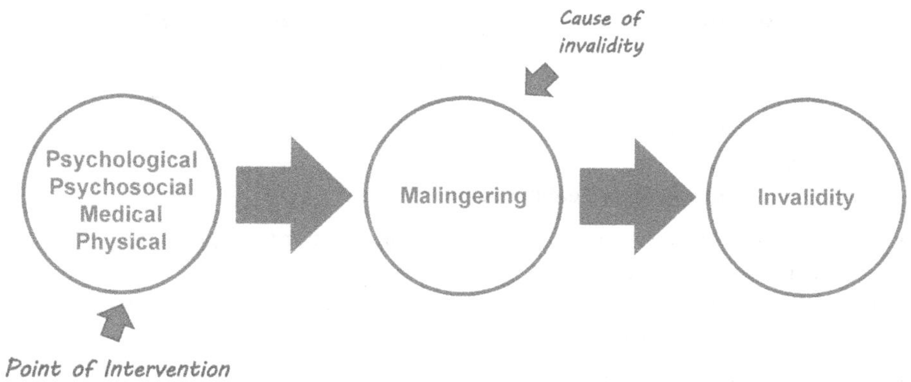

FIGURE 9.4. Theoretical model of malingering to avoid an adverse situation in clinical practice.

indicates you are experiencing depression, and I think that it would be helpful to treat this depression." In other instances, where appropriate, it could be stated, "While the cognitive test data are invalid, I can tell you that there is very strong research indicating that cognitive recovery occurs within 3 months from a mild head injury. When symptoms persist beyond that, such as they are for you, other factors are contributing. For you, I believe that depression is a contributing factor." Yet another potential hard shift could be phrased as "While testing is invalid, I do think that there are issues going on that can be improved. We've discussed x and working on improving that will likely be useful."

Overall, when moving forward, there is often opportunity to provide psychoeducation, discuss avenues for treatment, and/or discuss whatever else is clinically justified based on what is believed to be truly present and in need of treatment (see Table 9.5). In our clinical experience, essentially all patients agree with the need to focus on the recommendations, and they frequently express gratitude toward the clinician for the evaluation. While it is reasonable to assume that some patients will not follow up even after agreeing with the need for the intervention, research has indicated that some patients do follow up with interventions and, when completed, tend to benefit from the interventions (Goedendorp et al., 2013; Jurick et al., 2020). Furthermore, rates of invalid testing have been found to decline after treatment (Jurick et al., 2020), which suggests that the interventions might have adequately addressed underlying issues that drove certain patients to invalidate testing initially.

CLOSING REMARKS

In concluding this chapter, we wish to re-emphasize that it is natural and appropriate to feel apprehensive when preparing to provide feedback to patients who invalidate testing. With that being acknowledged, it is our clinical experience that by

TABLE 9.5. Potential Avenues to Suggest When Moving Forward in Step 4

- Provide psychoeducation and expected outcomes (e.g., regarding an injury such as mild traumatic brain injury) to:
  - Minimize iatrogenesis
  - Correct misattribution
  - Encourage more accurate treatment goals
- Discuss valid psychosocial, psychological, or medical factors that appear to:
  - Impact the patient's well-being
  - Motivate or relate to the patient's invalid approach (avoid contextualizing these factors as directly causing the invalid performance unless indicated)
- Provide treatment recommendations:
  - Psychotherapy
  - Psychotropic medication consultation
  - Social supports
  - Informational resources
  - Healthy lifestyle changes
  - Workups for conditions that may be present and impacting the patient's quality of life (e.g., sleep apnea)
  - Intervention for conditions that are known to be impacting the patient's quality of life (e.g., pain management, sleep management, substance abuse treatment)

demonstrating a combination of compassion, thoroughness, objectivity, and commitment to clinical care, risks of negative consequences can be minimized and, most importantly, the opportunity to provide help to the patient can be maximized. The firm-beneficent feedback approach has been outlined in this chapter. Steps of this approach start before the feedback session, as the clinician needs to conduct a clinical interview that sets the stage for successful feedback. During the feedback session, the patient's history should be summarized back to them in an intentional and skillful manner. Test invalidity should then be clearly communicated, but details about how the invalidity was identified should not be discussed. A hard shift then occurs, with the clinician discussing aspects of the patient's life that could realistically see benefit if some form of intervention were to occur. This could include providing psychoeducation on pertinent topics, discussing avenues for treatment of validity presented issues, and/or discussing anything else that is clinically justified.

CHAPTER 10

Managing Invalidity in Clinical Reports

Strategies and Examples

Just as providing oral feedback to patients who invalidate testing might feel daunting, writing reports for patients who invalidate testing might create some degree of unease for the clinician. This feeling can occur for a variety of reasons but possibly the most common reason is because the neuropsychologist realizes that the report will likely contain information that has the potential to be viewed negatively (i.e., the patient invalidated testing), and the patient has the legal right to request, receive, and read the neuropsychological report. Indeed, in our experience, a healthy minority of individuals who invalidate testing do request copies of their reports.

In Schroeder and Martin (2022a), we provided validity-related considerations for report writing by sections of the neuropsychological report (i.e., Introductory Disclaimer, Background History/Presenting Problem, Behavioral Observations, Procedures/Tests Administered, Test Results, and Conclusions). In the following paragraphs, we highlight key points from Schroeder and Martin (2022a), and we provide additional new information when appropriate. We also summarize these key points in Table 10.1.

SECTIONS OF THE REPORT

Introductory Disclaimer

Some clinicians have an Introduction Disclaimer section at the beginning of their reports which state that the evaluation is a nonforensic one. The disclaimer might read something along the lines of "This is a nonforensic clinical evaluation. The report is intended for health care purposes, not forensic purposes." or "This is a

TABLE 10.1.	Validity-Related Considerations for the Written Report by Section of the Report

Introductory disclaimer of the report
• We view this section as unnecessary: Patients have a legal right to use the report how they wish; making the disclaimer does not prevent subpoenas for records; the statement could leave a negative impression that the report is less reliable than other reports.
Background history/presenting problem
• While it can be easy to slip into a negative tone when writing about patients who invalid testing, it is important not to do so. • Inconsistencies in reporting should be noted but written in neutral and nonaccusatory language. • Consider how the tone of the report will be received by the reader (e.g., referring provider, patient, or third party): A negative tone can make a reader less amenable to the content; a negative tone can upset the patient, potentially increasing the likelihood of "retaliation." • Proofread the report from the perspective of the referring provider and the patient before finalizing the report: Do *not* change the content of the report based on how others might respond but change the tone of the report if appropriate.
Behavioral observations
• It is appropriate to make statements regarding the perception of the patient's engagement with and effort toward testing. • It is typically not appropriate to use behavioral observations (without validity test analysis) to form final conclusions of validity status.
Procedures/tests administered
• List which validity tests were administered. • Consider using only acronyms of validity tests if these validity tests include the word malingering or validity within the title of the test.
Test results
• Do not provide detailed information related to validity tests that could lead to compromises in trade secrets and test security. • Discuss the outcome of validity testing (e.g., testing is valid, indeterminate, or invalid). • Do not use a determination of indeterminate validity status in place of an invalid determination if invalidity is clearly present. • Consider minimizing or eliminating discussion of test scores when testing is invalid so that findings will not be misused by others.
Conclusions
• Acknowledge invalidity and do not explain away invalid findings by citing unlikely causes. • Acknowledge limitations in conclusions due to invalid test taking, when appropriate. • Do not refrain from making conclusions if conclusions can be confidently made. • Make recommendations based on findings that are believed to be accurate. • Make diagnoses, or rule out diagnoses, when they can be confidently made. • It is common to refrain from making a conclusion of malingering although clear statements of invalidity should be made.

nonforensic clinical evaluation only. If forensic opinions are requested, I reserve the right to review additional records and obtain additional information." While it is not necessarily wrong to include such a section, we do not provide this type of disclaimer for a variety of reasons. First, patients have a right to use the report how they wish. Second, adding the disclaimer does not prevent subpoenas for records or the ability to use the report in a legal case. Third, the statement could suggest that the clinical report is less complete or less reliable than a forensic report, which could leave a negative impression on the reader. Finally, reviewing additional records to address forensic issues after conducting a nonforensic evaluation would create a multiple relationship, which is typically discouraged (Martin, Schroeder, Boone, & Bush, 2022b). Instead, if an opinion is requested in a forensic arena regarding a clinical evaluation that has already been completed, the clinician should be aware that they are being asked to serve as a fact witness, which indicates that they should limit their testimony to the findings, conclusions, and information available from their initial evaluation (Sweet & Klipfel, 2022).

Background History/Presenting Problem

In the Background History/Presenting Problem section of the report, it can sometimes be easy to slip into a negative tone when writing about individuals who invalidate testing, especially when patients are flagrant in their feigning approaches, challenging in interpersonal interactions, and/or suspected of malingering. With that said, we believe that it is essential for clinicians to be impartial and noncritical when writing the background history (and the rest of the clinical report). In addition, when inconsistencies in a patient's reported history occur (e.g., the patient reports losing consciousness when medical records clearly indicate an absence of a loss of consciousness), we believe that the inconsistencies should be documented but they should be written in neutral and nonaccusatory language. This is because inconsistent reporting is not always due to lying or malingering. For example, cognitive impairment, psychiatric disorders, and substance use can all result in inaccurate reporting, and sometimes medical records can be wrong. Additionally, even cognitively normal individuals do not have "perfect" memories and can be inaccurate in their recall of past events even when significant (consider, for example, the well-documented propensity for inaccuracies in witness testimonies). Even when inaccurate reporting appears due to lying or malingering, though, clinicians should avoid adopting an adversarial tone in the report, as doing so can make a reader (e.g., the referral source, the patient, or a third party) less amenable to the content. This is especially true if the reader is an individual who has a positive relationship with the patient (e.g., consider a long-standing PCP) and has never found the patient to be deceptive before.

In addition to considering how a referring provider might perceive the report, it is important to consider how the patient might perceive the report because, again, the patient can legally have access to the report. We do *not* recommend that the clinician change the content of the report to assuage the patient, but we do recommend that the writer consider how the tone of the report might be perceived by the patient. If the patient disagrees with the conclusions made by the clinician, the patient is probably less likely to become angry if the tone of the report is noncritical and objectively worded as opposed to if the patient both disagrees with the content and perceives the clinician as being disparaging in his or her writing. When proofreading a report, a helpful exercise is to consider how the writing will be viewed by those who might read it. In this regard, our recommendation is to proofread the report from the perspective of the referring provider, the patient, and other potential future providers (e.g., neuropsychologists, neurologists, mental health providers) before considering the report final. Doing so will increase the likelihood that the final product will be perceived as objective, appropriately comprehensive, and being written in a neutral and nonoffensive tone.

Behavioral Observations

In the Behavioral Observations section of the report, it is important to document observations of engagement with testing, effort toward testing, and possible signs of feigning (if any). At the same time, and as noted elsewhere in this book, it is inappropriate to simply rely on observations and clinical judgment alone to determine validity status. Statements such as "the patient appeared positively engaged with testing" or "the patient appeared to put forth positive effort toward all tasks" can be appropriate; however, such observations should not be relied on exclusively when determining that a patient provided valid performance given the clear empirical research that clinical judgment alone is a poor predictor of validity status (Dandachi-FitzGerald et al., 2017; Faust et al., 1988; Heaton et al., 1978). Consequently, statements such as "the patient appeared to put forth adequate effort *so the results of testing are judged to be an accurate indication of the patient's true ability*" should not be included in the report.

Procedures/Tests Administered

Most clinicians likely have a Procedures/Tests Administered section in their reports that documents which tests were administered to their patient. Questions have been asked as to whether a clinician should document which validity tests were administered in addition to the cognitive tests. Professional consensus statements do recommend that neuropsychologists list the names of validity tests that were utilized so that another clinician can understand the basis of the conclusions and know which tests were administered in the event that a reevaluation is needed (Heilbronner et al., 2009; Sweet et al., 2021). Furthermore, nearly 90% of validity testing experts report that they "often" or "always" list validity tests in their tests administered section of the report (Schroeder, Martin, & Odland, 2016).

We, ourselves, list in our reports the stand-alone validity tests that were administered during the evaluation. For tests that include words like malingering (e.g., Test of Memory Malingering) or validity (e.g., Medical Symptom Validity Test), though, we only use the acronym (e.g., TOMM and MSVT) as opposed to the full name. We do this so that a patient who does not know that it is standard practice to include validity tests in all evaluations does not see the names of the tests and infer that the clinician preemptively thought that he or she would be malingering or performing invalidly.

Test Results

In the Test Results section, some clinicians discuss validity test results by test name, some clinicians provide scores of validity test results, and others neither discuss validity tests by name nor provide validity test scores. There is currently no consensus on the most preferable method of reporting on validity tests in the Test Results section and this is true even among validity assessment experts (Martin et al., 2015; Schroeder et al., 2016). For example, it has been found that 35% of experts report they frequently refer to validity tests by name when discussing test results, while 65% of experts do so infrequently (Schroeder et al., 2016). Furthermore, 52% of experts indicated that they are likely to report validity test scores in some form within the results section of the report, while 48% are unlikely to do so. We, ourselves, typically do not provide names of validity tests or scores in the Test Results section of our clinical reports. Instead, we provide basic descriptions of validity test outcomes. Our rationale is that such information could potentially be used by patients to attempt to evade detection in the future, and it does not provide incremental benefit in documenting that data are invalid. Additionally, the only type of reader who would be capable of appropriately interpreting actual validity test performances would be another neuropsychologist, who can always refer to or request the data summary sheet (depending on whether it is the neuropsychologist's practice to customarily include a data summary sheet with the report).

Regardless of how clinicians report validity test results in the Test Results section of their reports, it is imperative that descriptions do not compromise trade secrets and test security (Boone et al., 2022b). For example, clinicians should not describe administration formats and test stimuli in such a detailed manner that the descriptions could allow a reader to figure out which test is a validity test and then perform well on it on subsequent evaluations. Likewise, cutoff scores for validity tests should generally be avoided in reports, as a savvy reader could use that information to later pass the same validity test or coach others on how many errors can be made without being identified as invalidly performing testing.

Regardless of how clinicians report validity test results in the Test Results section, a formal "outcome" of the validity of test results should be made either in this section or the Conclusions section of the report. Some clinicians might prefer to only include a description of the test results in the Test Results section, in which case, the following examples could potentially be used to describe valid test findings:

> "As part of standard test procedure, empirically validated performance validity indices were interspersed throughout the neuropsychological testing session. The patient's performances on the indices were not suggestive of invalidity."

> "As part of standard test procedure, empirically validated performance validity indices were interspersed throughout the neuropsychological testing session. The patient passed six of six stand-alone and embedded validity tests, which is not suggestive of invalidity."

Other clinicians might include qualitative observations of validity status with the quantitative findings. This makes some sense, especially when remembering that validity tests emphasize specificity over sensitivity, and it is possible to pass validity tests while still performing invalidly (Martinez et al., 2021). The following statements are examples of how a clinician might incorporate both validity test findings and qualitative observations into a conclusion about the validity of testing:

> "As part of standard test procedure, empirically validated performance validity indices were interspersed throughout the neuropsychological testing session. The patient's performances on the indices were not suggestive of invalidity. Additionally, qualitative observations made during the evaluation were not suggestive of invalidity. As a result, the test findings are believed to be valid and an accurate depiction of the patient's cognitive abilities."

> "As part of standard test procedure, empirically validated performance validity indices were interspersed throughout the neuropsychological testing session. The patient passed six of six stand-alone and embedded validity tests. Additionally, qualitative observations made during the evaluation were not suggestive of invalidity. As a result, the test findings are believed to be valid and an accurate depiction of the patient's cognitive abilities."

In instances where testing is invalid, the following descriptions might be used to describe the findings:

> "As part of standard test procedure, empirically validated performance validity indices were interspersed throughout the neuropsychological testing session. The patient performed beyond cutoffs on multiple validity indices. Consequently, testing is invalid and uninterpretable as the patient's cognitive test performances are not representative of his cognitive capability."

> "As part of standard test procedure, empirically validated performance validity indices were interspersed throughout the neuropsychological testing session. The patient performed beyond cutoffs on five of six stand-alone and embedded validity indices. Consequently, testing is invalid as it is not representative of the patient's cognitive capability."

> "As part of standard test procedure, empirically validated performance validity indices were interspersed throughout the neuropsychological testing session. The patient performed beyond cutoffs on multiple validity indices. Additionally,

he produced highly variable and atypical scores on cognitive testing, which do not provide a consistent documentation of capabilities. Consequently, testing is invalid as it does not accurately represent the patient's cognitive capability."

"As part of standard test procedure, empirically validated performance validity indices were interspersed throughout the neuropsychological testing session. The patient performed beyond cutoffs on two stand-alone and three embedded validity indices. Consequently, the test results are determined to be invalid. Low cognitive test scores cannot be accurately interpreted, and low average and average-range test scores might even underestimate the patient's cognitive ability."

Finally, there might be occasional instances when it is unclear whether testing is valid or invalid despite appropriately using multiple validity tests. This could be, for example, due to the patient (1) passing validity tests but producing very atypical cognitive test scores that might suggest invalidity, (2) passing validity tests but behaviorally showing multiple significant signs that made the clinician question whether optimal effort was being provided, or (3) failing validity tests but it is unclear whether those particular tests were failed due to invalidity, significant cognitive impairment, language or cultural factors, or other causes. In these scenarios, the clinician might make statements such as the following:

"While the patient did not score beyond validity test cutoffs, he scored very atypically on cognitive tests given the injury in question. This raises the possibility that testing might be invalid and not representative of his cognitive capabilities."

"The patient passed validity tests but multiple qualitative observations during testing suggested that her engagement might have been limited at times. Given these observations, it is unclear whether all obtained test results are valid."

"The patient scored just beyond cutoffs on two of six validity tests. It is unclear whether this finding is due to an invalid test-taking approach or cognitive impairment resulting from the patient's documented severe brain injury. Because of this, the validity of the test scores must be considered indeterminate."

With regard to the indeterminate validity status designation, it is important to point out that validity tests (especially when used in aggregate) typically have excellent classification accuracy rates, so it should be uncommon to use this designation in reports. Furthermore, we note that an indeterminate classification status should not be used in place of an invalid classification just because a clinician might not want to say that testing is invalid. This would be an inappropriate use of the determination and, likely, and unethical practice.

After determining if testing is valid, the clinician will need to report the cognitive test findings. When testing is valid, the clinician can report the cognitive test findings in his or her typical manner. When testing is indeterminate, though, the clinician will need to decide whether to report the cognitive test results or not. Our practice would be to provide the test results, with a cautionary statement, if cognitive scores are largely consistent with expectations given the known injury or suspected disease. In this instance, we might make a statement such as "Because the validity of the test results is indeterminate, caution must be taken in interpreting the cognitive test findings. With that said, the following scores were obtained."

If the validity of the testing is indeterminate and the pattern of cognitive test findings does not make practical sense, our approach is to not report any cognitive test scores in the Test Results section of the report. This is because the cognitive findings are unlikely to be accurate (even if we can't definitely say that they are invalid) and reporting scores for the reader might result in the reader arriving at inaccurate conclusions even if those inaccurate conclusions are not stated in the neuropsychologist's report. In this regard, more harm might be done by reporting the test scores than withholding discussion of them.

When testing is invalid, the clinician will need to decide whether to report the cognitive test results. In our practices, we typically take one of two approaches. If testing is invalid but the patient still produced a number of average-range or near average-range test scores, we explicitly state that testing is invalid and an underrepresentation of the patient's abilities. We then provide a brief discussion of cognitive domains where performances were within normal limits and cognitive domains where performances were "below normal limits." By taking this approach, the clinician can establish that the patient is capable of, minimally, functioning within age-appropriate ranges in various cognitive domains, which, in some instances, can help to rule out significant cognitive impairment and/or certain diagnostic conditions. Furthermore, by simply stating that the patient performed "below normal limits" in other cognitive domains, we are removing the risk that a reader, who might ignore the statement that testing is invalid, will interpret specific scores on their own. When taking this approach, we typically report scores in general terms and by domain in order to avoid providing details on low scores, which might be inappropriately interpreted by the reader. Examples of such statement are as follows:

> "Although invalid, the patient still scored within or near the average range on tests of executive functioning and memory. Such performances might still underrepresent his true levels of functioning, but they rule out the possibility of significant cognitive impairment in these cognitive domains."

> "While validity measures indicate concern about an underperformance on testing, the patient scored within or near the average range on many tests of genuine cognitive ability. Although such findings might underrepresent the patient's true abilities, they demonstrate that the patient is, minimally, able to perform within typical age-related limits across several cognitive domains. Specifically, on most tests of executive functioning, the patient scored within the average to high average ranges. On tests of memory, scores were somewhat more variable, yet

performances were average on at least some tests of learning, delayed recall, and delayed recognition. Furthermore, low average or average-range performances were seen across most tests of attention, mental processing speed, visuospatial ability, and verbal expression."

When testing is invalid and few to no cognitive test scores are within an average range, we completely withhold discussing the cognitive test results. This is because some professionals disregard the statement that testing is invalid, and they interpret the scores on their own. As an example of this, one of us has previously written a report where it was clearly documented that testing was invalid and cognitive test scores underrepresented the patient's true capabilities. Test scores were then provided, which included a full-scale IQ score that fell in the range suggestive of an intellectual disability. The patient had no history of academic or functional difficulties, and it was made clear that the cognitive test scores were not an accurate portrayal of the patient's true capability. Despite this, it was later discovered that the referring therapist interpreted the low IQ score as being valid, and she stated in her own report that the neuropsychological test results indicated that the patient has an intellectual disability. It was at this point that the clinician decided not to report scores in reports when testing is invalid.

Conclusions

In the Conclusions section of reports where testing is invalid, some clinicians simply note that testing is invalid and cannot be interpreted. They then avoid making additional conclusions and/or recommendations. In our own practices, however, we find that there are often further conclusions that can be made, recommendations that are still justified for the patient, and/or guidance that may be helpful for the patient's other providers. With that said, if making additional statements outside of the fact that testing is invalid, the clinician should appropriately address any limitations that there might be. For example, it may be important in certain cases to state that "The obtained test data are invalid and cannot speak to the presence or absence of underlying cognitive deficits." In cases where underlying deficits are possible given the patient's medical or symptom history, a probabilistic statement could be made that describes the possibility for underlying deficits. Examples of such statements include:

"While testing was invalid, there is clear evidence from the medical record that the patient sustained a severe traumatic brain injury, and cognitive deficits may indeed be present. Recovery is often described as occurring over the 12 months following the injury, which indicates that ongoing recovery from any cognitive deficits that might be present could still occur."

"Although testing was invalid, the patient's recent MRI revealed evidence of a chronic left cerebellar stroke and moderate microvascular ischemic disease. Given these neuroimaging findings, the possibility of cognitive impairment cannot be excluded; however, the nature and degree of the patient's cognitive impairment could not be determined given clear evidence of underperformance on testing."

In cases where cognitive deficits are unexpected (e.g., an individual being seen months after a single mild concussion), the clinician can discuss recovery curve expectations and data on cognitive outcomes. When other non-neurological causes of persisting complaints are strongly suspected, these could also be noted. Providing this discussion could help the reader of the report to understand that reported cognitive symptoms are not neurological in etiology. An example of this would be as follows:

"As already described, validity measures indicate that neurocognitive testing does not accurately reflect the patient's cognitive capability. With that said, a large body of empirical research shows that neurocognitive dysfunction after a single uncomplicated concussion resolves within days to weeks after the injury. Indeed, the *Diagnostic and Statistical Manual of Mental Disorders, Fifth Edition*, notes that, when symptoms persist month to years after this type of mild injury, other causes of symptom complaints need to be considered. In this patient's case, he has findings of clinical depression, and he reports having severely disrupted sleep. Thus, these factors are much more likely the cause of the patient's ongoing cognitive complaints, particularly since empirical research indicates that, at this time point, there should be no ongoing neurocognitive dysfunction as a result of the injury itself."

In certain other cases, the clinician might be able to speak to the likelihood of specific questioned diagnoses, even in the presence of invalid data. Examples include:

"The patient was referred after expressing concern for Alzheimer's disease to her primary care provider. As the patient performed beyond cutoffs on multiple performance validity indicators, her low scores on testing cannot be interpreted due to psychometric evidence of underperformance. With that said, the patient performed within the average range or better on many tests of delayed memory recall and recognition. Such findings, particularly in the context of the patient's younger age, suggest an exceedingly low likelihood that her reported memory symptoms are due to Alzheimer's disease."

"The patient, who has no previous diagnosis of ADHD, was referred for a neuropsychological evaluation by his PCP after requesting that he be prescribed stimulant medication to treat ADHD. Validity testing indicates both underperformance on tests of cognitive functioning and overreport of symptoms on psychological and behavioral questionnaires. Although I am, therefore, unable to interpret his neuropsychological test data, this evaluation also included a thorough interview of the patient's current and lifelong functioning and review of his academic and medical records. From the information provided by the patient and his records, his reported difficulties with attention and motivation did not present until his late 20s. Because ADHD is a developmental disorder and DSM-5 symptom criteria requires that symptoms be present in childhood, he would not meet diagnostic criteria for the condition."

The examples provided in the previous paragraphs show that, even when testing is invalid, clinicians can sometimes confidently discuss (1) known or highly suspected injuries/illnesses, (2) established recovery curves and empirical data on cognitive outcomes, (3) normal range performances that rule out significant cognitive impairment, (4) factors and findings that are inconsistent with certain diagnoses, and/or (5) valid conditions that better explain complaints. Additionally, treatment recommendations can sometimes be made with a high degree of confidence even when testing is invalid. Recommendations might include a workup for possible conditions that may be affecting cognition (e.g., sleep apnea when the patient reports symptoms consistent with sleep apnea), treatment for psychiatric conditions for which there is sufficient valid information to suggest that they are truly present (e.g., psychotropic medication and/or psychotherapy for validly presented depression), self-help resources for reported behavioral issues (e.g., books on sleep hygiene for someone who reports having poor sleep habits), discussion of modifiable protective factors for cognitive health (e.g., the importance of exercise, nutrition, and cognitive stimulation), etc. When reaching conclusions and making recommendations, though, it is important that the clinician differentiate these from the invalid findings. That is, the clinician should avoid reaching conclusions or making recommendations based on invalid findings, and the clinician should also refrain from attributing invalid findings to noncredible explanations (e.g., refrain from attributing invalidity to depression when recommending treatment of depression). The following statement is an example of how one might do so.

"While sleep issues are not believed to be the cause of the patient's invalid test findings, the patient does have documented untreated sleep apnea. Treating this condition could potentially result in some benefit to the patient's cognition, mood, and energy on a day-to-day basis."

Finally, the clinician should consider which, if any, diagnoses might be provided in the report. We recommend that only clinical diagnoses that are strongly suspected or known be provided in reports when testing is invalid. Furthermore, sometimes it might be appropriate to indicate that the provided diagnoses are rule-out diagnoses given that testing is invalid. Along those lines, a statement such as the following might be included.

"Based on the patient's documented history of depressive symptoms, behavioral observations that included depressed affect and tearfulness, and his current presentation overall, I strongly suspect that depression is present. Given that testing was invalid, though, the evaluation results cannot completely verify a specific depressive disorder or its severity. For that reason, I am providing a rule out diagnosis of an unspecified depressive disorder."

In addition to diagnoses of clinical conditions, one might question if a determination/diagnosis of malingering should be made when testing is invalid and nontest factors (e.g., pursuit of an external incentive) point toward the possibility of malingering. The updated AACN consensus statement on validity assessment indicates that a determination of malingering can be made but it is up to the clinician as to whether and how it is reported (Sweet et al., 2021). As discussed in Chapter 8, we tend not to make conclusions of malingering in clinical reports. With that said, we also refrain from discrediting and explaining away validity test failure as being due to unlikely explanations (e.g., attention lapses, fatigue, depression). Instead, we note that testing was invalid, the test findings are inconsistent with expected cognitive outcomes and/or documented functional abilities, and the test results are not reflective of the patient's cognitive ability.

Per Martin et al. (2024), most North American neuropsychologists and validity assessment experts refrain from reaching conclusions of malingering in clinical reports as well. Specifically, it was found that only about 10% of both neuropsychologists and experts reported often or always using the term when malingering is suspected in their clinical evaluations. A separate survey of North American neuropsychologists (described in Schroeder & Martin, 2022a) was conducted to obtain more nuanced data on the topic. This second survey again found that most clinicians do not use the term malingering in nonforensic cases, but the term is more likely to be used in some clinical situations than others. Specifically, only 2% of neuropsychologists indicated that they would use the term when the cause of invalidity was unknown, 11% of clinicians would use the term when malingering was believed to be present but co-occurring pathology was also present, and 27% of providers noted that they would use the term when malingering was believed to be present and no co-occurring pathology was present. While the percentage of neuropsychologists willing to discuss malingering in clinical reports was higher in the last scenario, it is still noteworthy that nearly three-fourths of clinicians still avoid utilizing this label regardless of their suspicion for it.

In Martin et al. (2024), we asked clinicians who frequently use the term malingering why they use the term. As discussed in Chapter 8, the most commonly cited responses were (1) adhering to criteria for malingering, (2) because they believe it to be present, (3) to limit potential harm caused by malingering and/or benefit patient care, and (4) it is the responsibility of the clinician to communicate the most accurate explanation for the invalidity. Similarly, we asked clinicians who infrequently use the term malingering why they refrain from using the term. The most commonly cited explanations were (1) it is difficult to know and/or prove the cause, motivation, or intent behind invalid test performance, (2) using the term malingering could interfere with the clinical/therapeutic relationship, (3) malingering is a pejorative word and/or controversial term, (4) it is difficult to identify an external incentive in the case, and (5) using the term malingering provides no incremental benefit to the report.

The fifth point noted above could raise the question "What other statements are made in the report if using the term malingering provides no incremental benefit?" In the same survey (Martin et al., 2024), we found that the two most commonly made statements, endorsed by almost 90% of North American neuropsychologists and 100% of validity experts, are that test "data are invalid" and "test results are inconsistent with the severity of the reported injury." In thinking about these statements, the terminology used would appear accurate and, at the same time, the statements seem fairly benign as there are no direct inferences being made that the patient intentionally misrepresented their functioning.

CLOSING REMARKS

In concluding this chapter, we provide a clinical report of a patient who failed validity testing in order to demonstrate how a full clinical report might "come together" (see Appendix 10.1). In this case, two of two stand-alone performance validity tests (PVTs) were failed (Test of Memory Malingering Trial 1 = 32 and Dot Counting Test E-score = 24), and two of six embedded PVTs were failed (Logical Memory Recognition = 17 and Brief Visuospatial Memory Test—Revised Recognition Hits = 4). Additionally, a symptom validity scale on the Minnesota Multiphasic Personality Inventory–2nd Edition–Restructured Form was indicative of overreported somatic and/or cognitive complaints (FBS-r = 92). Thus, in total, five validity tests indicated the presence of invalid cognitive findings. While invalid test taking was clear in this particular case, the reason behind the invalidity was somewhat less clear. The patient was on private disability, and it was suspected that she might have believed that performing poorly was required to maintain disability, particularly since she had no desire to return to work. The patient denied that a disability review was ongoing or planned, but it is known that hidden external incentives surrounding disability do exist (Schroeder et al., 2022). Nonetheless, no firm external incentive could be identified.

In this case, underlying mild cognitive dysfunction was suspected as being a real possibility and mood-related factors were believed to be present even though testing was invalid. Consequently, this report provides an example of how clinical reports might be written when (1) testing is invalid and (2) underlying conditions are believed to be present. We emphasize, though, that specific content and verbiage should be based on multiple factors that include the context of the clinical evaluation, examination of possible external incentives, and outcomes of the evaluation. Consequently, statements within the sample report should not necessarily be "cut and paste" into other reports, especially when the context or outcomes related to the evaluations differ.

APPENDIX 10.1

Neuropsychological Report

Patient: Jane Doe

Date of Birth: xx/xx/xxxx

Date of Evaluation: xx/xx/xxxx

REFERRAL: The patient is a 57-year-old, left-handed, Native American, female with a history of left thalamic stroke. She was referred for a clinical neuropsychological evaluation by Referring Doctor, MD, to assess neuropsychological functioning, better understand the degree of cognitive and mood disturbances, and participate in treatment planning.

PROCEDURES: Available medical records were obtained and reviewed. A clinical interview was conducted with the patient. The following neuropsychological tests were administered by a psychometrist: Test of Premorbid Functioning, Wechsler Adult Intelligence Scale—4th Edition (subtests: Vocabulary, Similarities, Block Design, Matrix Reasoning, Digit Span, Arithmetic, Coding, Symbol Search), Wechsler Memory Scale—4th Edition (subtests: Logical Memory I & II, Visual Reproduction I & II), Brief Visuospatial Memory Test—Revised, Hopkins Verbal Learning Test—Revised, Delis–Kaplan Executive Function System (subtests: Trail Making, Verbal Fluency, Color–Word Interference, Tower), Neuropsychological Assessment Battery (subtest: Naming), Sentence Repetition Test, TOMM, Dot Counting Test, State–Trait Anxiety Inventory, and Minnesota Multiphasic Personality Inventory—2nd Edition—Restructured Form. The testing was scored and interpreted, a final session was held with the patient, and this report was written.

BACKGROUND INFORMATION: The patient reported that she noticed an acute onset of right-hand weakness on (7 months ago). She was working from home and writing at her table. She lost grip of her pen, which fell, rolled off the table, and landed on the floor. The patient stood up to go get the pen, but her right leg was weak, and she almost fell. She cautiously made her way to her couch to relax and see if her symptoms would go away. Around 20 minutes later, her husband came into the room to talk with her. The patient struggled to speak fluently, but she ultimately expressed that she was not feeling well and had right-sided bodily weakness. Her husband took her to the emergency department for workup. Medical records indicate that a head CT showed a vague area of slightly diminished density in the left basal ganglia. A follow-up brain MRI showed an acute to subacute ischemic infarct of the left thalamus. Following hospitalization, the patient was discharged to (a rehabilitation hospital). She underwent physical therapy, occupational therapy, and speech therapy (initially inpatient and, later, outpatient). Her final speech therapy note indicated that she showed significant improvement over the course of her therapy. At the time of speech therapy discharge, it was stated that the patient had occasional speech production and word-finding errors, but her occasional issues were considered within functional limits.

During the current evaluation, the patient reported that, since completing speech therapy, she has seen some improvement in her speech, but she still experiences frequent issues with word finding. Outside of word finding, she reports having issues with

(continued)

short-term memory that started after the stroke. When asked about her physical functioning, she reported that she has residual right-sided weakness, but she is able to use her hand and leg well enough that she can adequately perform most nondemanding activities. With that said, she tends to fatigue much easier than she used to. Consistently, a review of recent neurology records supports the presence of residual right-sided weakness and complaints of fatigue. When asked about her mood, the patient reported that she has anxiety, and she thinks that she is depressed. She elaborated on this and indicated that she is fearful that she will have another stroke, she is frustrated that she is not back at her baseline functioning, and she feels guilty about getting fatigued easily, which causes her to ask for help with certain activities. When queried further for symptoms of depression, the patient indicated that she feels sad and empty, she experiences some sense of worthlessness, and she has fleeting thoughts of death. Active suicidal ideation, however, was denied, and she expressed protective factors as being her husband and religious beliefs.

Additional medical history is significant only for being overweight. The patient reported that doctors told her that being overweight and having a high level of stress were likely factors that led to her stroke. Prior to the stroke, the patient noted that she was an executive within her company, and this job caused a significant amount of stress on a daily basis. Other than stress, her psychiatric history was unremarkable. She has never participated in psychotherapy, and she has never been prescribed psychotropic medication. She denied drinking alcohol, using tobacco, using marijuana, or using other illicit substances. She periodically drinks caffeine, but this is generally limited to one to two cups of coffee in the mornings. Neurological history is insignificant outside of the stroke. At present, the only medication that she is taking is aspirin 81 mg.

Psychosocial history indicates that the patient was born and raised in (urban area in the Midwest region of the United States). She denied experiencing abuse, neglect, or other traumas during her childhood. To the best of her knowledge, she met developmental milestones within normal limits. Scholastic achievement is significant for graduating from high school and earning a bachelor's degree in business. As noted above, she worked as an executive within her company prior to her stroke. Since her stroke, she has not returned to work. When asked about her future employment plans, she reported that she does not think that she can currently meet the demands of the job, so she does not plan to return to work. She is on private disability through her employer, and she indicated that there are no current or planned reviews to potentially change her disability status. She lives with her husband in City, State. She has no children.

BEHAVIORAL OBSERVATIONS: The patient was casually dressed, well groomed, and appeared her stated age. She ambulated independently but her gait appeared somewhat effortful due to right-sided weakness. Furthermore, a mild right-sided facial droop was observed. She was polite, and she was an active part of the clinical interview. She was able to recall details from her history. Her speech was fluent and normal in volume, rate, prosody, and articulation. Phraseology was ordinary. She spoke in complete and grammatically accurate sentences; no word-finding problems or paraphasic errors were noted. She was able to comprehend casual interview questions and formal test instructions without difficulty. Thought processes were logical and coherent. There was no evidence of delusions or hallucinations. Affect appeared depressed. The patient was tearful throughout

(continued)

the evaluation, and she often avoided eye contact. During testing, the patient complained of testing being challenging, she completed tests slowly, and she periodically appeared to give up easily on tests including easy tests.

NEUROPSYCHOLOGICAL TEST RESULTS: As part of standard test procedure, empirically validated performance validity indices were interspersed throughout the neuropsychological testing session. The patient performed beyond cutoffs on four of these validity indices, and this cannot be attributed to her history of stroke, current residual right-sided weakness, or symptoms of depression. Consequently, the test results are determined to be invalid, which entails that her low cognitive test scores cannot be interpreted, and any low average or average-range test scores should also be considered as possibly underestimating her cognitive capability.

Premorbid abilities were formally estimated using an equation that utilizes demographic variables, and premorbid abilities were estimated as being average. On tests of current ability, the patient performed within the average range on an attention span test. Performances on tests of working memory were variable, ranging from average to below normal limits. Mental processing speed performances were variable but below normal limits. The patient's performances on expressive verbal abilities ranged from average to low average. Specifically, she scored in the average range on a vocabulary test, in the low average range on a confrontation naming test, and in the low average range on verbal fluency tests. Her sentence repetition score was in the low average range. Word reading was measured as being average. Verbal comprehension was informally assessed and determined to be within normal limits. Visuospatial performances were variable, ranging from average to below normal limits. Performances on tests of verbal learning and recall were variable, ranging from average to below normal limits. Performances on tests of visuospatial learning and recall were also variable, ranging from average to below normal limits. Executive functioning performances were generally near normal limits on accuracy-based measures but were below normal limits on speed-based measures.

Psychological testing was also administered. Validity scales suggest that the patient may be underreporting emotional symptoms while overreporting cognitive and/or somatic symptoms. Regarding emotional symptoms, testing indicated the presence of mild depression. Beyond having symptoms of depression, the patient endorsed having some stress and worry.

SUMMARY and CONCLUSIONS: Medical records document that the patient had a stroke on (7 months ago). A head CT showed a vague area of slightly diminished density in the left basal ganglia, and a follow-up brain MRI demonstrated an acute to subacute ischemic infarct of the left thalamus. The patient sustained unilateral motor weakness and speech issues as a result. With regard to her speech, speech therapy notes indicate that significant improvement had occurred with only occasional speech production and word-finding errors, which were determined as being within functional limits, remaining at discharge. During the current neuropsychological clinical interview, the patient reported that she continues to have word-finding problems and right-sided weakness (right-sided weakness was observed and also documented in recent neurology notes). She also added that she experiences short-term memory difficulties, anxiety, and depression.

(continued)

On formal neurocognitive testing, the patient performed beyond cutoffs on multiple empirically validated performance validity indices. Additionally, an empirically validated symptom validity scale indicated an overreporting of cognitive and/or somatic concerns. Consequently, the neurocognitive test results are invalid, and the presence, nature, and extent of possible cognitive deficits cannot be conclusively stated. With that being said, from a neuropsychological standpoint, it is certainly possible that the patient could have some residual cognitive weaknesses, as it would not be uncommon for cognitive symptoms to persist after a stroke of this nature occurring 7 months ago. If the patient is experiencing any residual cognitive weaknesses, however, they are likely no more than mild in severity. This is because the patient scored no lower than low average on all verbal/language tests (the cognitive domain that was reportedly most impacted), and she demonstrated the ability to score within the average range in all cognitive domains except for mental processing speed. Thus, at worst, the patient might have a mild neurocognitive disorder.

Beyond raising the possibility that the patient might have some mild residual cognitive weaknesses, I have clearer and greater concerns about her emotional health. On psychological testing, the patient likely underreported her emotional symptoms. Even with this probable underreporting of emotional symptoms, psychological testing indicated the presence of depression, and stress and worry were also suggested. Furthermore, during the clinical interview, the patient reported that she is fearful that she will have another stroke, she is frustrated that she is not back to her baseline functioning, and she feels guilty about becoming easily fatigued, which causes her to ask for help with certain activities. When queried further for symptoms of depression, the patient indicated that she feels sad and empty, she experiences some sense of worthlessness, and she has fleeting thoughts of death. Behaviorally, the patient was tearful throughout the evaluation, and her affect was depressed. Thus, a depressive disorder diagnosis (with mixed anxiety) appears warranted.

A final session was held with the patient, and the aforementioned findings and impressions were provided to her. It was reviewed that she had a stroke, the stroke appears to have had an impact on her physical functioning, and it is possible that there may be ongoing mild cognitive issues, but my greatest neuropsychological concern is with regard to her emotional health. Therefore, I recommended that treatment focus on addressing the depression and anxiety that are believed to be present.

DIAGNOSTIC IMPRESSION:

- Unspecified Depressive Disorder, with mixed anxiety
- R/O Mild Neurocognitive Disorder, secondary to stroke

RECOMMENDATIONS:

- I recommended that the patient pursue psychotherapy. She seems to be experiencing a depressed mood with mixed anxiety, and she does not appear to be coping well with her current symptoms. After discussing this, the patient was in agreement to pursue therapy, and I initiated a referral.
- I encouraged the patient to talk with her prescribing provider about potentially starting

(continued)

a trial of an antidepressant medication. The patient was initially hesitant to do so, but she is now willing to discuss the possibility of this with her prescribing provider.

- Unless otherwise indicated by her physician, I would recommend that the patient start participating in aerobic exercise. Aerobic exercise has been found helpful for reducing anxiety, improving mood, improving cognitive clarity, and improving general health status. If needed, reengaging with a physical therapist or engaging with a skilled personal trainer might be considered to ensure that the patient is safely exercising given her reported right sided weakness.
- Finally, I recommended the book *Brain Injury Survival Kit: 365 tips, tools, and tricks to deal with cognitive function loss.* The book discusses a number of helpful topics such as the necessity of having adequate diet, exercise, rest, and stress reduction if one wants to perform at their maximal cognitive capabilities. I explained to the patient that this book can be useful for individuals with cognitive difficulties for a variety of reasons, not just those with traumatic brain injuries.

Thank you for involving me in the care of this patient.

Neuropsychologist

CHAPTER 11

Putting It All Together

A Case Demonstration

In this final chapter, we walk though the case of a patient that was evaluated within a clinical context. She engaged in the evaluation in a noncredible manner, which included producing invalid test results. We discuss pertinent information related to the case during each step of the evaluation (as explored in each of the previous chapters), and we provide our conceptualization of the case at each step to help demonstrate how all of the information comes together for a final conclusion. To maintain confidentiality of the patient, personal identifying information has been altered although the general background history, observations, test findings, impressions, and final conclusions remain consistent with the actual case.

THE CASE OF MS. SMALLS

Preparatory Work

The neuropsychologist received a clinical referral to evaluate Ms. Smalls. In an initial review of the records, it was seen that the patient was a 49-year-old, left-handed, biracial (White and Black), female who was recently honorably discharged from the U. S. Air Force. She is now a veteran, and she began seeing providers at her local Veterans Administration medical center (VAMC). In talking to her physician at the VAMC, she reported that she sustained a concussion 14 years ago while in the Air Force, and she feels like her memory has been worsening since then. At her request, her physician referred her for the current neuropsychological evaluation to better understand the memory issues and assist in developing a treatment plan.

The referring provider documented Ms. Smalls' report of her concussion in his medical records. Specifically, Ms. Smalls described hitting her head on the exterior of a plane while deployed in Iraq. She stated that she was sitting under the aircraft when an extremely loud banging noise occurred, causing her to jump up and hit the top of her head on the metal exterior of the plane. She noted that she lost consciousness, but she was not sure how long the loss of consciousness might have been. After becoming alert again, she decided not to seek medical attention and, instead, continued to carry out her duties for the day. The next day, she developed a headache, "foggy" thinking, and memory issues. Her memory issues have reportedly persisted, with worsening effects occurring over time. No evaluation or treatment had been previously sought, but she is now wanting to look into these issues as she has recently been discharged from the Air Force, and she is "transitioning back into civilian life."

Ms. Smalls underwent an MRI of the brain approximately 3 months before the neuropsychological evaluation, and the imaging study was read as being unremarkable. Labs were also obtained, and they were unremarkable. Medical history, outside of the reported concussion, was significant for insomnia and anxiety with onset reportedly occurring around the same time as the head injury. Ms. Smalls had not sought treatment for any of these conditions until recently starting psychotherapy and being prescribed an SSRI. Records indicated that she was not receiving service-connected disability, and there were no indications of her seeking disability, being involved in litigation, or having other external incentives. Likewise, there were no indications of a legal history, drug use history, or work-related problems.

In conceptualizing the case at this point, the clinician found it odd from a neurological perspective that Ms. Smalls was reporting having memory problems that have persisted—and worsened—since sustaining a single concussion 14 years ago, as literature does not suggest that this is a likely neurological outcome from a single concussion (Carroll et al., 2004; Rohling et al., 2011). With that said, it was thought that anxiety and insomnia could very well be contributing to her complaints, especially since these issues started around the same time, which happened to be during a stressful situation (i.e., deployment to a war zone). At the same time, the clinician considered the possibility that Ms. Smalls' reported symptoms might be noncredible and feigned. This is because she reported having ongoing symptoms which are not neurologically expected (as just described). Furthermore, she had a history of concussion and literature indicates that individuals with concussions are thought to invalidate testing at relatively high rates even in clinical settings (Martin & Schroeder, 2020). Additionally, while Ms. Smalls did not have a known external incentive, it was recognized that she was a veteran, and she was pursuing evaluation for an injury that occurred while she was in the Air Force, which could potentially result in award of service-connected disability benefits. For these reasons, it was thought that there was some risk that Ms. Smalls might invalidate neuropsychological testing.

Clinical Interview

Ms. Smalls arrived for the clinical interview alone, and she was approximately 20 minutes early for the appointment. She did not have any documents (e.g., history questionnaire) with her for the clinician to review, but she had a number of medical records in her medical chart that were previously reviewed. In walking from the waiting room to the clinician's office, Ms. Smalls did not spontaneously engage in conversation, but she appropriately responded to questions. Initial observations of Ms. Smalls were that she was casually dressed, was well groomed, and appeared her stated age. No physical abnormalities (e.g., gait problems) were observed, and she made appropriate eye contact. No abnormalities with receptive or expressive language were noted. She seemed mildly anxious.

After sitting down in the office, Ms. Smalls was asked about her understanding for the evaluation. She stated that she previously experienced a "brain injury," and she is being seen because it resulted in memory problems. The clinician noted that this is the same referral question that he had read, and he expressed interest in wanting to learn more from Ms. Smalls. Open-ended questions were asked, including those related to having her describe the incident. Ms. Smalls described the incident similar to how she described it to the referring provider, adding additional details when prompted for them. For example, when asked, Ms. Smalls reported having full memory for everything leading up to the head injury (i.e., no retrograde amnesia) and she remembers the rest of her day after getting up off the ground. When asked about any improvement in symptoms, she reported that her memory problems never improved at all and, in fact, they have significantly worsened over time. In addition to having memory issues, she reported struggling to some degree with attention and focus. Interestingly, despite her cognition significantly worsening, Ms. Smalls reported that she recently started a new full-time job, it is going well, and she is also taking advanced college courses in which she is typically earning A grades.

When asked how she has been transitioning in her move from military to civilian life, Ms. Smalls noted that it has been smooth. She added, though, that she is still establishing care with her local health care providers, and she is a little frustrated about how long it has been taking to get all of her "VA paperwork" completed. When asked what VA paperwork she needs to get completed still, she reported that she is seeking service-connected disability and is in the process of collecting documentation for that. When asked what condition she is trying to get disability for, she reported that she is pursuing disability related to her brain injury. At this point, the clinician informed Ms. Smalls that her provider referred her for the current evaluation due to the report of a previous brain injury and current cognitive symptoms, but the evaluation is for clinical purposes and not disability purposes. She expressed an understanding in that distinction, and she stated that she wanted to continue to pursue the evaluation as she wanted help dealing with her memory problems.

Ms. Smalls was asked about her other medical and psychiatric history. She reported that she periodically gets headaches (which she also linked to her concussion), she struggles with sleep, and she has anxiety. When asked about her sleep, she noted that she rarely slept while in Iraq due to hypervigilance, and her sleep has been horrible ever since then. When asked in what way her sleep is horrible, she reported that her brain "won't turn off" at night so it takes her anywhere from 1 to 3 hours to fall asleep. She denied having nightmares, but she reported that she awakens after a couple of hours of sleep and struggles to fall back to sleep. Consequently, she only sleeps 4 to 6 hours per night. Likely related to this, her daytime energy was described as being poor.

When asked about health habits, Ms. Smalls stated that she very infrequently exercises, and her job is primarily a sitting "desk job." She doesn't get very hungry either, so she typically skips breakfast, and she sometimes skips lunch. When asked how long her appetite has been poor, she reported that her appetite seemed to change around the time she was deployed to Iraq. Despite having a poor appetite, she denied noticing any changes to her senses of taste or smell.

Ms. Smalls was asked about her psychiatric history. She reported that she might have had a little anxiety throughout much of her life, but anxiety became problematic while she was in Iraq due to fears of potential attack (no attacks occurred during her tour in Iraq). Since returning from Iraq, her anxiety has continued to be high, and she periodically experiences panic-like symptoms. The primary trigger that she identified for her panic-like symptoms is being in crowded public locations. Because of this, she tries to avoid crowds when possible. She denied feeling depressed or having much negative emotionality. She also denied experiencing any significant intrusive thoughts and experiences. All other psychiatric symptomatology was denied as well. Suicidal ideation was also denied. As previously noted, Ms. Smalls just recently started therapy for anxiety, and she was also recently prescribed an SSRI.

Ms. Smalls was asked more about her psychosocial history. She reported that she was born and raised on the West Coast, but she has been living in the Midwest since discharge from the military. When asked why she decided to move to the Midwest, she reported that the cost of living was lower, and she has a cousin in the area with whom she has a close and positive relationship. Ms. Smalls is single (never married), and she has no children. She is living alone and reported that living alone is going well. She denied having any significant stressors, including work, financial, or relationship stressors.

After the previously described information was obtained, the clinician began wrapping up the clinical interview. In doing so, the clinician first provided a brief overview of the issues as discussed by Ms. Smalls. In this case, it was stated:

> "In briefly summarizing what we just talked about, it sounds like things went downhill when you were deployed to Iraq. While in Iraq, you hit your head pretty hard on the exterior of a plane, and you've been experiencing memory issues since then. Your memory has worsened over time; although, positively, work and school are going well. You've undergone an MRI of your brain, which was normal, and now we are looking into your experience of memory difficulties by doing a different type of testing. In addition to memory issues, you rarely slept while in Iraq and your sleep has been poor since then. You were also constantly on alert for potential threats while in Iraq, and anxiety has been problematic since then. Your appetite has also been poor, and you're not getting much physical activity. Is that a good summary of the high points that we discussed? Also, is there anything that we didn't discuss that you feel we should discuss?"

Ms. Smalls agreed with the summary, and she stated that she was unable to think of anything else that needed to be discussed but would alert the clinician to new information if she thinks of any.

The clinician, next, stated "I always like to ask patients what they think might be the cause of their problems. I know that you described hitting your head. Do you feel that is the sole cause of your memory difficulties? Or do you feel like something else might be contributing as well?" Ms. Smalls reported that the "brain injury" seems to be the primary factor contributing to her memory difficulties, but she has noticed that her memory seems to be a little worse when she is anxious. The clinician reinforced that anxiety can sometimes impact memory on a day-to-day basis, and he noted that we would be looking at anxiety during this evaluation as well as her memory. Finally, the clinician stated "So the primary goal of the evaluation, as I see it, is to look into your memory difficulties and then discuss ways to hopefully try to help. Is that your primary goal as well? Also, do you have any other goals for this evaluation that you would like to me try to address?" Ms. Smalls agreed with the goal and stated that she had no other goals that she wished the clinician to address.

The clinical interview was concluded by stating:

> "Unless you would like to take a brief break first, we will move into the testing part of the evaluation. You will be working with my technician for this part, and I will introduce you to him shortly. Before doing so, though, I want to discuss the testing a little bit more. My technician will ask you to do a number of different interactive activities like doing memory games and puzzles. Some of the test items will be very easy for you, some of the items will be very challenging, and others will be in between those two extremes. You might get a 100% on some of the tests, but you won't get a 100% on all of the tests. Nobody gets all items correct. This is because the tests are often designed so that we can identify where your abilities stop, as all of us have abilities that stop at some point. This type of testing helps to ensure that we can identify even mild difficulties that a person might be experiencing with memory, attention, and other thinking abilities. Your job is just to do the best that you can, regardless of whether test items are easy or challenging. By doing your best, we can get accurate and valid results. Conversely, if a person were to underperform on any tests to try to demonstrate areas of weakness, that will only muddy the pattern of results that we obtain, making it less likely that a diagnosis of a clinical condition could be made. So, it is really important that you do your best on all tests. Do you have any questions about this, and would you like to take a quick break before we begin testing?"

Ms. Smalls indicated that she had no questions, and she did not need a break.

Throughout the entirety of the clinical interview (discussed above), rapport was being developed, trust was being built, a genuine interest in learning about Ms. Smalls and her symptoms was displayed, and no degree of skepticism was demonstrated even when potentially conflicting pieces of information were being obtained.

Furthermore, the clinician intentionally questioned Ms. Smalls about external incentives but this information came about in a natural manner by asking pertinent probing, but nonthreatening, questions that built off prior nonthreatening questions. We have found that questioning patients about external incentives in this manner seems to lead to their endorsement more frequently than if asking direct questions such as "Are you seeking disability?" This might be due to the fact that patients have developed rapport and have let their guard down due to the nature of the clinically applied and nonthreatening questionings.

After the clinical interview concluded, the clinician's conceptualization was even stronger than before. The clinician felt confident that the head injury reported by Ms. Smalls resulted in no more than a concussion, at worst. Given that this occurred more than a decade ago and symptoms have been worsening since then, it was believed that the head injury was not the cause of her cognitive difficulties. The clinician believed that anxiety was likely present and sleep issues were also likely present, and these factors seemed like they were more likely issues contributing to any cognitive difficulties that she might have.

In addition to considering the possibility that anxiety and sleep issues might be contributing, it was considered that there were multiple risk factors for invalidity. As already mentioned, Ms. Smalls had a history of concussion, and she reported having ongoing symptoms when neurologically based symptoms would not typically be expected. Furthermore, a notable discrepancy was identified during the clinical interview. Specifically, Ms. Smalls reported that her memory problems were quite noticeable and problematic for her but, conversely, she stated that she was doing well at a new job and excelling in advanced college courses. Finally, through her responses to questions during the clinical interview, it was discovered that she was pursuing an external incentive (i.e., service-connected disability) related to the "brain injury," which could have been a motivating factor for seeking the current evaluation. While she was in agreement that the current evaluation was related to clinical services and not disability pursuit, she also stated that she was in the process of collecting paperwork to move her disability claim forward. Additionally, in looking at the referral paperwork a second time, it appeared clear that the referral was at the request of Ms. Smalls and not a spontaneous referral from her physician. For all of these reasons, there were concerns about the possibility that invalidity might occur during testing.

Selecting The Test Battery

The clinician constructed a test battery that allowed for evaluation of all cognitive domains, psychiatric disturbance, and sleep disturbance. Additionally, performance validity tests (PVTs) and symptom validity tests (SVTs) were included. When choosing PVTs, both the Test of Memory Malingering (TOMM) and Medical Symptom Validity Test (MSVT) were chosen because Ms. Smalls reported that her greatest cognitive concerns centered around memory. Only Trial 1 of the TOMM was administered because it has good classification accuracy statistics supporting its usage

(Martin et al., 2020; Schroeder et al., 2019c), and only administering this one subtest reduced test administration time. In addition to the two memory-based PVTs, the Dot Counting Test was administered. This test was administered because it is brief, and it assesses for noncredible attention problems—Ms. Smalls reported also having some attention issues. A number of embedded PVTs were interspersed throughout the test battery as well, which included Reliable Digit Span (RDS), the Effort Index (EI) from the Repeatable Battery for the Assessment of Neuropsychological Status (RBANS), an embedded validity index in the Brief Visuospatial Memory Test—Revised (BVMT-R), and an embedded validity test in the Color–Word subtest from the Delis–Kaplan Executive Functioning System (D-KEFS). Thus, in total, seven PVTs were included and examined within the test battery.

Regarding SVTs, embedded validity scales on the Minnesota Multiphasic Personality Inventory–2—Restructured Form (MMPI-2-RF) were utilized. These validity scales allow for examination of possible overreported psychiatric, somatic, and cognitive disturbances. Additionally, while it was not suspected that an underreporting of symptoms was going to occur, the MMPI-2-RF validity scales also include underreporting-based SVTs.

Administering the Tests

The clinician's technician administered the testing in a specific order. Stand-alone PVTs were administered early in the test battery and before cognitive tests that measure the same cognitive domain (e.g., administering the TOMM before the BVMT-R). The embedded PVTs were interspersed throughout the rest of the test battery. After cognitive testing was completed, the MMPI-2-RF (which included multiple embedded SVTs), PTSD Checklist for the DSM-5, and Epworth Sleepiness Scale were administered in that order.

During testing, it became readily apparent that Ms. Smalls was engaging with testing in a noncredible manner. As recommended in Chapter 7 of this book, she was not given *additional* prompts to do her best, as doing so could result in more sophisticated feigning. Also, the remainder of the test battery was administered despite Ms. Smalls' noncredible performance, as having a full dataset can sometimes be helpful in addressing issues even when testing is invalid.

The technician made various observations during testing. First, Ms. Smalls easily understood all test instructions and never asked for them to be repeated or elaborated upon. Second, it was observed that she seemed to not try very hard during testing, particularly on memory-based tests. Despite this, Ms. Smalls repeatedly made statements that the memory-based tests were challenging—even making these comments during easy tasks such as the TOMM and recognition memory tests. Conversely, she appeared to be much more engaged and effortful when performing "hands on" tasks (e.g., Block Design and Tower), which she stated that she enjoyed. It was also noted that, at no point during testing, did anxiety or other psychiatric factors appear to impact Ms. Smalls' performances. Likewise, although she yawned twice during testing, there were no observations of excessive sleepiness impacting her performances. Outside of the issues reported above, testing moved along smoothly, and Ms. Smalls did not request any breaks.

Identifying Invalidity and Interpreting Findings

Ms. Smalls' PVT results are provided in Table 11.1. She was identified as performing invalidly by five of the seven examined PVTs. Specifically, she failed the TOMM by performing well beyond cutoffs on both TOMMe10 and Trial 1. She also failed the easy validity subtests of the MSVT and, given that there was no suspicion for organic cognitive impairment, her genuine memory impairment profile did not need to be examined. It can be seen, though, that she would not meet criteria for a genuine memory impairment profile if calculated. On embedded PVTs, she clearly failed the RBANS EI and the BVMT-R embedded validity index. On the D-KEFS Color–Word validity index, Ms. Smalls would obtain a passing score when using a cutoff of ≤18, but she would obtain a failing score when using a cutoff of ≤20, which has been validated with a brain injury sample that was primarily comprised of individuals with mild traumatic brain injuries (Eglit et al., 2020).

Pertinent cognitive test results produced by Ms. Smalls are presented in Table 11.2. While invalid, they were still examined. Ms. Smalls produced low average scores on tests of attention. She typically scored in or near the average range on tests of mental processing speed, although she scored well below that on the RBANS Coding subtest. Likewise, she typically scored in or near the average range on language tests, although she scored well below that on the RBANS Semantic Fluency subtest (of note, she scored within the average range on the D-KEFS Category Fluency subtest). Ms. Smalls scored within the average to high average ranges on visuospatial tests. Both verbal and visual memory performances were generally quite poor with

TABLE 11.1. PVT Results

Test	Scores
Test of Memory Malingering	TOMMe10 = 5, Trial 1 = 31
Dot Counting Test	E-score = 12
Medical Symptom Validity Test	IR, DR, & CNS = 80%; PA = 80%; FR = 45%
Reliable Digit Span	RDS score = 8
RBANS Effort Index	Index score = 4
BVMT-R Recognition Hits	Raw score = 2
D-KEFS Color Word	Validity score = 19

Note. IR = Immediate Recognition; DR = Delayed Recognition; CNS = Consistency, PA = Paired Associates; FR = Free Recall; RDS = Reliable Digit Span; RBANS = Repeatable Battery for the Assessment of Neuropsychological Status; BVMT-R = Brief Visuospatial Memory Test—Revised; D-KEFS = Delis–Kaplan Executive Function System.

TABLE 11.2. Neurocognitive Test Results

Cognitive domain/test	Scores
Premorbid ability	
Test of Premorbid Functioning	Demographic IQ Estimate = 112
Test of Premorbid Functioning	Reading IQ Estimate = 110
Test of Premorbid Functioning	Combined IQ Estimate = 113
Attention/working memory	
Digit Vigilance Test Errors	*T*-score = 43
RBANS Digit Span	Scaled Score = 6
WAIS-IV Digit Span	Scaled Score = 7
Processing speed	
WAIS-IV Symbol Search	Scaled Score = 9
RBANS Coding	Scaled Score = 4
Digit Vigilance Test Time	*T*-score = 44
Trail Making Test Part A	*T*-score = 39
Language	
WAIS-IV Vocabulary	Scaled Score = 9
RBANS Picture Naming	Cumulative % = >75%
RBANS Semantic Fluency	Scaled Score = 2
D-KEFS Letter Fluency	Scaled Score = 9
D-KEFS Category Fluency	Scaled Score = 10
Visuospatial	
WAIS-IV Block Design	Scaled Score = 13
RBANS Figure Copy	Scaled Score = 9
RBANS Line Orientation	Cumulative % = >75%
Verbal memory	
RBANS List Learning	Scaled Score = 7
RBANS Story Memory	Scaled Score = 5
RBANS List Recall	Cumulative % = ≤2%
RBANS List Recognition	Cumulative % = ≤2%
RBANS Story Recall	Scaled Score = 4
Visual memory	
RBANS Figure Recall	Scaled Score = 3
BVMT-R Total Recall	*T*-score = 33
BVMT-R Delayed Recall	*T*-score = <20
BVMT-R Recognition Discrimination	Cumulative % = <1%
Executive functioning	
Trail Making Test Part B	*T*-score = 39
Verbal Fluency: Category Switching	Scaled Score = 12
Color–Word: Inhibition Time	Scaled Score = 4
Color–Word: Inhibition Errors	Scaled Score = 12
Color–Word: Inhibition-Switching Time	Scaled Score = 6
Color–Word: Inhibition-Switching Errors	Scaled Score = 10
Tower: Total Achievement	Scaled Score = 13

Note. RBANS = Repeatable Battery for the Assessment of Neuropsychological Status; WAIS-IV = Wechsler Adult Intelligence Scale—4th Edition; D-KEFS = Delis–Kaplan Executive Function System; BVMT-R = Brief Visuospatial Memory Test—Revised.

scores often falling within the below average to exceptionally low ranges. Finally, executive functioning scores were typically in the low average to high average ranges with the exception of speed-based performances on the Color–Word subtest.

Ms. Smalls' MMPI-2-RF validity, higher-order, and restructured clinical scale scores are provided in Table 11.3. She left no question on the inventory unanswered, and her scores on the content nonresponsiveness scales did not indicate issues with content inconsistent responding. Her overreporting validity scales were not suggestive of an exaggeration or feigning of psychiatric or somatic symptoms, but they

TABLE 11.3. MMPI-2-RF Results

MMPI-2-RF scale	Scores
VRIN-r	*T*-score = 63
TRIN-r	*T*-score = 50
F-r	*T*-score = 70
Fp-r	*T*-score = 77
Fs	*T*-score = 74
FBS-r	*T*-score = 89
RBS	*T*-score = 101
L-r	*T*-score = 62
K-r	*T*-score = 38
EID	*T*-score = 54
THD	*T*-score = 39
BXD	*T*-score = 36
RCd	*T*-score = 60
RC1	*T*-score = 74
RC2	*T*-score = 50
RC3	*T*-score = 51
RC4	*T*-score = 46
RC6	*T*-score = 43
RC7	*T*-score = 53
RC8	*T*-score = 52
RC9	*T*-score = 38

Note. VRIN-r = Variable Response Inconsistency; TRIN-r = True Response Inconsistency; F-r = Infrequent Responses; Fp-r = Infrequent Psychopathology; Fs = Infrequent Somatic Responses; FBS-r = Symptom Validity; RBS = Response Bias Scale; L-r = Uncommon Virtues; K-r = Adjustment Validity; EID = Emotional/Internalizing Dysfunction; THD = Thought Dysfunction; BXD = Behavioral/Externalizing Dysfunction; RCd = Demoralization; RC1 = Somatic Complaints; RC2 = Low Positive Emotions; RC3 = Cynicism; RC4 = Antisocial Behavior; RC6 = Ideas of Persecution; RC7 = Dysfunctional Negative Emotions; RC8 = Aberrant Experiences; RC9 = Hypomanic Activation.

were suggestive of an exaggeration or feigning of cognitive symptoms. Underreporting validity scales indicated no concerns about underreporting of symptoms. The higher-order scales were not clinically elevated, but Ms. Smalls reported having a high degree of somatic complaints on the restructured clinical scales. Finally, while not reported in the table, she also endorsed having a high degree of anxiety (*T*-score = 70 on the Anxiety specific problems scale).

Lastly, the PTSD Checklist for DSM-5 (PCL-5) and Epworth Sleepiness Scale were examined. When looking at recently created PCL-5 SVTs (Schroeder & Bieu, 2024), there was no evidence of invalid responding on the PCL-5. Ms. Smalls scored 30 on the checklist, which falls just short of the cutoff that is often suggested for a diagnosis of PTSD. When looking at her specific item endorsements, she failed to endorse enough intrusive symptoms and negative emotionality symptoms for a symptomatically based diagnosis of PTSD. On the Epworth Sleepiness Scale, Ms. Smalls scored 12, which suggests the presence of mild excessive daytime sleepiness.

Overall, the clinician deemed neuropsychological testing invalid. This decision was made based on multiple considerations. First, a single concussion in the distant past would not be expected to cause the very poor memory test scores that were obtained (Carroll et al., 2004; Rohling et al., 2011). Likewise, anxiety and mild daytime sleepiness would not be expected to cause the very poor memory test scores (Orff, Desmond, Nowakowski, & Perlis, 2007; Uiterwijk, Stargatt, Humphrey, & Crowe, 2022). Beyond this, the obtained test scores were highly discrepant from Ms. Smalls' reported daily functioning. Specifically, despite producing scores that would suggest a need for significant assistance in daily activities, she reported that there was no impairment in instrumental activities of daily living, and, beyond that, she indicated that she was learning and doing well at a new job, and she was excelling in advanced college courses.

In addition to the neurocognitive findings not fitting with Ms. Smalls' history and presentation, her validity test results clearly indicated invalidity. She failed five of seven PVTs, and the PVT failures could not be reasonably explained as being false-positive findings. Research indicates that a single concussion that occurred in the distant past will not cause failure on the PVTs that she failed (Eglit et al., 2020; Olsen, Schroeder, Heinrichs, & Martin, 2019; Martin et al., 2020; Resch et al., 2022; Shura et al., 2018). Furthermore, when thinking if there might be other unidentified neurological factors going on that might lead to PVT false-positive findings, this possibility was felt to be exceedingly unlikely. This is because, as noted above, Ms. Smalls did not demonstrate evidence of significant cognitive impairment in daily life, and she was doing well at learning a new job and passing challenging college courses. Psychiatric factors were not believed to be the cause of Ms. Smalls' PVT failures either. This is because she did not demonstrate significant psychiatric symptoms during testing, research indicates that anxiety does not cause PVT failures (Marshall & Schroeder, 2022), and a somatic symptom disorder (which could potentially be suggested by the MMPI-2-RF results) is also unexpected to cause these particular PVT failures (Graver & Boone, 2022). Likewise, daytime sleepiness was not believed to be the cause of the PVT failures, as Ms. Smalls had no issues staying alert during testing and research indicates that sleepiness generally does not result PVT failure (Schroeder & Martin, 2022d). In addition to all of those considerations, it was recognized that Ms. Smalls failed five of seven PVTs in total, and this aggregated PVT outcome is associated with essentially a 0% false-positive rate (Larrabee, 2014; Martin, Schroeder, & Olsen, 2022a).

Again, neuropsychological testing was believed to be invalid. The clinician then thought about reasons for the invalidity (outside of a possibility of a false-positive error which was already determined to be exceptionally unlikely). Poor effort and minimal engagement in testing were not thought to be the cause. This is because Ms. Smalls did not appear to be minimally engaged, and she did not appear to put forth poor effort outside of when completing memory tests (during which Ms. Smalls reported that testing was challenging, which would *suggest* that she was engaged and making an effort). Furthermore, her SVT failures could not be explained by poor effort, as simply providing poor effort would not cause her to complete questionnaires in such an atypical manner that they would be suggestive of an intentional misrepresentation of her cognitive functioning. Finally, factitious disorder was thought to be unlikely, as well, since there was nobody in Ms. Smalls' life that she was trying to deceive other than the examiner, and her attempt to deceive the examiner did not appear to be primarily for the purpose of eliciting attention, care, or nurturance.

Malingering as a cause of invalidity was thought to fit Ms. Smalls' clinical picture better than any other explanation. This is because there was evidence of feigning identified during the evaluation, as Ms. Smalls failed multiple PVTs and SVTs, and there were marked discrepancies between her self-report (working and doing well in advanced college courses) and her obtained test performances (exceptionally low memory test scores). Furthermore, an external incentive was identified as being present, the patient reported that she was collecting paperwork to support her disability claim of brain injury, and she could have seen the clinical report as providing documentation of brain injury-related cognitive difficulties.

While it was believed that Ms. Smalls was likely malingering during the evaluation, the clinician also considered whether other, unrelated, factors might be impacting Ms. Smalls' daily life. The first consideration was whether she had an anxiety or trauma disorder. Regarding anxiety, Ms. Smalls reported having anxiety during the clinical interview, and she appeared mildly anxious during the evaluation. Additionally, her report of symptoms on the MMPI-2-RF did indicate that a clinical degree of anxiety was present. While one might wonder if she was feigning anxiety (like her cognitive deficits), no evidence of feigned psychiatric symptoms was observed. There were no atypical or inconsistent reports of anxiety during the clinical interview. Furthermore, Ms. Smalls completed the MMPI-2-RF and psychiatric validity scales in a manner that did not indicate the presence of exaggeration or feigning of psychiatric symptoms.

With regard to a formal anxiety- or trauma-related diagnosis, PTSD was considered given that anxiety became problematic while Ms. Smalls was deployed to a war zone. She reported being chronically on alert while in the war zone, although no specific traumatic events occurred. Her PCL-5 score fell just short of the cutoff that is typically used for consideration of a diagnosis, and her symptom-based complaints did not reach the threshold for problematic issues with intrusive symptoms or negative alterations in cognitions and mood. Likewise, she generally denied experiencing intrusive symptoms and negative alterations in cognitions and mood during the clinical interview. For these reasons, a diagnosis of PTSD was not provided.

Another trauma-related condition that was considered was an adjustment disorder with anxiety. This condition did not fit, though, as Ms. Smalls had been away from the stressor for more than 6 months and her symptoms have persisted. Conversely, her symptoms seemed to fit the best with a generalized anxiety disorder diagnosis. She reported having excessive anxiety and worry that occurred more days than not for more than 6 months. Her anxiety and worry centered around a range of events and activities, and she found it difficult to control her anxiety and worry. She reported feeling keyed up, she noted having concentration difficulties that were linked to anxiety, and she reported having sleep disturbance linked to her brain being unable to "turn off." For these reasons, and because there was no evidence of exaggerated or feigned anxiety, a diagnosis of generalized anxiety disorder was made.

Finally, somatically related conditions were considered. First, a somatic symptom disorder was considered given Ms. Smalls' MMPI-2-RF findings. In considering the various somatic symptom and related disorders listed in the *Diagnostic and Statistical Manual of Mental Disorders, 5th Edition*, though, she did not appear to fit within any of the diagnostic criteria. For this reason, she was not given a diagnosis of somatic symptom disorder or other disorders characterized by somatization (e.g., illness anxiety disorder). Next, a sleep disorder, specifically, insomnia disorder, was considered in the differential diagnosis. Ms. Smalls reported having limited sleep quantity due to having difficulty initiating and maintaining sleep. These sleep issues resulted in daytime fatigue and some degree of distress. The sleep issues were a persistent problem for Ms. Smalls, and they were not due to limited opportunities for sleep or the effects of a substance. Consequently, a diagnosis of insomnia disorder, with mental disorder (generalized anxiety disorder) was made. Importantly, however, although the patient was diagnosed with this, neither her anxiety nor her sleep difficulties were thought to be the cause of her invalid performance because of the reasons previously discussed.

In conclusion, there was evidence that cognitive deficits were feigned but there was no evidence that Ms. Smalls feigned anxiety or a sleep disturbance. When considering differential diagnoses based on her specific symptoms, the following diagnoses were made: (1) generalized anxiety disorder and (2) insomnia disorder, with mental disorder (generalized anxiety disorder). There could be a realistic argument for making a diagnosis of malingering as well, but this diagnosis was not made. This is because, while it was strongly suspected that Ms. Smalls feigned her cognitive symptoms in an attempt to obtain an external incentive (i.e., service-connected disability), it could not be incontrovertibly proven. Furthermore, making a diagnosis of malingering was thought to provide limited incremental benefit to the evaluation given the write-up of noncredible cognitive findings and report that we would not expect cognitive issues after a single concussion. Finally, making a diagnosis of malingering can interfere with the clinical relationship and potentially make Ms. Smalls more likely to dismiss all findings and recommendations, including those for treatment of anxiety and insomnia.

Providing Feedback

In preparing for feedback with Ms. Smalls, the clinician was prepared to tell her that the cognitive test results were invalid, that he would not expect cognitive deficits following a remote concussion, that generalized anxiety and insomnia are thought to be present, and that the generalized anxiety and insomnia are likely factors contributing to day-to-day hardships and experiences of cognitive difficulties. The clinician was then prepared to discuss treatment recommendations related to the diagnoses of generalized anxiety disorder and insomnia disorder.

Upon meeting with Ms. Smalls for the feedback appointment, the clinician showed interest in, and care for, her by asking her how she has been since they met last week. In addition to asking this question, the clinician genuinely listened and responded to her statements. Next, the clinician briefly summarized the issues leading to the neuropsychological evaluation. Specifically, the clinician stated:

> "Dr. Rodriguez referred you to see me, and we met last week to talk and do some testing. You described hitting your head on the exterior of a plane while in Iraq. You believe that you lost consciousness, but you're not sure how long you might have been out. After becoming alert, you got up and carried out the rest of your activities. The following day, though, you developed a headache, foggy thinking, and memory difficulties. You described that those memory difficulties have worsened over time, and you've also noticed some issues with attention and concentration. In looking into this, you recently underwent an MRI of the brain, the results of which were normal. In addition to your cognitive concerns, you reported having heightened anxiety since being in Iraq, and you've experienced poor sleep since then as well. We did an evaluation to further look into all of that. Would you say, is that a fairly accurate summary of our discussion last week?"

Ms. Smalls agreed with the summary and had no additional input. The clinician then shifted to discussing the test results. Specifically, he stated:

> "Well good. I now want to go over your test results. You probably recall that you did a lot of testing. Additionally, you probably recall that you didn't just take one memory test, you took multiple memory tests. We administered multiple tests that measure the same cognitive, or thinking, ability to ensure that we have accurate and reliable findings. When looking at your test results, we saw variability in some of your test performances. For example, on one verbally based test you

> scored pretty poorly but on another very similar test, you scored well within normal limits. Additionally, on some memory tests, your performances were atypical in that we saw low scores, but these low scores were not in a pattern that fits with a history of brain injury. In fact, the variability and atypical findings indicate that the test results are invalid. What that means is that we do not have a reliable pattern of results to interpret. I can tell you, though, that research confidently indicates that people should neurologically recover from a concussion within a few weeks to months after the concussion. When that is not the case, secondary factors are typically the cause of having prolonged symptoms. Secondary factors are non-neurological factors that can lead to ongoing issues. Common secondary factors include anxiety and sleep disturbances, which you have. The questionnaires that you completed do indicate the presence of a clinically significant degree of anxiety and the presence of daytime sleepiness. So, putting all of the information together, research tells us that you should have neurologically recovered from a concussion by now. Fitting with that, your brain MRI was normal, and your neuropsychological testing did not point toward issues related to brain damage. Instead, I think that anxiety and daytime sleepiness from insomnia are causes of your cognitive concerns. And fitting with that, you noted that anxiety started while you were in Iraq and your sleep issues started after you began experiencing anxiety. So, I think we need to move forward by treating the anxiety and sleep issues. Does that make sense?"

Ms. Smalls reported that the findings made sense to her. She never questioned the invalidity, and she did not try to argue that her cognitive complaints are due to the concussion from 14 years ago.

Next, the clinician began talking about treatment options for anxiety and insomnia. The clinician recommended that Ms. Smalls continue with both psychotherapy and psychotropic medication management. It was noted that the neuropsychological findings would be put in Ms. Smalls' medical record so that her therapist could see the diagnoses and ensure that their treatment plan fit with her problems. Likewise, her prescribing provider could see the diagnoses, and it is possible that he might prescribe a medication to help with the insomnia in addition to anxiety. In addition, the clinician recommended that Ms. Smalls try to improve her diet, as limited and poor nutrition can result in cognitive inefficiencies in daily life. Exercise was also discussed, as exercise can sometimes help to reduce anxiety, improve sleep, and improve cognitive clarity. Finally, it was reinforced that the clinician does not see evidence of permanent brain damage, and he expects that Ms. Smalls will see improvement in her daily functioning if her anxiety reduces, her sleep improves, and her diet and exercise improve. Ms. Smalls reported that she understood and would move forward with the recommendations. The clinician asked if she had any additional questions or concerns, and she reported that she did not. Consequently, the feedback session ended, and Ms. Smalls left the office.

The preceding paragraphs demonstrate an application of the Martin and

Schroeder model for providing feedback when testing is invalid. Rapport building and information gathering started in the clinical interview (Step 1). At the time of the feedback session, a brief summary of issues was reported (Step 2). The information fit with Ms. Smalls' narrative of symptoms, and the summary included information that helped to set the stage for the evaluation findings (i.e., normal neuroimaging, problematic anxiety that started at the same time as her symptom complaints, and issues with sleep being present). A brief discussion of the testing was then provided with clear communication that the cognitive testing was invalid (Step 3). No further discussion was provided of the invalid findings after that, and a hard shift occurred (Step 4). The clinician began talking about anxiety and insomnia as problematic issues for Ms. Smalls, without attributing her invalid cognitive test scores to her anxiety and insomnia. Finally, recommendations were made and an opportunity for questions was provided. Ms. Smalls appeared to receive the information well, and no aggressive or challenging statements or actions were made by her.

Report Writing

A copy of Ms. Smalls' neuropsychological report is presented in Appendix 11.1. Negative tones were avoided in the report, and objective information was provided. While a diagnosis of malingering was not made, it was clearly stated that testing was invalid and not representative of her cognitive capability, and the report was written in such a way that it will not support a claim of Ms. Smalls' prior concussion resulting in a disability. Finally, treatment recommendations were made for clinical conditions that were believed to be real and present.

CLOSING REMARKS DISCUSSION

The case discussed in this chapter provides a demonstration of how we obtain and incorporate new information at each step of the evaluation process, conceptualize cases of invalidity as the evaluation progresses, identify invalidity via both validity tests and extra test information, and address invalidity in clinical settings. Each patient will be different and specific approaches and discussions might differ, but the general outline described above is typical of our evaluations. In our experiences, nearly all patients agree with our conclusions, and they frequently thank us for the evaluation and input. Personally, we typically feel as though the information provided to our patients was just as (and, on some occasions, even more) successfully received than in cases where valid data were obtained and discussed. We hope that the information presented throughout this book will help the reader conduct confident, evidence-based evaluations and receive similarly positive feedback from their patients.

APPENDIX 11.1

Neuropsychological Report

PATIENT: Ms. Smalls

DATE OF BIRTH: XX/XX/XXXX

DATE OF EVALUATION: XX/XX/XXXX

REFERRAL: Ms. Smalls is a 49-year-old, left-handed, biracial, female with a reported history of a remote concussion. She was referred for a clinical neuropsychological examination by Dr. Benny Rodriguez to assess neuropsychological functioning, assist in differential diagnosis of memory complaints, and participate in treatment planning.

PROCEDURES: Medical records were reviewed. A clinical interview was conducted with Ms. Smalls. The following neuropsychological tests were administered by a psychometrist: Wechsler Test of Adult Reading, Wechsler Adult Intelligence Scale–4th Edition (subtests: Vocabulary, Block Design, Digit Span, Symbol Search), Repeatable Battery for the Assessment of Neuropsychological Status, Brief Visuospatial Memory Test–Revised, Digit Vigilance Test, Trail Making Test, Delis–Kaplan Executive Function System (subtests: Verbal Fluency, Color–Word Interference, Tower), TOMM (subtest: Trial 1), MSVT, Dot Counting Test, Minnesota Multiphasic Personality Inventory—2nd Edition—Restructured Format, PTSD Checklist for DSM-5, and Epworth Sleepiness Scale. The testing was scored and interpreted, this report was written, and a feedback session was held with Ms. Smalls.

BACKGROUND INFORMATION: Ms. Smalls is an U. S. Air Force veteran. She reported that, 14 years ago, she hit her head on the exterior of a parked aircraft while in Iraq. When asked more about this, she stated she recalls everything leading up to the hit. She reported that she was sitting under the aircraft when an extremely loud banging noise occurred, causing her to jump up and hit the top of her head on the metal exterior of the plane. She thinks that she lost consciousness, but she is not sure how long the loss of consciousness might have been. After becoming alert again, she decided not to seek medical attention and, instead, continued to carry out her duties for the day. She recalls carrying out all of her duties, and she does not have any gaps in her memory other than when she thinks she was unconscious. The next day, though, she developed a headache, foggy thinking, and memory issues. She did not seek medical attention that day either, but she alerted her superior that she wasn't feeling the best. From that point forward, she feels like her memory has been poor, and it has worsened further over time, with significant issues currently being present. In addition to memory issues, Ms. Smalls reported that she has noticed herself having some attention and focus issues. An MRI of the brain was conducted on XX/XX/XXXX, and it was interpreted as being normal.

When asked about instrumental activities of daily living, Ms. Smalls denied having any significant issues with driving her automobile, managing her finances, managing her medications, cooking, or managing appointments. Regarding employment, Ms. Smalls was recently discharged from the Air Force, and she has started a full-time job as a civilian. She reported that this job is completely new to her, but she enjoys it, and it is going well. In addition to working full-time, she has enrolled in college, and she is taking

(continued)

advanced level courses. She reported that school has been going well, and she is primarily earning As in her classes, otherwise earning only an occasional B.

When asked about psychiatric history, Ms. Smalls reported that, in retrospect, she probably had a mild degree of anxiety throughout much of her life. This anxiety significantly worsened, though, when she was deployed to Iraq. She stated that she was always on high alert due to the potential threat of attack, and she got limited and poor quality sleep each night. While she was hyperalert due to being in a war zone, no specific traumas occurred. Ms. Smalls reported that her anxiety has continued to be high since then. She reported that she dislikes being in large public places, which will worsen her anxiety. This is the only trigger for her anxiety that she has noticed. She denied having nightmares and other intrusive thoughts related to her experiences in Iraq, and she denied having negative thoughts or feelings associated with her time in Iraq. Instead, she just feels anxious "almost all the time." She noted that she worries about a number of topics, and she struggles to "turn off" her brain at night, which interferes with sleep. She will struggle to fall asleep, and she will awaken in the middle of the night. Overall, she estimates that she gets about 4 to 6 hours of sleep each night. In addition, she added that she has noticed that anxiety can make it hard for her to focus at times, especially when her anxiety spikes. She recently started engaging in psychotherapy, and she was also recently prescribed an SSRI (Lexapro, which is her only prescribed medication). She denied feeling depressed, experiencing psychotic symptomatology, or having suicidal ideation. She also denied having any history of substance-use problems.

Medical history is significant for periodic headaches, which Ms. Smalls attributes to her prior head injury. Ms. Smalls also reported occasionally having some back problems, but she indicated that this is a long-standing issue that is likely unrelated to her military duties. When asked about exercise, she reported that she does not regularly engage in any. Furthermore, her job is a sitting desk job, so she gets very limited physical activity during the day. She added that even if she tried to exercise, she is tired during the day, so she would struggle to find the motivation. When asked about appetite, Ms. Smalls stated that her appetite has been poor since being in Iraq. She doesn't usually eat breakfast, and she might sometimes only eat one meal per day. She thinks that she has probably lost about 10 pounds over the past year. No changes in her senses of taste or smell were endorsed.

Psychosocial history indicates that Ms. Smalls was born and raised on the West Coast. She denied experiencing any significant stressors or traumas during her childhood. She did well in school, and there were never concerns about her having a learning or attention problem. She received an associate degree before enlisting in the Air Force. She is now pursuing a bachelor's degree and plans to pursue a master's degree after graduating. Consequently, she is taking advanced level courses to help bolster her transcript and make her a more competitive master's candidate. As described above, school is going well for her. In addition to being a student, Ms. Smalls is holding a full-time job. She reported that this job is new to her, but the job is going well. Regarding income, Ms. Smalls reported that she is pursuing a service-connected disability for the concussion that she sustained 14 years ago, but she is not currently service connected. Thus, her income is coming from her job. She is single (never married), and she has no children. She is living alone in suburb in the Midwest.

(continued)

Neuropsychological Report *(page 3 of 4)*

BEHAVIORAL OBSERVATIONS: Ms. Smalls was casually dressed, well groomed, and appeared her stated age. She ambulated independently and without gait, balance, or postural abnormalities observed. No resting or action tremor was observed. Eye contact was appropriate. Ms. Smalls did not spontaneously start conversations, but she responded to questions appropriately, and she was an active part of the clinical interview. Her speech was normal in volume, rate, and prosody. Phraseology was ordinary. She spoke in complete and grammatically accurate sentences; no paraphasic errors were noted. She was able to comprehend casual interview questions and formal test instructions without difficulty. Ms. Smalls never asked for test instructions or test stimuli to be repeated or elaborated upon. Thought processes were logical and coherent. There was no evidence of delusions or hallucinations. Affect was mildly anxious, but anxiety did not appear to impact Ms. Smalls' test engagement. Ms. Smalls completed testing without any breaks, and she did not demonstrate any signs of significant fatigue (although she yawned twice). She periodically seemed to give up easily during testing, particularly on memory tests, during which time she reported that memory-based tests were challenging.

TEST RESULTS: As part of standard neurocognitive test procedure, empirically derived performance validity indices were interspersed throughout the neurocognitive test battery. Ms. Smalls performed beyond cutoffs on five of seven validity tests. Additionally, there was a high degree of variability periodically seen among some tests that measure the same cognitive ability. For example, Ms. Smalls scored within normal limits on a semantic fluency test, but she scored well below expected limits on another semantic fluency test. In sum, these findings indicate that neurocognitive testing is invalid and not reflective of Ms. Smalls' cognitive capability.

As part of the standard psychological test procedure, empirically derived symptom validity indices were included on a self-report questionnaire. Results from symptom validity scales indicate overreporting of cognitive symptoms, but Ms. Smalls' report of somatic and psychological symptoms was valid. She endorsed having a high degree of somatic concerns, and she also endorsed having clinically significant anxiety. On a PTSD checklist, her total score was just below the common clinical cutoff, and her symptom endorsement failed to show significant intrusive symptoms and experiences with negative alterations in cognitions and mood. On a sleepiness scale, Ms. Smalls endorsed having mild daytime sleepiness.

SUMMARY and CONCLUSIONS: Ms. Smalls reported that she hit her head on the exterior of a parked aircraft while deployed in Iraq 14 years ago. She thinks that she lost consciousness, but she is not sure how long the loss of consciousness might have been. She has no amnesia surrounding the event other than for the brief period of time when she believes that she was unconscious. The next day, she had a headache, foggy thinking, and memory difficulties, but she did not seek medical attention. She feels like her memory has worsened since then, with significant memory issues currently being present. She also reported having heightened anxiety and poor sleep starting while in Iraq, and these issues have persisted since that time. A recent MRI of the brain was interpreted as being normal.

(continued)

On neurocognitive testing, Ms. Smalls performed beyond cutoffs on multiple standard validity indices, and there was a high degree of variability seen among some tests that measure the same cognitive ability. This variability and failure of multiple validity indices indicate that the test results are invalid and cannot be interpreted to represent Ms. Smalls' actual cognitive capabilities. On psychological testing, results from symptom validity scales indicated overreporting of cognitive symptoms, but her report of somatic and psychological concerns was valid. She endorsed having some somatic complaints, a clinically significant degree of anxiety, and mild daytime sleepiness.

Overall, although neurocognitive testing cannot be interpreted since Ms. Smalls' test results were invalid, I do not believe that her remote concussion is causing cognitive difficulties. Her brain MRI was normal, and empirical research indicates that cognitive recovery is expected over a few weeks to months after an uncomplicated concussion. When symptoms persist beyond a few weeks to months, non-neurological factors are typically the cause of one's prolonged symptoms. Common non-neurological factors that can contribute to ongoing symptom complaints include psychiatric distress and sleep disturbances, and Ms. Smalls has both generalized anxiety and insomnia. Thus, in sum, I see no evidence that Ms. Smalls' remote concussion is causing cognitive difficulties, but she does have anxiety and insomnia, which are likely negatively impacting her daily functioning.

A final session was held with Ms. Smalls and the neuropsychological findings and impressions were discussed. Moving forward, I recommended that treatment focus on Ms. Smalls' generalized anxiety and insomnia. If improvement in anxiety and sleep can be seen, I would expect improvement in her daily functioning. Ms. Smalls recently started psychotherapy, and I suggested that she continue with therapy to address her anxiety. Techniques for reducing anxiety at bedtime might also be discussed in therapy. In addition to therapy, Ms. Smalls was recently prescribed an SSRI. I recommended that she continue working with her psychotropic medication provider, and there might be discussion about possible medication management for insomnia if the SSRI were to not be helpful in that regard. Furthermore, exercise can sometimes help to reduce anxiety, improve sleep, and improve cognitive clarity, and I recommended that she try to gradually increase the amount of exercise that she gets. Finally, I recommended that Ms. Smalls try to improve her diet, as limited and poor nutrition can result in cognitive inefficiencies in daily life.

DIAGNOSTIC IMPERSSIONS:

- Generalized Anxiety Disorder
- Insomnia Disorder, with mental disorder (generalized anxiety disorder)
- I do not see evidence of cognitive dysfunction due to a remote history of concussion

Thank you for involving me in the care of this patient.

Neuropsychologist

References

Abeare, C. A., Hurtubise, J. L., Cutler, L., Sirianni, C., Brantuo, M., Makhzoum, N., & Erdodi, L. A. (2021). Introducing a forced choice recognition trial to the Hopkins Verbal Learning Test–Revised. *The Clinical Neuropsychologist, 35*(8), 1442–1470.

Aguilar, C., Bailey, C., Karyadi, K. A., Kinney, D. I., & Nitch, S. R. (2023). The use of performance validity tests among inpatient forensic monolingual Spanish-speakers. *Applied Neuropsychology: Adult, 30*(6), 671–679.

Alverson, W. A., O'Rourke, J. J., & Soble, J. R. (2019). The Word Memory Test genuine memory impairment profile discriminates genuine memory impairment from invalid performance in a mixed clinical sample with cognitive impairment. *The Clinical Neuropsychologist, 33*(8), 1420–1435.

Alwes, Y. R., Clark, J. A., Berry, D. T. R., & Granacher, R. P. (2008). Screening for feigning in a civil forensic setting. *Journal of Clinical and Experimental Neuropsychology, 30*, 133–140.

American Psychiatric Association. (2000). *Diagnostic and statistical manual of mental disorders* (4th ed., text rev.). Arlington, VA: Author.

American Psychiatric Association. (2022). *Diagnostic and statistical manual of mental disorders* (5th ed., text rev.). Arlington, VA: Author.

American Psychological Association. (2017). *Ethical principles of psychologists and code of conduct.* Retrieved from *www.apa.org/ethics/code/index.aspx.*

An, K. Y., Kaploun, K., Erdodi, L. A., & Abeare, C. A. (2017). Performance validity in undergraduate research participants: A comparison of failure rates across tests and cutoffs. *The Clinical Neuropsychologist, 31*(1), 193–206.

Ardolf, B. R., Denney, R. L., & Houston, C. M. (2007). Base rates of negative response bias and malingered neurocognitive dysfunction among criminal defendants referred for neuropsychological evaluation. *The Clinical Neuropsychologist, 21*(6), 899–916.

Armistead-Jehle, P., Grills, C. E., Bieu, R., & Kulas, J. (2016). Clinical utility of the Memory Complaints Inventory to detect invalid test performance. *The Clinical Neuropsychologist, 30*(4), 610–628.

Armistead-Jehle, P., Ingram, P. B., & Morris, C. S. (2020). Personality assessment inventory cognitive bias scale: Validation in a military sample. *Archives of Clinical Neuropsychology, 35*(7), 1154–1161.

Armistead-Jehle, P., & Shura, R. D. (2022). Memory complaints inventory: Review of psychometric properties. *Psychological Injury and Law, 15*(1), 104–112.

Arnold, G., Boone, K. B., Lu, P., Dean, A., Wen, J., Nitch, S., & McPherson, S. (2005). Sensitivity and specificity of finger tapping test scores for the detection of suspect effort. *The Clinical Neuropsychologist, 19*(1), 105–120.

Ashendorf, L. (2019). Rey auditory verbal learning test and Rey–Osterrieth complex figure test performance validity indices in a VA polytrauma sample. *The Clinical Neuropsychologist, 33*(8), 1388–1402.

Ashendorf, L., Clark, E. L., & Humphreys, C. T. (2021). The Rey 15-item memory test in U.S. veterans. *Journal of Clinical and Experimental Neuropsychology, 43*(3), 324–331.

Axelrod, B. N., Miller, J. B., & LaBuda, J. A. (2021). Embedded performance validity scores in standard memory tests. In *Assessment of feigned cognitive impairment: A neuropsychological perspective* (pp. 124–145). Guilford Press.

Bain, K. M., & Soble, J. R. (2019). Validation of the Advanced Clinical Solutions Word Choice Test (WCT) in a mixed clinical sample: Establishing classification accuracy, sensitivity/specificity, and cutoff scores. *Assessment, 26*(7), 1320–1328.

Beck, A. T., Steer, R. A., & Brown, G. K. (1996). *Manual for the Beck depression inventory-II.* Psychological Corporation.

Ben-Porath, Y. S. (2012). *Interpreting the mmpi-2-rf.* University of Minnesota Press.

Ben-Porath, Y. S., & Tellegen, A. (2011). *MMPI-2-RF (Minnesota Multiphasic Personality Inventory–2 Restructured Form) manual for administration, scoring, and interpretation.* University of Minnesota Press.

Benge, J. F., Wisdom, N. M., Collins, R. L., Franks, R., LeMaire, A., & Chen, D. K. (2012). Diagnostic utility of the Structured Inventory of Malingered Symptomatology for identifying psychogenic non-epileptic events. *Epilepsy & Behavior, 24*(4), 439–444.

Bernstein, M. T., Resch, Z. J., Ovsiew, G. P., & Soble, J. R. (2021). A systematic review and meta-analysis of the diagnostic accuracy of the advanced clinical solutions word choice test as a performance validity test. *Neuropsychology Review, 31*(2), 349–359.

Bianchini, K. J., Aguerrevere, L. E., Curtis, K. L., Roebuck-Spencer, T. M., Frey, F. C., Greve, K. W., & Calamia, M. (2018). Classification accuracy of the Minnesota Multiphasic Personality Inventory–2 (MMPI-2)—Restructured form validity scales in detecting malingered pain-related disability. *Psychological Assessment, 30*(7), 857.

Bianchini, K. J., Curtis, K. L., & Greve, K. W. (2006). Compensation and malingering in traumatic brain injury: A dose-response relationship? *The Clinical Neuropsychologist, 20*(4), 831–847.

Bianchini, K. J., Mathias, C. W., & Greve, K. W. (2001). Symptom validity testing: A critical review. *The Clinical Neuropsychologist, 15*(1), 19–45.

Bigler, E. D. (2015). Neuroimaging as a biomarker in symptom validity and performance validity testing. *Brain Imaging and Behavior, 9*, 421–444.

Binder, L. M. (1993). *Portland Digit Recognition Test manual.* Private Publication.

Binder, L. M. (2019). The patient–psychologist relationship and informed consent in neuropsychological evaluations. *The Clinical Neuropsychologist, 33*(6), 988–1015.

Binder, L. M., & Chafetz, M. D. (2018). Determination of the smoking gun of intent: Significance testing of forced choice results in social security claimants. *The Clinical Neuropsychologist, 32*(1), 132–144.

Binder, L. M., Larrabee, G. J., & Millis, S. R. (2014). Intent to fail: Significance testing of forced choice test results. *The Clinical Neuropsychologist, 28*(8), 1366–1375.

Blaskewitz, N., Merten, T., & Brockhaus, R. (2009). Detection of suboptimal effort with the Rey complex figure test and recognition trial. *Applied Neuropsychology, 16*(1), 54–61.

Blevins, C. A., Weathers, F. W., Davis, M. T., Witte, T. K., & Domino, J. L. (2015). The posttraumatic stress disorder checklist for *DSM-5* (PCL-5): Development and initial psychometric evaluation. *Journal of Traumatic Stress, 28*(6), 489–498.

Board of Directors. (2007). American Academy of Clinical Neuropsychology (AACN) practice guidelines for neuropsychological assessment and consultation. *The Clinical Neuropsychologist, 21*(2), 209–231.

Boccaccini, M. T. & Hart, J. R. (2018). Response style on the Personality Assessment Inventory and other multiscale inventories. In R. Rogers & S. D. Bender (Eds.), *Clinical assessment of malingering and deception* (4th ed., pp. 257–279). Guilford Press.

Boone, K. B. (2013). *Clinical practice of forensic neuropsychology: An evidence-based approach.* Guilford Press.

Boone, K. B. (2017). Self-deception in somatoform conditions: Differentiating between conscious and nonconscious symptom feigning. In K. B. Boone (Ed.), *Neuropsychological evaluation of somatoform and other functional somatic conditions: Assessment primer* (pp. 3–42). Routledge.

Boone, K. B. (Ed.). (2021). *Assessment of feigned cognitive impairment* (2nd ed.). Guilford Press.

Boone, K. B., Lu, P., & Herzberg, D. S. (2002a). *The dot counting test manual.* Western Psychological Services.

Boone, K. B., Salazar, X., Lu, P., Warner-Chacon, K., & Razani, J. (2002b). The Rey 15-item recognition trial: A technique to enhance sensitivity of the Rey 15-item memorization test. *Journal of Clinical and Experimental Neuropsychology, 24*(5), 561–573.

Boone, K. B., Sherman, D., Mishler, J., Daoud, G., Cottingham, M., Victor, T. L., . . . Wright, M. (2022a). Cross-validation of RAVLT performance validity indicators and the RAVLT/RO discriminant function in a large known groups sample. *The Clinical Neuropsychologist, 36*(8), 2342–2360.

Boone, K. B., Sweet, J. J., Byrd, D. A., Denney, R. L., Hanks, R. A., Kaufmann, P. M., . . . Suhr, J. A. (2022b). Official position of the American Academy of Clinical Neuropsychology on test security. *The Clinical Neuropsychologist, 36*(3), 523–545.

Boress, K., Gaasedelen, O. J., Croghan, A., Johnson, M. K., Caraher, K., Basso, M. R., & Whiteside, D. M. (2022). Replication and cross-validation of the personality assessment inventory (PAI) cognitive bias scale (CBS) in a mixed clinical sample. *The Clinical Neuropsychologist, 36*(7), 1860–1877.

Boucher, C. M., Giromini, L., Roth, R. M., & Erdodi, L. A. (2024). The Beck Depression Inventory—Second Edition as a Symptom Validity Test: Importing European Cutoffs to the USA. *Psychological Injury and Law, 17*(2), 1–12.

Bovin, M. J., Marx, B. P., Weathers, F. W., Gallagher, M. W., Rodriguez, P., Schnurr, P. P., & Keane, T. M. (2016). Psychometric properties of the PTSD checklist for Diagnostic and Statistical Manual of Mental Disorders–Fifth Edition (PCL-5) in veterans. *Psychological Assessment, 28*(11), 1379–1391.

Briere, J. (2011). *Trauma Symptom Inventory-2 professional manual.* Lutz, FL: Psychological Assessment Resources.

Buddin, W. H. Jr., Schroeder, R. W., Hargrave, D. D., Von Dran, E. J., Campbell, E. B., Brockman, C. J., . . . Baade, L. E. (2014). An examination of the frequency of invalid forgetting on the Test of Memory Malingering. *The Clinical Neuropsychologist, 28*(3), 525–542.

Bush, S. S., Ruff, R. M., Tröster, A. I., Barth, J. T., Koffler, S. P., Pliskin, N. H., . . . Silver, C. H. (2005). Symptom validity assessment: Practice issues and medical necessity NAN policy & planning committee. *Archives of Clinical Neuropsychology, 20*(4), 419–426.

Canivet, C., Choi, B., Karasek, R., Moghaddassi, M., Staland-Nyman, C., & Östergren, P. O. (2013). Can high psychological job demands, low decision latitude, and high job strain predict disability pensions? A 12-year follow-up of middle-aged Swedish workers. *International Archives of Occupational and Environmental Health, 86*, 307–319.

Carone, D. A., Iverson, G. L., & Bush, S. S. (2010). A model to approaching and providing feedback to patients regarding invalid test performance in clinical neuropsychological evaluations. *The Clinical Neuropsychologist, 24*(5), 759–778.

Carroll, L., Cassidy, J. D., Peloso, P., Borg, J., Von Holst, H., Holm, L., . . . Pépin, M. (2004). Prognosis for mild traumatic brain injury: results of the WHO Collaborating Centre Task Force on Mild Traumatic Brain Injury. *Journal of Rehabilitation Medicine, 36*(0), 84–105.

Chafetz, M. D. (2008). Malingering on the social security disability consultative exam: Predictors and base rates. *The Clinical Neuropsychologist, 22*(3), 529–546.

Chafetz, M. D. (2010). Symptom validity issues in the psychological consultative examination for social security disability. *The Clinical Neuropsychologist, 24*(6), 1045–1063.

Chafetz, M. D. (2011). The psychological consultative examination for social security disability. *Psychological Injury and Law, 4*(3), 235–244.

Chafetz, M. D., Bauer, R. M., & Haley, P. S. (2020). The other face of illness—deception: Diagnostic criteria for factitious disorder with proposed standards for clinical practice and research. *The Clinical Neuropsychologist, 34*(3), 454–476.

Chafetz, M. D., Prentkowski, E., & Rao, A. (2011). To work or not to work: Motivation (not low IQ) determines symptom validity test findings. *Archives of Clinical Neuropsychology, 26*(4), 306–313.

Chafetz, M., & Underhill, J. (2013). Estimated costs of malingered disability. *Archives of Clinical Neuropsychology, 28*(7), 633–639.

Clark, L. R., Stricker, N. H., Libon, D. J., Delano-Wood, L., Salmon, D. P., Delis, D. C., & Bondi, M. W. (2012). Yes/no versus forced-choice recognition memory in mild cognitive impairment and Alzheimer's disease: Patterns of impairment and associations with dementia severity. *The Clinical Neuropsychologist, 26*(7), 1201–1216.

Condor, R., Allen, L., & Cox, D. (1992). *Computerized assessment of response bias test manual.* Cognisyst.

Dahlstrom, W., Welsch, G., & Dahlstrom, L. (1972). *An MMPI handbook: Vol. I. Clinical interpretation.* University of Minnesota Press.

Dandachi-FitzGerald, B., Duits, A. A., Leentjens, A. F., Verhey, F. R., & Ponds, R. W. (2020). Performance and symptom validity assessment in patients with apathy and cognitive impairment. *Journal of the International Neuropsychological Society, 26*(3), 314–321.

Dandachi-FitzGerald, B., Merckelbach, H., & Merten, T. (2022). Cry for help as a root cause of poor symptom validity: A critical note. *Applied Neuropsychology: Adult, 31*(4), 1–6.

Dandachi-FitzGerald, B., Merckelbach, H., & Ponds, R. W. (2017). Neuropsychologists' ability to predict distorted symptom presentation. *Journal of Clinical and Experimental Neuropsychology, 39*(3), 257–264.

Daugherty, J. C., Querido, L., Quiroz, N., Wang, D., Hidalgo-Ruzzante, N., Fernandes, S., . . . Valera, E. (2021). The coin in hand–extended version: Development and validation of a multicultural performance validity test. *Assessment, 28*(1), 186–198.

Davis, J. J. (2022). Validity assessment within the rehabilitation setting. In R. W. Schroeder & P. K. Martin (Eds.), *Validity assessment in clinical neuropsychological practice: Evaluating and managing noncredible performance* (pp. 280–299). Guilford Press.

Davis, J. J., & Millis, S. R. (2014). Examination of performance validity test failure in relation to number of tests administered. *The Clinical Neuropsychologist, 28*(2), 199–214.

Davis, K., Carbone, R., Fredericks, J., Lujan, J., & Basdeo, A. (2021). *What makes a good doctor: A qualitative study of patient perspectives.* UIWSOM 2021 Community Engagement Project. Available at *www.researchgate.net/profile/Ryan-Carbone-3/publication/348899293_What_Makes_a_Good_Doctor_A_Qualitative_Study_of_Patient_Perspectives/links/60733ec592851c8a7bbe83de/What-Makes-a-Good-Doctor-A-Qualitative-Study-of-Patient-Perspectives.pdf*

De Boer, A. B., Phillips, M. S., Barwegen, K. C., Obolsky, M. A., Rauch, A. A., Pesanti, S. D., . . . Soble, J. R. (2023). Comprehensive analysis of MMPI-2-RF symptom validity scales and performance validity test relationships in a diverse mixed neuropsychiatric setting. *Psychological Injury and Law, 16*(1), 61–72.

Dean, A. C., Victor, T. L., Boone, K. B., Philpott, L. M., & Hess, R. A. (2009). Dementia and effort test performance. *The Clinical Neuropsychologist, 23*(1), 133–152.

Denning, J. H. (2012). The efficiency and accuracy of the Test of Memory Malingering Trial 1, errors on the first 10 items of the Test of Memory Malingering, and five embedded measures in predicting invalid test performance. *Archives of Clinical Neuropsychology, 27*(4), 417–432.

Denning, J. H. (2021). When 10 is enough: Errors on the first 10 items of the Test of Memory Malingering (TOMMe10) and administration time predict freestanding performance validity tests (PVTs) and underperformance on memory measures. *Applied Neuropsychology: Adult, 28*(1), 35–47.

Denning, J. H. (2023). When failing one performance validity test matters. *Applied Neuropsychology: Adult*, 1–12.

Denning, J. H., & Shura, R. D. (2019). Cost of malingering mild traumatic brain injury-related cognitive deficits during compensation and pension evaluations in the veterans benefits administration. *Applied Neuropsychology: Adult, 26*(1), 1–16.

DeRight, J., & Jorgensen, R. S. (2015). I just want my research credit: Frequency of suboptimal effort in a non-clinical healthy undergraduate sample. *The Clinical Neuropsychologist, 29*(1), 101–117.

Detullio, D., Messer, S. C., Kennedy, T. D., & Millen, D. H. (2019). A meta-analysis of the Miller Forensic Assessment of Symptoms Test (M-FAST). *Psychological Assessment, 31*(11), 1319.

Donders, J., & Vos, M. (2023). Utility of CVLT–3 response bias as a measure of performance validity after traumatic brain injury. *The Clinical Neuropsychologist, 37*(1), 91–100.

Dorociak, K. E., Schulze, E. T., Piper, L. E., Molokie, R. E., & Janecek, J. K. (2018). Performance validity testing in a clinical sample of adults with sickle cell disease. *The Clinical Neuropsychologist, 32*(1), 81–97.

Drane, D. L., Ojemann, J. G., Kim, M. S., Gross, R. E., Miller, J. W., Faught Jr, R. E., & Loring, D. W. (2016). Interictal epileptiform discharge effects on neuropsychological assessment and epilepsy surgical planning. *Epilepsy & Behavior, 56*, 131–138.

Eglit, G. M., Jurick, S. M., Delis, D. C., Filoteo, J. V., Bondi, M. W., & Jak, A. J. (2020). Utility of the D-KEFS Color Word Interference Test as an embedded measure of performance validity. *The Clinical Neuropsychologist, 34*(2), 332–352.

Erdodi, L. A., Abeare, C. A., Medoff, B., Seke, K. R., Sagar, S., & Kirsch, N. L. (2018a). A single error is one too many: The Forced Choice Recognition Trial of the CVLT-II as a measure of performance validity in adults with TBI. *Archives of Clinical Neuropsychology, 33*(7), 845–860.

Erdodi, L. A., Kirsch, N. L., Sabelli, A. G., & Abeare, C. A. (2018b). The Grooved Pegboard Test as a validity indicator—A study on psychogenic interference as a confound in performance validity research. *Psychological Injury and Law, 11*, 307–324.

Erdodi, L. A., Seke, K. R., Shahein, A., Tyson, B. T., Sagar, S., & Roth, R. M. (2017). Low scores on the Grooved Pegboard Test are associated with invalid responding and psychiatric symptoms. *Psychology & Neuroscience, 10*(3), 325.

Etherton, J. L., Bianchini, K. J., Ciota, M. A., & Greve, K. W. (2005a). Reliable Digit Span is unaffected by laboratory-induced pain: Implications for clinical use. *Assessment, 12*(1), 101–106.

Etherton, J. L., Bianchini, K. J., Greve, K. W., & Ciota, M. A. (2005b). Test of Memory Malingering performance is unaffected by laboratory-induced pain: Implications for clinical use. *Archives of Clinical Neuropsychology, 20*(3), 375–384.

Fals-Stewart, W., & Lucente, S. (1997). Identifying positive dissimulation by substance-abusing individuals on the Personality Assessment Inventory: A cross-validation study. *Journal of Personality Assessment, 68*(2), 455–469.

Faust, D., Hart, K. J., Guilmette, T. J., & Arkes, H. R. (1988). Neuropsychologists' capacity to detect adolescent malingerers. *Professional Psychology: Research and Practice, 19*(5), 508.

Fazio, R. L., Sanders, J. F., & Denney, R. L. (2015). Comparison of performance of the Test of Memory Malingering and Word Memory Test in a criminal forensic sample. *Archives of Clinical Neuropsychology, 30*(4), 293–301.

Fernandez, K., Boccaccini, M. T., & Noland, R. M. (2008). Detecting over-and underreporting of psychopathology with the Spanish-language Personality Assessment Inventory: Findings from a simulation study with bilingual speakers. *Psychological Assessment, 20*(2), 189.

Ferreira, I., Fernandes, S., Querido, L., Pires, R., Daugherty, J. C., Hidalgo-Ruzzante, N., & Pérez-García, M. (2022). Validation of the coin in hand—extended version among older adults with and without dementia. *Archives of Clinical Neuropsychology, 37*(1), 91–103.

Filone, S., & DeMatteo, D. (2017). *Assessing "credible fear": A psychometric examination of the Trauma Symptom Inventory-2 in the context of immigration court evaluations* (Vol. 29, No. 6, p. 701). American Psychological Association.

Fink, J. W. (2017). Beyond the tests: Record review, interview, and observations in forensic neuropsychology. In S. S. Bush, G. J. Demakis, & M. L. Rohling (Eds.), *APA Handbook of forensic neuropsychology* (pp. 41–56). American Psychological Association.

Fokas, K. F., & Brovko, J. M. (2020). Assessing symptom validity in psychological injury evaluations using the MMPI-2-RF and the PAI: An updated review. *Psychological Injury and Law, 13*(4), 370–382.

Frederick, R. I. (1997). *Validity Indicator Profile manual.* NCS Assessments.

Fuermaier, A. B., Dandachi-Fitzgerald, B., & Lehrner, J. (2023). Validity assessment of early retirement claimants: Symptom overreporting on the Beck Depression Inventory–II. *Applied Neuropsychology: Adult,* 1–7.

Gaasedelen, O. J., Whiteside, D. M., Altmaier, E., Welch, C., & Basso, M. R. (2019). The construction and the initial validation of the Cognitive Bias Scale for the Personality Assessment Inventory. *The Clinical Neuropsychologist, 33*(8), 1467–1484.

Gaasedelen, O. J., Whiteside, D. M., & Basso, M. (2017). Exploring the sensitivity of the Personality Assessment Inventory symptom validity tests in detecting response bias in a mixed neuropsychological outpatient sample. *The Clinical Neuropsychologist, 31*(5), 844–856.

Galioto, R., Dhima, K., Berenholz, O., & Busch, R. (2020). Performance validity testing in multiple sclerosis. *Journal of the International Neuropsychological Society, 26*(10), 1028–1035.

Gasquoine, P. G., Weimer, A. A., & Orta, M. (2019). Specificity rates for non-clinical, bilingual, Mexican Americans with California Verbal Learning Test3, verbal fluency, and Rey 15-IR performance validity measures. *The Clinical Neuropsychologist, 33*(8), 1445–1454.

Gervais, R. O., Ben-Porath, Y. S., Wygant, D. B., & Green, P. (2007). Development and validation of a Response Bias Scale (RBS) for the MMPI-2. *Assessment, 14*(2), 196–208.

Gervais, R. O., Russell, A. S., Green, P., Allen, L. M., Ferrari, R., & Pieschl, S. D. (2001). Effort testing in patients with fibromyalgia and disability incentives. *The Journal of Rheumatology, 28*(8), 1892–1899.

Goedendorp, M. M., van der Werf, S. P., Bleijenberg, G., Tummers, M., & Knoop, H. (2013). Does neuropsychological test performance predict outcome of cognitive behavior therapy for Chronic Fatigue Syndrome and what is the role of underperformance? *Journal of Psychosomatic Research, 75*(3), 242–248.

Goette, W. F., & Goette, H. E. (2019). A meta-analysis of the accuracy of embedded performance validity indicators from the repeatable battery for the assessment of neuropsychological status. *The Clinical Neuropsychologist, 33*(6), 1044–1068.

Graver, C. J., & Boone, K. B. (2022). Validity assessment in patients with somatic symptom and related disorders. In R. W. Schroeder & P. K. Martin (Eds.), *Validity assessment in clinical neuropsychological practice: Evaluating and managing noncredible performance* (pp. 357–377). Guilford Press.

Gray, M. J., Elhai, J. D., & Briere, J. (2010). Evaluation of the Atypical Response scale of the Trauma Symptom Inventory-2 in detecting simulated posttraumatic stress disorder. *Journal of Anxiety Disorders, 24*(5), 447–451.

Green, P. (2003). *Manual for the Word Memory Test for Windows.* Paul Green Publishing.

Green, P. (2004). *Medical Symptom Validity Test (MSVT) for Microsoft Windows: User's manual.* Paul Green Publishing.

Green, P. (2008). *Green's Nonverbal Medical Symptom Validity Test (NV-MSVT) for Microsoft Windows: User's manual 1.0*. Green's Publishing.

Green, P. (2019). *Users' manual for the Memory Complaints Inventory (MCI)*. Green's Publishing.

Green, P., Flaro, L., & Courtney, J. (2009). Examining false positives on the Word Memory Test in adults with mild traumatic brain injury. *Brain Injury, 23*(9), 741–750.

Green, P., & Merten, T. (2013). Noncredible explanations of noncredible performance on symptom validity tests. In D. A. Carone & S. S. Bush (Eds.), *Mild traumatic brain injury: Symptom validity assessment and malingering* (pp. 73–110). Springer.

Green, P., Montijo, J., & Brockhaus, R. (2011). High specificity of the Word Memory Test and Medical Symptom Validity Test in groups with severe verbal memory impairment. *Applied Neuropsychology, 18*(2), 86–94.

Greene, R. L. (1988). The relative efficacy of F-K and the obvious and subtle scales to detect overreporting of psychopathology on the MMPI. *Journal of Clinical Psychology, 44*(2), 152–159.

Greiffenstein, M. F., Baker, W. J., & Gola, T. (1994). Validation of malingered amnesia measures with a large clinical sample. *Psychological Assessment, 6*(3), 218.

Greve, K. W., & Bianchini, K. J. (2006). Should the Retention trial of the Test of Memory Malingering be optional? *Archives of Clinical Neuropsychology, 21*(1), 117–119.

Greve, K. W., Bianchini, K. J., & Doane, B. M. (2006). Classification accuracy of the Test of Memory Malingering in traumatic brain injury: Results of a known-groups analysis. *Journal of Clinical and Experimental Neuropsychology, 28*(7), 1176–1190.

Greve, K. W., Bianchini, K. J., Etherton, J. L., Ord, J. S., & Curtis, K. L. (2009a). Detecting malingered pain-related disability: Classification accuracy of the Portland Digit Recognition Test. *The Clinical Neuropsychologist, 23*(5), 850–869.

Greve, K. W., Binder, L. M., & Bianchini, K. J. (2009b). Rates of below-chance performance in forced-choice symptom validity tests. *The Clinical Neuropsychologist, 23*(3), 534–544.

Greve, K. W., Heinly, M. T., Bianchini, K. J., & Love, J. M. (2009c). Malingering detection with the Wisconsin Card Sorting Test in mild traumatic brain injury. *The Clinical Neuropsychologist, 23*(2), 343–362.

Greve, K. W., Ord, J., Curtis, K. L., Bianchini, K. J., & Brennan, A. (2008). Detecting malingering in traumatic brain injury and chronic pain: A comparison of three forced-choice symptom validity tests. *The Clinical Neuropsychologist, 22*(5), 896–918.

Guilmette, T. J., Hart, K. J., Giuliano, A. J., & Leininger, B. E. (1994). Detecting simulated memory impairment: Comparison of the Rey Fifteen-Item Test and the Hiscock forced-choice procedure. *The Clinical Neuropsychologist, 8*(3), 283–294.

Gunner, J. H., Miele, A. S., Lynch, J. K., & McCaffrey, R. J. (2012). The Albany consistency index for the test of memory malingering. *Archives of Clinical Neuropsychology, 27*(1), 1–9.

Hall, J. R., Balldin, V. H., Gamboa, A., Edwards, M. L., Johnson, L. A., & O'Bryant, S. E. (2018). Texas Mexican American adult normative studies: Normative data for the Repeatable Battery for the Assessment of Neuropsychological Status (RBANS). *Developmental Neuropsychology, 43*(1), 27–35.

Hall, J. T., & Ben-Porath, Y. S. (2022). The MMPI-2-RF validity scales: An overview of research and applications. In R. W. Schroeder & P. K. Martin (Eds.), *Validity assessment in clinical neuropsychological practice: Evaluating and managing noncredible performance* (pp. 150–178). Guilford Press.

Hampson, N. E., Kemp, S., Coughlan, A. K., Moulin, C. J., & Bhakta, B. B. (2014). Effort test performance in clinical acute brain injury, community brain injury, and epilepsy populations. *Applied Neuropsychology: Adult, 21*(3), 183–194.

Hanley, J. R., Baker, G. A., & Ledson, S. (1999). Detecting the faking of amnesia: A comparison of the effectiveness of three different techniques for distinguishing simulators from patients with amnesia. *Journal of Clinical and Experimental Neuropsychology, 21*(1), 59–69.

Heaton, R. K., Smith, H. H., Lehman, R. A., & Vogt, A. T. (1978). Prospects for faking believable deficits on neuropsychological testing. *Journal of Consulting and Clinical Psychology, 46*(5), 892.

Heilbronner, R. L., Sweet, J. J., Morgan, J. E., Larrabee, G. J., Millis, S. R., & Conference Participants 1. (2009). American Academy of Clinical Neuropsychology Consensus Conference Statement on the neuropsychological assessment of effort, response bias, and malingering. *The Clinical Neuropsychologist, 23*(7), 1093–1129.

Heinly, M. T., Greve, K. W., Bianchini, K. J., Love, J. M., & Brennan, A. (2005). WAIS Digit Span-based indicators of malingered neurocognitive dysfunction: Classification accuracy in traumatic brain injury. *Assessment, 12*(4), 429–444.

Henry, G. K., & Gornbein, J. (2022). Posttraumatic stress disorder and noncredible symptom reporting on the Trauma Symptom Inventory-2. *Applied Neuropsychology: Adult, 29*(1), 100–105.

Hopwood, C. J., Orlando, M. J., & Clark, T. S. (2010). The detection of malingered pain-related disability with the Personality Assessment Inventory. *Rehabilitation Psychology, 55*(3), 307.

Horner, M. D., Denning, J. H., & Cool, D. L. (2022). Self-reported disability-seeking predicts PVT failure in veterans undergoing clinical neuropsychological evaluation. *The Clinical Neuropsychologist*, 1–15.

Howe, L. L., Anderson, A. M., Kaufman, D. A., Sachs, B. C., & Loring, D. W. (2007). Characterization of the Medical Symptom Validity Test in evaluation of clinically referred memory disorders clinic patients. *Archives of Clinical Neuropsychology, 22*(6), 753–761.

Huber, B. N., Jones, R. G., Capps, S. C., & Buchanan, E. M. (2022). Memory complaints inventory profiles: Differentiating neurocognitive impairment, depression, and noncredible performance. *Applied Neuropsychology: Adult, 29*(2), 234–243.

Jones, A., Ingram, M. V., & Ben-Porath, Y. S. (2012). Scores on the MMPI-2-RF scales as a function of increasing levels of failure on cognitive symptom validity tests in a military sample. *The Clinical Neuropsychologist, 26*(5), 790–815.

Jurick, S. M., Crocker, L. D., Merritt, V. C., Hoffman, S. N., Keller, A. V., Eglit, G. M., . . . Jak, A. J. (2020). Psychological symptoms and rates of performance validity improve following trauma-focused treatment in veterans with PTSD and history of mild-to-moderate TBI. *Journal of the International Neuropsychological Society, 26*(1), 108–118.

Kalfon, T. B. O., Gal, G., Shorer, R., & Ablin, J. N. (2016). Cognitive functioning in fibromyalgia: The central role of effort. *Journal of Psychosomatic Research, 87*, 30–36.

Kapur, N. (1994). The coin-in-the-hand test: A new "bed-side" test for the detection of malingering in patients with suspected memory disorder. *Journal of Neurology, Neurosurgery, and Psychiatry, 57*(3), 385.

Kashluba, S., Paniak, C., & Casey, J. E. (2008). Persistent symptoms associated with factors identified by the WHO Task Force on Mild Traumatic Brain Injury. *The Clinical Neuropsychologist, 22*(2), 195–208.

Kelly, P. J., Baker, G. A., Van den Broek, M. D., Jackson, H., & Humphries, G. (2005). The detection of malingering in memory performance: The sensitivity and specificity of four measures in a U.K. population. *British Journal of Clinical Psychology, 44*(3), 333–341.

Kirkwood, M. W., Peterson, R. L., Baker, D. A., & Connery, A. K. (2017). Parent satisfaction with neuropsychological consultation after pediatric mild traumatic brain injury. *Child Neuropsychology, 23*(3), 273–283.

Kulas, J. F., Axelrod, B. N., & Rinaldi, A. R. (2014). Cross-validation of supplemental Test of Memory Malingering scores as performance validity measures. *Psychological Injury and Law, 7*(3), 236–244.

Kuncel, N. R., Credé, M., & Thomas, L. L. (2005). The validity of self-reported grade point averages, class ranks, and test scores: A meta-analysis and review of the literature. *Review of Educational Research, 75*(1), 63–82.

Lanca, M., Giuliano, A. J., Sarapas, C., Potter, A. I., Kim, M. S., West, A. L., & Chow, C. M. (2020). Clinical outcomes and satisfaction following neuropsychological assessment for adults: A community hospital prospective quasi-experimental study. *Archives of Clinical Neuropsychology, 35*(8), 1303–1311.

Lange, R. T., Pancholi, S., Brickell, T. A., Sakura, S., Bhagwat, A., Merritt, V., & French, L. M. (2012). Neuropsychological outcome from blast versus non-blast: Mild traumatic brain injury in U.S. military service members. *Journal of the International Neuropsychological Society, 18*(3), 595–605.

Larrabee, G. J. (1990). Cautions in the use of neuropsychological evaluation in legal settings. *Neuropsychology, 4*(4), 239.

Larrabee, G. J. (2003). Detection of malingering using atypical performance patterns on standard neuropsychological tests. *The Clinical Neuropsychologist, 17*(3), 410–425.

Larrabee, G. J. (2012a). *Forensic neuropsychology. A Scientific approach* (2nd ed.). Oxford University Press.

Larrabee, G. J. (2012b). Mild traumatic brain injury. In G. J. Larrabee (Ed.), *Forensic neuropsychology: A scientific approach* (2nd ed., pp. 231–259). Oxford University Press.

Larrabee, G. J. (2012c). Performance validity and symptom validity in neuropsychological assessment. *Journal of the International Neuropsychological Society, 18*(4), 625–630.

Larrabee, G. J. (2014). False-positive rates associated with the use of multiple performance and symptom validity tests. *Archives of Clinical Neuropsychology, 29*(4), 364–373.

Larrabee, G. J. (2022). Synthesizing data to reach clinical conclusions regarding validity status. In R. W. Schroeder & P. K. Martin (Eds.), *Validity assessment in clinical neuropsychological practice: Evaluating and managing noncredible performance* (pp. 193–210). Guilford Press.

Larrabee, G. J., Rohling, M. L., & Meyers, J. E. (2019). Use of multiple performance and symptom validity measures: Determining the optimal per test cutoff for determination of invalidity, analysis of skew, and inter-test correlations in valid and invalid performance groups. *The Clinical Neuropsychologist, 33*(8), 1354–1372.

Leese, M. I., Finley, J. C. A., Basurto, K. S., VanLandingham, H. B., Piszczor, J. P., Bianco, J. M., Phillips, M. S., Cerny, B. M., Schroeder, R. W., & Soble, J. R. (in press). Analysis of skew, examination of intercorrelations, and determining the optimal threshold for performance invalidity when 10 performance validity tests are administered during a neuropsychological evaluation. *Journal of Clinical and Experimental Neuropsychology.*

Lewis, J. L., Simcox, A. M., & Berry, D. T. R. (2002). Screening for feigned psychiatric symptoms in a forensic sample by using the MMPI-2 and the Structured Inventory of Malingered Symptomatology. *Psychological Assessment, 14*, 170–176.

Lezak, M. D., Howieson, D. B., Bigler, E. D., & Tranel, D. (2012). *Neuropsychological assessment.* Oxford University Press.

Lippa, S. M. (2022). The nuts and bolts of incorporating validity assessment in clinical evaluations. In R. W. Schroeder & P. K. Martin (Eds.), *Validity assessment in clinical neuropsychological practice: Evaluating and managing noncredible performance* (pp. 179–192). Guilford Press.

Loring, D. W., Marino, S. E., Drane, D. L., Parfitt, D., Finney, G. R., & Meador, K. J. (2011). Lorazepam effects on Word Memory Test performance: A randomized, double-blind, placebo-controlled, crossover trial. *The Clinical Neuropsychologist, 25*(5), 799–811.

Lu, P. H., Boone, K. B., Cozolino, L., & Mitchell, C. (2003). Effectiveness of the Rey-Osterrieth Complex Figure Test and the Meyers and Meyers recognition trial in the detection of suspect effort. *The Clinical Neuropsychologist, 17*(3), 426–440.

Marion, B. E., Sellbom, M., & Bagby, R. M. (2011). The detection of feigned psychiatric disorders using the MMPI-2-RF overreporting validity scales: An analog investigation. *Psychological Injury and Law, 4*(1), 1–12.

Marshall, P., & Happe, M. (2007). The performance of individuals with mental retardation on cognitive tests assessing effort and motivation. *The Clinical Neuropsychologist, 21*(5), 826–840.

Marshall, P. S., & Schroeder, R. W. (2022). Validity assessment in patients with psychiatric disorders. In R. W. Schroeder & P. K. Martin (Eds.), *Validity assessment in clinical neuropsychological practice: Evaluating and managing noncredible performance* (pp. 319–356). Guilford Press.

Martin, P. K., Hunter, B. P., Rach, A. M., Heinrichs, R. J., & Schroeder, R. W. (2017). Excessive decline from premorbid functioning: Detecting performance invalidity with the WAIS-IV and demographic predictions. *The Clinical Neuropsychologist, 31*(5), 829–843.

Marshall, P., Schroeder, R., O'Brien, J., Fischer, R., Ries, A., Blesi, B., & Barker, J. (2010). Effectiveness of symptom validity measures in identifying cognitive and behavioral symptom exaggeration in adult attention deficit hyperactivity disorder. *The Clinical Neuropsychologist, 24*(7), 1204–1237.

Martin, P. K., & Schroeder, R. W. (2020). Base rates of invalid test performance across clinical non-forensic contexts and settings. *Archives of Clinical Neuropsychology, 35*(6), 717–725.

Martin, P. K., & Schroeder, R. W. (2021a). Feedback with patients who produce invalid testing: Professional values and reported practices. *The Clinical Neuropsychologist, 35*(6), 1134–1153.

Martin, P. K., & Schroeder, R. W. (2021b). Language tests as performance validity tests. In K. B. Boone (Ed.), *Assessment of feigned cognitive impairment: A neuropsychological perspective* (2nd ed., pp. 248–263). Guilford Press.

Martin, P. K., & Schroeder, R. W. (2022a). A framework for providing clinical feedback when patients invalidate testing. In R. W. Schroeder & P. K. Martin (Eds.), *Validity assessment in clinical neuropsychological practice: Evaluating and managing noncredible performance* (pp. 47–69). Guilford Press.

Martin, P. K., & Schroeder, R. W. (2022b). Malingering: Maintaining a perspective of clinical care when patients feign. In R. W. Schroeder & P. K. Martin (Eds.), *Validity assessment in clinical neuropsychological practice: Evaluating and managing noncredible performance* (pp. 31–46). Guilford Press.

Martin, P. K., Schroeder, R. W., Boone, K. B., & Bush, S. S. (2022b). Ethical considerations associated with validity assessment in clinical evaluations. In R. W. Schroeder & P. K. Martin (Eds.), *Validity assessment in clinical neuropsychological practice: Evaluating and managing noncredible performance* (pp. 86–103). Guilford Press.

Martin, P. K., Schroeder, R. W., & Odland, A. P. (2015). Neuropsychologists' validity testing beliefs and practices: A survey of North American professionals. *The Clinical Neuropsychologist, 29*(6), 741–776.

Martin, P. K., Schroeder, R. W., & Odland, A. P. (2024). Neuropsychological validity assessment beliefs and practices: A survey or North American neuropsychologists and validity assessment experts. *Archives of Clinical Neuropsychology*, acae102.

Martin, P. K., Schroeder, R. W., & Olsen, D. H. (2022a). Performance validity in the dementia clinic: Specificity of validity tests when used individually and in aggregate across levels of cognitive impairment severity. *The Clinical Neuropsychologist, 36*(1), 165–188.

Martin, P. K., Schroeder, R. W., Olsen, D. H., Maloy, H., Boettcher, A., Ernst, N., & Okut, H. (2020). A systematic review and meta-analysis of the Test of Memory Malingering in adults: Two decades of deception detection. *The Clinical Neuropsychologist, 34*(1), 88–119.

Martin, P. K., Schroeder, R. W., Wyman-Chick, K. A., Hunter, B. P., Heinrichs, R. J., & Baade, L. E. (2018). Rates of abnormally low TOPF word reading scores in individuals failing versus passing performance validity testing. *Assessment, 25*(5), 640–652.

Martinez, K. A., Sayers, C., Hayes, C., Martin, P. K., Clark, C. B., & Schroeder, R. W. (2021). Normal cognitive test scores cannot be interpreted as accurate measures of ability in the context of failed performance validity testing: A symptom-and detection-coached simulation study. *Journal of Clinical and Experimental Neuropsychology, 43*(3), 301–309.

Martínez-Horta, S., Pagonabarraga, J., De Bobadilla, R. F., García-Sanchez, C., & Kulisevsky, J. (2013). Apathy in Parkinson's disease: more than just executive dysfunction. *Journal of the International Neuropsychological Society, 19*(5), 571–582.

McCaul, C., Boone, K. B., Ermshar, A., Cottingham, M., Victor, T. L., Ziegler, E., . . . Wright, M. (2018). Cross-validation of the Dot Counting Test in a large sample of credible and non-credible patients referred for neuropsychological testing. *The Clinical Neuropsychologist, 32*(6), 1054–1067.

Merten, T., Kaminski, A., & Pfeiffer, W. (2020). Prevalence of overreporting on symptom validity tests in a large sample of psychosomatic rehabilitation inpatients. *The Clinical Neuropsychologist, 34*(5), 1004–1024.

Meyers, J. E., Galinsky, A. M., & Volbrecht, M. (1999). Malingering and mild brain injury: How low is too low. *Applied Neuropsychology, 6*(4), 208–216.

Meyers, J., & Meyers, K. (1995). *Rey complex figure and recognition trial: Professional manual.* Psychological Assessment Resources.

Meyers, J. E., & Volbrecht, M. E. (2003). A validation of multiple malingering detection methods in a large clinical sample. *Archives of Clinical Neuropsychology, 18*(3), 261–276.

Miller, H. A. (2001). *Miller Forensic Assessment of Symptoms Test: Professional manual.* Psychological Assessment Resources.

Mittenberg, W., DiGiulio, D. V., Perrin, S., & Bass, A. E. (1992). Symptoms following mild head injury: expectation as aetiology. *Journal of Neurology, Neurosurgery & Psychiatry, 55*(3), 200–204.

Mittenberg, W., Patton, C., Canyock, E. M., & Condit, D. C. (2002). Base rates of malingering and symptom exaggeration. *Journal of Clinical and Experimental Neuropsychology, 24*(8), 1094–1102.

Moore, R. C., Davine, T., Harmell, A. L., Cardenas, V., Palmer, B. W., & Mausbach, B. T. (2013). Using the repeatable battery for the assessment of neuropsychological status (RBANS) effort index to predict treatment group attendance in patients with schizophrenia. *Journal of the International Neuropsychological Society, 19*(2), 198–205.

Morey, L. C. (2007). *Personality Assessment Inventory professional manual* (2nd ed.). Psychological Assessment Resources.

Morse, C. L., Douglas-Newman, K., Mandel, S., & Swirsky-Sacchetti, T. (2013). Utility of the Rey-15 recognition trial to detect invalid performance in a forensic neuropsychological sample. *The Clinical Neuropsychologist, 27*(8), 1395–1407.

National Center for PTSD. (n.d.). Va.Gov | Veterans Affairs. *www.ptsd.va.gov*

Nelson, N. W., Lee, C., & Sweet, J. J. (2021). Validity indicators within executive function measures: Use and limits in detection of response bias. In K. B. Boone (Ed.). *Assessment of feigned cognitive impairment: A neuropsychological perspective* (2nd ed., pp. 146–174). Guilford Press.

Nguyen, C. T., Green, D., & Barr, W. B. (2015). Evaluation of the MMPI-2-RF for detecting over-reported symptoms in a civil forensic and disability setting. *The Clinical Neuropsychologist, 29*(2), 255–271.

Nussbaum, S. H., Ales, F., Giromini, L., Watson, M., & Erdodi, L. (2023). Cross-Validating the Atypical Response Scale of the TSI-2 in a Sample of Motor Vehicle Collision Survivors. *Psychological Injury and Law*, 1–20.

Olsen, D. H., Schroeder, R. W., Heinrichs, R. J., & Martin, P. K. (2019). Examination of optimal embedded PVTs within the BVMT-R in an outpatient clinical sample. *The Clinical Neuropsychologist, 33*(4), 732–742.

Ord, A. S., Miskey, H. M., Lad, S., Richter, B., Nagy, K., & Shura, R. D. (2021a). Examining embedded validity indicators in Conners continuous performance test-3 (CPT-3). *The Clinical Neuropsychologist, 35*(8), 1426–1441.

Ord, A. S., Shura, R. D., Sansone, A. R., Martindale, S. L., Taber, K. H., & Rowland, J. A. (2021b). Performance validity and symptom validity tests: Are they measuring different constructs? *Neuropsychology, 35*(3), 241.

Orff, H. J., Drummond, S. P., Nowakowski, S., & Perlis, M. L. (2007). Discrepancy between subjective symptomatology and objective neuropsychological performance in insomnia. *Sleep, 30*(9), 1205–1211.

Pachet, A. K., Malcolm, D. N., Liu, I., Brown, C., Vanderveen, S., & Tan, A. (2022). Classification of performance validity and symptom validity using the Trauma Symptom Inventory-2. *Applied Neuropsychology: Adult, 31*(6), 1444–1451.

Palermo, C. A., & Brand, B. L. (2019). Can the Trauma Symptom Inventory-2 distinguish coached simulators from dissociative disorder patients? *Psychological Trauma: Theory, Research, Practice, and Policy, 11*(5), 477.

Pankratz, L. (2003). More hazards: Hypnosis, airplanes, and strongly held beliefs. *Skeptical Inquirer, 27*(3), 31–36.

Paul, R. H., Brickman, A. M., Navia, B., Hinkin, C., Malloy, P. F., Jefferson, A. L., . . . Flanigan, T. P. (2005). Apathy is associated with volume of the nucleus accumbens in patients infected with HIV. *The Journal of Neuropsychiatry and Clinical Neurosciences, 17*(2), 167–171.

Peak, A. M., Marceaux, J. C., Chicota-Carroll, C., & Soble, J. R. (2024). Cross-validation of the Trail Making Test as a non-memory-based embedded performance validity test among veterans with and without cognitive impairment. *Journal of Clinical and Experimental Neuropsychology, 46*(1), 16–24.

Pearson, N. C. S. (2009). *Advanced clinical solutions for WAIS-IV and WMS-IV: Administration and scoring manual.* The Psychological Corporation.

Peck, C. P., & Oakes, H. J. (2022). Validity assessment for clinical patients with workers' compensation claims. In R. W. Schroeder & P. K. Martin (Eds.), *Validity assessment in clinical neuropsychological practice: Evaluating and managing noncredible performance* (pp. 400–417). Guilford Press.

Pignolo, C., Giromini, L., Ales, F., & Zennaro, A. (2023). Detection of feigning of different symptom presentations with the PAI and IOP-29. *Assessment, 30*(3), 565–579.

Pliskin, J. I., DeDios Stern, S., Resch, Z. J., Saladino, K. F., Ovsiew, G. P., Carter, D. A., & Soble, J. R. (2021). Comparing the psychometric properties of eight embedded performance validity tests in the Rey Auditory Verbal Learning Test, Wechsler Memory Scale Logical Memory, and Brief Visuospatial Memory Test–Revised recognition trials for detecting invalid neuropsychological test performance. *Assessment, 28*(8), 1871–1881.

Postal, K. S., & Armstrong, K. (2013). *Feedback that sticks: The art of effectively communicating neuropsychological assessment results.* Oxford University Press.

Poynter, K., Boone, K. B., Ermshar, A., Miora, D., Cottingham, M., Victor, T. L., . . . Wright, M. (2019). Wait, there's a baby in this bath water! Update on quantitative and qualitative cut-offs for Rey 15-Item Recall and Recognition. *Archives of Clinical Neuropsychology, 34*(8), 1367–1380.

Rabin, L. A., Paolillo, E., & Barr, W. B. (2016). Stability in test-usage practices of clinical neuropsychologists in the United States and Canada over a 10-year period: A follow-up survey of INS and NAN members. *Archives of Clinical Neuropsychology, 31*(3), 206–230.

Reedy, S. D., Boone, K. B., Cottingham, M. E., Glaser, D. F., Lu, P. H., Victor, T. L., . . . Wright, M. J. (2013). Cross validation of the Lu and colleagues (2003) Rey-Osterrieth Complex Figure Test effort equation in a large known-group sample. *Archives of Clinical Neuropsychology, 28*(1), 30–37.

Rees, L. M., Tombaugh, T. N., & Boulay, L. (2001). Depression and the test of memory malingering. *Archives of Clinical Neuropsychology, 16*(5), 501–506.

Resch, Z. J., Rhoads, T., Ovsiew, G. P., & Soble, J. R. (2022). A known-groups validation of the medical symptom validity test and analysis of the genuine memory impairment profile. *Assessment, 29*(3), 455–466.

Rey, A. (1941). L'Examen psychologie dans las cas d'encephalopathie traumatique. *Archives de Psychologie, 23*(112), 286–340.

Rey, A. (1964). *L'examen clinique en psychologie.* Presses Universitaires de France.

Reznek, L. (2005). The Rey 15-item memory test for malingering: A meta-analysis. *Brain Injury, 19*(7), 539–543.

Rogers, R. (1990). Development of a new classificatory model of malingering. *The Bulletin of the American Academy of Psychiatry and the Law, 18*(3), 323–333.

Rogers, R. (2018). An introduction to response styles. In R. Rogers & S. D. Bender (Eds.), *Clinical assessment of malingering and deceptions* (4th ed., pp. 3–17). Guilford Press.

Rogers, R., Bagby, R. M., & Vincent, A. (1994a). Factitious disorders with predominantly psychological signs and symptoms: A conundrum for forensic experts. *The Journal of Psychiatry & Law, 22*(1), 91–106.

Rogers, R., Gillard, N. D., Berry, D. T., & Granacher, R. P. (2011). Effectiveness of the MMPI-2-RF validity scales for feigned mental disorders and cognitive impairment: A known-groups study. *Journal of Psychopathology and Behavioral Assessment, 33*(3), 355367.

Rogers, R., Salekin, R. T., Sewell, K. W., Goldstein, A., & Leonard, K. (1998). A comparison of forensic and nonforensic malingerers: A prototypical analysis of explanatory models. *Law and Human Behavior, 22*(4), 353–367.

Rogers, R., Sewell, K. W., & Goldstein, A. M. (1994b). Explanatory models of malingering: A prototypical analysis. *Law and Human Behavior, 18*(5), 543–552.

Rohling, M. L. (2013). *When are your trial data real?* Poster presented at the 53rd annual conference of the American Society for Clinical Psychopharmacology (NCDEU), Hollywood, FL.

Rohling, M. L., Binder, L. M., Demakis, G. J., Larrabee, G. J., Ploetz, D. M., & Langhinrichsen-Rohling, J. (2011). A meta-analysis of neuropsychological outcome after mild traumatic brain injury: Re-analyses and reconsiderations of Binder et al., Frencham et al., and Pertab et al. *The Clinical Neuropsychologist, 25*(4), 608–623.

Rohling, M. L., Green, P., Allen, L. M., III., & Iverson, G. L. (2002). Depressive symptoms and neurocognitive test scores in patients passing symptom validity tests. *Archives of Clinical Neuropsychology, 17*(3), 205–222.

Rosado, D. L., Buehler, S., Botbol-Berman, E., Feigon, M., León, A., Luu, H., . . . Pliskin, N. H. (2018). Neuropsychological feedback services improve quality of life and social adjustment. *The Clinical Neuropsychologist, 32*(3), 422–435.

Rudman, N., Oyebode, J. R., Jones, C. A., & Bentham, P. (2011). An investigation into the validity of effort tests in a working age dementia population. *Aging & Mental Health, 15*(1), 47–57.

Ruiz, I., Raugh, I. M., Bartolomeo, L. A., & Strauss, G. P. (2020). A meta-analysis of neuropsychological effort test performance in psychotic disorders. *Neuropsychology Review, 30*, 407–424.

Salazar, X. F., Lu, P. H., Wen, J., & Boone, K. B. (2007). *The use of effort tests in ethnic minorities and in non-English-speaking and English as a second language populations.* Psychological Corporation

Schroeder, R. W. (2022). *Identifying, explaining, and managing noncredible neuropsychological presentations in clinical practice.* Colorado Neuropsychological Society Spring 2022 Conference, Virtual Meeting.

Schroeder, R. W., Baade, L. E., Peck, C. P., VonDran, E. J., Brockman, C. J., Webster, B. K., & Heinrichs, R. J. (2012a). Validation of MMPI-2-RF validity scales in criterion group neuropsychological samples. *The Clinical Neuropsychologist, 26*(1), 129–146.

Schroeder, R. W., & Bieu, R. K. (2024). Exploration of PCL-5 symptom validity indices for detection of exaggerated and feigned PTSD. *Journal of Clinical and Experimental Neuropsychology, 46*(2), 152–161.

Schroeder, R. W., & Chafetz, M. (2022). Validity assessment for clinical patients pursuing Social Security disability. In R. W. Schroeder & P. K. Martin (Eds.), *Validity assessment in clinical neuropsychological practice: Evaluating and managing noncredible performance* (pp. 378–399). Guilford Press.

Schroeder, R. W., Clark, H. A., & Martin, P. K. (2022). Base rates of invalidity when patients undergoing routine clinical evaluations have social security disability as an external incentive. *The Clinical Neuropsychologist, 36*(7), 1902–1914.

Schroeder, R. W., & Marshall, P. S. (2010). Validation of the Sentence Repetition Test as a measure of suspect effort. *The Clinical Neuropsychologist, 24*(2), 326–343.

Schroeder, R. W., & Marshall, P. S. (2011). Evaluation of the appropriateness of multiple symptom validity indices in psychotic and non-psychotic psychiatric populations. *The Clinical Neuropsychologist, 25*(3), 437–453.

Schroeder, R. W., & Martin, P. K. (2021). Forced-choice performance validity tests. In K. B. Boone (Ed.), *Assessment of feigned cognitive impairment: A neuropsychological perspective* (pp. 34–63). Guilford Press.

Schroeder, R. W., & Martin, P. K. (2022a). Incorporation of validity assessment and validity findings when writing clinical reports. In R. W. Schroeder & P. K. Martin (Eds.), *Validity assessment in clinical neuropsychological practice: Evaluating and managing noncredible performance* (pp. 70–85). Guilford Press.

Schroeder, R. W., & Martin, P. K. (2022b). Validity assessment in clinical settings: How it differs from forensic settings and why it is important. In R. W. Schroeder & P. K. Martin (Eds.), *Validity assessment in clinical neuropsychological practice: Evaluating and managing noncredible performance* (pp. 3–10). Guilford Press.

Schroeder, R. W., & Martin, P. K. (2022c). Validity assessment within the memory disorders/dementia clinic. In R. W. Schroeder & P. K. Martin (Eds.), *Validity assessment in clinical neuropsychological practice: Evaluating and managing noncredible performance* (pp. 254–279). Guilford Press.

Schroeder, R. W., & Martin, P. K. (2022d). Explanations of performance validity test failure in clinical settings. In R. W. Schroeder & P. K. Martin (Eds.), *Validity assessment in clinical neuropsychological practice: Evaluating and managing noncredible performance* (pp. 11–30). Guilford Press.

Schroeder, R. W., & Martin, P. K. (Eds.). (2022e). *Validity assessment in clinical neuropsychological practice: Evaluating and managing noncredible performance.* Guilford Press.
Schroeder, R. W., & Martin, P. K. (2021). Forced-choice performance validity tests. In K. B. Boone (Ed.), *Assessment of feigned cognitive impairment: A neuropsychological perspective* (pp. 34–63). Guilford Press.
Schroeder, R. W., & Martin, P. K. (Eds.). (2022). *Validity assessment in clinical neuropsychological practice: Evaluating and managing noncredible performance.* Guilford Press.

Schroeder, R. W., Martin, P. K., Heinrichs, R. J., & Baade, L. E. (2019b). Research methods in performance validity testing studies: Criterion grouping approach impacts study outcomes. *The Clinical Neuropsychologist, 33*(3), 466–477.

Schroeder, R. W., Martin, P. K., & Odland, A. P. (2016). Expert beliefs and practices regarding neuropsychological validity testing. *The Clinical Neuropsychologist, 30*(4), 515–535.

Schroeder, R. W., Martin, P. K., & Walling, A. (2019a). Neuropsychological evaluations in adults. *American Family Physician, 99*(2), 101–108.

Schroeder, R. W., Olsen, D. H., & Martin, P. K. (2019c). Classification accuracy rates of four TOMM validity indices when examined independently and jointly. *The Clinical Neuropsychologist, 33*(8), 1373–1387.

Schroeder, R. W., Peck, C. P., Buddin, W. H. Jr., Heinrichs, R. J., & Baade, L. E. (2012b). The Coin-in-the-Hand Test and dementia: More evidence for a screening test for neurocognitive symptom exaggeration. *Cognitive and Behavioral Neurology, 25*(3), 139–143.

Schroeder, R. W., Spector, J., Snodgrass, M., & Bieu, R. K. (2025). *Validation of PCL-5 symptom validity indices in a cross-cultural forensic sample.* Manuscript in preparation.

Schroeder, R. W., Twumasi-Ankrah, P., Baade, L. E., & Marshall, P. S. (2012c). Reliable digit span: A systematic review and cross-validation study. *Assessment, 19*(1), 21–30.

Schwartz, E. S., Erdodi, L., Rodriguez, N., Ghosh, J. J., Curtain, J. R., Flashman, L. A., & Roth, R. M. (2016). CVLT-II forced choice recognition trial as an embedded validity indicator: A systematic review of the evidence. *Journal of the International Neuropsychological Society, 22*(8), 851–858.

Scimeca, L. M., Holbrook, L., Rhoads, T., Cerny, B. M., Jennette, K. J., Resch, Z. J., . . . Soble, J. R. (2021). Examining Conners continuous performance test-3 (CPT-3) embedded performance validity indicators in an adult clinical sample referred for ADHD evaluation. *Developmental Neuropsychology, 46*(5), 347–359.

Sellbom, M., & Bagby, R. M. (2008). Validity of the MMPI-2-RF (restructured form) Lr and Kr scales in detecting underreporting in clinical and nonclinical samples. *Psychological Assessment, 20*(4), 370.

Sellbom, M., & Bagby, R. M. (2010). Detection of overreported psychopathology with the MMPI-2 RF form validity scales. *Psychological Assessment, 22*(4), 757.

Sellbom, M., Wygant, D., & Bagby, M. (2012). Utility of the MMPI-2-RF in detecting noncredible somatic complaints. *Psychiatry Research, 197*(3), 295–301.

Sharland, M. J., & Gfeller, J. D. (2007). A survey of neuropsychologists' beliefs and practices with respect to the assessment of effort. *Archives of Clinical Neuropsychology, 22*(2), 213–223.

Sherman, E. M., Slick, D. J., & Iverson, G. L. (2020). Multidimensional malingering criteria for neuropsychological assessment: A 20-year update of the malingered neuropsychological dysfunction criteria. *Archives of Clinical Neuropsychology, 35*(6), 735–764.

Shura, R. D., Brearly, T. W., Rowland, J. A., Martindale, S. L., Miskey, H. M., & Duff, K. (2018). RBANS validity indices: A systematic review and meta-analysis. *Neuropsychology Review, 28*(3), 269–284.

Shura, R. D., Denning, J. H., Armistead-Jehle, P., & Axelrod, B. N. (2022a). Validity assessment within Veterans Affairs and active duty settings. In R. W. Schroeder & P. K. Martin

(Eds.), *Validity assessment in clinical neuropsychological practice: Evaluating and managing noncredible performance* (pp. 235–253). Guilford Press.

Shura, R. D., Ingram, P. B., Miskey, H. M., Martindale, S. L., Rowland, J. A., & Armistead-Jehle, P. (2023). Validation of the Personality Assessment Inventory (PAI) Cognitive Bias (CBS) and Cognitive Bias Scale of Scales (CB-SOS) in a post-deployment veteran sample. *The Clinical Neuropsychologist, 37*(7), 1548–1565.

Shura, R. D., Miskey, H. M., Rowland, J. A., Yoash-Gantz, R. E., & Denning, J. H. (2016). Embedded performance validity measures with postdeployment veterans: Cross-validation and efficiency with multiple measures. *Applied Neuropsychology: Adult, 23*(2), 94–104.

Shura, R. D., Ord, A. S., & Worthen, M. D. (2022b). Structured inventory of malingered symptomatology: A psychometric review. *Psychological Injury and Law, 15*(1), 64–78.

Shura, R. D., Rowland, J. A., Miskey, H. M., Ord, A. S., Magnante, A. T., VA Mid-Atlantic MIRECC Workgroup, & Martindale, S. L. (2023). Symptom validity indices in the Posttraumatic Stress Disorder Checklist for DSM-5. *Journal of Traumatic Stress, 36*(5), 919–931.

Silk-Eglit, G. M., Stenclik, J. H., Miele, A. S., Lynch, J. K., & McCaffrey, R. J. (2015). Rates of false-positive classification resulting from the analysis of additional embedded performance validity measures. *Applied Neuropsychology: Adult, 22*(5), 335–347.

Sleep, C. E., Petty, J. A., & Wygant, D. B. (2015). Framing the results: Assessment of response bias through select self-report measures in psychological injury evaluations. *Psychological Injury and Law, 8*, 27–39.

Slick, D. J., & Sherman, E. M. S. (2013). Differential diagnosis of malingering. In D. A. Carone & S. S. Bush (Eds.), *Mild traumatic brain injury: Symptom validity assessment and malingering* (pp. 57–72). Springer.

Slick, D. J., Sherman, E. M., & Iverson, G. L. (1999). Diagnostic criteria for malingered neurocognitive dysfunction: Proposed standards for clinical practice and research. *The Clinical Neuropsychologist, 13*(4), 545–561.

Smith, G. E., Petersen, R. C., Ivnik, R. J., Malec, J. F., & Tangalos, E. G. (1996). Subjective memory complaints, psychological distress, and longitudinal change in objective memory performance. *Psychology and Aging, 11*(2), 272–279.

Smith, K., Boone, K., Victor, T., Miora, D., Cottingham, M., Ziegler, E., . . . Wright, M. (2014). Comparison of credible patients of very low intelligence and non-credible patients on neurocognitive performance validity indicators. *The Clinical Neuropsychologist, 28*(6), 1048–1070.

Sobel, N., Babikian, T., & Boone, K. B. (2021a). Intelligence tests as performance validity measures. In K. B. Boone (Ed.). *Assessment of feigned cognitive impairment: A neuropsychological perspective* (2nd ed., pp. 94–110). Guilford Press.

Soble, J. R., Bain, K. M., Bailey, K. C., Kirton, J. W., Marceaux, J. C., Critchfield, E. A., . . . O'Rourke, J. J. (2019). Evaluating the accuracy of the Wechsler Memory Scale-(WMS-IV) logical memory embedded validity index for detecting invalid test performance. *Applied Neuropsychology: Adult, 26*(4), 311–318.

Soble, J. R., Santos, O. A., Bain, K. M., Kirton, J. W., Bailey, K. C., Critchfield, E. A., . . . González, D. A. (2018). The Dot Counting Test adds up: Validation and response pattern analysis in a mixed clinical veteran sample. *Journal of Clinical and Experimental Neuropsychology, 40*(4), 317–325.

Soble, J. R., Webber, T. A., & Bailey, K. C. (2021b). An overview of common performance validity tests for practicing clinicians: Cutoffs, classification accuracy, and administration times. In R. W. Schroeder & P. K. Martin (Eds.), *Validity assessment in clinical neuropsychological practice: Evaluating and managing noncredible performance* (pp. 126–149). Guilford Press.

Strauss, E., Sherman, E. M., & Spreen, O. (2006). *A compendium of neuropsychological tests: Administration, norms, and commentary.* American Chemical Society.

Strutt, A. M., Scott, B. M., Shrestha, S., & York, M. K. (2011). The Rey 15-item memory test and Spanish-speaking older adults. *The Clinical Neuropsychologist, 25*(7), 1253–1265.

Strutt, A. M., & Stinson, J. M. (2022). Performance validity testing with culturally diverse individuals and non-native English speakers: The need for a cultural perspective in neuropsychological practice. In R. W. Schroeder & P. K. Martin (Eds.), *Validity assessment in clinical neuropsychological practice: Evaluating and managing noncredible performance* (pp. 211–232). Guilford Press.

Stulemeijer, M., Vos, P. E., Bleijenberg, G., & Van der Werf, S. P. (2007). Cognitive complaints after mild traumatic brain injury: Things are not always what they seem. *Journal of Psychosomatic Research, 63*(6), 637–645.

Suchy, Y. (2019). Introduction to special issue: Current trends in empirical examinations of performance and symptom validity. *The Clinical Neuropsychologist, 33*(8), 1349–1353.

Suesse, M., Wong, V. W., Stamper, L. L., Carpenter, K. N., & Scott, R. B. (2015). Evaluating the clinical utility of the Medical Symptom Validity Test (MSVT): A clinical series. *The Clinical Neuropsychologist, 29*(2), 214–231.

Suhr, J. A. (2015). *Psychological assessment: A problem-solving approach.* Guilford Press.

Suhr, J. A., & Gunstad, J. (2007). Coaching and malingering: A review. In G. J. Larrabee (Ed.), *Assessment of malingered neuropsychological deficits* (pp. 287–311). Oxford University Press.

Suhr, J. A., Lee, G. J., & Angers, K. (2022). Validity assessment in academic evaluations. In R. W. Schroeder & P. K. Martin (Eds.), *Validity assessment in clinical neuropsychological practice: Evaluating and managing noncredible performance* (pp. 300–318). Guilford Press.

Sweet, J. J., Heilbronner, R. L., Morgan, J. E., Larrabee, G. J., Rohling, M. L., Boone, K. B., . . . Conference Participants. (2021). American Academy of Clinical Neuropsychology (AACN) 2021 consensus statement on validity assessment: Update of the 2009 AACN consensus conference statement on neuropsychological assessment of effort, response bias, and malingering. *The Clinical Neuropsychologist, 35*(6), 1053–1106.

Sweet, J., J., & Klipfel, K. M. (2022). Forensic primer for the nonforensic neuropsychologist: When clinicians participate in forensic proceedings. In R. W. Schroeder & P. K. Martin (Eds.), *Validity assessment in clinical neuropsychological practice: Evaluating and managing noncredible performance* (pp. 439–462). Guilford Press.

Tan, J. E., Slick, D. J., Strauss, E., & Hultsch, D. F. (2002). How'd they do it? Malingering strategies on symptom validity tests. *The Clinical Neuropsychologist, 16*(4), 495–505.

Thomas, K. M., Hopwood, C. J., Orlando, M. J., Weathers, F. W., & McDevitt-Murphy, M. E. (2012). Detecting feigned PTSD using the personality assessment inventory. *Psychological Injury and Law, 5*(3–4), 192–201.

Tombaugh, T. N. (1996). *Test of memory malingering.* Multi-Health Systems, Inc.

Tversky, A., & Kahneman, D. (1974). Judgment under uncertainty: Heuristics and biases. *Science, 185*(4157), 1124–1131.

Tylicki, J. L., Rai, J. K., Arends, P., Gervais, R. O., & Ben-Porath, Y. S. (2021). A comparison of the MMPI-2-RF and PAI overreporting indicators in a civil forensic sample with emphasis on the Response Bias Scale (RBS) and the Cognitive Bias Scale (CBS). *Psychological Assessment, 33*(1), 71.

Tyson, B. T., Pyne, S. R., Crisan, I., Calamia, M., Holcomb, M., Giromini, L., & Erdodi, L. A. (2023). Logical memory, visual reproduction, and verbal paired associates are effective embedded validity indicators in patients with traumatic brain injury. *Applied Neuropsychology: Adult*, 1–10.

Tyson, B. T., Shahein, A., Abeare, C. A., Baker, S. D., Kent, K., Roth, R. M., & Erdodi, L. A. (2023). Replicating a meta-analysis: The search for the optimal word choice test cutoff continues. *Assessment, 30*(8), 2476–2490.

Uiterwijk, D., Stargatt, R., Humphrey, S., & Crowe, S. F. (2022). The relationship between cognitive functioning and symptoms of depression, anxiety, and post-traumatic stress disorder in adults with a traumatic brain injury: a meta-analysis. *Neuropsychology Review, 32*(4), 758–806.

U.S. Department of Veterans Affairs. (2019, January 19). Compensation. Retrieved from *www.benefits.va.gov/compensation/types-compensation.asp*

Van Dyke, S. A., Millis, S. R., Axelrod, B. N., & Hanks, R. A. (2013). Assessing effort: Differentiating performance and symptom validity. *The Clinical Neuropsychologist, 27*(8), 1234–1246.

Van Egmond, J., & Kummeling, I. (2002). A blind spot for secondary gain affecting therapy outcomes. *European Psychiatry, 17*(1), 46–54.

Van Egmond, J., Kummeling, I., & aan Balkom, T. (2005). Secondary gain as hidden motive for getting psychiatric treatment. *European Psychiatry, 20*(5–6), 416–421.

Victor, T. L., Boone, K. B., Serpa, J. G., Buehler, J., & Ziegler, E. A. (2009). Interpreting the meaning of multiple symptom validity test failure. *The Clinical Neuropsychologist, 23*(2), 297–313.

Wang, E. W., Rogers, R., Giles, C. L., Diamond, P. M., Herrington-Wang, L. E., & Taylor, E. R. (1997). A pilot study of the Personality Assessment Inventory (PAI) in corrections: Assessment of malingering, suicide risk, and aggression in male inmates. *Behavioral Sciences & the Law, 15*(4), 469–482.

Webber, T. A., Sullivan-Baca, E., Modiano, Y. A., Taiwo, Z., & Grabyan, J. M. (2022). Validity of informant report interpretations: Role of examinee performance and symptom invalidity. *Psychological Assessment, 34*(2), 125.

Weiss, R. A., & Rosenfeld, B. (2017). Identifying feigning in trauma-exposed African immigrants. *Psychological Assessment, 29*(7), 881.

Westervelt, H. J., Brown, L. B., Tremont, G., Javorsky, D. J., & Stern, R. A. (2007). Patient and family perceptions of the neuropsychological evaluation: How are we doing? *The Clinical Neuropsychologist, 21*(2), 263–273.

Whiteside, D., Wald, D., & Busse, M. (2011). Classification accuracy of multiple visual spatial measures in the detection of suspect effort. *The Clinical Neuropsychologist, 25*(2), 287–301.

Widows, M. R., & Smith, G. P. (2005). *SIMS: Structured Inventory of Malingered Symptomatology: Professional manual.* PAR Inc.

Wisdom, N. M., Callahan, J. L., & Shaw, T. G. (2010). Diagnostic utility of the Structured Inventory of Malingered Symptomatology to detect malingering in a forensic sample. *Archives of Clinical Neuropsychology, 25*(2), 118–125.

Wooley, C. N., & Rogers, R. (2015). The effectiveness of the personality assessment inventory with feigned PTSD: An initial investigation of Resnick's model of malingering. *Assessment, 22*(4), 449–458.

Wygant, D. B., Anderson, J. L., Sellbom, M., Rapier, J. L., Allgeier, L. M., & Granacher, R. P. (2011). Association of the MMPI-2 restructured form (MMPI-2-RF) validity scales with structured malingering criteria. *Psychological Injury and Law, 4*, 13–23.

Wygant, D. B., Ben-Porath, Y. S., Arbisi, P. A., Berry, D. T., Freeman, D. B., & Heilbronner, R. L. (2009). Examination of the MMPI-2 restructured form (MMPI-2-RF) validity scales in civil forensic settings: Findings from simulation and known group samples. *Archives of Clinical Neuropsychology, 24*(7), 671–680.

Yeh, T. C., Chou, Y. C., Weng, J. P., Yeh, H. W., Kao, Y. C., Chiang, W. S., . . . Tzeng, N. S. (2019). Detection of malingering in the memory of patients with dementia: A pilot study on coin-in-the-hand test in a Northern Taiwan Memory Clinic. *Journal of Medical Sciences, 39*(2), 81–89.

Young, G. (2019). The cry for help in psychological injury and law: Concepts and review. *Psychological Injury and Law, 12*(3), 225–237.

Young, J. C., Roper, B. L., & Arentsen, T. J. (2016). Validity testing and neuropsychology practice in the VA healthcare system: Results from recent practitioner survey. *The Clinical Neuropsychologist, 30*(4), 497–514.

Youngjohn, J. R., Lees-Haley, P. R., & Binder, L. M. (1999). Comment: Warning malingerers produces more sophisticated malingering. *Archives of Clinical Neuropsychology, 14*(6), 511–515.

Index

Note. t or *f* following a page number indicates a table or a figure.

B

C

D

E

M

N

O

P

Q

R

T

U

V

W

Y